CLASSICAL STUDIES

Reference Sources in the Humanities Series
James Rettig, Series Editor

CLASSICAL STUDIES
A GUIDE TO THE REFERENCE LITERATURE

FRED W. JENKINS

1996
Libraries Unlimited, Inc.
Englewood, Colorado

For Nancy

LIBRARIES UNLIMITED, INC.
P.O. Box 6633
Englewood, CO 80155-6633
(800) 237-6124

Library of Congress Cataloging-in-Publication Data

Jenkins, Fred W.
    Classical Studies : a guide to the reference literature / Fred W. Jenkins.
        ix, 263 p. 17x25 cm.
        Includes bibliographical references and index.
        ISBN 1-56308-110-5
        1. Reference books--Classical philology--Bibliography.
    2. Reference books--Civilization, Classical--Bibliography.
    3. Civilization, Classical--Bibliography. 4. Classical philology--
    Bibliography. I. Title.
    Z7016.J4 1996
    [PA91]
    016.88--dc20   95-52209
                                                              CIP

CONTENTS

PREFACE

When I was first at work on this manual Stanley Morison observed that it sounded like the sort of book which might be a serviceable thing by the time it reached its fifth edition.

John Carter
ABC for Book Collectors

This book is a guide to the reference literature of classical studies. Its focus is on bibliographical and information resources, not on general scholarship in the field. While other works, such as Halton and O'Leary's *Classical Scholarship*,[1] offer introductory surveys of modern classical scholarship, no recent English-language work is devoted exclusively to basic and specialized reference sources for classics. In preparing this volume, I have kept several audiences in mind. Foremost, the book is designed for reference librarians and library users (both students and that now endangered species, the general reader). While it is not intended for working classical scholars, I hope they also find it of use, especially when venturing beyond their specialties.

In general, I have attempted to include the best and most up-to-date reference materials for the study of the Greek and Roman civilizations from the Bronze Age through the sixth century A.D. These include works on art and archaeology, history, language and literature, and philosophy. In addition, readers will find a number of works on the history of classical scholarship and on the *Nachleben* (i.e., later influence) of the classics. Ancient Near Eastern studies, patristics, medieval Latin, Neo-Latin, and Byzantine studies receive attention only insofar as they relate to classical studies proper.[2] Because of the relatively early professionalization of classical studies and their international character, this volume contains somewhat more older and foreign-language works than do most in this series. While giving preference to English-language works whenever possible, I have included many important titles in French, German, Italian, and Spanish. Coverage is reasonably complete through the end of 1994; a few works published in 1995 are also noted.

Following the basic principles of the series, I have listed only book-length works in this guide; works appearing in periodicals are generally ignored. Electronic publications, which are of growing importance in classical studies, are fully treated in these pages.[3] A number of bibliographical databases and electronic journals are noted in the appropriate chapters. I have also provided a separate chapter on resources available through the Internet.

I have arranged the material into three sections. The first part, "Bibliographical Resources," offers guidance in locating bibliographical citations, abstracts, and reviews. Some of the items cited may also aid in locating copies of scarcer works. A few categories of material, such as catalogs of manuscripts and incunabula and bibliographies of the works of individual classical scholars, have been excluded. The second part, "Information Resources," notes works that will help in answering specific questions. These include an array of dictionaries, encyclopedias, handbooks, and the like. This part also includes a discussion of Internet resources and a list of core periodicals. The final part describes relevant organizations and research centers. With a few exceptions, it seemed most useful to base chapters on type of work rather than subject. Full subject access is, however, provided through the appropriate index. Each chapter includes a headnote that clarifies its scope and provides advice to the reader.

In listing individual works, I have typically cited the most complete or best edition in its original printing; the most recent reprint edition, when one exists, is also noted. As for works that appeared simultaneously under multiple imprints, I have usually preferred the U.S. one. Citations are based on the title pages of the works (or its nearest equivalent for electronic publications); I have eschewed mindless consistency in presenting these. However, in the index, authors' names are regularized under the most commonly used form. The annotation accompanying each entry describes the work and frequently offers some evaluation or comparison to similar works. Related works are fully cross-referenced.

Many have contributed to the completion of this work. I should first like to thank James Rettig, my editor, both for offering the opportunity to write it and for his guidance and patience during its composition. *Superest ut nec te consilii nec me paeniteat obsequii.*[4]

I am grateful for much support and encouragement from my institution and colleagues. The University of Dayton granted me an indispensable sabbatical leave during the fall of 1993. Dean Edward Garten generously provided travel funds and other support. Many colleagues at Dayton supplied help and encouragement; I would particularly like to mention Nicoletta Hary, Anita Johnson, Linda Simons, and Susan Tsui. Thanks are also due to the interlibrary loan staff for their many efforts on my behalf.

Many friends and colleagues at other universities also contributed a great deal. Jean Wellington and Michael Braunlin of the University of Cincinnati Classics Library supplied invaluable assistance in tracking down and obtaining various works. Jean also discussed the content of several chapters with me, while Michael generously gave me the benefit of his extensive knowledge of ancient numismatics. Gail Hueting of the University of Illinois Library answered a number of bibliographical queries and provided hospitality during my visits to Illinois. She also kindly read and commented on early drafts of several chapters. Thomas Izbicki, Johns Hopkins University Library, shared with me his bibliographical materials on late and medieval Latin. Blake Landor of the University of Florida provided valuable assistance in the Sisyphean task of keeping up with developments on the Internet.

The Academic Library Association of Ohio awarded me its 1993 Research Award, which helped fund travel to several libraries. In addition to Cincinnati and Illinois, I have used the libraries of Ohio State University, the University of Chicago, and the University of Michigan. I am grateful to these institutions and their staffs.

In closing, I thank my wife and colleague, Nancy Courtney, to whom this work is dedicated. In addition to cheerfully and patiently enduring its composition, she read and improved a large part of the manuscript. Needless to say, all remaining defects of this book are due solely to the author, who is, among other things, stubborn.

Notes

1. See entry 9 for discussion of Halton and O'Leary. Those comfortable in French or German will also find the works of Poucet (entry 22) and Gullath (entry 8) useful guides to the literature of classical studies.

2. A number of introductory works and guides to the literature are already available for these related fields, although some are in need of updating. Those interested in patristics might consult Berthold Altaner, *Patrology* (New York: Herder, 1961) or Johannes Quasten, *Patrology* (Utrecht: Spectrum, 1950-1960). For medieval Latin, Karl Strecker's handbook, *Introduction to Medieval Latin*, translated and revised by Robert B. Palmer (Berlin: Weidmann, 1957), is a helpful guide; broader treatments of medieval studies include James M. Powell, *Medieval Studies: An Introduction*, 2d ed. (Syracuse, NY: Syracuse University Press, 1992) and Everett U. Crosby, *Medieval Studies: A Bibliographical Guide* (New York: Garland, 1983). Jozef Ijsewijn's *Companion to Neo-Latin Studies* (1st ed., Amsterdam: North-Holland, 1977; 2d ed., Louvain, Belgium: Louven University Press, 1990-) covers Latin after the Middle Ages. Unfortunately, there are no general guides or bibliographies for Ancient Near Eastern studies or Byzantine studies. However, those with an interest in Byzantine Greek will find Robert Browning's *Medieval and Modern Greek* (London: Hutchinson, 1969) a useful volume.

3. Those interested in the historical development of this area should refer to Jon Solomon, ed., *Accessing Antiquity: The Computerization of Classical Studies* (Tucson, AZ: University of Arizona Press, 1993). The quarterly newsletter, *Computing and the Classics* (Newark, Ohio: Ohio State University, 1984-) is a good source of current information. Subscriptions are free; contact the editor, Joseph Tebben, 147 Adena Hall, Ohio State University-Newark, 1179 University Drive, Newark, Ohio 43055. For information on the Internet, see the headnote to chapter 15.

4. Pliny, *Epistulae* I.1.2.

PART 1

BIBLIOGRAPHICAL RESOURCES

CHAPTER  1

GENERAL BIBLIOGRAPHICAL AND RESEARCH GUIDES

This chapter includes general bibliographies and guides to study and research. These works cover classical studies as a whole or a major department of it, such as Greek or Latin literature or ancient history. Some of them are reasonably current works that will serve the needs of both students and scholars. Others are antiquarian works that will chiefly interest bibliographers and historians of scholarship. Coverage of English-language works is relatively complete, while those in other languages are treated more selectively. These self-contained works tend to focus on books, although many include citations of journal articles as well. Their contents can be updated with the aid of the indexes and review journals found in chapters 2 and 3.

1.   Bengtson, Hermann. **Introduction to Ancient History**. Translated from the 6th edition by R. I. Frank and Frank D. Gilliard. Berkeley, CA: University of California Press, 1970. 213pp. ISBN 0-520-01723-4. LC 78-118685.

This is a translation of *Einführung in die Alte Geschichte* (now in its seventh German edition), the standard introductory work on the subject for German university students. The translators have adapted the work somewhat to better meet the needs of the English-reading student. In particular, they have revised the general bibliography to include more English-language works.

Bengtson discusses the scope of ancient history and briefly outlines the history of the study of antiquity from the Renaissance to the present. He then covers such basics as chronology, geography, anthropology, source materials, archaeology, and subdisciplines of ancient history (epigraphy, papyrology, and numismatics). Each section consists of a short introduction to the topic followed by a bibliographical essay. A final chapter covers reference works and periodicals. A general bibliography (without annotations) follows. Name and subject indexes conclude the work. Although now two decades old, Bengtson is still useful. The only comparable work is Petit's *Guide de l'étudiant en histoire ancienne* (entry 20), which is itself based on earlier editions of Bengtson.

2.   Defradas, Jean. **Guide de l'étudiant helleniste**. Paris: Presses Universitaires de France, 1968. 156pp. LC 75-371371.

A guide for French students of Greek language and literature, this work begins with some discussion of the role and nature of Greek studies in French colleges and universities. An extensive bibliographical survey follows. Defradas first covers research methods and key general works on Greek language, literature, and culture. He then lists the major Greek authors in chronological sequence, with references to important editions and secondary works. Finally, he discusses several ancillary disciplines: palaeography and textual criticism, papyrology, epigraphy, and archaeology. For each he provides an overview of the field and a very selective bibliography. Defradas comments, sometimes extensively, on most of the works cited. There is the expected bias in favor of French-language titles, although many German and English works are also mentioned. Indexes cover subjects, ancient authors, and modern authors. This work is a companion volume to those of Grimal on Latin studies (entry 7) and Petit on ancient history (entry 20).

3.   Dibdin, Thomas Frognall. **An Introduction to the Knowledge of Rare and Valuable Editions of the Greek and Latin Classics. Together with an Account of Polyglot Bibles, Polyglot Psalters, Hebrew Bibles, Greek Bibles and Greek Testaments, the Greek Fathers, and the Latin Fathers**. 4th ed. London: Harding and Lepard, 1827; reprint, Hildesheim, Germany: Georg Olms, 1977. 2v. LC 03-25381.

Itself something of a classic, Dibdin's work is well known to antiquarian book dealers and collectors. Dibdin is primarily of use to those working with early printed editions of the classics, especially bibliographers and historians of scholarship. Bibles appear first and are listed by date of printing. Editions of the Greek fathers, and then the Latin, follow. These are arranged by the author's dates. Finally, Dibdin treats the Greek and Latin classics. This section, by far the largest, is arranged alphabetically by author. Dibdin covers nearly all of the important early editions, from the beginning of printing to around 1820. His extensive annotations include much information on the editors and printers. He often discusses the history of a particular edition and its relation to earlier and contemporary editions. Dibdin also devotes much space to the aesthetic aspects of the books, such as paper and typography.

4.   Engelmann, Wilhelm, ed. **Bibliotheca Scriptorum Classicorum**. 8. Aufl., umfassend die Literatur von 1700 bis 1878, neu bearb. von E. Preuss. Leipzig, Germany: Verlag von Wilhelm Engelmann, 1880-1882; reprint, Hildesheim, Germany: Georg Olms, 1959. 2v. LC 01-16689.

Engelmann continues the work of Fabricius (entries 5-6) and Schweiger (entry 24). His first volume covers Greek literature, the second Latin. Each is divided into two sections: collected editions (by genre) and individual authors (alphabetically). There are a few cross-references for variant forms; no index is provided. Coverage is mainly philological. *Bibliotheca* lists editions, translations, commentaries, and critical literature (monographs and articles). Editions and translations far outnumber critical works. Occasionally a brief annotation or contents note accompanies an entry, but these are rare. Although not very satisfactory in either scope or organization, Engelmann remains the primary bibliographical resource for eighteenth- and nineteenth-century classical scholarship. Users should not neglect the additions and corrections at the end of each volume (volume 2 has additions for both volumes). *Bibliotheca* is continued by Klussmann (entry 13).

5.   Fabricius, Johann Albert. **Ioannis Alberti Fabricii ... Bibliotheca Graeca, sive, Notitia Scriptorum Veterum Graecorum Quorumcumque Monumenta Integra aut Fragmenta Edita Exstant tum Plerorumque e Mss. ac Deperditis ab Auctore Tertium Recognita et Plurimis Locis Aucta.** Editio Quarta variorum curis emendatior atque auctior curante Gottlieb Christophoro Harles; accedunt b. I. A. Fabricii et Christoph. Augusti Heumanni supplementa inedita. Hamburgi: Apud Carolum Ernestum Bohn, 1790-1809; reprint, Hildesheim, Germany: Georg Olms, 1966-1970.12v. LC 02-6671.

Bibliotheca Graeca has appeared in numerous editions and printings, of which this is the most complete. Most others are serviceable as well. Fabricius's work is part handbook or history of Greek literature and part bibliography. He provides extensive references to ancient literature, early editions of Greek authors, and scholarly works on Greek literature. Fabricius proceeds in roughly chronological order from the beginnings of Greek literature to the fall of Constantinople (A.D. 1453); chapters cover authors or (occasionally) genres. Thus, it is necessary to know the approximate date of an author to locate the relevant discussion. Users should also bear in mind that the dating of some authors has changed since the time of Fabricius. Lack of an index further complicates matters. Although somewhat difficult to consult, *Bibliotheca* remains a valuable source for early work on the classics.

6.   Fabricius, Johann Albert. **Jo. Alberti Fabricii Bibliotheca Latina, sive, Notitia Auctorum Veterum Latinorum, Quorumcumque Scripta ad Nos Pervenerunt, Distributa in Libros IV. Supplementis, Quae Antea Sejunctim Excusa Maximo Lectorum Incommodo Legebantur, Suis Quibusque Locis nunc Primum Insertis.** Venetiis: Apud Sebastium Coleti, 1728. 2v.

Fabricius completed *Bibliotheca Latina*, which is available in several editions, in 1697. It is a much less ambitious and less valuable work than his later *Bibliotheca Graeca* (entry 5). It consists of a chronological listing of Latin authors. Fabricius provides a brief biographical note on each, followed by a list of works with citations of their various editions. There is no index. *Bibliotheca Latina* can be helpful to those working with early editions of the Latin authors. Otherwise, it is primarily of antiquarian interest.

7.   Grimal, Pierre. **Guide de l'étudiant latiniste.** Paris: Presses Universitaires de France, 1971. 319pp. LC 71-576893.

Written by a distinguished Latinist, this work is intended as a guide for French university students. The first part provides a complete survey of Latin studies in France (ca. 1970), including a discussion of content, approaches, and methods at each level of formal education, and an overview of ancillary and related disciplines, such as numismatics, archaeology, and palaeography. The second part is a bibliographical guide. Its chapters successively cover fundamental reference works, studies of the language, Latin authors (editions and selected secondary works), and Roman history and civilization. Grimal presents the bibliographical chapters in the form of review essays. He provides critical commentary on nearly all of the works mentioned. Although geared toward the French reader, Grimal includes many works in English and German. Indexes cover ancient authors, historical persons, subjects, and modern authors. Companion volumes by Defradas (entry 2) and Petit (entry 20) cover Greek studies and ancient history respectively.

8.   Gullath, Brigitte, and Heidtmann, Frank. **Wie finde ich altertumswissenschaftliche Literatur: Klassische Philologie, Mittel- und Neulatein, Byzantinistik, Alte Geschichte und Klassische Archäologie**. Berlin: Arno Spitz, 1992. 346pp. (Orientierungshilfen; Bd. 23). ISBN 3-87061-207-X.

This recently published guide to research covers not only classical studies but also medieval Latin, Neo-Latin, and Byzantine studies. The first chapter provides a brief introduction to libraries and bibliographical research from a German viewpoint; the tenth is a glossary of bibliographical terms. The eight chapters in between cover a wide range of reference and general works in all of the standard languages of scholarship. Each deals with a broad general area: general works on classical studies, classical philology, medieval Latin and Neo-Latin, Byzantine studies and modern Greek philology, ancient history, classical archaeology, related fields (chiefly Near Eastern studies), and important periodicals. These chapters are extensively subdivided by form (e.g., handbooks, bibliographies). The 1,323 entries, which include articles as well as books, provide an effective general guide to reference literature and bibliographical apparatus of classical studies and related fields. The coverage of the related fields is not always as strong as for classics; the Ancient Near East receives particularly cursory coverage. Many entries receive brief descriptive annotations; these tend to be very short. A good general index concludes the work. This work and that of Poucet and Hannick in French (entry 22) are the best general bibliographical guides to research in classical studies.

9.   Halton, Thomas P., and Stella O'Leary. **Classical Scholarship: An Annotated Bibliography**. White Plains, NY: Kraus International Publications, 1986. 396pp. ISBN 0-527-37436-9; 0-527-37437-7pa. LC 82-48984.

Although originally intended as an update to Martin R. P. McGuire's *Introduction to Classical Scholarship* (entry 16), this book differs substantially from its predecessor. It is strictly a bibliography that covers both reference works and (very selectively) the monographic literature. Most entries include annotations that are generally useful, although content and quality vary greatly. References to scholarly reviews are also included in entries for monographs. The work is arranged into 15 major subject chapters, each of which is further subdivided as appropriate. There are author and subject indexes. Few items published after 1980 are included. As a guide to classical scholarship, this work is aimed primarily at advanced undergraduate and graduate students in the field. It is helpful for those seeking a quick orientation to the literature on a specific author or subdiscipline of classical studies. Readers who want an orientation to the field as a whole (and are willing to deal with French or German) will be better served by Poucet and Hannick (entry 22) or Gullath (entry 8). Poucet and Hannick in particular offers a well-structured guide to the literature of classical studies.

10.   Hoffmann, S. F. W. **Bibliographisches Lexicon der gesammten Literatur der Griechen**. 2. ungearb., durchaus verm., verb., und fortgesetzte Ausgabe. Leipzig, Germany: A. F. Böhme, 1838-1845; repr., Amsterdam: Adolf M. Hakkert, 1961. 3v. LC 5-16151.

Primarily of interest to antiquarians and historians of scholarship, Hoffmann provides a bibliographical guide to early work on Greek literature. He covers the authors in alphabetical sequence. Under each he lists editions and translations (from the first printed edition) as well as scholarly studies (chiefly from the eighteenth and nineteenth centuries, occasionally as far back as the sixteenth). There are very few annotations, and these only remark briefly on the contents or attribution of a work. Hoffman provides a more comprehensive bibliography for Greek studies in the early modern period than either Moss (entry 17) or Dibdin (entry 3), but is much less entertaining to read.

11.　　**Introduzione allo studio della cultura classica**. Milano: Mazorati Editore, 1972-1975. 3v. LC 73-359159.

This Italian introduction to classical studies consists of many short review essays by individual scholars. The volumes treat successively literature, linguistics and philology, and "subsidiary sciences." Coverage of literature is broken down by period, genre, and (less consistently) language. Some attention is given to Byzantine Greek and medieval Latin literature. The second volume is devoted mainly to traditional philological topics such as grammar, metrics, and textual criticism. The subsidiary sciences of volume 3 include archaeology, numismatics, geography, papyrology, linguistics, and so on. The organization of material is odd; for example, mythology and philosophy are placed in the linguistics and philology volume. While the quality of the essays varies, most provide a serviceable introduction and a good, though now dated, working bibliography for their topics. Indexes to subjects and modern authors appear at the end of the third volume.

12.　　Irmscher, Johannes, ed. **Einleitung in die klassischen Altertumswissenschaften: ein Informationsbuch**. Berlin: VEB Deutscher Verlag der Wissenschaften, 1986. 356pp. ISBN 3-326-00005-7.

Designed to meet the needs of East German university students, *Einleitung in die klassischen Altertumswissenschaften* offers a collection of brief introductory sketches on various aspects of classical studies. Most of the topics are predictable (e.g., classical archaeology, lexicography, numismatics), but some, such as Assyriology and classical studies, might not be expected in an introductory survey. There is a strong emphasis on ethnography and comparative studies throughout. Each essay defines its topic, reviews the state of studies (usually ca. 1980), and provides a short bibliography. Although there are the occasional intrusions of Marxist interpretation—which are to be expected of a work published in the former German Democratic Republic—this remains a handy work for readers of German.

13.　　Klussmann, Rudolf, ed. **Bibliotheca Scriptorum Classicorum et Graecorum et Latinorum: Die Literatur von 1878 bis 1896 einschliesslich umfassend**. Leipzig: O. R. Reisland, 1909-1913; repr., Hildesheim, Germany: Georg Olms, 1976. 2v. in 4. LC 10-9097.

Klussmann follows the pattern of Engelmann (entry 4), whose work he continues. His first volume covers Greek authors, the second Latin writers. Books and journal articles are cited without annotation. There are fewer editions and translations and far more critical works than in Engelmann. As in other works, there is a literary and philological bias; for example, history is covered only under entries for ancient historical authors. The size of Klussmann's work also illustrates the vast increase in scholarly activity in the classics in the late nineteenth century: He required more pages for 18 years than Engelmann needed to cover 178. Klussmann was originally published in *Bursian's Jahresbericht* (entry 48). For subsequent bibliography see Lambrino (entry 14).

14.   Lambrino, Scarlat, ed. **Bibliographie de l'antiquité classique, 1896-1914**. Paris: Société d'Edition "Les Belles Lettres," 1951. 761pp. (Collection de bibliographie classique). LC 52-001454.

Undertaken at the suggestion of Jacques Marouzeau, Lambrino's bibliography links Marouzeau's own *Dix années de bibliographie classique* (entry 15) and their predecessor Klussmann (entry 13). Lambrino planned two volumes: *Auteurs et textes* and *Matières et disciplines*. Of these, only the first was published. It is arranged alphabetically by ancient author, with Greek and Latin authors interfiled. Lambrino includes editions and critical studies. There are no abstracts or annotations, nor an index of modern authors, which was presumably reserved for the second volume.

15.   Marouzeau, J. **Dix années de bibliographie classique: bibliographie critique et analytique de l'antiquité gréco-latine pour la périod 1914-1924**. Paris: Société d'Edition "Les Belles Lettres," 1927-1928. 2v. (Collection de bibliographie classique). LC 28-27582.

Marouzeau compiled *Dix années* to remedy the bibliographical chaos brought about by World War I and subsequent events. His first volume, *Auteurs et textes*, covers editions and studies of individual classical authors in an alphabetical arrangement. The second volume, *Matières et disciplines*, covers general and topical works (e.g., history, archaeology, philology, history of scholarship) in a broad subject arrangement. Marouzeau includes citations of both monographs and articles, and provides brief abstracts in French. He also cites scholarly reviews under monographic titles. *Dix années* offers comprehensive coverage of scholarship for the period. For subsequent years see *L'Année philologique* (entry 26), which Marouzeau also founded. For previous years see Lambrino (entry 14).

16.   McGuire, Martin R. P. **An Introduction to Classical Scholarship: A Syllabus and Bibliographical Guide**. New and rev. ed. Washington, DC: Catholic University of America, 1961. 257pp. LC 61-66521.

Designed for beginning graduate students, McGuire's work takes the form of a syllabus for an introductory course in research methods and bibliography. Its arrangement is topical. Each section provides an overview of a particular area of classical studies and includes a bibliography. The final section is a general bibliography of ancient history and Greek and Latin authors (including early Christian history and literature) arranged by subject and genre. There is an index of modern scholars. The bibliographical portions have been superseded by Halton and O'Leary, *Classical Scholarship* (entry 9).

17.   Moss, Joseph William. **A Manual of Classical Bibliography: Comprising a Copious Detail of the Various Editions of the Greek and Latin Classics and of the Critical and Philological Works Published in Illustration of Them, with an Account of the Principal Translations into English, French, Italian, Spanish, German, etc**. 2d ed. London: Henry G. Bohn, 1837; repr., Port Washington, NY: Kennikat Press, 1969. 2v.

The scope of Moss's work, which covers the classical authors in alphabetical order, is well described by its copious subtitle. His style of citation is abbreviated, sometimes extremely so. Moss provides annotations that discuss content, publication history, bindings, and typography and often give the price of a copy as found in a bookseller's catalog of his era. While it can be of use in tracking down old editions and translations, Moss is primarily of antiquarian interest. The miscellaneous and frequently opinionated contents of the annotations will still interest bibliographers and historians of scholarship.

18.   Nairn, J. A. **J. A. Nairn's Classical Handlist**. 3d ed., rev. and enlarged. Oxford, England: B. H. Blackwell, 1953. 164pp. LC 54-14555.

First published in 1931 under the title *A Handlist of Books Relating to the Classics and Antiquity*, this book has been updated twice by the staff of B. H. Blackwell. Nairn provides an unannotated list of works in classical studies. The list, which is arranged by subject, includes editions and translations of classical authors, reference works, and selected secondary works. There is an index of authors. Although completely out of date, it can still be useful for locating citations of older works.

19.   Ooteghem, J. van. **Bibliotheca Graeca et Latina: á usage des professeurs des humanités gréco-latines**. Namur, Belgium: Editions de la Revue "Les Etudes classiques," 1969. 3ème éd. 384, 107pp. LC 70-851007.

In spite of its Latin title, this work is written in French. It is intended as a guide to classical bibliography for college teachers. Van Ooteghem divides the work into three sections. The first, which he calls *Indications préliminaires*, includes general works, bibliographical works, geography, Greek and Roman history, literary history, grammar, lexicography, and metrics. The two remaining parts cover Greek and Latin authors respectively. Van Ooteghem lists the authors alphabetically; under each he notes editions and studies. These are subarranged by work and topic as needed. There are some annotations, which usually serve to clarify content and, less often, to evaluate. His focus is on major, commonly studied authors. The bibliography includes nineteenth- and twentieth-century works in English, French, German, and Italian, as well as Greek and Latin. Although van Ooteghem does gather a large amount of basic material, his work is somewhat dated. Gullath (entry 8), Poucet (entry 22), and Halton and O'Leary (entry 9) are all better guides to classical bibliography.

20.   Petit, Paul. **Guide de l'étudiant en histoire ancienne**. 3ème éd. Paris: Presses Universitaires de France, 1969. 239pp. LC 78-481208.

Petit seeks to provide a guide to the study of ancient history for the French university student. He uses Bengtson (entry 1) as his model. The format of the two works is much the same. Bengtson is somewhat stronger in his coverage of technical aspects of the subject (e.g., chronology) and at least as good, if not better, in other areas as well. English-speaking students will, no doubt, prefer the translation of Bengtson. Thus, Petit is chiefly of use to those interested in a French approach to the subject.

21.   Platnauer, Maurice, ed. **Fifty Years (and Twelve) of Classical Scholarship: Being Fifty Years of Classical Scholarship, Revised with Appendices**. 2d ed. New York: Barnes and Noble, 1968. 523pp. LC 68-141561.

A reprint of the 1954 edition, this book consists of the original chapters followed by appendices that cover the intervening years. Each chapter was written by a distinguished British academic who surveyed the state of scholarship in a field; whenever possible the same person prepared the appendix to the chapter. Numerous bibliographical references are given. Emphasis is on philological and literary studies; most chapters cover literary genres (e.g., Greek tragedy). The chapters on the Greek and Roman historians provide coverage of historical studies in general, while archaeology is given short shrift. Although now dated, *Fifty Years* remains a good overview of classical scholarship as of 1968. An attractive feature is its narrative treatment of topics. However, the lack of an index is a major drawback.

22.   Poucet, Jacques, and J.-M. Hannick. **Introduction aux études classiques: guide bibliographique**. Louvain-le-Neuve, Belgium: Ciaco, 1989. (Etudes classiques). 242pp. ISBN 2-87085-182-0.

This recent French guide to the literature deserves to be more widely known and used. It was designed to serve as a bibliographical introduction to the field for Belgian university students in classical studies. Poucet and Hannick divide their work into two major parts. The first begins by presenting an overview of literary, epigraphical, papyrological, archaeological, and numismatic source materials. It then provides a good orientation to the standard series of classical texts, the various collections and *corpora* of ancient writings, and the frequently arcane publications of the documentary and material remains of antiquity. This part also briefly discusses the literature of such subdisciplines as textual criticism, geography, and chronology. The second part covers reference works. These are covered by form: encyclopedias and dictionaries, works on the languages, bibliographies, manuals, reviews, and collections (chiefly the major monographic series and periodicals). Useful notes and comments are often found at the beginning of sections. Poucet and Hannick also provide annotations to many of the individual works cited. These vary in length from a brief descriptive phrase to several paragraphs outlining the history and contents of a particular work. This well-thought-out volume will furnish undergraduate and graduate students with a sound working knowledge of the literature of classical studies. An electronic version, *Bibliotheca Classica Selecta*, is now under construction. It generally follows the format of the printed work, but also includes direct links to other Internet resources. The URL is http://www.fusl.ac.be/Files/General/BCS/BCS.html.

23.   Rees, B. R., ed. **Classics: An Outline for the Intending Student**. London: Routledge & Kegan Paul, 1970. 125pp. ISBN 0-7100-6914-6; 0-7100-6915-4pa.

Although distinctly British in orientation and now a bit old, Rees's introduction to classical studies for beginning undergraduates is still useful as an overview of college studies in classics. Separate chapters cover classical literature, ancient philosophy, history, archaeology, and the influence of the classics on English literature. Each chapter, by a specialist in the field, offers a narrative summary of the (then) current state of its subject, followed by a short bibliography of major works. Author and subject indexes are included.

24.   Schweiger, F. L. A. **Handbuch der classischen Bibliographie**. Leipzig: Friedrich Fleischer, 1830-1834; repr., Bryn Mawr, PA: Scholasticus Press, 1993. 2v. in 3. LC 02-6104.

Schweiger devotes the first volume of his *Handbuch* to Greek authors and the second to Latin. His arrangement is alphabetical, usually by author, although the occasional topical heading is also included (e.g., "Byzantina," which gathers Byzantine historians and chroniclers). Schweiger includes editions, commentaries, translations, and scholarly studies from the beginning of printing to about 1820. Some entries have brief annotations that are mainly of a bibliographical nature. Schweiger's coverage overlaps with that of Fabricius (entries 5-6) and of Engelmann (entry 4) and fills the gap between them. Schweiger also lists many useful sources of earlier bibliography in his *Vorwort* (foreword). Schweiger, along with Fabricius, is a basic source for pre-nineteenth-century classical bibliography.

25.   Van Keuren, Frances. **Guide to Research in Classical Art and Mythology**. Chicago: American Library Association, 1991. 307pp. ISBN 0-8389-0564-1. LC 91-11122.

Van Keuren's work is a guide to library research in classical art and architecture. Mythology is treated primarily as it relates to art, although some attention is devoted to mythology in literature. The book is divided into three parts. The first, "General Research," covers general works on Greek, Etruscan, and Roman art in successive chapters. The second part surveys works on mythology in both ancient and later art and literature. The third surveys particular media (e.g., Greek sculpture, Etruscan mirrors, Roman Republican coins) in a series of topical chapters.

Van Keuren's intention is to provide a step-by-step guide to doing research in the field. Each chapter begins with a detailed discussion of a single major reference work on the topic in question. This is followed by a section of complementary references, which includes brief descriptions of a number of related general and reference works. A third section discusses handbooks on the subject. The final section of each chapter, on supplementary sources, describes a wide range of monographs dealing with more specialized aspects of the subject. The user is expected to work through the chapter and the titles described in a systematic way, although it is possible to make more informal use of it. Good author-title and subject indexes provide help to the less-systematic reader.

This is an excellent tool for learning and teaching research methods in classical art and archaeology. It also provides a valuable overview of the structure of the literature in the field. Van Keuren's work should not, however, be regarded as a complete bibliographical guide to the field, because she is quite selective and omits a number of significant works.

CHAPTER 2

INDEXES AND ABSTRACTS

This chapter includes indexes to the periodical literature and other regularly updated bibliographical resources. Most appear annually (or are at least intended to), although a few are issued more frequently. While most indexes in classical studies remain in print form at the present, several computer databases are available, and others are being prepared. Along with review journals (treated in chapter 3), these represent the most current sources of bibliography. A number of older, now defunct indexes and abstracts are also listed below because of their important retrospective coverage.

26. **L'Année philologique: Bibliographie critique et analytique de l'antiquité gréco-latine.** 1925- . Paris: Société d'Edition "Les Belles Lettres," 1928- . ISSN 0184-6949.

L'Année philologique indexes all aspects of classical studies in an annual volume, which usually appears on a two- to three-year delay. Its scope is international. Originally a strictly French venture, it now has editorial offices in the United States and Germany as well as in Paris. Entries cover both books and articles; analytical entries are made for articles in festschriften and other collections. Each entry includes a brief descriptive abstract that may be in English, French, or German depending on which office indexed it. Book entries also cite scholarly reviews and are repeated with citations of new reviews from year to year (generally up to five years).

Organization has remained the same since this title's inception. The first and longest section is devoted to works on individual ancient authors and texts, and is arranged alphabetically by ancient author (with cross-references when needed). Subsequent sections, with appropriate subdivisions, cover major areas of classical scholarship: literary history, linguistics and philology, history of texts, archaeology, history, law, philosophy, sciences, history of scholarship, pedagogy, bibliography and reference works, and festschriften. A detailed table of contents facilitates subject access. Early volumes had only an index of modern authors. Over the years, additional indexes have been added: nonliterary ancient authors, collective titles (i.e., title entries in the authors and texts section), humanists (classical scholars as subjects), and geographical names.

L'Année philologique is the basic and indispensable tool for research in classical studies. For earlier coverage see J. Marouzeau, *Dix années de bibliographie classique* (entry 15), and its predecessors. The American Philological Association (entry 641) is currently sponsoring a project to make *L'Année* available on CD-ROM under the title *Database of Classical Bibliography*. However, due to restrictions imposed by the French publishers, the electronic version will not include the current three years of the print version. Thus, the computerized version will always lag five to six years in its coverage. The first release of the electronic version is scheduled to appear in 1995 and will cover the years 1976-1988; retrospective coverage will be expanded in subsequent releases.

27. **Archäologische Bibliographie**. 1913- . Berlin: G. Reimer, 1914-1918; Berlin: Walter de Gruyter, 1918- . ISSN 0341-8308. LC 38-4011.

The Deutsches Archäologisches Institut produces this annual bibliography, which continues bibliographies previously published in the "Archäologische Anzeiger" section of the *Jahrbuch des Deutschen Archäologischen Instituts* (1889-1912). The volumes for 1913-1972 were issued as supplements to the *Jahrbuch*. The *Bibliographie* provides comprehensive coverage of Greco-Roman archaeology and some coverage of Near Eastern archaeology as well. It includes books, articles, and reviews. Only citations are given; there are no abstracts. Arrangement is topical; a brief table of contents shows the major subject divisions. Recent volumes have included a "*Systematische Gliederung*," which gives a detailed listing of all subject categories and their subdivisions. There is an index of authors and reviewers in each volume.

One of the great virtues of *Archäologische Bibliographie* is its timeliness. The volume for each year is ordinarily published the following year. While it offers much less information than *Fasti Archaeologici* (entry 34), it appears years sooner. Users of the *Archäologische Bibliographie* should also note DYABOLA (entry 33), another product of the Deutsches Archäologisches Institut. DYABOLA is an electronic bibliographical database that covers much of the same material from 1956 on.

28. **Bibliographie internationale de l'Humanisme et de la Renaissance**. 1965- . Genève: Librairie Droz, 1966- . ISSN 0067-7000. LC 68-2326.

This annual bibliography is produced under the auspices of the Fédération Internationale des Sociétés et Instituts pour l'Etude de la Renaissance. Coverage is best for work on the fifteenth and sixteenth centuries, although there is some attention to the fourteenth and seventeenth centuries as well. The work is divided into two parts. The first covers persons and anonymous works (e.g., humanists and their works). The second part offers subject access that is divided into broad topical categories that are further subdivided. An index provides author access; there is also an index of persons treated as subjects (which includes only those who do not receive entries in the first part). There are no abstracts; the *Bibliographie* provides only citations. Early volumes were rather slender efforts, but recent ones have offered much fuller coverage of the literature. While of secondary interest to classicists, this is a very useful source for materials on the history of scholarship and the influence of the classics.

29. **Bibliographie papyrologique**. 1932- . Bruxelles: Fondation Egyptologique Reine Elisabeth, 1932- . ISSN 0964-7104.

30. **Electronic Bibliographie Papyrologique**. Version 2.0. Alpharetta, GA: Scholars Press, 1995. 3 computer disks.

Unlike most of the indexes in this section, which tend to be issued annually in bound volumes, the *Bibliographie papyrologique* is published on index cards approximately six times yearly. Each "issue" includes about 100 cards. It covers papyrological works (both books and articles). While the *Bibliographie* offers the fullest and most current coverage available for papyrological studies, it is difficult to consult. Cards must be arranged by either author or subject (unless two sets are used), and the other form of access is then lost. The title is best used as a current awareness service.

The electronic version, which has been developed by the American Society of Papyrologists (entry 642) in collaboration with the Fondation Egyptologique Reine Elisabeth, promises to alleviate many of the difficulties of the card format. It is produced with Pro-Cite and is intended to be used with that software, although it can be exported to other database programs. The cuurent version, 2.0, covers the years 1976 to 1994. Future versions will expand retrospective coverage.

31. **Bibliotheca Classica Orientalis: Dokumentation der altertumswissenschaftlichen Literatur der Sowjetunion und der Länder der Volksdemokratie**. Herausgegeben vom Institut für Griechische-Römische Altertumskunde bei der Deutschen Akademie der Wissenschaft zu Berlin. 1956-1969. Berlin: Akademie Verlag, 1956-1969. 14v.

A survey of Eastern European publications in classical and Byzantine studies, this periodical covered publications from the former USSR, Albania, Bulgaria, Hungary, Poland, Rumania, and Czechoslovakia. East Germany was added with volume 10 (that volume also included retrospective coverage of East German publications for 1956-1964). Most of the bibliographical citations for Slavic items include a German translation of the title; those for Russian entries also include the Romanized form of the author's name. Many, but by no means all, of the entries are annotated. The annotations are both descriptive and evaluative; all are in German. Arrangement is by subject within 18 broad categories. Often there are only one or two entries per subject in an issue. An index to the first 10 volumes appeared with volume 11 as a *"Registerheft"*; annual author and subject indexes appeared in each subsequent volume.

32. **Bulletin analytique d'histoire romaine**. 1962- . Strasbourg: Association pour l'étude de la civilisation romaine, 1965- . ISSN 0525-1044. LC 93-33397.

This annual publication abstracts articles on Roman history and archaeology. The first volume covered works published in Belgium, France, and Switzerland. Subsequent volumes have gradually added other countries and now provide reasonably good coverage of Europe. The *Bulletin* is arranged into three broad sections: sources, general history, and regional history. Each of these is further divided into numerous subsections. The detailed table of contents neatly outlines the structure of the whole. Each volume includes an index of names mentioned in the titles of articles; different typefaces are used to distinguish authors, other persons, places, and so forth. The abstracts, which are in French, generally give a good description of the original works. The *Bulletin* covers a wide range of materials, not all of which are included in *L'Année philologique* (entry 26). It is particularly useful for ferreting out obscure publications on a particular locality or archaeological site. Unfortunately, the publication schedule is erratic, to say the least. A gap occurs between the volumes for 1974-1975 and 1985 (which was published in 1992).

33.   Deutsches Archäologisches Institut. **DYABOLA**. Ennepetal, Germany: Biering und Brinkmann, 1992- .

DYABOLA (Dynamisch anwachsende Datenbank zu den Objekten und zur Literatur der Altertums- und Kunstwissenschaften) is a computerized version of the subject catalog of the Deutsches Archäologisches Institut in Rome. It covers a wide range of books, journal articles, and reviews on classical, early Christian, Byzantine, and medieval art and archaeology. It also includes works on the Ancient Near East. DYABOLA offers a number of search capabilities: author, exact title, title keyword, keyword (i.e., any proper name, ancient or modern), and subject (through the built-in hierarchical list of subject terms). While the rather cumbersome interface sometimes requires an inordinate number of steps and has several peculiarities (e.g., exact title searches must include any initial articles), this database is a valuable tool for research in classical archaeology and related fields. Because the electronic form begins with 1956, the old printed catalog (entry 202) remains useful for its coverage of earlier works. At present, DYABOLA includes works published through 1993, so it is reasonably up-to-date. Annual updates are planned. The database is currently available on a series of floppy disks that must be loaded onto a hard drive; a CD-ROM version is reportedly in preparation.

34.   **Fasti Archaeologici: Annual Bulletin of Classical Archaeology**. 1946- . Firenze, Italy: Sansone, 1948- . LC 90-40828.

Produced by the International Association for Classical Archaeology, this work attempts to provide full coverage of activities and publications in Greco-Roman archaeology. It was originally an annual publication, but 1969-1970 and subsequent volumes have appeared biennially as double volumes. Each volume is divided into six sections: generalia; prehistoric and classical Greece; Italy before the Roman Empire; the Hellenistic world and the provinces of the Eastern Roman Empire; the Roman West; and late antiquity. Each of these is divided into topical and geographical subsections. Contents include brief reports of ongoing excavations and recent discoveries (often accompanied by illustrations and maps), as well as summaries of new publications. There are indexes for authors (ancient and modern), geographical terms, and subjects. Although intended to appear on a one-year delay, *Fasti Archaeologici* is currently about 10 years behind schedule. It is an excellent source of information, but not at all timely. For current coverage it is necessary to consult *Archäologische Bibliographie* (entry 27).

35.   **International Guide to Classical Studies: A Quarterly Index to Periodical Literature**. 1961-1973. Darien, CT: American Bibliographic Service, 1961-1973.

Sometimes issued under the title *ABS International Guide to Classical Studies*, this work provides a listing of articles by author. There are no annotations, although occasional clarification is provided for uninformative titles. A fairly detailed subject index follows the listings. There are also indexes of reviews and reviewers. Cumulative indexes appear at the end of each volume. The *International Guide* covers only a selection of the more prominent journals; *L'Année philologique* (entry 26) renders it superfluous. Publication ceased with the death of Stanford Becker, "sole research bibliographer and Director of American Bibliographic Service" (v.12, no.1-4, p.1).

36.   **Klassieke Bibliographie: Maandlisten van Tijdschriftartikeleen met Driemaandelijksche Lijsten van Nieuwe Boekwerken in de Buma-Bibliotheek en in andere Nederlansche Bibliotheken.** 1929-1950. Utrecht, Netherlands, 1929-1950. 22v. LC 31-2181.

Several Dutch scholars and librarians collaborated in the production of this annual index. They list articles first and then books. The editors' organizational principles are obscure: citations are in short alphabetical clusters that are arranged in no particular order. Only citations are provided; there are no abstracts. There are author and keyword indexes at the end of each volume. Publication apparently ceased in 1950. *L'Année philologique* (entry 26) provides far superior coverage for the period in question.

37.   Malitz, Jürgen. **Gnomon bibliographische Datenbank: Internationales Informationssystem für die klassische Altertumswissenschaft.** München: C. H. Beck, 1994- . ISSN 0945-9790 (manual). ISBN 3-406-38194-4 (computer disks).

Produced by Beck (the publisher of *Gnomon* [entry 46]) and the Katholische Universität Eichstätt, this bibliographical database covers all aspects of classical studies. The initial release indexes all reviews, personal notes, and obituaries found in volumes 1 (1925) to 63 (1993) of *Gnomon*, as well as the listings found in that journal's *Bibliographische Beilage* from 1990 onward. In addition, for the years 1987 onward, the database indexes reviews from a number of other major journals; these include *Anzeiger für die Altertumswissenschaft* (entry 42), *American Journal of Archaeology* (entry 526), *Classical Review* (entry 45), *Göttingische Gelehrte Anzeigen, Journal of Hellenic Studies* (entry 557), and *Journal of Roman Studies* (entry 559). Altogether, the first release covers more than 200 periodicals and lists more than 120,000 books and articles. Search options include author, year, journal, and subject descriptor. The author indexing lacks authority control. The database does contain a German-language thesaurus of 3,000 subject descriptors that can be viewed in either alphabetical or hierarchical formats. Subsequent releases are to include an English version of this thesaurus. The interface itself is cumbersome and requires some practice to use effectively. There are a number of searching peculiarities, such as the need to use diacritics to ensure proper retrieval.

The initial version consists of 10 floppy disks and a manual. Both the manual and search menus are bilingual (German and English). Current system requirements include an IBM-compatible personal computer, DOS 3.3 or higher, 384K of RAM, and a hard drive with at least 65MB of free space. Updates and revisions will be published annually.

At the present time, the *Gnomon bibliographisches Datenbank* is the only general classical database of its kind. The printed version of *L'Année philologique* (entry 26) covers a much wider range of materials and provides abstracts. It remains to be seen how the forthcoming CD-ROM edition of *L'Année* will compare with the *Gnomon* database. Preliminary indications suggest that for the immediate future, *Gnomon* will both cover a wider span of years and generally be more current, but that the *L'Année* CD-ROM will offer superior information and access for the years that it covers.

38.   Matheson, Philippa M. W., and Robert Kallet-Marx. **TOCS-IN: Tables of Contents of Journals of Interest to Classicists**. Toronto, 1992- . URL: gopher://gopher.lib.virginia.edu/11/alpha/tocs or gopher://.epas.utoronto.ca/1ftp%3aftp.epas.utoronto.ca%40/pub/tocs-in

Based at the University of Toronto, TOCS-IN is a project to provide online access over the Internet to the tables of contents of journals in all areas of classical studies, including ancient history and archaeology. Material is supplied by volunteer contributors and then entered by Matheson and Kallet-Marx. Currently TOCS-IN covers about 145 journals; nearly all major titles are included. Files are divided into broad subject categories: general classics, archaeology, religion and Near Eastern studies, and miscellaneous. Within these categories, arrangement is alphabetical by title. TOCS-IN is best used as a current awareness service; it is much more up-to-date than such traditional sources as *L'Année philologique* (entry 26). Those who lack access to libraries with extensive periodical holdings will find this an exceptionally valuable resource.

TOCS-IN can be accessed by several means. The easiest is by gopher. A searchable copy of the archive (with WAIS indexing) is maintained at the University of Virginia; this can be reached by gophering to gopher.lib.virginia.edu and following the path: alphabetical organizations/tocs-in. The files are also available at numerous other gopher sites (see those listed in chapter 15). Files are also available by ftp from the original archive in Toronto; to do so, ftp to ftp.epas.utoronto.ca and follow the path pub/tocs-in.

39.   **Nestor**. Madison, WI: Institute for Research in the Humanities, University of Wisconsin, 1957-1977; Bloomington, IN: Program in Classical Archaeology, Indiana University, 1978- . ISSN 0228-2812. LC 84-2227.

Originally an irregular publication, *Nestor* now appears monthly (except July-September). It covers current work in Minoan and Mycenaean studies. The bulk of each issue is devoted to a bibliography (unannotated) of current publications in the field. There are also conference notices and summaries and occasionally brief accounts of work in progress. *Nestor* is an excellent source for currrent information on developments in Greek Bronze Age archaeology.

In addition, the cumulative *Nestor* bibliography of more than 30,000 entries is now available in machine-readable form as a series of structured ASCII files. It may be obtained on floppy disks (in either IBM/PC or Apple versions) from the publisher. The files may also be obtained over the Internet via ftp; to do so, ftp to cica.cica.indiana.edu; login as "anonymous" and use your full E-mail address as your password. The path to the appropriate files is /pub/archaeology.

40.   Rounds, Dorothy. **Articles on Antiquity in Festschriften: An Index**. Cambridge, MA: Harvard University Press, 1962. 560pp. LC 62-7193.

Rounds's work ranges over the Ancient Near East, Greece, Rome, and the Byzantine Empire. She provides an author/title index of articles in festschriften published between 1863 and 1954. All significant words in the titles are indexed. There are also entries for the festschriften themselves (the only full citation made) under the names of institutions and individuals honored. There are many cross-references for topical words and variant forms of proper names. While there is no subject index as such, the full indexing of title words plus the numerous cross-references approximate one.

In some ways Rounds is a bit cumbersome to use. Author and title entries require further reference to the actual festschrift entry to find full bibliographic details. The style of the entries tends to be somewhat telegraphic. Although many of these festschrift articles can be found through other sources (e.g., *L'Année philologique* [entry 26]), Rounds is a valuable tool for tracking down the contents of these difficult works. Her indexing is especially helpful when dealing with a fragmentary citation.

41. **The Year's Work in Classical Studies**. 1906-1947. London: John Murray, 1907-1919; Bristol, England: J. W. Arrowsmith, 1920-1950; repr., Amsterdam: J. Benjamins, 1969-1970. 34v. LC 08-12174.

The Classical Association (Great Britain; entry 647) sponsored this annual collection of review essays. It was intended to help teachers in the field keep up-to-date with scholarly advances. The essays, many written by distinguished scholars, covered recent developments and publications in such areas as Greek literature, Latin literature, Greek history, Roman history, philosophy, religion and mythology, papyrology, Greek archaeology, and Italian archaeology. Various other topics (e.g., Roman law, New Testament) appeared on a more occasional basis. Publication was suspended after the 1947 volume in deference to *L'Année philologique*'s (entry 26) superior coverage.

CHAPTER

REVIEW
JOURNALS

Here are listed journals whose primary function
is to provide notices and reviews of recent scholarly
works. These sources, while not as comprehensive as
some of the indexes noted in chapter 2, often provide
more current citations. For the works covered, they
frequently offer more detailed and critical descriptions
as well. The titles below also include several reviews
that are published electronically; these are usually the
most up-to-date sources for recent publications. Additional general information about electronic publications can be found in the introduction to chapter 15.

42. **Anzeiger für die Altertumswissenschaft**. 1948- . Wien: A. Sexl, 1948-1955;
     Innsbruck, Austria: Universitätsverlag Wagner, 1956- . ISSN 0003-6293.
     LC 53-29776.

This quarterly review, edited by the Osterreichischen Humanistischen Ge-
sellschaft, offers substantial, scholarly reviews of books in classical and Byzantine
studies, some brief reviews, and occasional review articles. Most reviews are in
German, although a few appear in French, English, or Italian. Unfortunately, despite
the quarterly publication schedule, the reviews are rarely timely.

43. **Bolletino di studi latini: Periodico semestrale d'informazione bib-
     liografica**. 1971- . Naples: Loffredo Editore, 1971- . ISSN 0006-6583.

Issued semiannually, this journal is chiefly devoted to reviews and bibliographical surveys, although it does include a few articles as well. A typical
number offers several review articles and bibliographical surveys, and around
20 scholarly reviews. These are followed by a survey of recent journal issues
that lists their contents and often supplies brief summaries. This survey provides
a convenient way to keep up with a wide range of Italian and other European
journals. Each issue concludes with a *Notiziario bibliografico* arranged by
subject, which notes recent books and articles. The first *Notiziario* each year lists
works about specific ancient authors, while the second covers works on topical
subjects. These bibliographies are similar to the *Bibliographische Beilage* in
Gnomon (entry 46); the listings in *Gnomon* are generally more current and

slightly fuller. Along with *Gnomon, Bollettino* is a good place to find items too recent to have appeared in *L'Année philologique* (entry 26).

44. **Bryn Mawr Classical Review**. 1990- . Bryn Mawr, PA: Bryn Mawr College and University of Pennsylvania, 1990- . ISSN 1055-7660 (print version); 1063-2948 (electronic version). LC 92-649894.

This relative newcomer is published both in electronic form and in a printed version. Reviews appear frequently but irregularly in the electronic version and are subsequently gathered into five or more printed issues per year. The reviews are all of a scholarly nature and sometimes of substantial length; their quality is uniformly high. Sometimes books are reviewed more than once by different reviewers; there are also occasional responses from authors. BMCR reviews books in all areas of classical studies; most of the works reviewed are in English, but there is some coverage of Western European scholarship as well. This is one of the most timely sources of substantive reviews.

To obtain an electronic subscription via the Internet, one should send the request "subscribe BMCR-L [yourname]" to listserv@cc.brynmawr.edu. The authoritative electronic archival text is maintained by the University of Virginia's Electronic Text Center (entry 616). The electronic backfile is also widely available through other gopher and World Wide Web sites, which are described in chapter 15.

45. **Classical Review**. 1887- (n.s. 1951-). Oxford, England: Oxford University Press, 1887- . ISSN 0009-840X. LC 10-32843.

Originally a monthly, this journal now appears semiannually. It provides reviews and notices of recent books in all areas of classical studies, with special emphasis on literary and historical studies. Works in Western European languages are frequently included. The reviews, which are generally written by highly qualified specialists, tend to be critical and scholarly. This is the best single English-language source for reviews of classical books, although the reviews rarely appear in a timely fashion. A general index of authors and reviewers and an *index locorum* (passages from ancient literature that are discussed) appear at the end of each volume. Two cumulative indexes have also appeared; one covers the old series (v. 1-64) and the other volumes 1-36 of the new series.

46. **Gnomon: Kritische Zeitschrift für die Gesamte klassische Altertumswissenschaft**. 1925- . Berlin: Weidmannsche Buchhandlung, 1925- . ISSN 0017-1417. LC 27-3554.

Gnomon currently appears eight times per year. Each issue includes major reviews of around eight to ten works and short reviews of perhaps a dozen more. Reviews are usually in German, although a few appear in English or French. Odd-numbered issues include the *Bibliographische Beilage*, which is paginated separately. This bibliography, which is arranged by subject, covers books and articles. There are no abstracts. While much less comprehensive than *L'Année philologique* (entry 26), these listings are far more timely. They provide a good tool for current awareness and for locating recent publications. Similar listings also appear in the *Bollettino di studi latini* (entry 43) under the title *Notizario bibliografico. Notizario* is generally not as timely or as extensive as *Bibliographische Beilage. Gnomon* also includes personal notes (e.g., birthdays and deaths of German classicists) and brief obituaries of major scholars. Annual indexes cover reviewers, authors, and subjects. *Gnomon* now also produces a computerized bibliographical database based on its backfiles (see entry 37).

47. **Ioudaios Review**. Lehigh, PA, 1991- . ISSN 1183-9937. URLs: http://www.lehigh.edu/lists/ioudaios-review or ftp://ftp.lehigh.edu/pub/list-serv/ioudaios-review

This review, which is associated with the *Ioudaios* electronic discussion group (entry 589), is published in electronic form over the Internet. It consists entirely of scholarly book reviews. The journal focuses on Hellenistic Judaism; it reviews nearly every significant new book on Jews in the Greco-Roman world. Both the issue for the current year and the full backfile are available at the World Wide Web site noted above. In addition to the full text of the journal, files and directories at that site provide background information about the journal and indexes of authors, reviewers, and titles. Individual reviews can also be obtained by anonymous ftp from the ftp address noted above.

48. **Jahresbericht über die Fortschritte der klassischen Altertumswissenschaft**. 1873-1956. Berlin: S. Calvary, 1873-1897; Leipzig: O. R. Reisland, 1898-1956. 285v. LC 28-6999.

Frequently referred to as *Bursian's Jahresbericht*, after its first editor Conrad Bursian, this periodical provided review essays on major authors or topics. In 1873 and 1874-1875 two volumes were issued; volume 1 of 1874/75 is titled *Die Fortschritte der Philologie*, volume 2 *Die Fortschritte der Altertumswissenschaft*. From 1876 each year consists of three volumes: *Griechische Klassiker* (later *Griechische Autoren*), *Lateinische Klassiker* (later *Lateinische Autoren*) and *Altertumswissenschaft*. Two supplements supply additional material: *Bibliotheca Philologica Classica* and *Biographisches Jahrbuch für Altertumskunde* (called from 1907 to 1924 *Biographisches Jahrbuch für die Altertumswissenschaft*). *Bibliotheca* offers a bibliography of books, articles, and dissertations dealing with all aspects of classical antiquity. The unannotated entries are arranged in subject categories. *Biographisches Jahrbuch* is a useful source of information on modern German classical scholars. It contains lengthy obituaries that often include full bibliographies, as well as biographies, of the deceased.

While the *Jahresbericht* long ago ceased publication, its many review essays and surveys remain a valuable source of retrospective bibliography. Its activities are continued in part by *Lustrum* (entry 49).

49. **Lustrum: Internationale Forschungsberichte aus dem Bereich des Klassischen Altertums**. 1956- . Göttingen, Germany: Vandenhoeck & Ruprecht, 1957- . ISSN 0024-7421.

Lustrum, which appears irregularly, continues in the vein of *Bursian's Jahresbericht* (entry 48). Issues consist of two or three review articles on particular authors, genres, or topics. Each article is prepared by a specialist in the field and usually surveys scholarship over an extended period of time. Most offer extensive bibliographies with some evaluative comment and discussion of trends. Often the more lengthy individual articles include an index. *Lustrum* is quite useful for keeping abreast of the literature on a wide range of authors and topics.

50. **Scholia Reviews**. 1992- . Durban, South Africa: Department of Classics, University of Natal, 1994- .

Also known as *Scholia E-Reviews*, this is an electronic version of reviews that appear in the printed journal, *Scholia*. It offers scholarly reviews of recent works in all aspects of classical studies. While the number of reviews is not large (currently around 12 to 15 per year), the reviews are made available in a timely manner. Subscribers receive each review by E-mail as soon as it is ready, often long before it appears in printed form. Subscription requests may be sent via the Internet to scholia@owl.und.ac.za. The backfiles are archived both at the University of Natal and at the University of Pennsylvania. These are available by ftp and by gopher. The URL for gopher access at the University of Pennsylvania is: gopher://ccat.sas.upenn.edu:5070/11/scholia.

CHAPTER

TOPICAL BIBLIOGRAPHIES

This chapter includes bibliographies and bibliographical surveys on particular topics within classical studies. Coverage here, as elsewhere in this volume, is limited to book-length works. Many bibliographies are also published as articles; *Lustrum* (entry 49), *Classical World* (entry 545), and *Aufstieg und Niedergang der römischen Welt* (entry 350) are good sources to check for these. A large number of bibliographies, including those appearing in periodicals, are listed by James H. Dee, "A Survey of Recent Bibliographies of Classical Literature," *Classical World* 73:5 (Feb. 1980): 275-90. To supplement and update materials found in the works below, one may consult the appropriate indexes and abstracts from chapter 2.

51.　Accardi, Bernard, et al., comps. **Recent Studies in Myths and Literature, 1970-1990: An Annotated Bibliography**. New York: Greenwood Press, 1991. 251pp. (Bibliographies and Indexes in World Literature, no.29). ISBN 0-313-27545-9. LC 91-18070.

　　While aimed primarily at students of British and American literature, this work is also of use to classicists. Its second chapter deals with myth in classical literature; others cover general works on myth and literature or specific periods of American or British literature. These chapters also include many studies on the use of classical myth in later literature. Some 1,081 works are cited; more than half discuss classical mythology in some way. Each entry includes a descriptive annotation. Many of these are fairly substantial, and a few include critical comments as well. Author and subject indexes are provided. Those interested in classical literature proper need only consult the second chapter, while readers concerned with the influence of classical myth in Anglo-American literature would do well to approach the work through the subject index. Users should also bear in mind that this bibliography is far from complete in its coverage.

52.　Arlen, Shelley. **The Cambridge Ritualists: An Annotated Bibliography of the Works by and about Jane Ellen Harrison, Gilbert Murray, Francis M. Cornford, and Arthur Bernard Cook**. Metuchen, NJ: Scarecrow Press, 1990. 414pp. ISBN 0-8108-2373-X. LC 90-47304.

Harrison, Murray, Cornford, and Cook were among the first to apply anthropological theories to the study of Greek literature, myth, and religion. Their works have had a lasting influence and continue to be read. Arlen, a reference librarian, has compiled an exhaustive bibliography of their writings and of works about them. She lists 2,019 items in five major sections: one for works dealing with the "Cambridge Ritualists" in general, and separate sections for each of the four scholars. These sections each open with a portrait, a biographical sketch, and an overview of current research on the scholar. Works by the individual follow, subarranged by form: books, translations, articles, letters, and reviews. A bibliography of critical and biographical writings about the scholar closes each section. Descriptive annotations accompany many but not all entries. Entries for books include citations of reviews. Numerous cross-references link related entries. Arlen provides author, title, and subject indexes. This bibliography is noteworthy both for its completeness and its ease of use.

53.   Beck, Frederick A. G. **Bibliography of Greek Education and Related Topics**. Sydney, Australia: F. A. Beck, 1986. 333pp. ISBN 0-9588450-0-X.

Although compiled by a well-known authority on ancient Greek education, this bibliography is disappointing. The work lacks focus; in addition to items specifically about Greek education, it also includes many "related" works on philosophy, rhetoric, literary criticism, the history of writing, and Greek athletics. While not entirely irrelevant, many of these are peripheral to the announced subject. Also, the book's organization is somewhat cumbersome. Beck provides subject access through a classified listing. The citations in this part are usually rather spare; sometimes they are not even sufficient to identify the work clearly. The second part of the book is an alphabetical author list, which includes fuller citations. Beck sometimes supplies annotations. In the case of books, these are frequently quotations from or summaries of reviews. Most of these annotations are in the author list, but a few are included with the classified entries. Users will need to check both listings to be sure they have all the relevant information about a given item. Beck does provide some aids for the user; these include an outline of his classification scheme and indexes to the classification, series and serials, and reviewers. While Beck offers full coverage of Greek education, most will find consulting his bibliography tedious and time-consuming.

54.   Bell, Albert A., Jr., and James B. Allis. **Resources in Ancient Philosophy: An Annotated Bibliography of Scholarship in English, 1965-1989**. Metuchen, NJ: Scarecrow Press, 1991. 799pp. ISBN 0-8108-2520-1. LC 91-39912.

This work is aimed primarily at college students and the reference librarians who work with them, although it will also be useful for teachers and scholars. Its more than 7,000 entries are arranged under 21 rubrics covering all the major philosophical schools and the most important individual philosophers of antiquity. Each of these is further subdivided into numerous sections. A particularly useful feature of the work is the provision of introductory notes for each chapter and section. These provide background information on the topic or individual covered and help orient nonspecialist users. The annotations provide brief summaries of works cited but rarely appraise them. Bell and Allis emphasize philosophical studies but also include a number of philological and historical items. This is an excellent single source on ancient philosophy for students and others who need primarily recent English-language works. For more detailed coverage and works in other languages, consult bibliographies listed under individual philosophers in chapter 6.

55. Bérard, François, Denis Feissel, Pierre Petitmengin, and Michel Sève. **Guide de l'épigraphiste: bibliographie choisie des épigraphies antiques et médiévales**. 2ème ed. Paris: Presses de l'Ecole Normale Supérieure, 1989. 354pp. (Bibliothèque de l'Ecole Normale Supérieure guides et inventaires bibliographiques, 2). ISBN 2-7288-0143-6. LC 89-183334.

Aimed at beginning students of Greek and Latin epigraphy, this selective bibliography lists 2,051 publications. While the authors emphasize published editions of inscriptions, they also offer ample coverage of handbooks, bibliographies, and the more important secondary literature. The overall arrangement is by type of work, with subarrangement by place or subject as appropriate. The bibliography provides a good working guide to study of Latin inscriptions through the fall of the western empire (A.D. 476) and Greek inscriptions through the fall of Byzantium (A.D. 1453). The compilers also include a more limited selection of works on "peripheral epigraphies," by which they mean inscriptions in a variety of languages and dialects, such as Minoan, Mycenaean, Egyptian, Coptic, Persian, and Etruscan. Medieval Latin inscriptions of the ninth to fifteenth centuries are also treated under this rubric. Although relatively few entries are annotated, useful notes and comments are scattered throughout the volume. The three indexes cover authors, places, and subjects.

56. Berkowitz, Luci, and Karl A. Squittier. **Thesaurus Linguae Graecae Canon of Greek Authors and Works**. 3d ed. New York: Oxford University Press, 1990. 471pp. ISBN 0-19-506037-7. LC 89-49454.

Originally designed as a working tool for the TLG project (see entry 464), the *Canon* has now grown to be an extremely useful bibliographical reference source. It lists the source editions for each Greek author and work included in the TLG database. The *Canon* now covers more than 3,000 Greek authors and more than 9,000 individual works. It includes virtually all extant Greek authors and texts from Homer to A.D. 600 and a considerable number of later Byzantine works as well. Entries are arranged alphabetically by author (or title for anonymous works). The TLG number, and century and place of origin, if known, are provided for each author. Individual works are then listed along with the selected edition for each. In most cases, the best available critical edition is cited. The *Canon*, which is indispensible to users of the TLG database, is also of great value to anyone seeking editions of particular Greek authors and works.

57. Bonser, Wilfrid. **A Romano-British Bibliography (55 B.C.-A.D. 449)**. Oxford, England: Basil Blackwell, 1964. 2v. LC 65-4078.

Bonser covers works on the period extending from Julius Caesar's first expedition to Britain in 55 B.C. to the arrival of Hengist and Horsa in A.D. 449. The 9,370 unannotated items cited include materials published before the end of 1959. Bonser has arranged these in a classified scheme. The first part covers topics, which are arranged under general headings and their various subdivisions. The second part covers works on specific archaeological sites. The second volume contains indexes to authors, subjects, personal names, and place-names. Many of the citations are to relatively obscure works published by local historical and antiquarian societies, which are often overlooked by more general sources of classical bibliography. Bonser is an indispensable work for the study of Roman Britain.

58. Boyle, Leonard E. **Medieval Latin Palaeography: A Bibliographical Introduction**. Toronto: University of Toronto Press, 1984. 399pp. (Toronto Medieval Bibliographies, 8). ISBN 0-8020-5612-1; 0-8020-6558-9pa. LC 85-157656.

Although primarily aimed at medievalists, this bibliography is of considerable value to anyone interested in the transmission of classical Latin literature and Latin palaeography. A leading scholar in the field (and now Prefect of the Vatican Library), Boyle modestly claims in the preface that the work is aimed only at beginners. This is not entirely true, because even specialists will find it a useful tool. Boyle has arranged his material in eight broad subject categories (with many subdivisions) that cover bibliographical and general works, the scripts, libraries, writing materials, scribes, the transmission and editing of texts, and research aids (general reference works). Many entries are accompanied by descriptive and evaluative annotations. In addition to a detailed general index, there is a special index of manuscripts.

59. Braswell, Susan. **Western Manuscripts from Classical Antiquity to the Renaissance: A Handbook**. New York: Garland, 1981. 382pp. (Garland Reference Library of the Humanities, v.139). ISBN 0-8240-9541-3. LC 79-7908.

The misleading subtitle of this book conceals a bibliography. Braswell covers all Western manuscripts, not just classical ones, through the Renaissance. She employs a topical arrangement, with chapters on such topics as bibliographical materials; libraries; microforms; incipits; special subjects; indexes, lists, catalogs, and *repertoria*; palaeography; diplomatics and archives; codicology; manuscripts and their contents; and textual criticism. Braswell provides descriptive annotations for most entries. Those interested in the history and transmission of classical texts will find much of value in this volume. However, anyone with specific interests in Latin palaeography would do well to consult Boyle's more specialized (and more learned) bibliography (entry 58).

✓ 60. Braund, Susan H. **Roman Verse Satire**. New York: Oxford University Press, 1992. 65pp. (New Surveys in the Classics, no.23). ISBN 0-19-922072-7. LC 92-221767.

This survey, like others in its series, is aimed primarily at undergraduates. Braund covers both general topics (e.g., the origins and characteristics of satire) and chief exponents of the genre (Lucilius, Horace, Persius, and Juvenal) in a series of brief essays. She reviews recent scholarship both in the text and in the detailed notes. Braund is highly selective and concentrates on recent English-language work.

✓ 61. Bremmer, Jan N. **Greek Religion**. New York: Oxford University Press, 1994. 111pp. (New Surveys in the Classics, no.24). ISBN 0-19-922073-5.

Bremmer, who has published extensively in this area, surveys recent scholarship on Greek religion. He takes Walter Burkert's *Griechische Religion der archaischen und klassischen Epoche* (Stuttgart, Germany: Kohlhammer, 1977) as his point of departure and focuses on subsequent work, although he also discusses important earlier studies. Bremmer organizes his survey under eight rubrics: general characteristics, gods, sanctuaries, ritual, mythology, gender, transformations, and the genesis of Greek religion. His approach follows the familiar format of this series: Each chapter consists of a critical discussion of recent trends and publications, with bibliographical details presented in notes at the end. Bremmer does depart from the series's normal practice of concentrating on English-language works and notes many valuable European-language publications. The index of names, subjects, and passages is detailed and includes all authors mentioned in the notes. Those seeking more extensive retrospective coverage should also consult Motte (entry 103).

62. Brockmeyer, Norbert, and Ernst Friedrich Schultheiss. **Studienbibliographie: Alte Geschichte**. Wiesbaden, Germany: Franz Steiner, 1973. 148pp. (Wissenschaftliche Paperbacks Studienbibliographien). LC 73-372193.

Intended as a guide for advanced students, this work deals with Ancient Near Eastern as well as Greek and Roman history. Books and articles are presented in a topical arrangement. Chapters cover general works, reference works, foundations (chronology, geography, ethnography, sociology, science and technology, the military, law, religion, politics, and historical theory), source materials, ancillary disciplines (epigraphy, numismatics, and papyrology), and secondary sources (editions and studies of the ancient historical writers). Brockmeyer and Schultheiss emphasize basic works and source materials. Their focus is firmly placed on ancient history; literature and archaeology are treated only to the extent that they provide historical sources. Annotations are not supplied. There are author, source, and subject indexes.

Bengtson (entry 1), which is available in English, is better as a general guide because of its narrative style and the many annotations in its bibliographical sections. However, Brockmeyer and Schultheiss include a number of works omitted by Bengtson. For those interested primarily in Roman history, Christ (entry 69) offers a more complete bibliography.

63. Brüggemann, Lewis William. **A View of the English Editions, Translations and Illustrations of the Ancient Greek and Latin Authors**. Stettin, Germany: J. S. Leich, 1797-1801; repr., New York: Burt Franklin, 1971. 2v. LC 06-25040.

Brüggemann focuses on works actually published in England, most of them being seventeenth- and eighteenth-century imprints. Greek and Latin authors are treated in separate sections, each arranged chronologically. Because the dating of a number of authors has changed since Brüggemann's day, some are found in peculiar locations. There are occasional annotations, and reviews are sometimes cited also. Brüggemann provides an index of authors. The main lists are in the first volume; the second volume is a supplement. Primarily of antiquarian interest, Brüggemann can be useful to bibliographers and historians of scholarship.

64. Calder, William M., III, and Daniel J. Kramer. **An Introductory Bibliography to the History of Classical Scholarship Chiefly in the XIXth and XXth Centuries**. Hildesheim, Germany: Georg Olms, 1992. 410pp. ISBN 3-487-09643-9. LC 93-150750.

This constitutes a catalog of books and reprints in the large personal library of Calder, who is one of the leading exponents of the study of the history of classical scholarship. The bibliography is divided into sections for general works, works on institutions, and works on individuals. Calder goes far beyond the strict confines of classical scholarship and includes much on the general intellectual and academic history of the period covered. He has supplied annotations for most entries. These, which vary in length, are usually both informative and entertaining. They are also opinionated, and not everyone will find the opinions to their liking. Calder brings together many obscure and hard-to-find references, including quite a few from sources not familiar to the average classicist.

65. Calhoun, George M., and Catherine Delamere. **A Working Bibliography of Greek Law**. Cambridge, MA: Harvard University Press, 1927; repr., Buffalo, NY: Wm. S. Hein, 1980. 144pp. (Harvard Series of Legal Bibliographies, 1). LC 27-27465.

Calhoun's bibliography focuses on the classical period; it is less comprehensive for Hellenistic and later Greek law. There is limited coverage for works published in the eighteenth century and earlier (Calhoun, in his preface, refers to other bibliographical sources for these). Works are presented in a single alphabetical list, arranged by author. There are neither annotations nor indexes. While dated and generally lacking in bibliographical amenities, Calhoun remains useful for his coverage of nineteenth- and early twentieth-century scholarship.

66. **Catalogus Dissertationum Philologicarum Classicorum: Verzeichnis von etwa 27400 Abhandlungen aus dem Gesamtgebiete der klassischen Philologie und Altertumskunde**. 2. Aufl. Leipzig: Buchhandlung Gustav Fock, 1910; repr. (with Editio III), New York: Johnson Reprint, 1963. 652pp.

67. **Catalogus Dissertationum Philologicarum Classicorum**. Editio III. Erläuterungschriften zu den griechischen und lateinischen Schriftstellern, enthaltend die Literatur aus den Jahren 1911-1936 und eine Auswahl früher erschiener Schriften. Leipzig: Buchhandlung Gustav Fock, 1937; repr. (with 2. Aufl.), New York: Johnson Reprint, 1963. 176pp.

A bookseller's catalog with a vengeance, the 2d edition of this compilation issued by the German bookseller Gustav Fock lists more than 27,000 dissertations and *Programmschriften* written by German scholars in either Latin or German. Most of the work in this academic genre is obscure and hard to find; some of it is valuable, but much is not worth the effort of finding. Fock's catalog is one of the few comprehensive tools for locating and verifying citations to these writings. Fock's citations tend to be rather spartan; information is often abbreviated. The catalog is arranged in broad subject categories: works on Greek authors and Latin authors (both A-Z), and *Altertumswissenschaft* (all other aspects of the study of classical antiquity, with further subdivision into language, history, archaeology, and so on). There is also a keyword subject index, but no access by author.

The catalog is continued to 1936 by the 3d edition. This edition contains nearly 6,000 further entries but is more restricted in scope. It supplies only sections on Greek and Latin authors, each arranged alphabetically. There is no index.

68. Christ, Karl. **Antike Numismatik: Einfuhrung und Bibliographie**. Darmstadt, Germany: Wissenschaftliche Buchgesellschaft, 1967. 107pp. LC 68-080573.

A general survey of ancient numismatics by a noted ancient historian, this work could equally well be treated as a handbook or a bibliography. Its chapters cover general works, Greek numismatics, Hellenistic numismatics, Roman numismatics, and special studies. Various topical subdivisions appear under each chapter. Brief narrative sections, which provide an overview of the various aspects of ancient numismatics, alternate with extensive bibliographical listings. There is a very selective subject index but no index of authors cited. Although now dated, Christ remains an excellent guide to earlier work in the field. For more recent works, see Clain-Steffanelli (entry 70).

69.	Christ, Karl, ed. **Römische Geschichte: Eine Bibliographie**. Darmstadt, Germany: Wissenschaftliche Buchgesellschaft, 1976. 544pp. ISBN 3-534-06074-1.

Intended for German students, this bibliography covers all aspects of Roman history. Its 8,232 unannotated entries are organized by subject. The major sections cover general works, special topics (e.g., law, religion, art), the history of the Roman republic, the collapse of the republic, the empire (31 B.C to A.D. 192), the crisis of the third century, and late antiquity. Each is subdivided further by topic and period. Christ includes books, articles, and dissertations in a variety of languages, although German is emphasized. He provides an excellent guide to twentieth-century work on Roman history through 1975. There is a subject index, but not, unfortunately, one for authors.

70.	Clain-Steffanelli, E. E. **Numismatic Bibliography**. München: Battenberg, 1985. 1848pp. ISBN 3-87045-938-7. LC 85-138945.

Although a general bibliography of numismatics, this work offers the most comprehensive and up-to-date bibliographical treatment of Greek and Roman numismatics available. Clain-Steffanelli lists 3,388 books, dissertations, articles, and catalogs dealing with the coinage of the classical world. Separate chapters cover Greece and Rome. Each begins with a section on general works and concludes with special topics (prices, coin types and iconography, minting techniques, etc.). Aside from these, the Greek material is arranged geographically and the Roman chronologically. Clain-Steffanelli occasionally adds a note to clarify content; otherwise, entries are not annotated. She also provides numerous cross-references. The extensive indexes cover authors, personal names, collectors, geographical terms, numismatic terms, and public collections. This bibliography is useful to those interested in economic history as well as students of ancient coinage.

✓	71.	Clark, Gillian. **Women in the Ancient World**. New York: Oxford University Press, 1989. 46pp. (New Surveys in the Classics, no.21). LC 89-194776.

Because publications on women in antiquity tend to be scattered under many more general rubrics, they can be difficult to find. Clark's survey provides both a good overview of the subject and a working guide to the literature. After an introduction, she presents a series of brief chapters covering major aspects of the lives of women in antiquity: the nature of women, domesticity, company, fertility, intelligence, power, money, religion, protection, and repression. Each discusses the major primary sources and reviews the current state of scholarship. Bibliographical details are given in the notes. Clark covers a wide range of recent publications (through mid-1988) in the field. As in other volumes in the series, preference is given to English-language publications. Additional material may be found in Goodwater (entry 86) and Vérilhac (entry 130a).

72.	Coulson, William D. E., and Patricia N. Freiert. **Greek and Roman Art, Architecture, and Archaeology: An Annotated Bibliography**. 2d ed., completely revised. New York: Garland, 1987. 203pp. (Garland Reference Library of the Humanities, v.580). ISBN 0-8240-8756-9. LC 84-48860.

Coulson and Freiert, both established archaeologists, aim their bibliography at four types of users: general readers, teachers, undergraduates, and graduate students. Their first seven chapters cover all major aspects of the subject: general works, the methodology and history of archaeology, Aegean prehistory, the Greeks, the Etruscans, the Romans, and sites of multiple periods.

In these chapters Coulson and Freiert list a wide array of scholarly books and the better popular books. The bibliography does not include articles. The vast majority of works noted are in English. Coulson and Freiert have supplied substantial annotations for each entry that provide clear descriptions and assessments. They have also added an eighth chapter, "Additional Resources," to the 2d edition, covering bibliographical resources (including a useful digression on publishers and distributors of archaeological works), monographic series, museum collections and publications, the classical tradition and its influence, and novels set in the ancient world. There is also an index of authors. This is an exceptionally well done bibliography.

73. Cousin, Jean. **Bibliographie de la langue latine, 1880-1948**. Paris: Société d'Edition "Les Belles Lettres," 1951. 375pp. (Collection de bibliographie classique). LC 51-8399.

Cousin's bibliography covers all aspects of the study of the Latin language. It is arranged by subject; major headings cover such topics as general linguistic works, the relation of Latin to other languages, the history of the language, writing and pronunciation, phonology, morphology, syntax, word order, stylistics, and lexicography. As Cousin worked closely with Jules Marouzeau, his coverage of works published in 1914 and later largely duplicates that of the corresponding sections of *Dix années* (entry 15) and *L'Année philologique* (entry 26). There are no annotations. Cousin does provide indexes to Latin words and to names (chiefly of Latin authors). His work is comprehensive for the years covered; for later bibliography see Cupaiuolo (entry 75).

74. Criniti, Nicola. **Bibliografia catilinaria**. Milano: Editrice Vita e Pensiero, 1971. 84pp. (Pubblicazioni dell'Università cattolica del S. Cruore. Saggi e ricerche, ser. 3: Scienze storiche, 6). LC 72-331657.

Criniti offers a relatively complete bibliography of works on the Catilinarian conspiracy, an event made prominent by the writings of Cicero and Sallust. The first part of the work lists more than 800 historical studies on the conspiracy, arranged by author. The second part is devoted to literary and artistic works (including novels, plays, operas, and graphic works) based on the life and conspiracy of Catiline. More than a hundred such works, arranged by form, are included. Indexes provide subject access to the whole bibliography and also allow for geographical and chronological approaches to the imaginative works in the second part.

75. Cupaiuolo, Fabio. **Bibliografia della lingua latina (1949-1991)**. Napoli: Loffredo Editore, 1993. 592pp. (Studi latini; v. 11).

Continuing the work of Cousin (entry 73), Cupaiuolo's bibliography closely follows his predecessor in scope and form. Cupaiuolo gathers a vast number of citations covering every aspect of the Latin language. He also includes many linguistic works that, while not directly concerned with Latin, are useful to students of the language. Arrangement is by subject, with chapters covering such topics as linguistics, origins of the Latin language, orthography and pronunciation, phonetics, morphology, syntax, stylistics, and lexicography. For those concerned primarily with a single author, Cupaiuolo has provided a chapter on the language and style of individual authors, which is subarranged alphabetically by ancient author. Many entries include brief descriptive annotations, and entries for books also list reviews. The lack of an index is a major drawback. There are occasional typographical errors and inaccuracies of citation as well, although not enough to seriously reduce the value of the work. Together, Cousin and Cupaiuolo provide an excellent guide to works on the Latin language.

76.   Donlan, Walter, ed. **The Classical World Bibliography of Greek and Roman History**. New York: Garland, 1978. 234pp. (Garland Reference Library of the Humanities, v.94). ISBN 0-8240-9879-X. LC 76-52511.

This volume gathers 14 bibliographical surveys that originally appeared in *Classical World* (entry 545) between 1954 and 1971. Three each of these are devoted to Herodotus (one general survey and two collectively covering 1954-1969), Thucydides (1942-1967), and Tacitus (1948-1967). The following are each covered by a single survey: Livy (1940-1958), Caesar (1935-1961), Philo and Josephus (1937-1959), Alexander the Great (1948-1967), and Julian the Apostate (1945-1964). These surveys normally are selective, although those on Philo and Josephus and Alexander the Great attempt completeness. All are by well-known specialists on the respective subjects. There is some variation in presentation, but most of the surveys are arranged topically, and all include descriptive and evaluative comments on the works cited. The compilation reflects a general bias in classical studies towards treating history through historical authors. It is a useful compendium for those seeking retrospective bibliographies on the ancient historians. A general index would have been helpful.

77.   Donlan, Walter, ed. **The Classical World Bibliography of Greek Drama and Poetry**. New York: Garland, 1978. 339pp. (Garland Reference Library of the Humanities, v.93). ISBN 0-8240-9880-3. LC 76-52510.

Donlan gathers 13 surveys that were published in *Classical World* (entry 545) between 1953 and 1976. There are two review articles on Homeric studies, one covering major trends in scholarship during 1939-1955, the other focusing on Homeric originality (listing studies published between 1928 and 1971). Greek tragedy is covered well, with two surveys each on Aeschylus (collectively covering 1947-1964) and Euripides (1940-1965), and one on Sophocles (1945-1956). Two articles cover work on Aristophanes and Old Comedy for 1946-1967. A complete bibliography of publications on Menander's *Dyskolos*, which was rediscovered and published in 1958, for 1959-1960 rounds out the drama section. Three essays surveying work on Greek lyric poetry for 1946-1975 conclude the volume. These are much more comprehensive than the other surveys and take up nearly half the book. All the surveys employ some form of subject arrangement and include descriptive and evaluative discussion of the works cited. Unless otherwise noted, they are selective bibliographies. Although they are not up-to-date, the surveys are a useful source of bibliography on important authors and genres in Greek literature. The lack of an index, however, is a major drawback.

78.   Donlan, Walter, ed. **The Classical World Bibliography of Philosophy, Religion, and Rhetoric**. New York: Garland, 1978. 396pp. (Garland Reference Library of the Humanities, v.95). ISBN 0-8240-9878-1. LC 76-52512.

In this volume Donlan collects some 19 surveys by various hands that appeared in *Classical World* (entry 545) between 1954 and 1973. The philosophical component begins with two reviews of work on the Pre-Socratics that covers 1945-1966 and a survey of work on Plato (1945-1955). There are three essays on Aristotle: one general survey for 1945-1955, and one each on the *Psychology* (1954-1964) and the *Poetics* (1940-1954). Surveys of work on Epicureanism (1937-1954), Hellenistic philosophy (1937-1957), and Lucretius (1945-1972) complete the section. The single survey dealing with religion covers works on early Roman religion for 1945-1952. No fewer than five bibliographical essays deal with Cicero; two are general (1939-1965), and three focus on the rhetorical and philosophical works of Cicero (1939-1967). Two surveys on the prose works of the younger Seneca (1940-1968) and two general reviews of scholarship on ancient rhetoric (1939-1963) conclude the volume. As with other volumes in this series, the surveys are arranged by subject and offer useful annotations or discussion of works noted. Most are selective in their coverage. As in Donlan's other compilations, an index is lacking.

79. Donlan, Walter, ed. **The Classical World Bibliography of Roman Drama and Poetry and Ancient Fiction**. New York: Garland, 1978. 387pp. (Garland Reference Library of the Humanities, v.97). ISBN 0-8240-9876-5. LC 76-52516.

This gathering of bibliographies that originally appeared in *Classical World* (CW) (entry 545) between 1953 and 1975 is something of a hodgepodge. Roman drama and poetry are represented by literature surveys on Plautus (1950-1964), Terence (1934-1958), Catullus (two items together covering 1934-1969), Horace (1945-1957), Propertius (1960-1972), Ovid (1958-1968), and Roman satire (three surveys covering 1937-1968). Under the rubric of ancient fiction are two general surveys (1937-1970), two review essays covering work on Petronius (1940-1968) and one on Apuleius (1938-1970). Two additional surveys deal with psychoanalytical studies of classical authors (1911-1960) and teaching the classics in translation (1924-1975). The surveys generally conform to the pattern of *CW* surveys: They are arranged by subject and include descriptive and evaluative comments. A few attempt relative completeness; most are selective. They remain useful, especially for those seeking retrospective bibliography on particular authors. No index is provided.

80. Drexhage, Hans-Joachim. **Deutschsprachige Dissertationen zur alten Geschichte, 1844-1978**. Wiesbaden, Germany: Franz Steiner, 1980. 142pp. ISBN 3-515-03197-9. LC 80-507083.

Drexhage lists more than 2,200 German-language dissertations on ancient history; he includes works from Austria, the Netherlands, Germany, Switzerland, and parts of Central Europe arranged in a single alphabetical sequence by author. Drexhage does not provide abstracts; nor does he note subsequent publication of dissertations as books. He does, however, provide good indexes that cover names of individuals and peoples (as subjects), geographical names, and topical subjects. Many of the earlier dissertations are also listed in the *Catalogus Dissertationum* (entries 66-67); Drexhage has marked these with an asterisk. Drexhage is a much more convenient source; only those seeking very obscure items will need to resort to the *Catalogus*. For German dissertations after 1978 see the lists of "Althistorische Dissertationen" in the annual publication *Chiron* (München: C. H. Beck, 1971-).

81. Faider, Paul. **Répertoire des éditions de scolies et commentaires d'auteurs latins**. Paris: Société d'Edition "Les Belles Lettres," 1931. 48pp. (Collections d'études, série scientifique, no.8). LC 41-36.

Faider deals with the relatively obscure area of ancient commentators on the Latin classics. These include both separate commentaries (e.g., Servius on Vergil) and marginalia (often called scholia) found in ancient and medieval manuscripts. Faider lists Latin authors alphabetically and cites under each editions of the relevant ancient commentators and scholiasts. Faider's headnotes often provide historical information and bibliography on individual commentators. The work is now badly dated; for example, new editions of Servius (on Vergil) and Asconius (on Cicero) have subsequently appeared. Faider does remain useful for tracking down the less-prominent scholiasts for whom we still often depend on nineteenth-century editions.

82. Fantuzzi, Marco. **Letterature greca antica, bizantina e neoellenica**. Milano, Italy: Garzanti, 1989. 471pp. (Strumenti di studio. Guide bibliografiche, v.1). ISBN 88-11-47506-6. LC 89-174152.

Despite the all-encompassing title, more than three-quarters of this work is devoted to ancient Greek literature. Coverage extends from the beginnings through the Greco-Roman era. The first chapter includes general works, periodicals, grammars and lexica, metrics, palaeography, papyrology, and mythology. Subsequent chapters cover periods and genres: archaic epic, lyric poetry (seventh-fifth centuries B.C.), archaic and classical prose and historiography, classical drama, artistic prose of the fourth century B.C., Plato and Aristotle, Hellenistic literature, and literature of the Greco-Roman era. All of these are further subdivided; the table of contents lays out the entire scheme. Each section lists standard editions and translations for the authors, along with a generous selection of the scholarly literature. Although the bibliography includes works in a variety of languages (including many items in English), it emphasizes those in Italian. For example, a number of well-known books that originally appeared in English are listed only in their Italian translations. Fantuzzi occasionally provides descriptive comments about the works cited. There is an index of names. This bibliography is relatively current, and its use requires little knowledge of Italian. While selective, it offers a good range of citations for most Greek authors.

✓ 83. Fay, George E. **A Bibliography of Etruscan Culture and Archaeology, 1498-1981**. Greeley: Museum of Anthropology, University of Northern Colorado, 1982-1983. 2v. (Occasional Publications in Classical Studies, no.1). LC 84-620585.

Fay, an anthropologist with no special expertise in Etruscan studies, compiled his bibliography chiefly from secondary sources and rarely examined the actual works. He covers all aspects of Etruscan history and culture; not surprisingly, most of the items deal with archaeology or epigraphy. Fay arranged materials alphabetically by author; subarrangement is by date of publication. The majority of the items listed are in Italian, although all pertinent languages are included. Fay provides no annotations nor does he supply an index. However, his two volumes contain more than 5,500 citations, including virtually everything found in Lopes Pegna's earlier bibliography (entry 99). While a number of libraries possess the first volume (A-J) of Fay's bibliography, far fewer hold the comparatively scarce second volume (K-Z).

✓ 84. Forman, Robert J. **Classical Greek and Roman Drama: An Annotated Bibliography**. Pasadena, CA: Salem Press, 1989. 239pp. (Magill Bibliographies). ISBN 0-89336-659-4. LC 89-10805.

Forman, an English professor, intends his work for "high school students, college undergraduates, and general readers as a guide to reading and research." He includes translations, commentaries, and critical works that are chosen both for basic importance and wide availability in libraries. Forman begins with a unit called "general studies" in which he gathers general works on classical drama. Few significant English-language works are omitted. Then Forman covers individual dramatists: Aeschylus, Aristophanes, Ennius, Euripides, Menander, Plautus, Seneca, Sophocles, and Terence. He offers a good selection of the available translations and scholarly literature. Occasionally he includes dated items or difficult technical works, but most of his choices are on target for his audience.

He also provides annotations that clearly indicate the content and value of each work. An author index concludes the volume.

✓ 85.   Garnsey, Peter, and Richard Saller. **The Early Principate: Augustus to Trajan**. Oxford, England: Clarendon Press, 1982. 42pp. (New Surveys in the Classics, no.15). ISBN 0-903035-12-X. LC 82-207445.

Garnsey and Saller survey recent work on the early Roman empire. They do so in a series of brief essays covering major topics, including politics, the empire, administration, society, economy, monarchy, and culture. Bibliographical citations are provided in the notes following each essay. Their overview, which is aimed at undergraduates, provides a good orientation and working bibliography for the period.

86.   Goodwater, Leanna. **Women in Antiquity: An Annotated Bibliography**. Metuchen, NJ: Scarecrow Press, 1975. 171pp. ISBN 0-8108-0837-4. LC 75-23229.

Goodwater covers both ancient sources and modern studies. The first part of her bibliography is an omnium-gatherum of classical works by or about women. These include, for example, Greek tragedies in which women figure prominently. Some of the sources are cited in Greek or Latin editions, while others are cited in translations of varying quality. The second part lists secondary works under four broad rubrics: general works, Greece, Etruscan women, and Rome. Goodwater's annotations describe the content of each work adequately but generally avoid evaluation. There are indexes of women of antiquity and of authors. While Goodwater supplies some 534 entries (147 in sources, the remainder in modern studies), users should bear in mind that much significant work has been done in this area since 1975. Gillian Clark's recent survey volume (entry 71) provides many more recent references, while Vérilhac's bibliography (entry 130a) is the most complete overall.

✓ 87.   Gwinup, Thomas, and Fidelia Dickinson. **Greek and Roman Authors: A Checklist of Criticism**. 2d ed. Metuchen, NJ: Scarecrow Press, 1982. 280pp. ISBN 0-8108-1528-1. LC 82-690.

"The purpose of this bibliography is to provide a comprehensive list of recent criticism of the authors of *belles-lettres* of ancient Greece and Rome." It is aimed at students in comparative and world literature and general humanities courses. The authors include only items in English and claim to place emphasis on newer works. Nearly 4,000 works are listed on authors ranging from Homer to St. Augustine. The bibliography begins with a list of general works covering Greek and Roman literary history, criticism, history, and art history. This strange list includes many first-rate titles intermingled with outdated items and a number of technical works unlikely to be of use to the intended audience. For example, students who read only English are rarely interested in metrical analyses of Greek tragic choruses. Many old works are cited in reprint editions without any indication of their true dates. The following section, which covers individual classical authors in alphabetical sequence, is little better. It mingles the excellent, the good, the mediocre, and the highly technical without discrimination; no annotations are provided to guide the unwary. There are no indexes. While students can find much of use here, they will also find much that is ill-suited to their needs.

88.   Herescu, N. I. **Bibliographie de la littérature latine**. Paris: Société d'Edition "Les Belles Lettres," 1943. 426pp. (Collection de bibliographie classique). LC 46-3765.

Herescu's work is a general bibliography for the study of Latin literature. His introduction lists bibliographical resources and selected reference works. The body of the work is arranged in chapters corresponding to the standard period divisions in Latin literature. Each begins with a section on general works and then lists individual authors. Under each author, Herescu lists extant manuscripts and gives references to facsimiles and studies of them. He then lists editions, translations, indexes, and secondary works. He includes both articles and books under secondary works, often subarranging these by topic. He also provides an index of Latin authors.

Herescu's bibliography is a good working guide for pre-1940 publications on Latin literature. It is more comprehensive than Leeman's *Bibliographia Latina Selecta* (entry 96) but less up-to-date.

89.   Householder, Fred W., and Gregory Nagy. **Greek: A Survey of Recent Work**. The Hague: Mouton, 1972. 105pp. (Janua Linguarum, Series Practica, 211). LC 73-161227.

Although no longer "recent," this volume provides a wide-ranging survey of much of the most significant work done on the Greek language in this century. Particular emphasis is given to studies published in the 1950s and 1960s, a time of exceptional activity in the field due to the decipherment of Linear B by Michael Ventris in 1952. Householder and Nagy review their material in narrative chapters covering generalities, phonology, morphology, syntax, etymology and vocabulary, and dialectology. Two bibliographies (the second a supplemental listing for works published in 1968-1972) provide full citations for all works discussed. Both authors are distinguished experts on the Greek language; their commentary is as valuable as the bibliography itself.

✓ 90.   Kallendorf, Craig. **Latin Influences on English Literature from the Middle Ages to the Eighteenth Century: An Annotated Bibliography of the Scholarship, 1945-1979**. New York: Garland, 1982. 141pp. (Garland Reference Library of the Humanities, v.345). ISBN 0-8240-9261-9. LC 82-9371.

Taking Highet's *The Classical Tradition* (entry 334) as his point of departure, Kallendorf surveys 35 years of scholarly work on Latin influences in English literature. His initial chapters cover basic works on the classical tradition and works on rhetoric and prose style. Subsequent chapters cover the various periods in chronological order from the Middle Ages to the eighteenth century. Each is subdivided by topic. Kallendorf's 769 annotated entries include books, chapters in books, and journal articles. Most annotations consist of brief summaries; a few offer critical comment. The majority of the works cited are in English. While Kallendorf's coverage is not exhaustive, he does provide more than adequate material for students and an excellent starting point for scholars.

91.   Karras, Margret, and Josef Wiesehöfer. **Kindheit und Jugend in der Antike: Ein Bibliographie**. Bonn, Germany: Rudolf Habelt, 1981. 123pp. ISBN 3-7749-1852-X. LC 81-167551.

Karras and Wiesehöfer list 1,270 works on children and youth in the Ancient Near East, Greece, and Rome, arranged under broad subject headings such as law, culture, play, and education. Each category is subdivided by culture (general, Greek, Roman, Egyptian, and other). The authors have included works in a variety of languages, although German and English predominate. Items cited range from scholarly works of general interest to highly technical epigraphical and papyrological publications. Author and subject indexes are provided. The pertinent sections of Krause (entry 94) cover some of the same material and are more up-to-date.

92. Kessels, A. H. M., and W. J. Verdenius. **A Concise Bibliography of Ancient Greek Literature**. Apeldoorn, Netherlands: Administratief Centrum, 1982. 2d ed., revised and enlarged. 145pp.

This bibliography is "intended to be used primarily by students and teachers of classics." Kessels and Verdenius first list bibliographical, reference, and general works. They then cover individual authors and genres in a roughly chronological sequence. They tend to include only major authors. Often authors are treated in groups; for example, all the tragedians are gathered under the heading "Tragedy." Kessels and Verdenius note editions, commentaries, indexes, and a selection of the scholarly literature (books only; no articles are included). There is a list of the major classical periodicals. The index covers mainly authors, although a few titles and subjects are found there also. This bibliography is not very detailed but will serve as an adequate general guide for students.

93. Kirk, Eugene P. **Menippean Satire: An Annotated Catalogue of Texts and Criticism**. New York: Garland, 1980. 313pp. (Garland Reference Library of the Humanities, v.191). ISBN 0-8240-9533-2. LC 79-7921.

For those interested in the history of the genre of Menippean satire, this work provides a comprehensive bibliographical resource. It attempts "to list exhaustively all Menippean satires written before 1660 in the languages of Western Europe, and all the criticism published in those same languages about Menippean satire, up to the present time." Kirk's introduction gives a good overview of the genre and its history in the course of explaining the scope and organization of his catalog. He then lists the authors of Menippean satire in roughly chronological sequence from Menippus of Gadara, the inventor of the form, to Abraham Cowley. Under each he notes all of their works that might be characterized as Menippean satire and cites modern editions and translations. The texts cited, as in the case of Petronius, do not always include the best critical editions. Kirk's annotations in the author listings include much biographical, bibliographical, and critical information. Kirk also provides, in a separate chapter, a selective bibliography of important Renaissance editions of the classical Menippean satires. The final chapter includes entries for more than 200 critical works on the genre, arranged alphabetically by author. Most of these are accompanied by brief summaries. An index of authors and subjects concludes the volume. This work is useful for the study of medieval and Renaissance literature as well as that of classical literature and its influence.

94. Krause, Jens-Uwe. **Die Familie und weitere anthropologische Grundlagen**. Unter Mitwirkung von Bertram Eisenhauer, Konstanze Szelényi und Susanne Tschirner. Stuttgart, Germany: Franz Steiner, 1992. 260pp. (Heidelberger althistorische Beiträge und epigraphische Studien, Bd.11; Bibliographie zur römischen Sozialgeschichte, 1). ISBN 3-515-06044-8. LC 93-243284.

This unannotated bibliography lists more than 4,000 works on such topics as demographics, women, marriage, family and relationships, sexuality, childhood, youth, the elderly, and death and burial. It covers Rome, the early Christians, and the early Byzantine empire. Krause and his fellow compilers have gathered their material from a wide range of sources in classics, history, religious studies, and anthropology. They include books, dissertations, and articles from journals and festschriften. The material is arranged by subject; author and subject indexes provide additional access. Krause's bibliography is an invaluable resource for research on Roman social history.

95. Kristeller, Paul Oskar. **Latin Manuscript Books Before 1600: A List of the Printed and Unpublished Inventories of Extant Collections**. 4th ed., rev. and enlarged by Sigrid Krämer. München: Monumenta Germaniae Historica, 1993. 941pp. (Monumenta Germaniae Historica. Hilfsmittel, 13). ISBN 3-88612-113-5.

Now in its 4th edition, this well-known work is a fundamental resource for anyone interested in classical, medieval, or Renaissance manuscripts. This edition covers works published through the summer of 1992. Its first section notes general works that give bibliographical or statistical information about manuscript collections; this part does not, as a rule, contain manuscript catalogs. The second section lists manuscript catalogs that cover libraries in more than one city. Both of these sections are arranged alphabetically by author or title. Catalogs and inventories of individual libraries are found in the third section; these are arranged alphabetically by city. The final section lists directories and guides to libraries and archives. Brief annotations accompany some entries. The lack of indexes is inexplicable.

96. Leeman, A. D. **Bibliographia Latina Selecta**. Operam praebentibus G. Bouma, H. Pinkster. Amsterdam: Adolf M. Hakkert, 1966. 173pp. LC 68-98448.

Leeman's compilation is a selective general bibliography on Latin language and literature. It is aimed primarily at European university students. The first part, which is arranged by topic, covers bibliography, reference works, linguistics, metrics, literary history, Roman law, palaeography and textual criticism, the history of scholarship, the influence of the classics, and collected editions. The second part is devoted to individual Latin authors, arranged chronologically. Leeman lists a selection of editions, translations, indexes, commentaries, and critical studies for each author, and includes only book-length works. There is an index of Latin authors.

Leeman shows a strong European bias in his selection of works and is now dated. For the most part, English-language students will be better served by consulting the bibliographies found at the end of the Latin volume of the *Cambridge History of Classical Literature* (entry 275).

97. Leitner, Helmut. **Bibliography to the Ancient Medical Authors**. Bern: Hans Huber, 1973. 61pp. ISBN 3-456-00322-6. LC 72-86911.

Leitner's general bibliography of editions and translations of the ancient medical writers arranges the authors alphabetically. Under each he lists individual works by title, followed by collected editions and collected translations. Leitner includes mostly twentieth-century editions; occasionally nineteenth-century ones are noted if they are the only or best edition of a given author. He covers the whole of antiquity from Hippocrates to Paulos of Aigina (seventh century A.D.). A couple of later authors are also included. Writers on veterinary medicine are excluded. Leitner is somewhat stronger on Greek than Latin writers. Additional material on Latin medical writers can be found in Sabbah's *Bibliographie des textes médicaux latins* (entry 122).

98. Lindenlaub, Marie-Luise. **Deutschsprachige Dissertationen zur Archäologie des Mittelmeerraums, 1945-1977**. Berlin: Deutsches Archäologisches Institut, 1979. 288pp. LC 80-482439.

Lindenlaub lists some 792 Austrian, German, and Swiss doctoral dissertations on the art and archaeology of the ancient Mediterranean region. These include works on Ancient Near Eastern, Greek, Roman, and early Christian archaeology, arranged by subject. Each entry includes the full citation for the dissertation, information on subsequent publication, the location of any published abstracts, and references to reviews. If the dissertation has been published, Lindenlaub describes the published version; if not, the actual dissertation. Lindenlaub also provides indexes of authors and institutions.

99. Lopes Pegna, Mario. **Saggio di bibliografia etrusca**. Firenze, Italy: Olschki, 1953. 89pp. (Biblioteca di bibliografia italiana). LC 53-37853.

This bibliography covers all aspects of Etruscan studies from 1498 through 1952. Lopes Pegna uses broad subject divisions to organize the citations: history, archaeology, and topography; linguistics and epigraphy; art; religion; technology and science; numismatics and metrology; and cartography. Within each division, entries are presented chronologically by date of publication. The works cited are in a variety of languages, with Italian being the most common. There are no annotations, but there is an index of personal and geographic names. Fay's much larger bibliography (entry 83) includes everything listed in this work plus many additional citations. However, Lopes Pegna offers certain advantages, such as access by subject.

100. Mathiesen, Thomas J. **A Bibliography of Sources for the Study of Ancient Greek Music**. Hackensack, NJ: Joseph Boonin, 1974. 59pp. (Music Indexes and Bibliographies). ISBN 0-913574-10-4. LC 74-169157.

Mathiesen attempts to gather all materials dealing with ancient Greek music. He covers all aspects of music: theory, notation, instruments, and metrics. His 949 entries represent works published from the fifteenth century to 1972. He includes editions and translations of relevant ancient texts, as well as modern books, articles, and theses. His entries are arranged in a single alphabetical sequence by author. There are few annotations, and these are primarily bibliographical in nature. Mathiesen does not provide any indexes. While lacking in amenities, his list does provide a helpful guide to this highly specialized field of study.

101. Moon, Brenda E. **Mycenaean Civilization, Publications Since 1935: A Bibliography**. London: University of London, Institute of Classical Studies, 1957. 77pp. (Bulletin of the Institute of Classical Studies. Supplement, no.3).

102. Moon, Brenda E. **Mycenaean Civilization, Publications 1956-60: A Second Bibliography**. London: University of London, Institute of Classical Studies, 1961. 130pp. (Bulletin of the Institute of Classical Studies. Supplement, no.12). LC 67-8205.

Moon's first volume covered Mycenaean civilization in a rather strict sense: "the Late Helladic culture centered in Greece c. 1600-1100 B.C." She further excluded works on Mycenaean language, literacy, and epigraphy. In her second compilation, she decided to include works on language and epigraphy (from 1953) and to expand the scope of the bibliography to include Minoan civilization during the same period (with retrospective coverage to 1936). No attempt was made to cover related areas such as Homeric or Near Eastern studies. Moon included books and periodical articles but not reviews or items in the popular press. She arranged entries alphabetically by author. Her "subject list" functions essentially as an index to the author listings. There is also a topographical index. Moon's two volumes provide a useful guide to an important period in Mycenaean studies.

103. Motte, André, Vinciane Pirenne-Delforge, and Paul Wathelet. **Mentor: Guide bibliographique de la religion grecque = Bibliographical Survey of Greek Religion**. Liège, France: Universitè de Liège, Centre d'Histoire des Religions, 1992. 781pp. (Kernos. Supplement, 2).

This selective bibliography covers works on Greek religion published prior to 1985. The lengthy introduction provides a guide to the primary sources, including ancient texts (editions, commentaries, indexes, and concordances), epigraphical and papyrological works, iconographical sources, and numismatic materials. The introduction also notes relevant general bibliographical and reference sources. A listing of 2,060 books and articles, arranged by author, comprises the main part of the volume. Substantial signed annotations, which both summarize and evaluate, accompany most entries. Nearly all of the annotations are in French. Although an odd and limited subject index appears at the end of the introduction, access by subject is generally inadequate. Otherwise, this work is a valuable guide to its subject. Casual inquirers and those who read only English may find Bremmer's survey (entry 61) more helpful.

104. Oates, John F., Roger S. Bagnall, William H. Willis, and Klaas A. Worp. **Checklist of Editions of Greek and Latin Papyri, Ostraca, and Tablets**. 4th ed. Atlanta, GA: Scholars Press, 1992. 94pp. (BASP Supplements, no.7). ISBN 1-55540-782-X. LC 92-33810.

The purpose of this work is "to provide a ready bibliography of all monographic volumes, both current and out-of-print, of texts written on papyrus, parchment, ostraca, or wood tablets." The focus is chiefly on documentary texts; literary texts are included, but there was no systematic effort to cover these exhaustively, because they can be found in Pack (entry 107). The *Checklist* serves several additional purposes as well. It supplies a standard list of abbreviations for papyrological publications. It also serves as a canon of volumes containing documentary texts that have been or will be entered in the *Duke Data Bank of Documentary Papyri* (entry 459). As in earlier editions, the *Checklist* notes whether each volume is currently in print and provides information about publishers. Guides are also provided to *corpora* of texts, monographic series, periodicals, and the proceedings of international congresses. An innovation with this edition is a list of "instrumenta," which is a guide to reference tools for papyrology. While chiefly of interest to working papyrologists, the *Checklist* is an indispensable resource for anyone who must traverse this thicket of highly technical publications and arcane abbreviations.

105. Oleson, John Peter. **Bronze Age, Greek, and Roman Technology: A Selected, Annotated Bibliography**. New York: Garland, 1986. 515pp. (Bibliographies of the History of Science and Technology, v.13; Garland Reference Library of the Humanities, v.646). ISBN 0-8240-8677-5. LC 85-45143.

Oleson covers primarily Greco-Roman technology but also includes some material on the Ancient Near East. His chronological limits extend from the Bronze Age to the sixth century A.D. He includes books and articles in English, French, German, Italian, and Spanish. Topical chapters cover all major aspects of technology: mining, food production, energy, engineering, manufacturing, transportation, record-keeping and standards, military technology, and cultural aspects of technology. In addition, two introductory chapters cover sources and general surveys. An index provides access by author. Oleson, who has himself done significant research in the field, provides strong annotations that describe and assess each entry. This wide-ranging bibliography includes works from many disciplines, including classical and Near Eastern studies, anthropology, and the history of science. It is an excellent guide to a rapidly developing aspect of ancient studies.

106. Oster, Richard E. **A Bibliography of Ancient Ephesus**. Metuchen, NJ: American Theological Library Association and Scarecrow Press, 1987. 155pp. (ATLA Bibliography Series, no.19). ISBN 0-8108-1996-1. LC 87-12617.

While intended primarily for New Testament scholars, this work is of value to anyone interested in this important Greco-Roman city in Asia Minor. Oster's scope covers "the ancient history, culture, and archaeological evidence of Ephesus." Works on archaeological excavations, inscriptions, and numismatics comprise the majority of his citations. The 1,535 numbered entries, which range in date from the eighteenth century to the 1980s, include books, dissertations, and journal articles. Oster arranges these by author; a subject index is also provided. Although the individual entries do not include annotations, Oster's introduction supplies a good overview of scholarly work on Ephesus.

107. Pack, Roger A. **The Greek and Latin Literary Texts from Greco-Roman Egypt**. 2d rev. and enlarged ed. Ann Arbor, MI: University of Michigan Press, 1965. 165pp. LC 65-10786.

Pack is a repertory of all Greek and Latin literary texts (defined broadly as all nondocumentary texts) that have been preserved in Egypt. It includes texts preserved on papyrus, parchment, ostraca, and wooden tablets. Pack lists Greek texts first, then the Latin ones. Under each language, he divides texts into those identified by author (arranged A-Z) and *adespota* (arranged by genre). Pack also adds a separate category under Latin for legal texts. For works of known authorship Pack identifies the passage, cites the edition, and gives the date, provenance, and material of the manuscript. He also cites any additional scholarly literature. For *adespota* Pack characterizes the passage by form and subject matter; cites the original publication; gives the date, provenance, and material; and notes other relevant studies. Pack remains the standard bibliography of literary papyri; scholars often cite the texts by their Pack number. Paul Mertens is now preparing a badly needed new edition.

108. Palmer, Henrietta R. **List of English Editions and Translations of Greek and Latin Classics Printed Before 1641**. London: For the Bibliographical Society, 1911; repr., Philadelphia: R. West, 1977. 119pp. LC 14-9902.

This work, alphabetical by author, is a traditional descriptive bibliography of translations of classical authors that were published in England between 1480 and 1640. In addition to bibliographical description, each entry includes a brief list of holding libraries (all British). A substantial introduction by Victor Scholderer surveys the activities and interests of translators in the period covered. Palmer is chiefly useful for research in bibliography and in the history of scholarship.

109. Paquet, L., M. Roussel, and Y. Lafrance. **Les Présocratiques: Bibliographie analytique (1879-1980)**. Montréal: Les Editions Bellarmine and Paris: Les Belles Lettres, 1988-1989. 2v. (Collection Noêsis; Collection d'études anciennes). ISBN 2-89007-647-4(v.1); 2-89007-686-5(v.2). LC 89-208837.

This bibliography covers a century of work on the Pre-Socratic philosophers. Its major divisions include bibliographical works; general studies; studies of themes, ideas, and terms; and particular studies. Particular studies include individual schools, such as the Milesians, and individual philosophers, such as Heraclitus. The bibliography includes editions, books, and articles. Annotations generally provide summaries and occasionally offer critical comments. Some of the summaries have been reprinted from *L'Année philologique* (entry 26). Entries for books also list reviews. The compilers have cited a full selection of the modern scholarly literature on the Presocratics. There is an index of modern authors.

110. Parks, George B., and Ruth Z. Temple. **The Literatures of the World in English Translation: A Bibliography. Vol. 2: The Greek and Latin Literatures**. New York: Frederick Ungar, 1968. 442pp. LC 68-31454.

This volume begins with a brief bibliography of reference and general works on classical antiquity. Greek literature is then covered in several chapters that include both collections and translations of individual authors. Authors are grouped into chronological divisions: early and classical, Hellenistic, Greek Christian, and Byzantine literature. Latin literature is covered in similar fashion, with period subsections for republican, imperial, medieval, and Neo-Latin literature. The work lists a full selection of translations, including older (as far back as the sixteenth century) and recent translations. There are occasional annotations. There is also a general index, although it is far from exhaustive; the names of many translators are omitted. Users should note that many translations have been published since 1968, and some represent substantial improvements over those listed here.

111. Peradotto, John. **Classical Mythology: An Annotated Bibliographical Survey**. Urbana, IL: American Philological Association, 1973. 76pp. (American Philological Association Bibliographical Guides).

Aimed at college-level teachers and students of classical myth, Peradotto's book has become a standard bibliographical reference for the subject. Although reprinted twice (most recently in 1981), it has never been revised and is now dated. However, it remains useful for its coverage of many valuable works published prior to 1973. This coverage is highly selective (only 212 items are listed) and limited to book-length works. Peradotto arranges his material in sections by form and topic. He begins with chapters on reference works and general surveys of myth. Then a series of topical chapters covers comparative mythology; myth in relation to such subjects as art, literature, psychology, anthropology, and religion; and the structural study of myth. At the end, Peradotto returns to form and treats general studies, specialized studies, and translations of the major ancient literary sources. In each section, bibliographical citations are listed at the beginning, followed by critical discussions that give a clear description of the contents and merits of each work. Peradotto supplies numerous cross-references between sections, an author-title index, and an index of publishers.

112. Pöschl, Viktor, Helga Gärtner, and Waltrout Heyke. **Bibliographie zur antiken Bilderspache**. Heidelberg: Carl Winter Universitätsverlag, 1964. 674pp. (Bibliothek der klassischen Altertumswissenschaften). LC 66-55568.

Pöschl and his assistants have compiled an unusual bibliography that deals with studies of metaphorical language in classical literature. The bibliography consists of two parts. The general section, *Allgemeine Literatur*, is arranged by topic (e.g., linguistics, mythology, literary history). The second part covers works on individual Greek and Latin authors and is arranged alphabetically by ancient author. Entries occasionally include a brief annotation, usually to clarify the content or to indicate what metaphor is discussed. A detailed index of metaphors follows so that one can find discussions of a particular metaphor in ancient literature. There is also an index of modern authors.

113. **Les provinces hellénophones de l'empire romain de Pompée au milieu du IIIe siècle ap. J.-C.: Recueil bibliographique à partir des analyses du BAHR (1962 à 1974)**. Strasbourg, France: AECR, 1986. 515pp. ISBN 2-904-337-16-4.

This bibliography is compiled from 13 volumes of the *Bulletin analytique d'histoire romaine* (entry 32) that cover 1962-1974. All entries concerning the Greek-speaking provinces of the Roman empire through the third century A.D. are gathered here in a geographical arrangement. Each province receives a separate chapter, while general works and those dealing with several provinces are found in an initial general chapter. Chapters are divided into two general sections: sources and historical studies. These are further subdivided by topic as appropriate to the material in each chapter. The scheme is neatly laid out in the table of contents. The lack of indexes is a major drawback; there is, for example, no author access. The strength of the work is in its abstracts, which are often lengthy and provide good descriptions of the items.

114. Quellet, Henri. **Bibliographia Indicum, Lexicorum, et Concordantium Auctorum Latinorum = Répertoire bibliographique des index, lexiques, et concordances des auteurs latines**. Hildesheim, Germany: Georg Olms, 1980. 262pp. ISBN 3-487-07014-6. LC 81-182390.

Despite the author's modest claims that he makes no pretense of being exhaustive, his work may be considered so for all practical purposes. He gathers some 1,097 works in his main list and addenda. Quellet includes indexes at the end of editions of texts, as well as separately published indexes, concordances, and lexica to the various Latin authors. He arranges his material alphabetically by Latin author. Symbols in the margin by each citation indicate the degree of completeness of the particular index. An appendix lists a number of related works (e.g., studies and compilations of Latin names of stars, animals). There is also an index to the names of the compilers of the indexes and lexica. A number of indexes and concordances have appeared since 1980; these must be sought in *L'Année philologique* (entry 26). Until computerized databases of Latin literature render printed indexes obsolete, Quellet will remain a useful tool for those interested in Latin language and lexicography.

115. **Les Religions dans le monde romain (200 av. J.C. à 200 ap. J.C.): Bibliographie analytique à partir des publications périodiques de 1962 à 1968 dépouillées par le Bulletin analytique d'histoire romaine**. Strasbourg, France: Association pour l'Etude de la Civilisation Romaine, 1975. 247pp.

This bibliography consists of entries drawn from the volumes of the *Bulletin analytique d'histoire romaine* (entry 32) for 1962-1968. This material has been rearranged into two large sections: publications of source material subdivided by type (literary, papyrological, epigraphical, archaeological, and numismatic) and studies, which are subdivided into broad subject categories. The limitations of the parent publication apply to this volume: It lists only journal articles from a restricted geographical area. It does, however, include citations from some European journals not indexed by more general sources, such as *L'Année philologique* (entry 26). There are a number of formal weaknesses in the bibliography. Entries retain their original numbers from the *Bulletin analytique*, which is confusing as these are now meaningless and have no relation to the present compilation. Also, there are no indexes. The abstracts, which are often substantial, are one of the few attractive features. This bibliography is of limited use and can only be recommended to specialists in Roman religion.

✓116.   Rhodes, P. J. **The Athenian Empire**. Oxford, England: Clarendon Press, 1985. 47pp. (New Surveys in the Classics, no.17). ISBN 0-903035-14-6. LC 85-220204.

Rhodes, a well-known specialist in Greek history, offers a succinct review of scholarly work on the Athenian empire. He concentrates on the period following 1924, when the first studies of the Athenian tribute lists began to appear. After a general introduction, brief essays summarize scholarship on various aspects of the development and fall of the empire; bibliographical details are relegated to the notes that follow each.

117.   Richard, Marcel. **Répertoire des bibliothèques et des catalogues de manuscripts grecques**. 2ème ed. Paris: Centre National de la Recherche Scientifique, 1958. 276pp. (Publications de l'Institut de Recherche et d'Histoire des Textes, 1). LC 68-33492.

118.   Richard, Marcel. **Répertoire des bibliothèques et des catalogues de manuscripts grecques. Supplément I (1958-1963)**. Paris: Centre National de la Recherche Scientifique, 1964. 76pp. (Documents, Etudes, et Répertoires publiées par l'Institut de Recherche et d'Histoire des Textes, 9).

These two volumes comprise the standard bibliography of catalogs and inventories of Greek manuscripts. Richard divides each volume into four sections: bibliography, specialized catalogs, regional catalogs, and cities and other places. The bibliography sections include only a few general works, which are arranged chronologically. Specialized catalogs, which are organized by topic, include catalogs of manuscripts on specific subjects, such as alchemy or medicine. The other sections are arranged by place. Richard includes both books and articles. Many of the entries are annotated; some of these notes include additional information about the manuscript collections that various scholars and librarians supplied directly to Richard. Each volume concludes with a detailed index.

119.   Riesenfeld, Harald, and Blenda Riesenfeld. **Repertorium Lexicographicum Graecum = A Catalogue of Indexes and Dictionaries to Greek Authors**. Stockholm: Almqvist & Wiksell, 1954. 95pp. LC 54-5571.

In spite of the Latin title, the introduction and commentary in this book are in English. In it the Riesenfelds gather "lexicographical material bearing upon Greek literature from its beginning to the end of the Byzantine epoch." They restrict themselves to literary material; papyri, inscriptions, and ostraca are generally ignored. The Reisenfelds arrange their material alphabetically by

Greek author. Their listings include indexes in editions as well as separately published indexes, concordances, and dictionaries. They are selective in the inclusion of earlier indexes, especially if a modern glossary or index is available. Coverage is strongest for classical and Hellenistic Greek authors and weakest for the Byzantines. This bibliography is a good starting point for locating indexes and lexica to individual Greek authors, although a large number have subsequently been published. The *Thesaurus Linguae Graecae* (entry 464) has replaced printed indexes to a large extent, although the dictionaries still remain useful.

120. Rollins, Alden M. **The Fall of Rome: A Reference Guide**. Jefferson, NC: McFarland, 1983. 130pp. ISBN 0-89950-034-X. LC 82-23918.

This bibliography suffers from the lack of a clear sense of its intended audience and purpose. The preface describes it as a "select and selectively annotated guide to twentieth-century literature in English on the fall of Rome," although a few French- and German-language items and some nineteenth-century publications are found in it. Rollins presents a farrago of popular and scholarly works; scholars will find it too general and incomplete to be of real use, while more general inquirers will find much that is unlikely to be accessible to them, such as doctoral dissertations. The 260 entries include standard historical treatises, popular books, articles from both learned and general periodicals, published lectures, reviews, and dissertations. Rollins arranges everything alphabetically by author. He provides fairly extensive annotations for most entries that supply good summaries, which are sometimes accompanied by useful commentary and references to related works. A brief index includes authors and subjects.

121. Rollins, Alden. **Rome in the Fourth Century A.D.: An Annotated Bibliography with Historical Overview**. Jefferson, NC: McFarland, 1991. 324pp. ISBN 0-89950-624-0. LC 91-52762.

The Roman empire of the fourth century A.D. is of interest to Byzantinists and medievalists as well as classicists. As a result, relevant publications are found in the literature of several disciplines. Rollins has gathered twentieth-century English-language materials through 1988. His more than 1,400 entries include books, dissertations, and articles arranged into 11 broad subject categories, such as politics and government, military matters, literature, and education. Together they cover virtually every aspect of fourth-century history and life. Rollins annotates most entries. The quality of these annotations varies. Some are merely one- or two-line summaries, while others are more detailed and offer evaluative remarks. Some book annotations also include citations for selected reviews. There is an index of subjects but not one for authors. Rollins is a handy guide to English-language works in this active area of research. Students especially will find this book useful.

122. Sabbah, Guy, Pierre-Paul Corsetti, and Klaus-Dietrich Fischer. **Bibliographie des textes médicaux latins: antiquité et haut moyen âge**. Saint-Etienne, France: Publications de l'Université, 1987. 174pp. (Centre Jean-Palerne, Memoires, 6). LC 92-234605.

This bibliography covers the Latin medical writers of antiquity and the Middle Ages. All the authors are listed in a single alphabetical sequence. Editions, commentaries, translations, indexes, concordances, and lexica are noted under each. The occasional annotations are primarily of a bibliographical nature. Sabbah and his collaborators cover many authors, including those on veterinary medicine, omitted by Leitner (entry 97). There are indexes of manuscripts and of modern authors.

123. Sargenti, Manlius, ed. **Operum ad Ius Romanum Pertinentium Quae ab Anno MCMXL ad Annum MCMLXX Edita Sunt Index Modo et Ratione Ordinatus**. Ticini, Italiae: Alma Ticinensis Universitas, Institutum Romani et Historiae Iuris, 1978. 3v.

124. Sargenti, Manlius. **Operum ad Ius Romanum Pertinentium Quae inde ab Anno MCMLXXI usque ad Annum MCMLXXX Edita Sunt Index Modo et Ratione Ordinatus**. Mediolani, Italiae: Cisalpino-Goliardico, 1988-1990. 3v. ISBN 88-205-0614-9(v.1); 88-205-0646-7(v.2); 88-205-0683-1(v.3).

The volume of publication on Roman law is well illustrated by Sargenti's massive bibliography for 1940-1970; a mere 30 years' work requires more than 2,000 pages. This is an exceptionally wide-ranging bibliography and includes many works whose relation to the study of Roman law is tangential. Sargenti arranges the citations by subject. His single alphabetical sequence includes general topics and technical terms of Roman law as headings. He lists books and articles; book reviews are sometimes cited under the entry for the work reviewed. There are no annotations, but there are indexes of subject headings and authors. The author index is particularly helpful; it gives both the subject heading and the page reference. The second work follows the pattern of Sargenti's earlier bibliography and extends coverage to 1980.

125. Scanlon, Thomas F. **Greek and Roman Athletics: A Bibliography**. Chicago: Ares Publishers, 1984. 142pp. ISBN 0-89005-522-X. LC 91-187821.

Scanlon's bibliography lists more than 1,600 works on sports in the ancient world. It includes works published in a variety of languages between 1573 and 1983. Work on ancient sports is interdisciplinary, and relevant material is often found in sources unfamiliar to classicists. Therefore, Scanlon gathers publications from such fields as physical education, sociology, and anthropology as well as from classical studies. He arranges the citations in broad subject categories, which he further subdivides as necessary. He does not provide annotations, but he cites reviews in entries for books. His substantial introduction discusses overall trends in the study of ancient sports and comments on a few specific works. An index of authors concludes the work.

125a. Sienkewicz, Thomas J. **The Classical Epic: An Annotated Bibliography**. Pasadena, CA: Salem Press, 1991. 265pp. (Magill Bibliographies). ISBN 0-89356-663-2. LC 90-48884.

Despite its broad title, this work deals only with Homer and Vergil. Sienkewicz designed the bibliography for students and general readers approaching Homer and Vergil for the first time; for the most part, he serves this audience well. His introduction offers a general appreciation of the two poets and some guidance for their readers, along with a short list of general works on epic poetry. The bibliography consists of two parts that cover Homer and Vergil respectively. Within each Sienkiewicz arranges entries by subject. The Homeric part covers general studies, historical background, bibliography, the authorship question, and broader literary studies of the Homeric poems, the *Iliad*, the *Odyssey*, and Homer's influence. The sections on the individual poems note editions and translations, as well as critical works. The Vergilian section is similarly arranged, including both general works on Vergil and works specifically on the *Aeneid*. Sienkewicz restricts himself to English-language works that are readily available. His entries include books, chapters in books, and journal articals. The accompanying annotations provide good descriptions of each item. There is an index of authors. This work is particularly useful for the study and teaching of Homer and Vergil at the secondary and college levels.

126. Smith, F. Seymour. **The Classics in Translation: An Annotated Guide to the Best Translations of the Greek and Latin Classics into English**. London: Scribner's, 1930; repr., New York: Burt Franklin, 1968. 307pp. LC 31-5075.

Smith provides separate alphabetical listings of Greek and Latin authors. He includes some Fathers of the Church, medical writers, and Renaissance authors in addition to the strictly classical. Brief annotations accompany most entries. Cross-references are made where appropriate, and an index of translators is provided. Smith's now dated work is still useful for identifying translations of minor authors and for finding translations by the famous and interesting. Many of the translations included are by well-known figures of English literary history.

✓ 127. Sparkes, Brian A. **Greek Art**. New York: Oxford University Press, 1991. 77pp. (New Surveys in the Classics, no.22). ISBN 0-19-922071-9. LC 92-183877.

Sparkes surveys scholarly work on ancient Greek art, with emphasis on the last 15 years. He cites primarily English-language studies. He discusses general works on Greek art in his introduction. The remaining chapters concentrate on sculpture and vase-painting; other art forms receive scant attention. Each chapter takes the form of a review essay, with the bibliographical citations relegated to the endnotes. While it does not cover all aspects of Greek art, Sparkes's work is readable and nicely illustrated. It is well suited to the needs of both undergraduates and graduate students.

127a. Suder, Wieslaw. **Geras: Old Age in Greco-Roman Antiquity: A Classified Bibliography**. Wroclaw, Poland: Profil, 1991. 169pp. ISBN 83-900102-2-4.

An interdisciplinary work, this bibliography covers publications in classics, medicine, sociology, and anthropology through 1989. Its 1,040 numbered citations include books, articles, and dissertations. While many are in English, works in French, German, Italian, and Spanish are also well represented. Suder arranges the entries alphabetically by author; an index provides subject access. There are no annotations.

128. Tarrant, Richard. **Greek and Latin Lyric Poetry in Translation**. Urbana, IL: American Philological Association, 1972. 62pp.

Tarrant reviews, in considerable detail, English translations of Greek and Latin lyric poetry. He intends the book to serve as a guide to those teaching or studying ancient literature in translation. His definition of lyric poetry is elastic and extends to pastoral (Theocritus and Vergil) and elegiac verse (Tibullus, Propertius, and Ovid) as well. Tarrant includes both anthologies and translations of individual poets. He has selected mainly translations from the 1950s and 1960s, although a few earlier ones are included. His discussion touches on both the accuracy and the literary quality of each translation. There are indexes of publishers and translators.

129. Thompson, Lawrence S. **A Bibliography of American Doctoral Dissertations in Classical Studies and Related Fields**. Hamden, CT: Shoestring Press, 1968. 250pp. LC 67-24191.

130. Thompson, Lawrence S. **A Bibliography of Dissertations in Classical Studies: American, 1964-1972; British, 1950-1972**. Hamden, CT: Shoestring Press, 1976. 296pp. ISBN 0-208-01457-8. LC 76-41178.

In the first volume, Thompson attempted to list all American dissertations in classics and related fields from the beginning of graduate study in America to the 1960s. He takes a very broad approach; in addition to works on virtually every aspect of classical studies, he notes many dissertations on early Christian topics. Altogether he lists 2,080 dissertations. He arranges his bibliography alphabetically by author. Each entry includes author, title, university, and date of submission. If a dissertation was subsequently published, Thompson gives publication information. He generally cites any published abstracts, including those in *Dissertation Abstracts* and in various journals. Indexes cover subjects, titles, topographical names, Greek words, and Latin words.

The second volume follows the pattern of the earlier one, except that it also extends coverage to Great Britain. It adds another 1,917 dissertations. Thompson lists only doctoral dissertations for America but includes British dissertations for all types of degrees. Once again, the indexing is unusually good. Thompson provides cumulative indexes for 1861-1972. Together his two volumes form a comprehensive guide to American dissertations in classical studies. More recent dissertations can, of course, be found in *Dissertation Abstracts International: Humanities and Social Science* (Ann Arbor, MI: University Microfilms International, 1969-). The *American Philological Association Newsletter* (see entry 641) lists both recently completed dissertations and those in progress in North American universities. The *Bulletin of the Institute of Classical Studies* (entry 537) performs a similar service for British dissertations.

130a. Vérilhac, A. M., and C. Vial. **La femme grecque et romain: Bibliographie**. Lyon: Maison de l'Orient, 1990. 209pp. (La femme dans le monde mediterraneen, v.2) (Travaux de la Maison de l'Orient, no.19). ISBN 2-903264-48-1.

In this bibliography, Vérilhac and Vial list some 3,300 works relating to women in classical antiquity. These include books, articles, selected dissertations, and editions of primary sources. Most are in English, French, German, or Italian. While a few nineteenth-century publications are noted, most works cited are more recent. The bibliography provides good coverage through the mid-1980s; the latest work cited is from 1986. Entries consist of full citations, alphanumeric subject classifications, and subject keywords. A few also include brief critical comments. Arrangement is alphabetical by author. Cross-references are supplied for works with multiple authors. Two indexes provide subject access. One is based on the broad alphanumeric subject classes assigned by the editors. The other is a keyword index that offers a more specific subject approach. This bibliography is much more detailed than the works of Clark (entry 71) and Goodwater (entry 86). It also provides better coverage of works in languages other than English.

131. Vermeule, Cornelius C. **A Bibliography of Applied Numismatics in the Fields of Greek and Roman Archaeology and the Fine Arts**. London: Spink, 1956. 172pp. LC 58-3889.

Vermeule is chiefly concerned with the use of coins in the study of Greek and Roman art, archaeology, and history. His 1,328 entries, which include both books and articles, are drawn from a wide range of publications in the fields of archaeology, history, and numismatics. He arranges these works by author under several broad subject headings. Brief annotations accompany many of the entries. These useful notes are chiefly descriptive but occasionally criticize the work in question or provide hints as to its possible use. In the case of books, they also note important reviews. There is a selective index of subjects. This bibliography is especially helpful to students of antiquity who are not numismatists but who work in areas where coins provide important source material.

132. Vogt, Joseph, and Heinz Bellen, eds. **Bibliographie zur antiken Sklaverei.** Neubearbeiten von Elisabeth Hermann. Bochum, Germany: Studienverlag Dr. N. Brockmeyer, 1983. 2v. ISBN 3-88339-363-0. LC 84-181935.

Vogt and Bellen have compiled a wide-ranging bibliography that covers slavery in the Ancient Near East and the classical world. There is token coverage of the Ancient Far East as well. The bulk of the material concerns the classical world. The bibliography deals with all aspects of slavery in antiquity, including works on the role of slaves in literature as well as more strictly historical studies. Many general works that touch on ancient slavery are also noted. These include works on such topics as ancient agriculture, manufacturing, and social organization. While not exhaustive, *Bibliographie zur antiken Sklaverei* is a major resource; this greatly expanded 2d edition includes 5,162 entries. There are no annotations. The citations are arranged in subject categories, with numerous cross-references provided. An extensive array of indexes appears in the second volume, covering Greek words, Latin words, personal names (as subjects), geographical names, subjects, and authors. This bibliography is best suited to those doing advanced research in the field; Wiedemann (entry 135) offers a good survey of recent and important work on ancient slavery for undergraduates and graduate students.

133. Warburg Institute. **Kulturwissenschaftliche Bibliographie zum Nachleben der Antike = A Bibliography of the Survival of the Classics.** Leipzig: B. G. Teubner, 1934 (v.1); London: Warburg Institute, 1938 (v.2); repr., Nendeln, Liechtenstein: Kraus Reprint, 1968. 2v.

Despite the English title and imprint of the second volume, virtually the entire text of this important bibliography is written in German. Although intended to be an ongoing project, the bibliography ceased publication after only two volumes, which cover 1931-1933. The volumes list 2,490 books and articles on all aspects of the influence of the classics on Western European civilization. Entries are organized under a number of topical and period headings. Each is accompanied by a long, scholarly annotation. The two indexes provide access by author and by personal name and subject. This bibliography is a valuable resource for anyone interested in the classical tradition or the history of classical scholarship.

134. White, K. D. **A Bibliography of Roman Agriculture.** Reading, England: University of Reading, 1970. 63pp. (Bibliographies in Agricultural History, no.1). ISBN 0-900724-03-X. LC 73-852088.

Compiled by one of the leading authorities on Roman agriculture, this working bibliography provides an excellent guide to the subject. The substantial introduction supplies an overview of the field and a reliable guide to the most important literary and archaeological source material. The bibliography brings together some 918 items from a wide range of publications in classical studies, history, and agriculture, arranged by subject; an outline of the classification scheme appears at the beginning of the bibliography. White supplies descriptive and evaluative annotations for many entries. There is no index.

135. Wiedemann, T. E. J. **Slavery**. Oxford, England: Clarendon Press, 1987. 51pp. (New Surveys in the Classics, no.19). ISBN 0-903035-48-0. LC 88-157411.

Wiedemann supplies a selective survey of work on slavery in antiquity. His emphasis is on recent studies, although he also includes significant earlier works. He divides his material into six topical chapters: historiographical issues, interpreting the evidence, slavery as a social institution, slaves as producers and servants, slaves in public service, and discontent and rebellion. These chapters follow the normal format of the series: a brief critical survey of scholarly work on each topic followed by bibliographical endnotes. Wiedemann provides a good overview of the field for students of ancient history. Those who need more extensive bibliographical coverage should consult Vogt and Bellen (entry 132).

CHAPTER  5

BIBLIOGRAPHIES OF INDIVIDUALS

Here are found bibliographies and bibliographical surveys that deal with an individual (or in a few cases, two or three individuals). Most of these are literary authors or philosophers, although a few are figures of primarily historical interest. Bibliographies of the works of individual classical scholars have been excluded. As in the previous chapter, only book-length bibliographies are noted. The reader should refer to the introductory note to that chapter for some sources for bibliographies published in periodicals. To supplement the bibliographies listed below with more current material, one should consult the appropriate author entry in the annual volumes of *L'Année philologique* (entry 26). The review journals listed in chapter 3 are also good sources of information concerning recent publications.

Aeschylus

136. Ireland, S. **Aeschylus**. Oxford, England: Clarendon Press, 1986. 41pp. (New Surveys in the Classics, no.18). ISBN 0-903035-15-4. LC 86-198700.

Ireland's survey aims "to provide an introductory guide to the main areas of Aeschylean scholarship in recent times." While focusing on recent English-language studies of Aeschylus, he also includes important older and foreign-language works. Ireland follows the general pattern of the series and organizes his material into several topical bibliographical essays that cover both general concerns and the individual plays of Aeschylus. He provides a readable and knowledgeable overview of Aeschylean studies, which is suitable for both undergraduate and graduate students. Those who require exhaustive bibliographical coverage will also need to consult Wartelle's large retrospective bibliography (entry 137).

137. Wartelle, André. **Bibliographie historique et critique d'Eschyle et de la tragédie grecque, 1518-1974**. Paris: Société d'Edition "Les Belles Lettres," 1978. 685pp. (Collection d'études anciennes). LC 79-346983.

This massive compilation begins with the 1518 *editio princeps* of Aeschylus and proceeds to list, in chronological order, editions, commentaries, translations, and studies through 1974. Arrangement within each year is alphabetical by author. Earlier works generally lack annotations; those provided tend to be bibliographical in nature. Many of the later works (especially those of the twentieth century) receive brief descriptive summaries and occasional critical comment. Book reviews are listed under the book entry. In addition to works specifically on Aeschylus, many more general studies of Greek tragedy are included as well. Separate indexes provide name and title access to authors, editions, and translations. There are also a subject index and an "index" that is a list of periodicals surveyed for the bibliography.

Alexander

138. Burich, Nancy J. **Alexander the Great: A Bibliography**. Kent, OH: Kent State University Press, 1970. 153pp. ISBN 0-87338-103-3. LC 72-114734.

Burich attempts to include "only those materials which make a real contribution to the knowledge about Alexander and his exploits." She has excluded the medieval Alexander legends, literary works, and most general reference and news items. Burich offers nearly 700 entries under four rubrics: bibliographic aids and general materials, classical sources, pre-nineteenth-century materials, and modern sources. The most useful parts of the book are the chapters on classical and modern sources. Burich supplies an impressive list of ancient sources for the study of Alexander; most entries suggest an edition or translation. In the case of a few items that deal only partly with Alexander, specific references would have helped. The section on modern sources provides a generous selection of scholarly work on Alexander through the early 1960s. Coverage of pre-nineteenth-century works is rather slim; many of those cited were not examined by the compiler. Some entries receive brief annotations that are usually descriptive in nature. There are no indexes.

Aristophanes

139. Ussher, R. G. **Aristophanes**. Oxford, England: Clarendon Press, 1979. 44pp. (New Surveys in the Classics, no.13). ISBN 0-903035-10-3. LC 80-492020.

Ussher surveys the state of Aristophanic studies, ca. 1979, in a series of short topical essays. Some of these will present a challenge to the Greekless reader, as they deal with technical aspects of Aristophanes's work and contain a considerable amount of untranslated Greek. Ussher covers a wide range of works, mostly published since 1950, in his extensive notes. He includes somewhat more foreign-language works than is typical for volumes in this series. Ussher is a good source of bibliography for advanced Greek students; he is of less use to those studying Aristophanes in translation.

Aristotle

140. Barnes, Jonathan, Malcolm Schofield, and Richard Sorabji. **Aristotle: A Selective Bibliography**. Oxford, England: Sub-Faculty of Philosophy, 1977. 88pp. (Study Aids, v.7). LC 79-322703.

This bibliography is "designed primarily to suit the interests of English-speaking philosophers.... First, we list relatively few studies that are exclusively historical or philological in character; secondly, we offer only a thin coverage of Aristotle's own scientific and antiquarian researches; thirdly, we refer to disproportionately few foreign publications." The authors also favor recent works. They have arranged their materials into 10 broad subject chapters covering the areas in which Aristotle worked. Many useful annotations and notes are scattered throughout the bibliography. Although now dated, this work is still a good orientation to the study of Aristotle. There is no index.

141. Cooper, Lane, and Alfred Gudeman. **A Bibliography of the *Poetics* of Aristotle**. New Haven, CT: Yale University Press, 1928. 193pp. (Cornell Studies in English, 11). LC 28-12280.

Compiled by two noted scholars, this is a helpful guide to the earlier literature on one of Aristotle's most influential works. It provides citations to approximately 1,500 items and is relatively complete through the mid-1920s. Material is arranged by form (Greek editions, translations, commentaries, and articles) and date of publication. All types of publication are included except book reviews. The authors have provided an author index and occasional cross-references; however, lack of subject access is a drawback.

142. Erickson, Keith V. **Aristotle's *Rhetoric:* Five Centuries of Philological Research**. Metuchen, NJ: Scarecrow Press, 1975. 187pp. ISBN 0-8108-0809-9. LC 75-5639.

Erickson's "five centuries" refer to the years 1475-1975. The almost 1,600 entries cover books, dissertations, and articles. Some reviews appear as entries, although no systematic effort is made to list them. Entries do not include annotations. Works are arranged alphabetically by author; the only index is a chronological one. Lack of subject access requires the user to browse the entire bibliography to locate works of interest. A work of the literary and historical significance of the *Rhetoric* really deserves better.

143. Schwab, Moise. **Bibliographie d'Aristote**. Paris: H. Welter, 1896; repr., New York: Burt Franklin, 1967. 380pp. LC 01-8386.

Useful for those seeking older works on Aristotle, Schwab's compilation is the last large-scale general bibliography of Aristotle. It lists some 3,742 items, including both editions and secondary works that range in date from the 1490s to the late nineteenth century. The initial chapters deal with biographical works, general studies, manuscripts, and complete editions of Aristotle's works. The remaining chapters cover Aritstotle's individual works, grouped by topic (e.g., logic, metaphysics, rhetoric). Schwab's infrequent annotations are mostly of a bibliographical nature. An index of authors is provided.

Callimachus

144. Lehnus, Luigi. **Bibliografia Callimachea, 1489-1988**. Genova, Italy: Università di Genova, Facoltà di Lettere, 1989. 398pp. (Pubblicazioni del D.AR.FI.CL.ET.; n.s., no.123). LC 90-202251.

Lehnus covers five centuries of Callimachean scholarship. His work is comprehensive and relatively recent, although not always easy to use. He has divided his material into two major sections. The first, which is confusingly called "Works" ("Opere"), includes not only editions and translations but also studies of specific works. After noting complete editions and translations, Lehnus proceeds one by one through the individual works of Callimachus. Subarrangement is chronological. The second part deals with topical studies (manuscripts, metrics, biography, etc.). In this section Lehnus provides extensive coverage of Callimachus's influence on later authors, which is perhaps the most important aspect of Callimachean studies for the majority of classicists. There are no annotations. While cross-references are occasionally provided, there are no indexes. The detailed table of contents provides some help in navigating the work, but not enough.

Catullus

145. Ferguson, John. **Catullus**. Oxford, England: Clarendon Press, 1988. 50pp. (New Surveys in the Classics, no.20). LC 88-190314.

For those who do not require the fullness of Harrauer (entry 146) or Holoka (entry 147), Ferguson's survey provides a convenient and highly readable guide to the high points of Catullan scholarship. His brief chapters cover the history of the text, Catullus's life, literary influences, the poems, and modern translations and Catullus's impact on subsequent literature. In each chapter Ferguson provides an overview of his subject and discusses the most important scholarly works on it. A good working bibliography appears at the end of the volume.

146. Harrauer, Hermann. **A Bibliography to Catullus**. Hildesheim, Germany: Gerstenberg, 1979. 206pp. (Bibliography to the Augustan Poetry, 3). ISBN 3-8067-0787-1. LC 80-450064.

Harrauer's work contains 2,931 numbered entries (more items are listed because of supplementary entries). It covers works published between 1500 and 1976, with a few entries for 1977 as well. Coverage through the eighteenth century is less than complete, owing to the defective bibliographical apparatus available for the period. Harrauer includes editions, translations, commentaries, books, and articles. Reviews are listed under the work reviewed. There are no annotations. The citations are arranged in 17 topical chapters; several of these are further subdivided. Works within a given category are subarranged chronologically. As in earlier volumes in this series (entries 181, 193), Harrauer provides outstanding indexing. The *index locorum* provides access to discussions of individual poems and even specific lines. The subject index offers access to additional subjects not brought out by the chapter arrangement and to discussions of particular Latin words. There is also an author index. Harrauer is generally superior to Holoka's bibliography of Catullus (entry 147), both because of the wider span of years covered and the superior access afforded. However, both must be used to obtain reasonably exhaustive coverage.

147. Holoka, James P. **Gaius Valerius Catullus: A Systematic Bibliography**. New York: Garland, 1985. 324pp. (Garland Reference Library of the Humanities, v.513). ISBN 0-8240-8897-2. LC 84-45404.

It is not clear why this work was published just six years after Harrauer's major bibliography of Catullus (entry 146). Holoka offers roughly the same number of entries, 3,111, and covers 1878 to 1981 (a few items published in 1982 and 1983 are included also). The citations are arranged in nine broad topical chapters; most of these are subdivided into a number of additional categories. Subarrangement within a category is chronological. Holoka includes editions, translations, books, and articles. Reviews are listed under the work reviewed. Some entries include brief descriptive annotations. Holoka also includes tables of contents for many of the books listed. There are some cross-references to related entries, but there is only an author index, which leaves one dependent on the chapter and section headings for other access. Holoka picks up a few items that Harrauer missed and carries the work five years later. Harrauer is generally better in breadth of coverage and provides far better access.

Epictetus

148. Oldfather, W. A. **Contributions Toward a Bibliography of Epictetus**. Urbana, IL: University of Illinois, 1927. 201pp. LC 28-2296.

149. Oldfather, W. A. **Contributions Toward a Bibliography of Epictetus. A Supplement**. Edited by Marian Harman. Urbana, IL: University of Illinois Press, 1952.

This selective yet extensive bibliography is a product of one of the foremost American classicists of the twentieth century. Oldfather arranged his material by form; chapters cover editions, translations, ancient commentaries, and modern criticism. He gives fairly full coverage of editions and translations. Subarrangement is by date for editions and by language for translations. For the earlier works, Oldfather often supplies reasonably complete title page transcriptions and notes libraries known to hold copies. Many entries are equipped with learned, critical annotations that deal with content and publishing history. Oldfather is most selective in his coverage of critical works, which are arranged alphabetically by author. His annotations of these entries range from brief summaries to scholarly discussions.

Oldfather had nearly finished the supplement before his death in a canoeing accident in 1945. His former student Marian Harman prepared the manuscript for publication. The supplement, which includes works published through 1946, follows the pattern of the original bibliography. In addition to some new items, it contains many updated, corrected, and expanded versions of entries from the original volume. A handlist of manuscripts of the *Encheiridion* of Epictetus has been appended. The supplement also includes indexes for both volumes; these cover editors, translators, and authors; printers and publishers; and places of publication. There is also a preliminary list of Epictetus manuscripts by W. H. Friedrich and C. U. Faye

Heraclitus

150. Roussos, Evangelos N. **Heraklit-Bibliographie**. Darmstadt, Germany: Wissenschaftliche Buchgesellschaft, 1971. 164pp. ISBN 3-534-05585-3. LC 72-317298.

In addition to works specifically about Heraclitus, this wide-ranging bibliography includes many general works on Greek literature and philosophy that touch on him. Both the philological and philosophical aspects of Heraclitean studies receive good coverage. Roussos arranges his material under three general headings: text, the teachings of Heraclitus, and influence. The text chapter includes sections on bibliography, texts (editions, translations, and commentaries), the life of Heraclitus, and technical studies (transmission, language, and style). The second chapter, which is divided into a number of topical sections, covers all major aspects of Heraclitus's thought. The final chapter covers the influence of Heraclitus on later philosophers from antiquity through Martin Heidegger. It is arranged into several chronological units. There are no annotations. Roussos provides chronological and author indexes.

Herodotus

151. Bubel, Frank. **Herodot-Bibliographie, 1980-1988**. Hildesheim, Germany: Olms-Weidmann, 1991. 63pp. (Altertumswissenschaftliche Texte und Studien, Bd.20). ISBN 3-487-09507-6.

Bubel's compilation, which is based on *L'Année philologique* (entry 26), contains roughly 600 works and is arranged in 19 broad subject categories. In addition to works published within the designated years, Bubel includes a few earlier books reviewed during that time. There are no annotations. Reviews are listed under the works reviewed. Bubel provides indexes to authors, names and subjects, and passages discussed. Although essentially a derivative work, Bubel is more convenient to use than the individual volumes of *L'Année philologique* and offers better access.

Hippocrates

152. Bruni Celli, Blas. **Bibliografía Hipocrática**. Caracas, Venezuela: Universidad Central de Venezuela, 1984. 500pp. LC 85-121395.

Completed just as the bibliography of Maloney and Savoie (entry 153) appeared, this work includes some 1,000 more entries (4,496 in all). Bruni Celli includes editions, translations, and secondary works from the earliest printed editions through the early 1980s. He arrranges these alphabetically by author or editor. Although Bruni Celli does not annotate his entries, he provides biographical notes for some early authors, occasional content notes (especially for partial editions of the *Corpus Hippocraticum*), and references to other bibliographies as applicable. The work is illustrated with small reproductions of title pages from early editions of the Hippocratic writings. In addition to name and subject indexes, Bruni Celli provides an index to editions of individual Hippocratic works and an index of cities and printers for the major editions. Bruni Celli seems to have been unable to decide whether he wanted to compile a bibliographical guide to the early editions or a guide to the Hippocratic literature in general. What he has produced is a useful, if not entirely satisfactory, combination of the two.

153. Maloney, G., and R. Savoie. **Cinq cents ans de bibliographique hippocratique**. Québec: Les Editions du Sphinx, 1982. 291pp. ISBN 2-920123-01-7. LC 82-210317.

Of interest to historians of medicine as well as classicists, this bibliography gathers five centuries of work on Hippocrates and the *Corpus Hippocraticum*. It lists some 3,332 works, including editions, commentaries, translations, and scholarly studies. The authors have covered all aspects of Hippocratic studies: historical, medical, and philological. Their coverage is relatively complete for works published in Western Europe and North America; publications from other regions are included, but no effort was made to do so comprehensively. They have arranged the citations chronologically, with the entries for each year subarranged alphabetically. The entries do not include any annotations or summaries. There is an index of authors, but no provision for subject access. Bruni Celli's slightly later work (entry 152) provides many additional citations and better subject access.

Homer

154. Hainsworth, J. B. **Homer**. Oxford, England: Clarendon Press, 1969. 44pp. (New Surveys in the Classics, no.3). LC 77-469334.

Hainsworth, a distinguished Homerist, reviews selected aspects of recent Homeric scholarship. He organizes these under text, comparison, craft, and art. The chapter on text discusses not only the history of the text but also the performance of the poem and the "Homeric Problem." Hainsworth's discussion of comparative studies of epic is a good introduction to the topic. Craft, of course, refers both to formulaic composition and to versification. The chapter on art covers several aspects of the interpretation and appreciation of Homer. A brief appendix lists the principal editions, commentaries, lexica, grammars, and translations. Hainsworth covers roughly the same span as Packard and Meyers (entry 155). Although he cites far fewer works, his review essays make a more coherent introduction to the scholarly literature.

155. Packard, David W., and Tania Meyers. **A Bibliography of Homeric Scholarship. Preliminary edition, 1930-1970**. Malibu, CA: Undena, 1974. 183pp. ISBN 0-8900-3005-7. LC 74-18918.

This bibliography is based on the yearly listings found in *L'Année philologique* (entry 26), with some expansions and corrections. Only citations are provided; there are no abstracts (although these can be found in the various volumes of *L'Année*). Packard and Meyers have arranged the entries in a single alphabetical list by author. They have also provided a classified subject index and an index to Homeric passages discussed in the various works. This derivative work offers both more and less than the corresponding sections of *L'Année*. Everything is gathered in a single volume with better access tools, but without the abstracts.

Horace

156. Doblhofer, Ernst. **Horaz in der Forschung nach 1957**. Darmstadt, Germany: Wissenschaftliche Buchgesellschaft, 1992. 205pp. (Erträge der Forschung, Bd.279). ISBN 3-534-04505-X. LC 93-156228.

Doblhofer reviews publications on Horace for 1957 to 1987. He also discusses a number of important works that appeared before 1957. His work takes the form of a series of topical review essays that cover all aspects of Horatian studies. These progess from general aspects (textual history, editions, biography, literary history, and criticism) to studies of specific works and poems. Doblhofer gives a good overview of the scholarship in each area. He indicates the scope of each item, sets it in the context of other works on the topic, and occasionally provides his own assessment of its value. The bibliography, which is arranged in sections corresponding to the review essays, includes 1,157 numbered items. There are indexes of persons and subjects. Doblhofer covers far more works than Williams (entry 157) and is much more current. However, some knowledge of German is required to make effective use of Doblhofer.

157. Williams, Gordon. **Horace**. Oxford, England: Clarendon Press, 1972. 49pp. (New Surveys in the Classics, no.6). LC 73-163573.

In this survey, a noted scholar of Augustan poetry covers the works of Horace in chronological order. Williams's introduction discusses general treatments of Horace. Subsequent chapters review scholarly work on the individual books of poetry. In each, Williams first notes the principal editions, commentaries, and major studies of the work, and then proceeds to studies of particular aspects of the poems. The majority of the publications cited are relatively recent, and many are in English, although Williams includes a generous selection of the most important older and foreign-language works as well.

Josephus

158. Feldman, Louis H. **Josephus: A Supplementary Bibliography**. New York: Garland, 1986. 696pp. (Garland Reference Library of the Humanities, v.645). ISBN 0-8240-8792-5. LC 84-48399.

Feldman intended this work as a supplement to Schreckenberg's bibliography (entries 160-161). Roughly half of Feldman's 3,500 entries are pre-1976 items missed by Schreckenberg. Another quarter are items listed by Schreckenberg for which Feldman provides additional information or corrections. The remaining entries provide coverage for 1976-1984. Feldman departs from Schreckenberg's chronological scheme and arranges his entries alphabetically by author; however, he continues to use Schreckenberg's numerical classification scheme and provides an index to it in order to facilitate subject access. Feldman's entries also include useful summaries and occasional critical remarks. He provides indexes to citations of Josephus and to Greek words discussed for this volume and for Schreckenberg's *Supplementband*, which lacked such indexes. Feldman also provides corrigenda for his *Josephus and Modern Scholarship* (entry 159). Together, the works of Schreckenberg and Feldman provide exhaustive coverage of works on Josephus and are a valuable resource for the study of Hellenistic Judaism in general.

159. Feldman, Louis H. **Josephus and Modern Scholarship (1937-1980)**. Berlin: Walter de Gruyter, 1984. 1055pp. ISBN 3-11-008138-5.

This work updates and expands the Josephus portion of Feldman's *Scholarship on Philo and Josephus (1937-1962)* (entry 169). Feldman uses a detailed subject classification scheme (neatly laid out by his table of contents) to organize about 3,500 entries. Bibliographical citations are listed at the beginning of each subject section. In the discussion that follows, Feldman summarizes and critically reviews the items. He covers the literature exhaustively for his period; he also includes some works published prior to 1937. There is a very full *index locorum*. Feldman also provides indexes of Greek, Latin, Hebrew, and other words discussed and of modern scholars. Most readers will prefer Feldman to Schreckenberg (entries 160-161) for the years covered as the discussion of works is in English. Also, only Feldman's work provides suitable subject access. However, Schreckenberg remains indispensable for his coverage of Josephan scholarship before 1937.

160. Schreckenberg, Heinz. **Bibliographie zu Flavius Josephus**. Leiden, The Netherlands: E. J. Brill, 1968. 336pp. (Arbeiten zur Literatur und Geschichte des hellenistischen Judentums, 1). LC 76-395269.

161. Schreckenberg, Heinz. **Bibliographie zu Flavius Josephus: Supplementband mit Gesamtregister**. Leiden, The Netherlands: E. J. Brill, 1979. 242pp. (Arbeiten zur Literatur und Geschichte des hellenistischen Judentums, 14). ISBN 90-04-05968-7.

Schreckenberg's original bibliography lists about 2,200 items, which include editions, commentaries, translations, and secondary works. He also cites many works on Judaism and ancient history in general, as well as works specifically on Josephus. Schreckenberg arranges his entries chronologically by date of publication, beginning with the *editio princeps* and extending to 1968. His coverage is reasonably complete through 1965. Annotations, some quite extensive, accompany many entries. Schreckenberg provides indexes of persons, passages of Josephus's works, and Greek works. He also employs a curious form of subject classification. The numbers 1-25 are assigned to various form and subject headings; Schreckenberg then places the appropriate numbers in the margin beside each entry. Their value is limited, however, because no index to these is provided.

Schreckenberg includes in the supplement all additional works on Josephus that came to his attention by March 1979. Together with the earlier volume, it can be considered reasonably complete through 1975. Schreckenberg follows a quite different plan of organization in the supplement. He places all secondary materials in a single alphabetical list, arranged by author. A second section includes editions (arranged chronologically) and translations (by language). Schreckenberg again annotates some entries. He also provides alphabetical and chronological indexes of authors, and a separate index of editors and translators of Josephus. Feldman's various bibliographies (entries 158-159) should be consulted for additional material.

Livy

162. Walsh, P. G. **Livy**. Oxford, England: Clarendon Press, 1974. 38pp. (New Surveys in the Classics, no.8). LC 75-324622.

Walsh, who has done notable work on Livy, offers a "general assessment" of recent scholarship on Livy in selected areas. In a series of brief review essays he covers Livy as an Augustan historian, as a historian of Rome, and as a literary artist. Walsh also provides a brief treatment of Livy's *Nachleben* (i.e., his influence) and studies of it. He provides fuller coverage of foreign-language scholarship, especially German works, than is typically found in volumes of this series. In fact, this attractive survey pulls together most of the significant work done on Livy in this century. An appendix lists the principal editions, commentaries, translations, and lexica.

[Longinus]

163. Marin, Demetrios St., comp. **Bibliography on the "Essay on the Sublime."** Printed Privately for the Author, 1967. 101pp. LC 68-118876.

Marin's bibliography covers work on the "Essay on the Sublime," which traditionally has been ascribed to Longinus, through the end of 1956. He also includes a number of items concerning other rhetoricians, such as Dionysius of Halicarnassus, for purposes of comparative study. Marin arranges his material by form and subject. The first section lists and briefly discusses the known manuscripts of the essay. The second includes general and specialized bibliographies. Editions, commentaries, and translations are found in the third chapter. The final section covers scholarly studies and is divided into several broad subject categories. Many of the entries include annotations that variously offer summaries, bibliographical information, or critical comment. Indexes of ancient and modern authors conclude the work. Marin is a useful, if dated, source of material on this problematic and important work.

Lucretius

164. Gordon, Cosmo Alexander. **A Bibliography of Lucretius**. 2d edition. London: St. Paul's Bibliographies, 1985. 323pp. ISBN 0-90675-06-0.

Gordon first published his bibliography in 1962; this reissue includes an introduction and notes by E. J. Kenney. This work is a traditional descriptive bibliography of editions and translations of Lucretius, extending from the *editio princeps* of 1473 to Konrad Müller's 1975 edition of *De Rerum Natura*. It includes much of interest to bibliographers, textual critics, and historians of scholarship. The well-designed index provides ready access by names of editors, illustrators, printers, and the like.

Menander

165. Arnott, W. Geoffrey. **Menander, Plautus, and Terence**. Oxford, England: Clarendon Press, 1975. 62pp. (New Surveys in the Classics, no.9). LC 77-367418.

Arnott's survey covers the three surviving writers of new comedy. He treats Menander in the first chapter, Plautus and Terence in the second. Each section begins with a brief general bibliography that lists the chief editions, commentaries, translations, and general works. Arnott then reviews the major areas of scholarly research in a series of sections. The notes to these sections provide many additional citations. In general, Arnott supplies a good overview of research in the area and a sound working bibliography of pre-1975 publications.

Ovid

166. Barsby, John. **Ovid**. Oxford, England: Clarendon Press, 1978. 49pp. (New Surveys in the Classics, no.12). LC 79-310588.

Barsby surveys work on Ovid since 1955, although he also includes a few significant older items. He focuses chiefly on readily available studies in English. Barsby notes general works in his introduction; subsequent chapters cover Ovid's various books of poetry. Each chapter provides a synthesis of recent scholarship, with bibliographical particulars relegated to the notes. While no longer current, Barsby's survey is well suited to the needs of students.

167. Paratore, Ettore. **Bibliografia Ovidiana**. Sulmona, Italy: Comitato per le Celebrazioni de Bimillenario, 1958. 169pp. LC 59-4252.

Paratore compiled this bibliography for the bimillenary of Ovid's birth. He arranged his material by form into seven chapters: incunabula (editions, complete and partial, to 1700, rather than the term's more normal meaning of pre-1501 imprints), editions (from 1700), translations, dissertations, books

and chapters in books, journal articles, and lexica. All are subarranged chronologically. Citations of early publications are abbreviated. There are no annotations of any sort. Paratore also failed to provide indexes. As a result, this work
is difficult to consult and of limited value.

Petronius

168. Schmeling, Gareth L., and Johanna H. Stuckey. **A Bibliography of
Petronius**. Lugduni Batavorum (Leiden, Netherlands): E. J. Brill, 1977.
239pp. (Mnemosyne Supplements, 39). ISBN 90-04-04753-0. LC 77-
550459.

This work, which the authors describe as a handlist, is something of a hybrid
between a traditional descriptive author bibliography and an annotated bibliography
of secondary works. The substantial introduction surveys the manuscript tradition
and printing history of Petronius, and provides brief historical overviews of translations and of Petronian scholarship from the Renaissance to the 1960s. The
bibliography is arranged into four sections. The first and shortest is devoted to
manuscripts of Petronius; these are arranged alphabetically by *sigla* and by location.
The second section covers printed books, by which the authors mean editions and
translations of Petronius, in chronological order. The third and longest section deals
with scholarly works on Petronius; these are arranged alphabetically by author. The
final section covers "Petroniana," works based on or influenced by Petronius (e.g.,
Fellini's *Satyricon*). Many entries include annotations providing bibliographical
information or a summary of the contents. This is a comprehensive bibliography
with more than 2,000 entries, but it is not always easy to use. Subject access, which
is provided through the short general index, is weak. Nor is there an index of
particular passages discussed in the secondary works. However, this is an indispensable tool for the study of Petronius. It is also nicely illustrated with reproductions
of title pages of early editions and of manuscript leaves.

Philo

169. Feldman, Louis H. **Scholarship on Philo and Josephus (1937-1962)**.
New York: Yeshiva University, n.d. 62pp. (Studies in Judaica).

The original version of this survey was printed in *Classical World* (entry
545) and was subsequently reprinted in one of the collected volumes of *Classical
World* bibliographies. This separate edition adds supplementary items and several indexes. Feldman attempts complete coverage for the specified years. The
material is arranged by subject; Feldman also provides descriptive and evaluative comments. There are indexes to ancient passages discussed; to Hebrew,
Greek, and Latin words; and to names of modern scholars. For Josephus, this
work is superseded by Schreckenberg (entries 160-161) and Feldman's other
bibliographies (entries 158-159).

Pindar

170. Gerber, Douglas E. **A Bibliography of Pindar, 1513-1966**. Cleveland, OH:
Case Western Reserve University for the American Philological Association,
1969. 160pp. (Philological Monographs, no.28). LC 68-8750.

Gerber lists editions, commentaries, translations, and studies of Pindar. He begins with the first printed edition in 1513 and attempts to cover all materials that had appeared by March of 1967. The citations are arranged into 30 sections by form and subject; many of these sections are further subdivided. When appropriate, items are included under more than one heading. Reviews are listed with the work reviewed. There are no abstracts, although Gerber sometimes reproduces the tables of contents for books. The lack of an index is a major defect of the work. It is otherwise a useful tool and appears to be reasonably complete for the years covered.

Plato

171. McKirahan, Richard D., Jr. **Plato and Socrates: A Comprehensive Bibliography, 1958-1973**. New York: Garland, 1978. 592pp. (Garland Reference Library of the Humanities, v.78). ISBN 0-8240-9895-1. LC 76-52670.

This bibliography is a continuation of H. F. Cherniss's bibliographies for 1950-1957 that appeared in the journal *Lustrum* (entry 49). McKirahan's more than 4,600 entries for only 15 years well illustrate the difficulty of keeping abreast of scholarship on Plato and Socrates. He has arranged the entries by subject; his table of contents effectively lays out the scheme. Within each category, works are subarranged chronologically. There are no annotations. Reviews are listed under the entry for the book reviewed. An author index concludes the volume. For additional coverage of Socrates see Navia and Katz (entry 186).

172. Ritter, Constantin. **Bibliographies on Plato, 1912-1930**. New York: Garland, 1980. 909pp. (Ancient Philosophy). ISBN 0-8240-9590-1. LC 78-66617.

This volume consists of reprints of six bibliographical surveys that originally appeared in *Bursian's Jahresbericht* (entry 48) between 1912 and 1930. All are in German. Together, they provide a fairly complete report of scholarly work on Plato during the first three decades of this century. The publisher has merely reprinted the original texts; no table of contents or index is provided (there is not even continuous pagination). As a result, the work is difficult to use. For this reason, and because of the language and date, Ritter is of use chiefly to professional scholars.

173. Saunders, Trevor J. **Bibliography on Plato's *Laws*, 1920-1976, with Additional Citations Through March 1979**. 2d ed. New York: Arno Press, 1979. 65pp. (History of Ideas in Ancient Greece). ISBN 0-405-12491-0. LC 79-16012.

Saunders includes only material that deals primarily with the *Laws*; more general works on Plato are excluded. He does admit a few works antedating 1920. Within his chronological limits, Saunders covers all aspects of work, both philological and philosophical, on the *Laws*. His material is divided into three sections: texts and translations, books and articles (subarranged into 13 categories by subject), and discussions of individual passages. The rare annotation serves chiefly to clarify content when titles are ambiguous. There are no indexes. Saunders provides a useful working guide, although most will want to use his work as a supplement to more general bibliographies of Platonic studies.

✓ 174. Skemp, J. B. **Plato**. Oxford, England: Clarendon Press, 1976. 63pp. (New Surveys in the Classics, no.10). LC 77-367770.

Skemp selectively reviews work on Plato from 1945 to 1975 in a series of brief bibliographical essays that cover all the major aspects of scholarship on Plato. While he emphasizes English-language studies, Skemp also includes major works in French and German. His summaries and valuations of the items discussed are helpful and reliable. Skemp, although far from comprehensive and now dated, remains a useful aid in grappling with the vast bibliography on Plato.

Plautus

175. Bubel, Frank, ed. **Bibliographie zu Plautus, 1976-1989**. Bonn: Rudolf Habelt, 1992. 53pp. ISBN 3-7749-2576-3.

Beginning where Hughes (entry 176) left off, Bubel gathers 14 years of work on Plautus. His 576 citations, which are drawn entirely from *L'Année philologique* (entry 26), include books, dissertations, and articles. He presents these in a topical arrangement. Reviews are cited under book titles, but no summaries or annotations are provided. Thus, readers who want abstracts will still need to consult the individual volumes of *L'Année philologique*. Bubel has done a good job of indexing the bibliography. Separate indexes cover specific passages of Plautus, names and subjects, linguistic topics, metrics, Latin words, and authors.

176. Hughes, J. David. **A Bibliography of Scholarship on Plautus**. Amsterdam: Adolf M. Hakkert, 1975. 154pp. ISBN 90-256-0769-1. LC 76-353120.

Hughes concentrates on works published since the mid-nineteenth century. He includes books, articles, and published theses; editions of Plautus's works and reviews are omitted. His 2,328 citations are arranged by subject. A detailed table of contents neatly lays out the headings. There are cross-references for works that fall into more than one category. Hughes does not provide annotations. An index of authors concludes the work. Hughes covers most of the significant work done on Plautus and a number of more general works on Roman comedy as well. Those who prefer a selective overview of Plautine studies might consult the nearly contemporary survey by Arnott (entry 165). For more recent materials see Bubel (entry 175).

Pliny the Elder

177. Le Bonniec, H. **Bibliographie de l'Histoire naturelle de Pline l'Ancien**. Paris: Société d'Edition "Les Belles Lettres," 1946. 58pp. (Collection d'études latines, série scientifique, 21). LC 48-2102.

Le Bonniec focuses on items appearing after 1800, although he includes a selection of important earlier works as well. Despite the publication date of 1946, coverage drops off after 1939; the latest publication listed in the bibliography is from 1941. Le Bonniec uses a subject arrangement. He begins with biographical works on the elder Pliny, then covers general works on the *Natural History* under such rubrics as sources, influence, manuscripts, and language and style. The bulk of the bibliography covers studies of individual books and passages of the *Natural History*. Many of these are also useful for the more general study of ancient science and technology. Le Bonniec occasionally supplies descriptive notes to clarify the content of a book or article. There are no indexes. Although sadly out-of-date, Le Bonniec remains a useful aid for the study of a comparatively neglected author.

Plotinus

178. Mariën, Bert. **Bibliografica critica degli studi Plotiniani: Con rassegna delle loro recensioni**. Riveduta e curata da V. Cilento. Bari, Italy: Laterza, 1949. 273pp.

Mariën offers extensive coverage of Platonism and Neoplatonism in general, as well as all aspects of Plotinus's life, work, and influence. The earliest work cited is Ficino's Latin translation of the works of Plotinus (1492), and many other early works are included, although most items cited date from the nineteenth and first half of the twentieth century. Mariën arranges his material by subject categories. Many entries include brief descriptive annotations. Reviews are listed under the appropriate book entries. The work is well indexed and includes supplementary subject indexes in addition to an author index. Mariën is useful for the study both of late antique philosophy and of Neoplatonism during the Renaissance. Because of its date, Mariën's compilation will be of interest chiefly to specialized scholars.

Plutarch

179. Scardigli, Barbara. **Die Römerbiographien Plutarchs**. München: C. H. Beck, 1979. 230pp. ISBN 3-406-07400-6. LC 80-493511.

Scardigli surveys the scholarly literature on Plutarch's *Lives* from 1935 through 1978; she covers only the Roman biographies. The introduction notes and discusses general works on Plutarch, biography as a genre in antiquity, and the *Lives*. Scardigli then devotes a separate chapter to each of the lives, from Romulus through Galba and Otho. For each she provides a brief narrative overview of recent work followed by bibliographical citations, which are divided into studies of particular passages and textual studies. Many additional relevant works are cited in the notes to the narrative passages. This is a useful source, but it does not lend itself to quick consultation because so much information is buried in the notes. The indexes of passages from ancient literature and of personal names are thorough and fully cover the notes as well as the text.

Propertius

180. Fedeli, P., and P. Pinotti. **Bibliografia properziana (1946-1983)**. Assisi, Italy: Tipografia Porziuncola, 1985. 111pp. (Atti Accademia properziana del Subasio, ser.6, no.9). LC 86-157091.

Published on the occasion of the bimillenary of Propertius's death, this work is a continuation of the bibliography in P. J. Enk's *Sex. Propertii Elegiarum Liber I (Monobiblos)* (Leiden: E. J. Brill, 1946). Fedeli and Pinotti organize their entries by form and subject. Entries for books include citations of reviews; otherwise there are no annotations. Items that fit under multiple headings are cross-referenced. There is an author index. The chief value of Fedeli and Pinotti is for coverage of works published since Harrauer compiled his bibliography (entry 181). Harrauer offers more comprehensive coverage of the literature before 1973 and better indexing.

181. Harrauer, Hermann. **A Bibliography to Propertius**. Hildesheim, Germany: H. A. Gerstenberg, 1973. 219pp. (Bibliography to the Augustan Poetry, 2). ISBN 3-8067-0352-3. LC 73-178623.

This work generally follows the plan of Harrauer's *Bibliography of the Corpus Tibullianum* (entry 193). It aims at complete coverage of work published after 1900; earlier work is covered selectively. Harrauer lists, without annotations, 1,833 items in 15 topical chapters. Subarrangement is chronological. Reviews are cited under the entry for the work reviewed. Occasionally a major review receives an additional, independent entry. A full set of indexes concludes the work. The *index locorum* clearly differentiates works on whole poems and on single lines and groups of lines. There are also subject and author indexes.

Ptolemy

182. Stahl, William Harris. **Ptolemy's *Geography*: A Select Bibliography**. New York: New York Public Library, 1953. 86pp. LC 54-10090.

Stahl gathers a generous selection from the vast literature on Ptolemy's *Geography*. His bibliography runs to 1,464 entries, although the actual number of works is somewhat less, as some items are cited more than once. It includes both books and articles. Stahl covers works published through 1948; he includes many important eighteenth- and nineteenth-century items as well as more recent studies. He arranges his material by subject and form. The major divisions include regional geography, Ptolemaic studies, mathematical geography, and maps. The appendices include bibliographies of editions, translations, and works on such topics as the history of the text and Ptolemy's sources. While there are no annotations, entries for books also list reviews. Stahl cites works under more than one heading when appropriate. An index of authors concludes the work.

Pythagoras

183. Navia, Luis E. **Pythagoras: An Annotated Bibliography**. New York: Garland, 1990. 381pp. (Garland Reference Library of the Humanities, v.1128). ISBN 0-8240-4380-4. LC 90-33296.

Navia's selective bibliography presents more than 1,000 works about Pythagoras and Pythagoreanism. He covers works in English, French, German, Italian, and Spanish. His eclectic assortment includes primarily philosophical and philological works, but also extends to Neoplatonic and theological works, and to the history of such fields as science and music. In addition, there is much on Pythagoras's considerable influence on later generations. Navia has conveniently arranged his material by form and subject. He also supplies annotations, often extensive, that give good descriptions of the works cited. Navia provides indexes of authors and of names as subjects. His book is a necessary guide to the diverse and far-flung publications relating to Pythagoras.

Sallust

184. Leeman, A. D. **A Systematical Bibliography of Sallust (1879-1964)**. Rev. and augmented edition. Lugduni Batavorum (Leiden, Netherlands): E. J. Brill, 1965. 109pp. (Mnemosyne Supplements, no.4).

Leeman lists about 1,000 items (his 1,252 numbered entries include a good many cross-references). He covers works in English, French, German and the

Scandinavian languages, Italian, Spanish, Russian, Greek, and Latin. He omits many school editions and limits his coverage of translations to the most important English, French, and German ones. Otherwise he aims for completeness within the specified dates; a number of important earlier editions and studies are also included. Leeman arranges his entries into seven broad categories by form and subject. Each of these has numerous subdivisions. Leeman tends to give summary bibliographic citations, although the information provided is usually sufficient to identify works. Many entries include brief descriptive annotations. Entries for books often provide the table of contents. Reviews are also cited under book entries. An author index concludes the volume. Although now badly in need of a supplement, Leeman remains an excellent resource.

Seneca

185. Motto, Anna Lydia, and John R. Clark. **Seneca, A Critical Bibliography, 1900-1980: Scholarship on His Life, Thought, Prose, and Influence**. Amsterdam: Adolf M. Hakkert, 1989. 372pp. ISBN 90-256-0959-7. LC 90-147965.

Motto and Clark, who are the leading American authorities on the younger Seneca, cover both general works on him and studies of his prose works and their influence; works dealing with his tragedies are generally excluded. They arrange their 1,759 entries into broad categories by form and subject. They also provide annotations for most items (except dissertations) that summarize and evaluate the work. An author index concludes the volume. Because of Seneca's lasting influence on Western literature and thought, even nonclassicists will find much of interest in this bibliography.

Socrates

186. Navia, Luis E., and Ellen L. Katz. **Socrates: An Annotated Bibliography**. New York: Garland, 1988. 536pp. (Garland Reference Library of the Humanities, v.844). ISBN 0-8240-5740-6. LC 88-10264.

Because Socrates's life and thought is known only through the works of his contemporaries, a bibliography on Socrates inevitably becomes a bibliography on numerous other ancients as well. While their focus always stays on Socrates, Navia and Katz cite many works concerning Aristophanes, Xenophon, and Plato (who are our major sources of information about Socrates) as well. Their scope is comprehensive in terms of forms and subjects, but coverage is selective within each category. They include works in English and in the standard Western European languages. No attempt is made to be exhaustive, which the authors note would result in "an unrealizable project." They do, however, cover a wide range of materials, including fiction, poetry, and drama about Socrates. Navia and Katz arrange their nearly 2,000 entries by form and subject; cross-references are made for works that fit in more than one category. Their annotations, which are strictly descriptive, do a good job of summarizing the works. There is an index of authors. This is an excellent working bibliography for the study of Socrates. One can also consult McKirahan's *Plato and Socrates* (entry 171), which lists far more citations covering a much shorter period of time.

187. Patzer, Andreas. **Bibliographia Socratica: Die wissenschaftliche Literatur über Sokrates von den Anfängen bis auf die neueste Zeit in systematisch-chronologischer Anordnung**. Freiburg, Germany: Karl Alber, 1985. 365pp. ISBN 3-495-47585-0. LC 86-100918.

Patzer's bibliography, with more than 2,300 entries, includes quite a few more items than Navia and Katz (entry 186). However, he provides no annotations. Patzer arranges his material by form and subject. There are four main sections: *Hilfsmittel* (bibliographies, surveys, and other auxiliary works), *Quellentexte* (editions and commentaries for all authors who are sources for the life and thought of Socrates), *Wissenschaftliche Literatur* (scholarly studies), and *Varia* (miscellaneous works on Socrates). Each includes numerous subdivisions; the overall scheme is made clear in the lengthy table of contents. *Wissenschaftliche Literatur*, which comprises nearly two-thirds of the book, is by far the largest part. Patzer provides cross-references as well as an index of names and subjects. He covers a wide range of works in a variety of languages. Although Navia and Katz will be the first choice for most readers of English, Patzer includes many additional citations and should also be consulted by anyone needing exhaustive coverage.

Sophocles

188. Buxton, R. G. A. **Sophocles**. Oxford, England: Clarendon Press, 1984. 38pp. (New Surveys in the Classics, no.16). ISBN 0-903035-13-8. LC 85-205399.

Buxton's survey is aimed chiefly at university students. He follows the standard approach of the series: brief topical essays present a synthesis of recent scholarship in the area, with bibliographical details supplied in the notes. Buxton cites English-language works as much as possible, but also includes important works in other languages. While touching on all major aspects of Sophoclean studies, Buxton gives emphasis to literary and dramatic criticism. He provides a good working introduction to the study of Sophocles and his plays.

Strabo

189. Biraschi, A. M., P. Maribelli, G. D. Massaro, and M. A. Pagnotta. **Strabone: Saggio di bibliografia, 1469-1978**. Perugia, Italy: Università degli Studi, 1981. 137pp. (Pubblicazioni degli Istituti di Storia Antica e di Storia Medioevale e Moderna della Facoltà di Lettere e Filosofia). LC 88-176341.

This bibliography covers works by and about Strabo from the publication of the earliest printed version (a Latin translation) in 1469 through 1978. The compilers have grouped their material in three sections: editions, translations, and studies. They have arranged entries within each of these chronologically. While the section devoted to secondary studies includes a number of items of historical and geographical interest, philological works predominate. There are no annotations. Indexes provide access by subject (only very broad terms) and author. There is also a brief and unsatisfactory *index locorum*, which covers only those passages expressly mentioned in the titles of works cited.

Tacitus

190. Goodyear, F. R. D. **Tacitus**. Oxford, England: Clarendon Press, 1970. 44pp. (New Surveys in the Classics, no.4). LC 79-570213.

Goodyear, who has done extensive work on Tacitus, offers a "personal synthesis" of the scholarly literature on his subject. His brief introduction notes many of the most significant general works on Tacitus and on the history of the early empire. The various chapters cover the minor works, the *Histories* and the *Annals*, Tacitus as a historian, and his language and style. Goodyear provides a good overview of twentieth-century Tacitean studies through the 1960s. He also notes, as the publication patterns require, more German-language works than is the norm for volumes in this series.

Terence

191. Cupaiuolo, Giovanni, ed. **Bibliografia terenziana (1470-1983)**. Napoli: Società Editrice Napoletana, 1984. 551pp. (Studi e testi dell'antichità, 16).

Cupaiuolo lists some 5,190 items, beginning with the first printed edition of Terence (1470). He devotes the first part of the bibliography to editions, commentaries, and translations. This is arranged into sections for complete editions, partial editions, and editions of individual plays. In each case, translations, which are arranged by language, follow the lists of editions. Cupaiuolo's coverage is exhaustive (2,794 editions and translations are noted). He also provides references to standard bibliographies and library catalogs under entries for earlier editions (primarily those of the fifteenth and sixteenth centuries) and to reviews for modern editions. In the second part, Cupaiuolo lists an extensive array of scholarly studies of Terence; these date mostly from the nineteenth and twentieth centuries. He arranges these by subject. Virtually every aspect of Terentian studies is covered in detail. In addition to items dealing specifically with Terence, Cupaiuolo also includes many general works that contain significant discussion of him. An index of names concludes the volume.

Thucydides

192. Dover, K. J. **Thucydides**. Oxford, England: Clarendon Press, 1973. 44pp. (New Surveys in the Classics, no.7). LC 74-171533.

Written by one of the leading Greek scholars of the twentieth century, this slender volume surveys the state of Thucydidean studies as of 1973. The first chapter lists and comments upon most important editions, commentaries, translations, and general works. Subsequent chapters deal with specific aspects of Thucydides's *History*: its authority, the text, style, composition, speeches, acts and intentions, judgment, and generalization. Each cites and discusses relevant studies. While in some ways this work is more a collection of brief essays than a bibliographical survey, it does provide a good overview of work on Thucydides during the first three-quarters of the century.

Tibullus

193. Harrauer, Hermann. **A Bibliography to the Corpus Tibullianum**. Hildesheim, Germany: H. A. Gerstenberg, 1971. 90pp. (Bibliography to the Augustan Poetry, 1). ISBN 3-8067-0014-1. LC 73-884445.

"It is the aim of this bibliography to offer a complete list of the literature on the *Corpus Tibullianum* since the year 1900. Older literature has only been included as far as it proved to be of importance for further scientific work...." The list consists of 1,111 works arranged in 21 topical chapters. Works are arranged chronologically within each chapter. Dates are inserted at intervals in the left margin as an aid to the reader. Entries for books include citations of reviews. There are no annotations. The subject arrangement is well thought out and logical. A full array of indexes is provided, including an unusually full *index locorum* and subject and author indexes.

Vergil

194. Donlan, Walter, ed. **The Classical World Bibliography of Vergil**. New York: Garland, 1978. 176pp. (Garland Reference Library of the Humanities, v.96). ISBN 0-8240-9877-3. LC 76-52514.

This compilation includes three general bibliographical surveys on Vergil covering 1940-1973 and "A Bibliographical Handlist on Vergil's *Aeneid* for Teachers and Students in Secondary Schools." All of these originally appeared in *Classical World* (entry 545). The surveys are each arranged into broad subject divisions. Many of these are further subdivided. The editor provides brief descriptions of the works cited. Although their primary emphasis is on English works, the surveys also cover many European-language publications. The "Handlist" is a general bibliography aimed at high school teachers. There are no indexes. While no longer up-to-date, this volume remains a useful entry into the vast scholarly literature on Vergil. It can be supplemented by the annual bibliographical surveys on Vergil that appear in *Vergilius*, the journal of the Vergilian Society of America (see entry 666). Those seeking earlier works should consult Mambelli (entry 195).

195. Mambelli, Giuliano. **Gli studi virgilani nel secolo xx**. Firenze, Italy: G. C. Sansone, 1940. 2v. (Guide bibliografiche dell'Istituto Nazionale di Cultura Fascista). LC 44-30789.

These two thick volumes cover work on Vergil between 1900 and 1939. Coverage is comprehensive through 1936, while that for subsequent years is less complete. Mambelli arranges his 3,952 entries by author; subarrangement is by date of publication. Some later items are found in the appendix rather than in the main list. Mambelli supplies descriptive annotations for most entries and notes reviews under entries for books. Indexes cover names, subjects, passages discussed, and journal titles. For works after 1939 see Donlan (entry 194) and Williams (entry 196).

196. Williams, R. D. **Virgil**. Oxford, England: Clarendon Press, 1967. 44pp. (New Surveys in the Classics, no.1). LC 68-104147.

Williams's aim in this work is to provide not a general bibliographical survey of Vergil, but a synthesis of "recent important work of a critical kind." Williams focuses almost entirely on works of literary criticism. He discusses mainly works of the 1950s and 1960s, without neglecting significant earlier works. A brief appendix lists the most useful editions, translations, and commentaries. Donlan's compendium (entry 194) offers a much wider approach to Vergilian bibliography.

CHAPTER  6

LIBRARY CATALOGS

For many years, printed library catalogs have been an important tool for gathering and verifying citations and for locating copies of specific items. Online access to library catalogs throughout the world has partially, but not completely, replaced this function. The printed catalogs listed below represent some of the major research collections for classical studies. Of course, not all libraries with important holdings in classics have produced printed catalogs. Many of these have now made their catalogs available to remote users through the Internet. Some of the more important North American collections for classical studies not included below can be found at Columbia University, the University of California at Berkeley, the University of Cincinnati (possibly the best overall collection in North America; particular strengths include Bronze Age and classical archaeology, Latin palaeography, and modern Greek studies), the University of Illinois (the personal libraries of Johannes Vahlen and Wilhelm Dittenberger form the basis of this collection, which is exceptionally strong in classical philology), the University of Michigan (notable for its comprehensive holdings in papyrology), and Yale University.

197. **Catalogo delle edizioni di testi classici esistenti nelle biblioteche degli istituti stranieri di Roma**. Roma: Unione Internazionale degli Istituti di Archeologia, Storia, e Storia dell'Arte in Roma, 1969. 544pp. LC 77-503139.

This work is a union list of editions of Greek and Latin authors held by the major foreign classical schools in Rome. It represents the combined holdings of some 18 institutions, such as the American Academy in Rome (entry 621), the British School at Rome (entry 625), and the Deutsches Archäologisches Institut (entry 630). The catalog includes Latin authors from the beginning through Isidore of Seville (A.D. 636) and Greek authors from the beginning through John of Damascus (A.D. 749). The authors (and, for anonymous works, titles) appear in a single alphabetical sequence. Under each author, collected editions come first and individual works follow alphabetically. Editions listed range from the beginning of printing through 1960; nineteenth- and twentieth-century editions comprise the bulk of the entries. One of the more helpful features is the inclusion of editions that appear in the various *corpora*, such as Migne's *Patrologia*, as well as those issued separately. This makes the work particularly useful for identifying editions of late and minor authors.

198. **Catalogue of the Gennadius Library, American School of Classical Studies at Athens**. Boston: G. K. Hall, 1968. 7v.

199. **Supplement**. Boston: G. K. Hall, 1973. 852pp.

200. **Second Supplement**. Boston: G. K. Hall, 1981. 833pp.

The Greek diplomat and scholar Joannes Gennadius (1844-1932) began this collection and presented it to the American School of Classical Studies at Athens (entry 623) in 1922. The collection covers all aspects of the history and culture of Greece from antiquity to the present. Its strengths are in Byzantine and modern Greek studies, although it includes many works on classical studies as well. The collection is exceptionally rich in early editions of classical and Byzantine authors, materials concerning the beginnings of classical archaeology (1750-1825), and travel books on Greece and the surrounding areas. The American School has regularly added to the holdings of the Gennadius Library in Byzantine and modern Greek studies, but not in classical studies, as that area is covered by the School's own working library.

The catalog, typical of G. K. Hall publications, reproduces the actual library catalog cards. These are presented in a single alphabetical sequence, with Greek and Roman alphabet headings interfiled. The catalog includes author and subject headings; title entries appear only for anonymous works. Numerous cross-references are provided.

201. **A Classified Catalogue of the Books, Pamphlets, and Maps in the Library of the Societies for the Promotion of Hellenic and Roman Studies**. London: Macmillan, 1924. 336pp. LC 25-5084.

Founded in 1879, the shared library of these two British societies (entries 664-665) is located in London and is now associated with the University of London's Institute of Classical Studies (entry 636). Its holdings cover all aspects of Greek and Roman studies: language, literature, history, archaeology, and philosophy. The library also includes some works on modern Greece and the Ancient Near East. This catalog, which was compiled by John Penoyre, shows the collection as it stood in 1924. Although the collection has grown substantially since then, the only supplements to appear have been the annual acquisitions lists of the library, which are not widely available. The catalog of 1924 is useful chiefly for finding nineteenth- and early twentieth-century imprints; its strengths include *corpora*, periodicals, and pamphlets. Its classified arrangement is generally sensible and easy to follow. It progresses from "instruments of study" (periodicals, collected works, reference works, and methodology) through language, literature, and history to geography (in a broad sense) and antiquities. A detailed outline of the classification scheme appears at the beginning of the volume. Lack of author and title indexes is a major drawback.

202. Deutsches Archäologisches Institut, Römische Abteilung. **Kataloge der Bibliothek des Deutschen Archaeologischen Instituts, Rom = Catalogs from the Library of the German Institute of Archaeology, Rome**. Boston: G. K. Hall, 1969. **Autoren- und Periodica Kataloge = Author and Periodical Catalogs**. 7v. LC 73-202658. Systematischer Katalog = **Classified Catalog**. 3v. LC 73-205023. **Zeitschriften-Autoren Katalog = Author Catalog of Periodicals**. 3v. LC 73-202659.

The Deutsches Archäologisches Institut (entry 630) traces its origins back to 1829. At the time this catalog was published, its library held more than 90,000 volumes and 1,300 periodicals. While the collection focuses on classical archaeology, it also includes many works on other aspects of classical studies, the Ancient Near East, European prehistory, and early Christian and Byzantine archaeology. The DAI's rich collection includes many now-scarce older works. Its catalog is a valuable bibliographical resource both for classicists and for archaeologists in general.

The catalog was published in three parts. The first and largest covers authors and periodicals. The entries for authors appear first; periodicals follow in a separate list by title. The second component is a classified subject catalog in three volumes. A detailed exposition of the classification scheme appears in the first volume. The final part, also in three volumes, provides author analytics for journal articles. Entries, which consist of reproduced catalog cards, supply basic bibliographical information. As these were prepared at different times and under varying rules, the amount and quality of information can vary. Many of the cards were handwritten and can be difficult to decipher. DYABOLA (entry 33), a new computerized version of the DAI's catalog, which currently covers works published since 1956, provides a better option for those seeking more recent publications. The printed catalog remains of great value for retrospective coverage.

203. Harvard University Library. **Ancient Greek Literature: Classification Schedules, Classified Listing by Call Number, Chronological Listing, Author and Title Listing**. Cambridge, MA: Harvard University Library, 1979. 638pp. (Widener Library Shelflist, 58). ISBN 0-674-03310-8. LC 79-9989.

This volume contains shelflist entries for 19,800 book-length works housed in the Widener Library at Harvard. It includes only works cataloged before July 1976 and covers anthologies of Greek literature and works by and about individual Greek authors. A few Greek authors, such as Euclid, whose works are primarily mathematical, are excluded. General works on ancient literature, including histories of Greek literature, will be found in the volume on classical studies (entry 206). The old Harvard classification system for Greek literature is outlined at the beginning to facilitate access to the classified listing. A separate listing provides author and title access. There is also a chronological listing of titles, although probably this will not interest most users. Entries provide spartan bibliographical data (generally author, title, place, and date), in keeping with older cataloging practices, which is useful for compiling retrospective bibliography and verifying citations. It includes a number of scarce and obscure works that will not readily be found elsewhere.

204. Harvard University Library. **Ancient History: Classification Schedule, Classified Listing by Call Number, Chronological Listing, Author and Title Listing**. Cambridge, MA: Harvard University Library, 1975. 363pp. (Widener Library Shelflist, 55). ISBN 0-674-03312-4. LC 75-21543.

This volume of the Widener Library Shelflist series covers both Ancient Near Eastern and classical history. It lists some 11,000 titles that were held by the Widener Library at Harvard as of 1975. More than half of these deal with Greece and Rome in some way. The classified listing follows the old, unique Harvard classification system, which is outlined at the beginning of the volume. Author and title access is also provided in a separate list. The work is mainly of use to those compiling exhaustive bibliographies or trying to verify difficult citations, although others may well find things of value in it.

205. Harvard University Library. **Archaeology: Classification Schedules, Classified Listing by Call Number, Chronological Listing, Author and Title Listing**. Cambridge, MA: Harvard University Library, 1979. 442pp. (Widener Library Shelflist, 56). ISBN 0-674-04318-9. LC 79-555.

The archaeology section of the Widener Library Shelflist series includes more than 14,000 book entries. It contains only works that had been cataloged by July of 1976. The volume covers archaeology in general; of particular interest here are the holdings in Greek, Roman, and Near Eastern archaeology. This volume also covers Greek and Latin palaeography and diplomatics, and ancient numismatics. As in the rest of the series, subject access is provided through a classified listing. An outline of the classification schedule appears at the front of the book. There is also an author and title listing. As with other volumes in the series, this one is especially useful for compiling retrospective bibliographies and verifying obscure citations.

206. Harvard University Library. **Classical Studies: Classification Schedules, Classified Listing by Call Number, Chronological Listing, Author and Title Listing**. Cambridge, MA: Harvard University Library, 1979. 215pp. (Widener Library Shelflist, 57). ISBN 0-674-13461-3. LC 79-948.

This catalog "includes works on the history and theory of classical scholarship, the history of classical literature (but not works about individual authors), classical arts and sciences, classical rhetoric, classical prosody, classical inscriptions, and classical mythology and religion." It contains entries for around 6,700 books. The arrangement of materials is the same as in other volumes of the series: separate listings provide subject, chronological, and author-title access. As with the other volumes of the Widener Library Shelflist, this is primarily of use for extensive bibliographical projects and verifying citations.

207. Harvard University Library. **Latin Literature: Classification Schedules, Classified Listing by Call Number, Chronological Listing, Author and Title Listing**. Cambridge, MA: Harvard University Library, 1979. 610pp. (Widener Library Shelflist, 59). ISBN 0-674-51295-2. LC 79-9985.

The Latin literature volume of the Widener Library Shelflist includes anthologies of Latin literature and works by and about individual authors. In addition to classical Latin literature, the volume covers medieval and modern Latin writers. A few authors whose works deal entirely with mathematics are excluded, as are the writings of the Latin Church Fathers. Literary histories are found in the volume for classical studies (entry 206). The organization of material follows the pattern typical of the series: an outline of the classification scheme, a list of entries classified by subject, a chronological list, and an author and title list. About 18,600 titles are listed; these represent works held and cataloged by the Widener Library at Harvard as of July 1976. This title is a valuable source for those doing in-depth bibliographical research on any aspect of Latin literature.

208. Southan, Joyce E. **A Survey of Classical Periodicals: Union Catalogue of Periodicals Relevant to Classical Studies in Certain British Libraries**. London: University of London, Institute of Classical Studies, 1962. 181pp. (Bulletin of the Institute of Classical Studies. Supplement, no.13). LC 65-9438.

Southan's union list of classical and related journals covers nearly all London libraries, but only university libraries from elsewhere in Great Britain. In addition to strictly classical periodicals, Southan lists many others in which materials of classical interest appear on a regular basis. She includes a limited number of academy and museum publications, but generally excludes local archaeological publications. Monographic series are also excluded, unless they appear as supplements to a journal. Entries are arranged alphabetically by the latest form of title; cross-references are made from earlier forms. The entries provide title, subtitles, previous titles, and place and date of publication. Southan also notes holding libraries; exact holdings are supplied for libraries with partial runs of a title. There is no index. Although somewhat old, Southan's work is still a useful guide. She includes many less-than-obvious titles in addition to the well-known ones. Her list can be useful in locating copies of the more obscure journals.

209. University of London Library. **The Palaeography Collection**. Boston: G. K. Hall, 1968. 2v. LC 74-152793.

This collection primarily contains works on the palaeography of Greek, Latin, and other Western European languages. It also holds works on all aspects of the medieval book and on archives and archival studies. Particular strengths include catalogs of manuscripts and published facsimiles of manuscripts. While the focus of the collection is not strictly classical, it includes much of interest to students of Greek and Latin palaeography, papyrology, and the transmission of classical literature. The first volume provides author listings, while the second is arranged by subject. The entries consist of reproduced library catalog cards that provide the basic bibliographical data for each title.

210. Warburg Institute. **Catalog of the Warburg Institute Library, University of London**. 2d ed. Boston: G. K. Hall, 1967. 12v.

211. Warburg Institute. **Catalog of the Warburg Institute Library, University of London: First Supplement**. Boston: G. K. Hall, 1971. 676pp.

The Warburg Institute (entry 639) promotes research on the survival and influence of classical antiquity in European civilization. The Institute library, which had its origin in the personal collection of Aby Warburg, is now the largest collection devoted to the *Nachleben* of the classical world. The catalog is arranged by subject, with each volume covering a broad area: social patterns, history, history of religion, history of science, history of philosophy, classical and vernacular literature, humanism, preclassical and classical art, and postclassical art (three volumes). Reference works and periodicals are listed in the final volume. The supplementary volume covers acquisitions for 1966-1970. Researchers in both the history of classical scholarship and the classical tradition will find the catalog a rich source of retrospective bibliography.

PART 2

INFORMATION RESOURCES

CHAPTER 7

GENERAL DICTIONARIES, ENCYCLOPEDIAS, AND HANDBOOKS

This chapter includes reference works that cover classical studies as a whole. The largest and most detailed of these, such as Pauly-Wissowa (entry 225), tend to be in German. All of the larger English-language classical dictionaries that are of real value will be found below also. In addition, a selection of the better smaller classical dictionaries are noted, although this category is not covered exhaustively. Finally, several handbooks that offer extended treatment of the broader aspects of classical civilization appear below. Works devoted to individual areas of study, such as literature or archaeology, or specific topics may be found in the four chapters that follow.

212.   Avery, Catherine B., ed. **The New Century Classical Handbook**. Editorial Consultant, Jotham Johnson. New York: Appleton-Century-Crofts, 1962. 1,162pp. LC 62-10069.

Aimed at students and general readers, this encyclopedia of classical civilization is widely available. Chronologically the handbook covers the period from the beginnings of Greek civilization to the end of the Julio-Claudian dynasty at Rome (A.D. 68). There are a few entries for the years immediately following, and none for anything after the early second century A.D. The book's more than 6,000 entries treat persons (both historical and mythological), literary works, monuments and works of art, and places. Entries for persons provide biographical and historical information. Articles for literary works consist of summaries, while those for monuments and art works are largely descriptive. Entries for places give both geographical and historical information. Emphasis is placed on how the material appeared to the ancients rather than on modern interpretations; hence, many of the articles deal more with legend than fact and can mislead those seeking accurate historical information. This problem is exacerbated by the errors of fact and interpretation found in some entries. There are no bibliographies, nor is an index provided. The *Oxford Classical Dictionary* (entry 218) is generally a better choice as an all-purpose encyclopedia of classical civilization, because it is more recent and offers reliable historical data. It also includes excellent short bibliographies at the end of most articles.

Around 1972, five smaller works based on material from *The New Century Classical Handbook* were issued. These cover biography, geography, mythology, Greek literature, and Greek art. In some cases these works include new material, in others not. For fuller descriptions see entries 354, 403, 283, 258 and 234 respectively.

213. Avi-Yonah, Michael, and Israel Shatzman. **Illustrated Encyclopaedia of the Ancient World**. New York: Harper & Row, 1975. 509pp. ISBN 0-06-010178-4. LC 73-14245.

Begun by the Israeli scholar Michael Avi-Yonah, this encyclopedia was completed after his death by his colleague Israel Shatzman. The work is aimed at students and general readers. Its approximately 2,300 articles cover all aspects of Greek and Roman civilization from the Bronze Age to late antiquity. The articles tend to be brief and to focus on factual information: historical and biographical information, descriptions of places and works of art, and summaries of myths and literary works. Most include one or two bibliographical references. There are a number of illustrations, including a few in color. Several maps and a series of chronological listings of kings and emperors of antiquity follow the main text. Numerous cross-references and a selective index make it relatively easy to navigate the encyclopedia. This is a useful work for students, although it lacks the depth and scholarly detail of the *Oxford Classical Dictionary* (entry 218).

214. Cotterell, Arthur, ed. **The Penguin Encyclopedia of Classical Civilizations**. New York: Viking, 1993. 290pp. ISBN 0-670-82699-5.

Aimed at a popular audience, this work provides overviews of the major civilizations of antiquity. Its chapters, each by a specialist in the field, cover Hellenic civilization (500-338 B.C.), the Hellenistic age (336-31 B.C.), Rome (510 B.C.-A.D. 476), the successive Persian empires (Achaemenid, Parthian, and Sassanian), India (500 B.C.-ca. A.D. 550), and China (481 B.C.-A.D. 316). Cotterell and his collaborators tend to focus on the "classical" periods of the civilizations and give little attention to their early phases. Each chapter includes a chronology, a general historical overview, and sections devoted to social, cultural, and economic history. The work is well written and includes numerous illustrations (some in color). A brief general bibliography and a selective index conclude the volume. The *Encyclopedia* will be most useful to readers and students seeking a concise general overview of one or more of the ancient civilizations represented. It can also be used to compare the various ancient societies, at least in broad outlines.

215. Daremberg, C., and E. Saglio, eds. **Dictionnaire des antiquités grecques et romaines d'après les textes et les monuments: contenant l'explication des termes qui se rapportent aux moeurs, aux institutions, a la religion, aux arts, aux sciences, au costume, au mobilier, a la guerre, a la marine, aux métiers, aux monnaies, poids et mesures, etc., etc., et en general a la vie publique et privée des anciens**. Paris: Hachette, 1877-1919; repr., Graz, Austria: Akademische Druck- u. Verlagsanstalt, 1969. 5v. in 10. LC 31-106232.

This famous work is well known for its unsurpassed coverage of the material culture of antiquity. Though outdated in many respects, it remains the best source of information on realia. A true dictionary of antiquities, it treats objects, institutions, and concepts, not people or places. Articles cover such things as furniture, cooking implements, jewelry, tools, political and religious institutions and offices, and Greek and Latin technical terms relating to government, the military, and various sciences and trades. The signed articles, by a variety of hands, offer clear, concise, and adequately detailed information on each topic. Each includes extensive references to the primary sources and to the then-current secondary literature. The work is fully illustrated with black-and-white engravings. Indexes are to be found in the final volume. An analytical table lists the lemmata under 17 broad subject headings. There are also indexes of Greek and Latin words and of ancient authors. In addition, Daremberg and Saglio provide many cross-references to link related articles. Written on a far larger scale and superior in quality to Smith's dictionary of antiquities (entry 230), Daremberg and Saglio continues to be the best single reference work for those interested in the material remains of antiquity. Those who can read only English will find Smith the most helpful general source in this area.

216. **Enciclopedia classica**. Direzione: G. Battista Pighi, Carlo del Grande, Paolo E. Arias. Torino, Italy: Società Editrice Internazionale, 1957- . LC 60-38597.

Fewer than half of the projected 14 volumes of this general handbook on the classical world have been published. Because volumes are issued in fascicles, even some of these have only appeared in part. The work consists of four parts (*sezioni*) that cover ancient history, Greek and Latin literature, archaeology, and special topics (e.g., ancient science and mythology). Volumes on Roman history, Greek antiquities, the Latin language, archaeology, Roman art, and Greek art have been published to date. A number of Italian scholars have contributed to the *Enciclopedia*; each is responsible for a whole volume or fascicle. Although on a much larger scale, the *Enciclopedia* is similar in design to the French work of Laurand (entries 221-222). Despite its incomplete state, it contains much valuable information on Greek and Roman civilization. The numerous illustrations are particularly noteworthy; these include many charts, plans, and aerial photographs not readily found elsewhere. Extensive bibliographical notes are supplied throughout the work; indexes appear at the end of each completed volume.

217. Grant, Michael, and Rachel Kitzinger. **Civilization of the Ancient Mediterranean: Greece and Rome**. New York: Scribner's, 1988. 3v. ISBN 0-684-18864-3(v.1); 0-684-18865-1(v.2); 0-684-18866-X(v.3). LC 87-23465.

Some 88 noted scholars have contributed 97 essays to this handbook on classical civilization. The work begins with a chronological table and summaries of Greek and Roman history from the first millenium B.C. to the late fifth century A.D. The essays, which focus on the economic, social, and cultural aspects of classical civilization, are then presented in a series of topical sections: Land and Sea (i.e., geography), Population, Agriculture and Food, Technology, Government and Society, Economics, Religion, Private and Social Life, Women and Family Life, Literary and Performing Arts, Philosophy, and Visual Arts. Each includes several essays. The writing, while scholarly, is readable and accessible to a general audience. There are many illustrations, and a substantial bibliographical note appears at the end of every essay. A detailed general index closes the work. This is an especially useful work for those seeking extended treatments of broad topics in Greek and Roman civilization.

218. Hammond, N. G. L., and H. H. Scullard, eds. **Oxford Classical Dictionary**. 2d ed. Oxford, England: Clarendon Press, 1970. ISBN 0-19-869117-3. LC 73-18819.

Designed to replace, on a smaller scale, Smith's dictionaries of classical antiquities, biography, and geography (entries 230, 392, and 416), the first edition (1949) of *Oxford Classical Dictionary* (OCD) established it as the standard general English-language reference work on the classical world. The 2d edition represents a thorough revision, with virtually every article reexamined and many new ones added. An index was also added to the 2d edition; this facilitates access to subjects treated under broader or related headings. Not all material was carried over from the first edition, so that the earlier edition occasionally remains useful.

The OCD covers the period from the beginnings of Greek civilization to the death of Constantine (A.D. 337). In general, coverage of the period after the second century A.D. is more selective. A few people and events of exceptional importance from after A.D. 337 are also included. The OCD includes articles on ancient authors, historical and mythological figures, places, events, objects, and concepts. These range in length from a brief one-line identification to several pages. Many articles include bibliographical notes that cite major primary sources and selected secondary works.

The OCD is strongest on people and places and weakest on realia (material culture). It also tends to emphasize the military and political aspects of history over the social and economic ones. However, the wide range of material it does cover and the high quality of its content make it the best work of its kind in English. For more extensive treatment of realia one should consult Smith (entry 230) or Daremberg and Saglio (entry 215). Readers of German will find the *Lexikon der Alten Welt* (entry 224) larger in both size and scope.

219. Klauser, Theodor, ed. **Reallexikon für Antike und Christentum: Sachwörterbuch zur Auseinandersetzung des Christentums mit der Antiken Welt**. Stuttgart, Germany: Hiersemann, 1950-. LC 54-20747.

220. Klauser, Theodor, ed. **Reallexikon für Antike und Christentum: Sachwörterbuch zur Auseinandersetzung des Christentums mit der Antiken Welt**. **Supplement**. Stuttgart, Germany: Hiersemann, 1985- . LC 85-182341.

This encyclopedia focuses on the civilization of the ancient Mediterranean world in relation to the early history of Christianity. Thus, it offers broad but selective coverage of the Ancient Near East and the classical world combined with detailed coverage of early Christianity through the sixth century A.D. It includes articles on a wide range of topics: individual biographies, literature, philosophy, religion, medicine, and general antiquities. These vary in length; most articles are fairly compact, but some are quite extensive. Many include a substantial bibliography. All entries are signed. While the list of contributors is international, most are German. Issued in fascicles, the *Reallexikon* is still far from complete. As of late 1994, 16 volumes, which cover A through Ianus, have appeared. Several supplements have also been published that include both new articles and additions and revisions to existing articles. While the *Reallexikon* does not provide encyclopedic coverage of the classical world, it is an invaluable resource for anyone seriously interested in ancient philosophy and religion, early Christianity, or late antiquity in general.

221. Laurand, L., and A. Lauras. **Manuel des études grecques et latines**. Paris: A. et J. Picard, 1955-1970. 2v.

222. Laurand, L. **Pour mieux comprendre l'antiquité classique: histoire et méthode historique, pedagogie, linguistique. Supplément au Manuel des études grecques et latines**. Paris: Auguste Picard, 1936.

After three-quarters of a century, this work has reached the point at which none of the volumes are in the same edition. The first, which is now in its 14th edition, treats Greece. The second, in its 4th edition, covers Rome. Each of these contains a geographical survey, an outline history, discussion of social and political institutions (including coverage of virtually every aspect of daily life), a history of the literature, and a grammar of the language. Each major unit includes its own detailed table of contents and indexes. Many bibliographies are provided throughout the two volumes. The supplement (still in its first edition) offers a summary account of methodology and the transmission of classical texts, followed by an extensive discussion of the influence of the classics in modern times, especially in France. The supplement includes a general index. The work is now dated but remains of interest both for the range of material covered in one place and for the French perspective, which is often different from that found in Anglo-Saxon works.

223. Lemprière, J. **Lemprière's Classical Dictionary of Proper Names Mentioned in Ancient Authors Writ Large**. 3d ed. London: Routledge & Kegan Paul, 1984. 675pp. ISBN 0-71020-068-4; 0-71020-843-Xpa. LC 83-22959.

Originally published in 1788 under the title *Bibliotheca Classica*, Lemprière has been frequently reprinted and widely used ever since. This edition has been revised by F. A. Wright. Lemprière has entries only for proper names, including historical and mythological persons, peoples, and geographic names. His articles are usually short, ranging in length from a sentence to (rarely) several columns. He provides basic biographical information for historical individuals, brief summaries of the relevant stories under mythical characters, and identifications of places. Entries for the more important places also include a capsule history. Many of the entries include references to relevant ancient sources. While Lemprière is more restricted in scope than the majority of works noted in this chapter, his dictionary is a useful companion for readers of classical literature.

224. **Lexikon der Alten Welt**. Zurich: Artemis, 1965. 3,523 cols. LC 67-105898.

Often called the *Artemis Lexikon*, this excellent work is compiled by an international (but primarily German) group of contributors. It includes the Ancient Near East as well as the classical world. Selective coverage of the Byzantine period is provided as well. Entries include people, places, material objects, and topical subjects. The quality of the articles sometimes varies, but is generally quite good. Most articles include brief bibliographies. Many photographs, line drawings, and figures illustrate the text. A number of maps (some in color) are also provided. The four appendices offer much helpful information; they include an alphabetical list of ancients with references to published ancient portraits of them, guidance in identifying and locating manuscripts from the Latin names commonly applied to them, a list of abbreviations of papyrological works (now superseded by the *Checklist of Editions of Greek and Latin Papyri,*

Ostraca, and Tablets [entry 104]), a list of the more important ancient sites and their excavators, a summary treatment of ancient weights and measures, and a small collection of famous sayings from Greek and Latin in both the original and German translation.

The *Artemis Lexikon* dwarfs the *Oxford Classical Dictionary* (OCD) (entry 218) in size and scope; it provides many more entries. It is the best one-volume encyclopedia of the ancient world. Those who can read German should use it in addition to the OCD.

225. Pauly, August Friedrich von. **Paulys Realencyclopädie der classischen Altertumswissenschaft**. Neue Bearbeitung unter Mitwirkung zahlreicher Fachgenosen herausgegeben von Georg Wissowa. Stuttgart, Germany: J. B. Metzler, 1893-1972. Reihe I, 47v. in 48; Reihe II, 19v. LC 01-2869.

226. **Paulys Realencyclopädie der classischen Altertumswissenschaft. Supplement**. Stuttgart, Germany: J. B. Metzler, 1903-1978. 15v.

227. Gartner, Hans, and Albert Wünsch. **Paulys Realencyclopädie der classischen Altertumswissenschaft: Neue Bearbeitung begonnen von Georg Wissowa fortgeführt von Wilhelm Kroll und Karl Mittelhaus ... Register der Nächtrage und Supplemente**. München: Alfred Druckenmüller, 1980. 250pp. LC 83-102992.

228. Murphy, John P. **Index to the Supplements and Supplementary Volumes of Pauly Wissowa's RE: Index to the Nachträge and Berichtigungen in Vols. I-XXIV of the First Series, Vols. I-X of the Second Series, and the Supplementary Vols. I-XIV of Pauly-Wissowa-Kroll's Realenzyklopädie, with an Appendix Containing an Index to Suppl. Vol XV (Final)**. 2d ed. Chicago: Ares, 1980. 144pp. ISBN 0-89005-174-7.

The massive *Realencyclopädie* is a fundamental reference work for every area of classical studies. It is frequently referred to as Pauly-Wissowa; citations commonly use the abbreviation *RE*, which is followed by the volume and column numbers. The basic encyclopedia was issued in two series, which cover A-Q and R-Z. Corrections and additions are found in the *Nachträge* located in the back of many of these volumes. The supplement, which is in 15 volumes, includes both new articles and revisions to existing articles.

The product of several generations of German scholars, Pauly-Wissowa covers all aspects of classical studies in great detail. Its entries include people, places, topical subjects, and Greek and Latin terms. Even relatively obscure individuals and places can be found in Pauly-Wissowa. While the articles vary in length, most are substantial. Some articles are actually short monographs. A valuable feature is the exhaustive listing of ancient sources for each subject.

Pauly-Wissowa is exceptionally difficult to use. In addition to requiring a solid knowledge of German, the organization is complex and often confusing. Although the arrangement of the basic set is alphabetical, one must also deal with the *Nachträge* and articles in the supplement. Sometimes even the basic encyclopedia can be challenging. For example, individual Romans are normally listed by the *gens* (family) name. The result is that dozens or, in some cases, hundreds of individuals are gathered under a particular name. While each is marked off and numbered in sequence, it can be a time-consuming process to find the one sought. In general, the best way to consult Pauly-Wissowa is to begin with one of the separately published indexes (Gartner or Murphy); this will help both in finding the appropriate article and in locating any relevant *Nachträge* or supplementary articles.

Both indexes provide an alphabetical list of article titles accompanied by references to corrections and supplements. Both also use a coding system to indicate the extent of the new material, which may range from minor additions to complete replacement of the original article. Gartner is the better choice, if available. His entries generally provide more information than do those of Murphy. Gartner also includes an alphabetical index of all contributors to both the original volumes and supplements to Pauly-Wissowa.

There is also an abridged version of Pauly-Wissowa, *Der Kleine Pauly* (entry 233), which is easier to use but includes much less information. Because it frequently includes references to the full articles in the original and its supplements, *Der Kleine Pauly* can also be used as a guide to the larger work.

229. Peck, Harry Thurston, ed. **Harper's Dictionary of Classical Literature and Antiquities**. New York: American Book, 1896; repr., New York: Cooper Square, 1962. 1,701pp. LC 01-20387.

This work is similar to Smith's dictionaries (entries 230, 392, and 416), although on a smaller scale. Its many entries deal with virtually every aspect of classical civilization: literature, mythology and religion, history, geography, and archaeology. It is particularly good for realia and topics dealing with everyday life in classical antiquity. Articles tend to be brief, although those on broader subjects occasionally run to several pages. Some articles also include bibliographies, although these are usually badly dated. Numerous line drawings and figures accompany the text; many provide handy illustrations of various artifacts. Despite its age, this work remains useful. More recent works, such as the *Oxford Classical Dictionary* (entry 218), should be preferred, but do not always include everything in the older works of Smith and Peck.

230. Smith, William, ed. **A Dictionary of Greek and Roman Antiquities**. London: John Murray, 1875. 1293pp. LC 16-7351.

Smith's dictionary of antiquities is a companion volume to his similar works on classical biography and geography. Like those works, it is available in many editions and printings; most late nineteenth- and early twentieth-century editions are usable. Its contributors include a number of eminent nineteenth-century British classical scholars. Although now badly out of date, it remains, along with Daremberg and Saglio (entry 215), one of the few reference sources for information about realia (i.e., the material culture of classical antiquity). Its articles cover physical artifacts, Greek and Latin technical terms (legal, military, architectural, etc.), festivals and events, weights, measures, and money. There are some illustrations and charts. Indexes cover Greek words, Latin words, and subjects. There is also a classified index that lists pertinent entries under broad subject headings. When possible, one should use the more current dictionaries and handbooks noted elsewhere in this chapter. However, for some material objects Smith or Daremberg and Saglio still provide the best general information available without recourse to highly specialized works. Those who have French should consult Daremberg and Saglio, which is generally considered to be the superior work.

231. Speake, Graham. **A Dictionary of Ancient History**. Oxford, England: Blackwell, 1994. 758pp. ISBN 0-631-18069-9. LC 93-1437.

Intended for students and general readers, this work covers not only Greek and Roman military and political history but also literature, philosophy, religion,

art, and society. Its chronological limits range from the first Olympics in 776
B.C. to the fall of the western Roman empire in A.D. 476. A few entries, which
cover the Greek bronze age or the Byzantine empire, fall outside these boundaries. A team of British historians and classicists prepared the articles; all are
signed. The entries include persons, places, events, and topics. Most tend to be
brief, often a single paragraph. Occasionally, treatment of major topics will
extend to a page or more. References for further study appear at the end of most
entries. Speake provides an extensive general bibliography, a number of genealogical tables and king lists, and a selection of maps at the end of the volume.
The maps are taken from the works of Levi (entry 430) and Cornell and Matthews
(entry 421). While there are no indexes, many cross-references are provided
throughout the body of the dictionary.

This work offers concise articles that supply basic information on a wide
range of subjects. Its treatment of these is rarely as full as that found in the *Oxford
Classical Dictionary* (entry 218), although it is a bit more current.

232. Warrington, John. **Everyman's Classical Dictionary, 800 B.C.-A.D.
337**. 3d ed. London: J. M. Dent, 1970. 537pp. LC 78-110947.

Aimed at students and general readers, this dictionary covers classical
civilization from Homer to Constantine. Early Christian matters are generally
considered out of scope. Warrington has an unusually large amount of front
matter. This includes a list of modern place-names with their ancient equivalents,
a list of the principal philosophical schools of antiquity, a genealogical table of
the Julio-Claudians, and a select bibliography of general works. A systematic
list of the entries gathers them under a number of broad subject headings, such
as geography and topography, Greek literature, and philosophy and science.
Only then does one reach the dictionary proper. The relatively short articles
emphasize the factual. There are many cross-references to related articles. No
bibliographies are provided in the entries. Warrington's dictionary is adequate
for its purpose, although most will be better served by the larger and fuller
Oxford Classical Dictionary (entry 218). Warrington's compact format makes
it handier as a companion to reading. Because there is little difference between
the various editions of this work, those who have access only to earlier ones need
not be unduly concerned.

233. Ziegler, Konrat, and Walther Sontheimer. **Der Kleine Pauly: Lexikon
der Antike auf der Grundlage von Pauly's Realencyclopädie der
classischen Altertumswissenschaft**. Stuttgart, Germany: Alfred Druckenmüller, 1964-1975. 5v. LC 66-780.

This greatly abridged version of *Pauly's Realencyclopädie* (entry 225) is
more current and easier to use than the original, but it covers much less than the
original work. The articles, which are all signed, are compact and informative.
All material has been updated and revised. There are entries for people, places,
and topical subjects. The articles range in length from a paragraph to several
pages. Nearly all include brief bibliographical notes. Corrections and additions
appear in the final volume. *Der Kleine Pauly* provides a middle option for those
who find the one-volume encyclopedias, such as the *Oxford Classical Dictionary*
(entry 218), too limited but who are not inclined to deal with the full-sized *Pauly*.
Because it often gives references to the articles in the more complex larger work,
Der Kleine Pauly can be used as an index to it.

CHAPTER  8

SPECIALIZED DICTIONARIES, ENCYCLOPEDIAS, AND HANDBOOKS

This chapter covers a wide range of reference works on specific aspects of classical studies. These include such works as dictionaries of mythology or quotations, handbooks and histories of classical literature, and standard works on ancient history, classical philosophy, and archaeology. While it is not possible to list all such works, the most useful will be found below. A selection of handbooks and manuals covering the more esoteric areas, such as epigraphy, palaeography, papyrology, and numismatics, are also noted (under ancillary disciplines). Reference works dealing with biography, geography, and the classical languages will be found in chapters 9 through 11.

Art and Archaeology

234. Avery, Catherine B., ed. **The New Century Handbook of Greek Art and Architecture**. New York: Appleton-Century-Crofts, 1972. 213pp. LC 72-187738.

Most of the articles in this volume are derived from the larger *New Century Classical Handbook* (entry 212), although a number of additions and revisions have been made. The work takes the form of a dictionary. Its articles provide basic factual information on artists, individual works of art, sites, and various technical terms. All are clearly written and aimed at a general audience. Numerous black-and-white illustrations accompany the text. The lack of bibliographies is the chief drawback. This handbook is most useful as a ready-reference work.

Those who want an extended discussion of a particular artistic medium should use Richter's handbook (entry 245) instead.

✓235. Boardman, John, ed. **The Oxford History of Classical Art**. New York: Oxford University Press, 1993. 406pp. ISBN 0-19-814386-9. LC 93-6825.

Designed as a companion volume to the *Oxford History of the Classical World* (entry 251), this work is aimed at a wide audience. Its various chapters, each by an expert in the field, cover broad chronological periods: preclassical Greece, the classical period, the Hellenistic period, Rome (republic and early empire), and the later Roman empire. Boardman also provides an introduction and a concluding chapter on the diffusion of classical art through the ancient Mediterranean world. No coverage is given to Bronze Age Greece or the Etruscans, and Christian art of the later empire receives little attention. Many illustrations (some in color) accompany the well-written text. A brief bibliography provides a good guide to the more important and accessible recent work on classical art. There is a general index. Although excellent as a single-volume survey of the field, Boardman does not offer the depth of coverage that some of the more specialized surveys do. Those interested primarily in Greek art will find more in Robertson (entry 246) and Pedley (entry 243); for Roman art, Henig (entry 242) offers more detailed treatment.

236. **Enciclopedia dell'arte antica classica e orientale**. Roma: Istituto della Enciclopedia italiana, 1958-1966. 7v. LC 58-37080.

237. **Supplemento**. Roma: Istituto della Enciclopedia italiana, 1973. 951pp.

238. **Atlante dei complessi figurati e degli ordini architettonici**. Roma: Istituto della Enciclopedia italiana, 1973. 1v. (various paging).

239. **Atlante delle forme ceramiche**. Roma: Istituto della Enciclopedia italiana, 1981-1985. 2v.

240. **Indici dei nomi e delle cose notevoli dei volumi I-VIII e del primo supplemento**. Roma: Istituto della Enciclopedia italiana, 1984. 629pp.

Produced under the general direction of the eminent art historian Ranuccio Bianchi Bandinelli, this encyclopedia covers art in the ancient Mediterranean world from prehistory to ca. A.D. 500. Covering artists, artistic subjects (including historical and mythological figures), places, and topics (e.g., amphitheatres, arches, types of pottery), its articles are both compact and informative; a short bibliographical note appears at the end of each. Many entries are also accompanied by illustrations (black-and-white for the most part). The *Enciclopedia* will serve both the casual inquirer and the specialist. Unfortunately, there is no comparable work in English.

Several supplementary volumes have appeared since the completion of the *Enciclopedia*. These include the *Supplemento*, which includes addenda to many existing articles and a number of new entries. The *Atlante dei complessi figurati* offers section-by-section illustrations of large works (e.g., Trajan's column, which alone occupies 31 pages of plates) and extensive illustrations of the architectural orders. The *Atlante delle forme ceramiche* is a technical typological work on the shapes of ancient pottery. The separate index volume provides an exhaustive index to people, places, and topics discussed in the *Enciclopedia* and the *Supplemento*.

241. Ginouvès, René, and Roland Martin. **Dictionnaire méthodique de l'architecture grecque et romaine**. Paris: De Boccard, 1985- . (Collection de l'Ecole Française de Rome, 84). ISBN 2-7283-0105-0(v.1); 2-7283-0239-8 (v.2). LC 86-179913.

This work-in-progress is essentially a guide to the terminology of Greek and Roman architecture. The first volume covers materials, construction techniques, and decorative techniques. The second deals with structural elements. Other aspects will be treated in future volumes. A classified subject arrangement is employed within each volume. Entries, which are under the French term, give a brief definition and the equivalent terms in German, English, Italian, modern Greek, ancient Greek, and Latin. The extensive footnotes contain many references to the scholarly literature on classical architecture. Numerous illustrations are provided in separate sections at the end of each volume. Each volume also includes its own bibliography and separate indexes of architectural terms for each language. This work is exceptionally useful for those working with scholarly publications in foreign languages, because relatively few bilingual dictionaries cover such technical terms.

242. Henig, Martin, ed. **A Handbook of Roman Art: A Comprehensive Survey of All the Arts of the Roman World**. Ithaca, NY: Cornell University Press, 1983. 288pp. ISBN 0-8014-1539-X; 0-8014-9242-4pa. LC 82-071591.

Henig and his contributors cover all aspects of Roman art. Early Roman art and that of the late empire are treated in separate chapters at either end of the book. Otherwise, chapters deal with the various artistic forms and media: architecture, sculpture, wall painting, mosaics, decorative metalwork and jewelry, coins, pottery, terra-cottas, glass, and epigraphy. Useful supplementary material includes a guide to the major pottery forms, a glossary, an excellent bibliography arranged by topic, and a general index. Well written and illlustrated, Henig serves as a handy reference work as well as a readable survey of Roman art.

243. Pedley, John Griffiths. **Greek Art and Archaeology**. New York: Harry N. Abrams, 1993. 367pp. ISBN 0-8109-3369-1. LC 92-9707.

Intended as an introduction to Greek art and archaeology, this work is an excellent general source of information on the subject. The readable and up-to-date text is accompanied by numerous well-chosen illustrations (chiefly black-and-white). Pedley covers architecture, sculpture, pottery, and wall painting from the Bronze Age through the Hellenistic period. He also provides some historical background on each period. The overall arrangement of the book is chronological, with subarrangement by categories of artwork. Pedley also includes a short chronology, a glossary, and a selective bibliography. A general index concludes the volume. For the categories of art not covered by Pedley, one should consult Richter's *Handbook of Greek Art* (entry 245).

244. Preston, Percy. **A Dictionary of Pictorial Subjects from Classical Literature: A Guide to Their Identification in Works of Art**. New York: Scribner's, 1983. 311pp. ISBN 0-684-17913-X. LC 83-4470.

Preston has compiled a dictionary of objects, creatures, activities, and distinguishing features found in representations of individuals and themes drawn from classical literature and mythology. His purpose is to provide not a catalog of paintings, drawings, and the like with classical themes or allusions, but rather a tool for identifying such themes and allusions. Entries include, for example, "castaway," "drinking," "falling," and "monster" (variously subdivided). Each notes what mythical or literary figure is associated with it and provides references to literary treatments in the ancient authors. There are a few illustrations. Preston is by no means exhaustive; he concentrates on the more important Greek and Roman literary works. His work is useful for identifying classical themes in later works of art and for bringing together material on particular topics. Preston makes liberal use of cross-references but does not provide an index. Those seeking works of art based on specific myths or historical events should consult Reid (entry 294) or Rochelle (entry 249).

245.   Richter, Gisela M. A. **A Handbook of Greek Art**. 9th ed. New York: Da Capo, 1987. 431pp. ISBN 0-306-80298-8. LC 87-6810.

Since it first appeared in 1959, Richter's *Handbook* has become a standard work. The 7th edition (1974) was the last to be revised by the author, who died in 1972. Subsequent editions have incorporated corrections and updated bibliographies, but are otherwise unchanged. Richter covers all aspects of Greek art from about 1100 B.C. to 100 B.C. She organizes her material into chapters by form and material: architecture, larger works of sculpture, statuettes, decorative metalwork, terra-cottas, engraved gems, coins, jewelery, paintings and mosaics, pottery, furniture, textiles, glass, ornament, and epigraphy. The text is readable and profusely illustrated (although all illustrations are black-and-white). Supplementary materials include maps, a substantial bibliography, a chronology of Greek sculptural works, and indexes of places and names. Richter covers a much wider range of materials than Pedley (entry 243) but is not as current. Pedley also covers Bronze Age Greece, which Richter omits.

246.   Robertson, D. S. **Greek & Roman Architecture**. 2d ed. New York: Cambridge University Press, 1969. 407pp. ISBN 0-521-06104-0; 0-521-09452-6pa. LC 76-407810.

Originally published in 1929 as *Handbook of Greek and Roman Architecture*, this highly regarded work covers all aspects of classical architecture. Chapters proceed in roughly chronological order from Minoan Crete, Troy, and pre-Mycenean Greece to the fourth century A.D. There are a few departures from the chronological scheme, such as the chapter on Greek and Roman houses. Many figures and illustrations are provided. Particularly useful appendices supply a selective chronological table of Greek, Etruscan, and Roman buildings from 1000 B.C. to A.D. 330 and a glossary of architectural terms. While now old, Robertson's focus on the essential and well-established facts has kept the work from becoming obsolete except in a few details. It remains an excellent source of general information on Greek and Roman architecture, although the bibliography (which has remained unaltered since the first edition) must be supplemented from other sources.

247.   Robertson, Martin. **A History of Greek Art**. New York: Cambridge University Press, 1975. 2v. ISBN 0-521-202779. LC 73-79317.

248.   Robertson, Martin. **A Shorter History of Greek Art**. New York: Cambridge University Press, 1981. 240pp. ISBN 0-521-23629-0; 0-521-28084-2pa. LC 80-41026.

Robertson's massive work, the largest and most comprehensive treatment of the subject by an individual writer in English, covers all Greek art (except for architecture) from the archaic period through the Hellenistic age. He intends the work for both scholars and general readers, and so translates all Greek and Latin.

The text, which comprises the first volume, proceeds chronologically and is intended to be read rather than consulted. The second volume contains the extensive bibliographical apparatus, illustrations, and indexes. The selection of illustrations has been faulted by some, because it does not include all of the important works discussed in the text. Those seeking information on a specific topic would do best to approach this work through the indexes. Because their organization is better suited to the casual inquirer, Richter (entry 245) and Pedley (entry 243) are better choices for most reference purposes. Their works also cover architecture. However, Robertson frequently offers better coverage of a particular topic or information not found in the other works.

The abridged version, which is intended for use as a textbook, retains the same chapter divisions, although the content is considerably reduced. Illustrations are integrated into the text. While Robertson generally refers readers to his larger work for more information, there is a brief bibliography. There is also a detailed general index.

249. Rochelle, Mercedes. **Mythological and Classical World Art Index: A Locator of Paintings, Sculptures, Frescoes, Manuscript Illuminations, Sketches, Woodcuts, and Engravings Executed 1200 B.C. to A.D. 1900 with a Directory of the Institutions Holding Them**. Jefferson, NC: McFarland, 1991. 279pp. ISBN 0-89950-566-X. LC 91-52503.

Rochelle provides a useful resource for anyone seeking art works depicting classical myth and history. Persons, gods, goddesses, and events appear as subjects. Under each Rochelle lists a selection of artworks. She arranges these chronologically by date of creation, "beginning with contemporaneous works and continuing through the Romantic movement." For each work Rochelle gives the title or a description, the artist's name (if known), date, museum holding the original, and references to published reproductions. A directory of museums (with addresses) and an index of artists follow the text. Although Reid (entry 294) supplies better and more complete information on classical myths in modern art, Rochelle covers a much wider range of material by including art works created before 1300 and historical subjects.

History

250. Bickermann, E. J. **Chronology of the Ancient World**. Ithaca, NY: Cornell University Press, 1980. 2d ed. 223pp. (Aspects of Greek and Roman Life). ISBN 0-8014-1282-X. LC 78-58899.

Bickermann first published his handbook more than 50 years ago under the title *Chronologie* (Leipzig: B. G. Teubner, 1933). It has since undergone extensive revision and expansion and has been translated into several languages. The first part of the work provides a general overview of the chronology of the ancient world, with particular emphasis on Greece, Rome, and Greco-Roman Egypt. Among other things, Bickermann discusses the astronomical basis and history of the various ancient calendars and the types of chronographic systems (regnal years, eponymous magistrates, etc.) used by the ancients. The second part is a collection of tables that include lists of astronomical data, kings, emperors, and magistrates. A synchronistic table brings together the most common systems of the classical world (Olympian years, the Varronian years *ab urbe condita*, and Egyptian mobile years) with modern equivalents. Bickermann also provides a chronological table of Greek and Roman history, which gives a year-by-year listing of major historical events from 776 B.C. to A.D. 476. There is a short general index. Bickermann is the most accessible general treatment of ancient chronology and is particularly good for students. Samuel (entry 256) covers much of the same ground but is geared more toward the working scholar.

✓ 251. Boardman, John, Jasper Griffin, and Oswyn Murray, eds. **The Oxford History of the Classical World**. New York: Oxford University Press, 1986. 882pp. ISBN 0-19-872112-9. LC 85-21774.

252. Boardman, John, Jasper Griffin, and Oswyn Murray, eds. **The Oxford History of Greece and the Hellenistic World**. New York: Oxford University Press, 1991. 520pp. ISBN 0-19-285247-7. LC 91-11926.

253. Boardman, John, Jasper Griffin, and Oswyn Murray, eds. **The Oxford History of the Roman World**. New York: Oxford University Press, 1991. 518pp. ISBN 0-19-285248-5. LC 91-11763.

The first item listed above is an excellent one-volume history of Greece and Rome designed for the student and general reader. It is also available in two separate paperback volumes. The three major sections cover Greece (from Homer to the rise of Alexander), Greece and Rome (essentially the Hellenistic period), and Rome (from Augustus to the fall of the empire in the west). In addition to political history, the work covers cultural and social history. The various chapters within each section include such topics as literature, philosophy, art and architecture, and religion as well as historical overviews. Each chapter is by a well-known scholar in the area and includes notes for further reading. The book is richly illustrated and includes a number of maps. A lengthy "table of events" at the end of the text provides a convenient chronology of the classical world. A general index concludes the volume.

This is a good choice for the layperson. Those who require more detailed and scholarly treatment should consult the *Cambridge Ancient History* (entry 255).

254. Bunson, Matthew. **Encyclopedia of the Roman Empire**. New York: Facts on File, 1994. 494pp. ISBN 0-8160-2135-X; 0-8160-3182-7pa. LC 91-38036.

Aimed at a broad general audience, Bunson covers the Roman world from approximately 59 B.C to A.D. 476. The front matter of his book includes a discussion of Roman names and a chronology of major military, political, and cultural events. The encyclopedia consists of roughly 1,900 entries. The compact articles cover people, places, important Latin terms (especially those relating to politics and the military), topics, and a few events. More than half of the entries are biographical. A handful of slightly longer entries deal with wider topics such as literature, medicine, and Christianity. The clear and readable articles are well suited to the needs of students and general readers, although their lack of bibliographies is a serious weakness. Appendices provide a list of Roman emperors, genealogical tables of the major imperial houses, and a glossary. The general bibliography is weak and not particularly well balanced. An index concludes the volume.

✓ 255. **Cambridge Ancient History**. 1st-3d eds. New York: Cambridge University Press, 1923- . Details for individual volumes:

V. 1, pt. 1: **Prolegomena and Prehistory.** 3d ed. 1971. 758pp. ISBN 0-521-07051-1. LC 75-85719.

V. 1, pt. 2: **Early History of the Middle East.** 3d ed. 1971. 1,058pp. ISBN 0-521-07791-5. LC 73-116845.

V. 2, pt. 1: **History of the Middle East and Aegean Region, 1800-1300 B.C.** 3d ed. 1973. 891pp. ISBN 0-521-08230-7. LC 75-85719.

V. 2, pt. 2: **The Assyrian and Babylonian Empires, the Eastern Mediterranean and the Black Sea, 1380-1000 B.C.** 3d ed. 1975. 1,128pp. ISBN 0-521-08691-4. LC 75-85719.

Plates to Volumes I-II. New ed. 1977. 181pp. ISBN 0-521-20571-9. LC 75-85719.

V. 3, pt. 1: **The Prehistory of the Balkans; the Middle East and Aegean World, Tenth to Eighth Centuries B.C.** 2d ed. 1982. 1,088pp. ISBN 0-521-22496-9. LC 75-85719.

V. 3, pt. 2: **The Assyrian and Babylonian Empires and Other States of the Near East, from the Eighth to the Sixth Centuries B.C.** 2d ed. 1992. ISBN 0-521-22717-8. LC 75-85719.

V. 3, pt. 3: **The Expansion of the Greek World, Eighth to Sixth Centuries B.C.** 2d ed. 1982. 554pp. ISBN 0-521-23447-6. LC 75-85719.

Plates to Volume III. New ed. 1984. 313pp. ISBN 0-521-24289-4. LC 75-85719.

V. 4: **Persia, Greece, and the Western Mediterranean, c. 525-479 B.C.** 2d ed. 1988. 960pp. ISBN 0-521-22804-2. LC 75-85719.

Plates to Volume IV. New ed. 1988. 264pp. ISBN 0-521-30580-2. LC 77-378456.

V. 5: **The Fifth Century B.C.** 2d ed. 1992. 619pp. ISBN 0-521-23347-X. LC 75-85719.

V. 6: **The Fourth Century B.C.** 2d ed. 1994. 1,077pp. ISBN 0-521-23348-8. LC 75-85719.

V. 7, pt. 1: **The Hellenistic World.** 2d ed. 1984. 641pp. ISBN 0-521-23445-X. LC 75-85719.

Plates to Volume VII, Part 1. New ed. 1984. ISBN 0-521-24354-8. LC 83-5186.

V. 7, pt. 2: **The Rise of Rome to 220 B.C.** 2d ed. 1990. 600pp. ISBN 0-521-23446-8. LC 75-85719.

V. 8: **Rome and the Mediterranean to 133 B.C.** 2d ed. 1989. 650pp. ISBN 0-521-23448-4. LC 75-85719.

V. 9: **The Last Age of the Roman Republic, 146-43 B.C.** 2d ed. 1994. 929pp. ISBN 0-521-25603-8. LC 75-85719.

V. 10: **The Augustan Empire, 44 B.C.- A.D. 70.** 1934. 1,058pp. ISBN 0-521-04492-8. LC 23-11667.

V. 11: **The Imperial Peace, A.D. 70-192.** 1936. 997pp. ISBN 0-521-04493-6. LC 23-11667.

V. 12: **The Imperial Crisis and Recovery, A.D. 193-324.** 1939. 850pp. ISBN 0-521-04494-4. LC 23-11667.

The first edition of the *Cambridge Ancient History* (CAH) appeared in 12 volumes with five volumes of plates (1923-1939); it has been under continuous revision, and as a result its parts are now in various editions. The above listing will serve as a guide both to the most current manifestation and to the contents of each volume. CAH counts among its contributors the leading British classical and Near Eastern scholars of several generations, along with a number of notable American and European scholars. It moves in a broad chronological procession through the history of the ancient Mediterranean world from the prehistoric era to A.D. 324 (when Constantine the Great became sole ruler of the Roman empire). The work covers political, social, economic, and cultural history. Volumes cover particular eras and sometimes regions. Within each volume, long chapters by various hands treat different regions, periods, and topics. Many maps and genealogical tables are provided. Each volume includes an extensive bibliography and a substantial index. Plates appear in separate volumes.

Designed for the use of scholars and advanced students, CAH is the most substantial and all-inclusive survey of ancient history available. The more casual inquirer may also find it of use. Its text is generally reliable and often authoritative, although the older volumes, which cover the Roman empire, badly need revision to take into account 50 years of active scholarship.

256. Samuel, Alan E. **Greek and Roman Chronology: Calendars and Years in Classical Antiquity**. München: C.H. Beck, 1972. 307pp. (Handbuch der Altertumswissenschaft, Abt.1, t.7). ISBN 3-406-03348-2. LC 72-185353.

Samuel covers the same ground as Bickermann (entry 250) but does so in much more detail. After a chapter on the astronomical background, he covers virtually all known Greek and Roman calendars in a series of chapters arranged by region and period. These include Greek astronomical calendars, Greek civil calendars, calendars of the Hellenistic kingdoms, the Roman calendar, and calendars of the eastern Roman provinces. The final two chapters cover Greek and Roman chronography. Indexes of subjects, months, and sources conclude the volume. In most cases, Samuel offers fuller and more detailed information than Bickermann. For example, his lists of Athenian archons and Roman consuls are more complete and include many notes and references to the scholarly literature. He also provides coverage of many local calendars, while Bickermann concentrates on the better-known and more widespread calendars. However, Bickermann is a more accessible guide for the layperson and student, and will generally fill their needs.

257. Scarre, Chris, ed. **Smithsonian Timelines of the Ancient World**. New York: Dorling Kindersley, 1991. 256pp. ISBN 1-56458-305-8. LC 93-18480.

The editor of this profusely illustrated work has adopted a liberal definition for "ancient world," and includes everything from prehistory through A.D. 1500. While the book is not primarily about the classical world, it does provide extensive coverage of Greek and Roman civilization. Each of the 18 chapters covers a span of years that can range from millenia for prehistoric eras to a few centuries for more recent periods. Chapters include a brief introduction, maps, timelines, and a short feature article on a topic from the period. The timelines cover four broad subject areas (food and environment, shelter and architecture, technology and innovation, and art and ritual) in five geographical regions (Americas, East Asia and Australasia, Middle East and South Asia, Europe, and Africa). Coverage of the classical world can be found under the relevant time periods in the sections on Europe, the Middle East, and Africa. The timelines present selected highlights rather than a comprehensive chronology of the various civilizations. They are chiefly useful for setting developments within particular cultures in a broader context. A selective index and a brief general bibliography conclude the volume. This visually appealing work is designed for the casual inquirer rather than the scholar.

Literature

258. Avery, Catherine B., ed. **The New Century Handbook of Greek Literature**. New York: Appleton-Century-Crofts, 1972. 213pp. LC 79-183797.

Drawn from the larger *New Century Classical Handbook* (entry 212), this work focuses specifically on Greek literature. Entries, which are all signed, cover authors, genres, and individual works. Nearly all major authors and a good many minor ones are included. The articles are arranged alphabetically. Their content consists largely of basic biographical information on the authors and summaries of literary works. A guide to pronunciation is provided, but there are neither bibliographical references nor an index. This work aims low and will satisfy the needs of only the most basic user. Howatson's *Oxford Companion to Classical Literature* (entry 273), which also covers Latin literature, is a far superior work and should be preferred.

259. Bardon, Henry. **La littérature latin inconnue**. Paris: Klincksieck, 1952-1956. 2v. LC 52-6573.

Most histories of Latin literature focus on the writers whose works have survived. Bardon's unique volume deals with those authors whose works are either totally lost or now exist only in fragments. He covers authors chronologically by period; periods are subdivided by literary genres. Bardon reconstructs what he can about each author from mentions in other authors and from any surviving fragments of their works. His notes provide full references to the ancient sources and to relevant secondary works. Some of the information found in Bardon is speculative. However, most of these authors receive short shrift from the standard literary histories, and many are omitted altogether. The only other readily available work that covers such authors in any detail is the large German history of Latin literature by Schanz-Hosius (entry 280). Each of Bardon's two volumes includes an index of ancient authors.

260. Brown, Andrew. **A New Companion to Greek Tragedy**. Totowa, NJ: Barnes & Noble, 1983. 209pp. ISBN 0-389-20389-0; 0-389-20396-3pa. LC 83-3842.

Designed to aid those reading Greek tragedy in English translation, Brown's work takes the form of a dictionary. He includes people and places from the plays, technical terms relating to Greek tragedy, and various topics concerning Greek life and religion. Brown concentrates on 15 widely read plays rather than dealing with the whole surviving corpus. Entries range from a line or two to several pages. A pronunciation guide is included when appropriate. Brown also provides illustrations and genealogical tables. A bibliography of translations and secondary works of interest to students and general readers concludes the volume. Many of its entries include short, sometimes pungent annotations. Brown's clear and forceful style and practical approach make this an excellent aid to the beginning reader of tragedy. Those requiring broader coverage of ancient drama as a whole should consult Harsh (entry 269) or Hathorn (entry 270).

261. Conte, Gian Biagio. **Latin Literature: A History**. Translated by Joseph B. Solodow. Revised by Don Fowler and Glenn W. Most. Baltimore, MD: Johns Hopkins University Press, 1994. 827pp. ISBN 0-8018-4638-2. LC 93-20985.

Based on the Italian original, which appeared in 1987, this history of Latin literature has been adapted to better meet the needs of English-speaking students. It provides an excellent survey of the major Latin authors and genres from the beginnings to the sixth century A.D. Conte divides his work into five parts: the early and middle republic, the late republic, the age of Augustus, the early empire, and the late empire. Within each of these parts, chapters cover authors and genres. The unit on the late empire, which is first subarranged chronologically and then by genre, is an exception to this pattern. Conte offers perhaps the best balanced treatment of Latin literature available. He provides ample historical background and biographical information about the authors, lists of their works (including dates and brief descriptions) and of ancient sources of information concerning them, and critical discussion of the works. Conte also supplies substantial annotated bibliographies throughout the volume. The appendices include chronological tables of Roman and Greek history and culture, an alphabetical listing of Greek authors and texts, a glossary of Latin political and social terminology, and a glossary of terms concerning rhetoric, metrics, and literary criticism. An index of names rounds out the volume. The physical design of the book is also exceptional: Clear typefaces, wide margins, and the use of marginal lemmata make the work easy to consult.

Conte is clearly the leading rival to the Latin volume of the *Cambridge History of Classical Literature* (entry 275), a work that focuses on the critical aspects of literary history and sometimes neglects to provide adequate background material. Those whose needs go beyond these two histories must refer to the much larger German work of Schanz-Hosius (entry 280).

262. Dihle, Albrecht. **Greek and Latin Literature of the Roman Empire: From Augustus to Justinian**. Translated by Manfred Malzahn. London: Routledge, 1994. 647pp. ISBN 0-415-06367-1. LC 93-45284.

Unlike the other literary histories in this chapter, Dihle treats both Latin and Greek literature. His temporal limits extend from the late first century B.C to the early sixth century A.D. Dihle's chapters are based on historical periods: the Julio-Claudian era, the Flavian era, the second century, the Severan era, the third century, the era of Diocletian and Constantine, and the Christian empire. Each contains a number of sections that cover genres or major authors. Dihle's work has many virtues. It offers much more extensive coverage of late antique authors than do Lesky (entry 277) and the two volumes of the *Cambridge History of Classical Literature* (entries 266 and 275). Lesser-known authors receive considerable attention. The book is also very readable; Dihle writes effectively for the general reader and the student. While the focus is on the actual literary works, Dihle provides ample historical and biographical background. His bibliography, which is keyed to chapters and pages, is brief but usually provides adequate starting points for further research. A general index concludes the volume.

263. Dihle, Albrecht. **A History of Greek Literature: From Homer to the Hellenistic Period**. Translated by Clare Krojzl. London: Routledge, 1994. 332pp. ISBN 0-415-08620-5. LC 93-45284.

Aimed at the student and general reader, this work covers Greek literature from Homer through the time of Augustus (for the later period, see entry 262). Dihle divides the volume into four chronological sections: archaic literature, classical literature of the fifth century B.C., classical literature of the fourth century B.C., and Hellenistic literature. Chapters within each section cover major authors and genres. While Dihle focuses on the more prominent authors, he also takes note of a number of minor figures as well. He provides the requisite biographical and historical information and a critical discussion of the literary works. His bibliography is relatively brief but provides a good basis for further study. An index closes the volume. This is a good choice for the casual reader or a beginning student; the more advanced may prefer Lesky (entry 277) or the appropriate volume of the *Cambridge History of Classical Literature* (entry 266).

264. Duff, J. Wight. **A Literary History of Rome: From the Origins to the Close of the Golden Age**. 3d ed. Edited by A. M. Duff. New York: Barnes & Noble, 1959. 543pp. LC 60-1962.

265. Duff, J. Wight. **A Literary History of Rome in the Silver Age: From Tiberius to Hadrian**. 3d ed. Edited by A. M. Duff. New York: Barnes & Noble, 1964; repr., Westport, CT: Greenwood Press, 1979. 599pp. LC 65-775.

The several editions of this old standby have endured nearly a century (the first appeared in 1909). While Duff is dated and represents the traditional approach of an earlier generation of scholars, his book remains a mine of useful basic information on Latin literature. In the first volume, Duff covers Latin literature from the earliest fragments to the close of the Augustan era; he continues the history to the mid-second century A.D. in the second. He provides historical background and biographical information for each author before briefly describing and commenting on their works. Duff aimed his works at those with some training in the classics. Although not inaccessible to the general reader, they do include much untranslated Latin. Each volume contains a bibliography (now very out-of-date) and a good general index. Conte (entry 261) and the second volume of the *Cambridge History of Classical Literature* (entry 275) are much more current works and are to be preferred as scholarly histories. They also go far beyond Duff's temporal limits to treat Latin literature as late as the sixth and fourth centuries A.D. respectively.

266. Easterling, P. E., and B. M. W. Knox. **Greek Literature**. New York: Cambridge University Press, 1985. 936pp. (**Cambridge History of Classical Literature, v.1**). ISBN 0-521-21042-9. LC 82-22048.

The product of a team of distinguished British and American scholars, this work is the best and most current scholarly history of classical Greek literature available in English. The substantial general introduction discusses books and readers in the Greek world. The work then proceeds in chronological sequence through the major authors and genres of ancient Greek literature. Coverage is fairly thorough from Homer through the second century A.D., but then becomes spotty. Nonnus of Panopolis, an epic poet of the fifth century A.D., is the latest writer discussed (in the epilogue). In a departure from the traditional approach of biography and summary, the primary focus of this work is genuinely literary. The reader will find much more actual discussion and appreciation of the works themselves than is typical in histories of Greek or Latin literature. Biographical details and bibliographies are relegated to an appendix of authors and works. The bibliographies note major editions, commentaries, and translations and recommend a few studies for further reading. In the case of a few authors, they supply a more substantial list of scholarly works. A second appendix provides a concise introduction to Greek meters. The volume concludes with an extensive general bibliography and a detailed index.

Those who want a more traditional approach to literary history (with more emphasis on biography and historical background) will prefer Lesky (entry 277) or Rose (entry 278). Dihle's two volumes (entries 262-263) occupy something of a middle ground in approach but are addressed more to the student and general reader than the scholar. Schmid and Stählin's massive work (entry 281) offers much more detail than either Lesky or Cambridge, but is available only in German.

267. **Enciclopedia virgiliana**. Roma: Istituto della Enciclopedia italiana, 1984-1991. 5v. in 6. LC 87-127100.

Few authors rate an encyclopedia devoted solely to their works and influence; Vergil appears to be the only Latin author thus far to have received this distinction. This work is modeled on the earlier *Enciclopedia dantesca* from the same publisher. In a single alphabetical sequence one finds articles on characters, places, expressions and words, objects, and topics found in Vergil's poems. There are also entries for earlier authors who influenced Vergil, later authors influenced by him, and noted Vergilian scholars. Virtually anything connected to Vergil, however tangentially, is likely to be found in the *Enciclopedia*. In some ways it forms an eccentric encyclopedia of classical and European culture. All articles are signed. The cast of contributors is international, although Italian scholars predominate. Many of the articles are quite extensive. Some are illustrated; all include bibliographies. The final volume includes the full text of Vergil's works (including minor and apocryphal writings) in the Latin original with a facing Italian translation. There is also a massive collection of testimonia pertaining to Vergil's life and works, drawn from writers dating from late antiquity through the fifteenth century. Indexes cover Latin words, illustrations, and contributors of articles.

✓ 268. Feder, Lillian. **Crowell's Handbook of Classical Literature**. New York: Crowell, 1964. 448pp. LC 64-18162. Reprinted as **The Meridian Handbook of Classical Literature**, New York: New American Library, 1986.

Designed as a guide for students and general readers interested in classical literature and its influence, this handbook summarizes many of the best-known classical writings and provides useful background information. Feder supplies entries for authors (chiefly biographical), works (summaries and criticism), places, and historical and mythical figures. Except for those that summarize major works (e.g., *The Odyssey*), entries tend to be brief; emphasis is on the factual and descriptive. Entries are gathered in a single alphabetical sequence. Although there is no index, there are numerous cross-references. Feder is generally a reliable guide to the major authors and works but provides little coverage for minor figures. She is particularly weak for the Hellenistic period of Greek literature, Silver Latin literature, and the literature of late antiquity. Howatson (entries 273-274) is more current than Feder and also supplies much more of the historical and cultural background material required for a proper understanding of classical literature.

✓ 269. Harsh, Philip Whaley. **A Handbook of Classical Drama**. Stanford, CA: Stanford University Press, 1944. 526pp. LC 44-4205.

Intended as an aid to modern readers who lack a background in classical studies, this work covers the major dramatic genres of antiquity: Greek tragedy, Old Comedy, New Comedy, Roman comedy, and Roman tragedy. For each, Harsh provides an introduction that describes its character, origins, subject matter, meters, and typical structure. His treatment of the surviving authors and their works follows. This includes a biography and general critical appreciation of each dramatist and individual discussions of his surviving plays. Harsh supplies both background information and critical commentary on the plays. The work includes extensive notes and bibliography and an index.

Although still useful for readers studying ancient drama at a basic level, 50 years of scholarship have left Harsh's book very dated, especially in its critical approaches. Even some of the factual material is now incorrect (e.g., the early dating of Aeschylus's *Suppliants* is no longer widely accepted). Hathorn (entry 270) is more current, though not entirely up-to-date himself. Hathorn's handbook is also rather different in character, because it is organized as a dictionary and focuses more on plot summaries and background information.

270. Hathorn, Richmond Y. **Crowell's Handbook of Classical Drama**. New York: Thomas Y. Crowell, 1967. 350pp. LC 67-12403.

Hathorn's work is a dictionary of ancient drama. His entries cover the playwrights, their individual works, characters from the plays, places, ancient technical terms relating to drama, and historical and cultural background material. The entries range from a sentence to several pages. Major dramatists receive extensive entries, while the articles on their individual works include both detailed summaries and some (often uninspired) critical commentary. Hathorn also includes brief entries on many minor dramatists and their works. He provides neither a bibliography nor an index. His handbook is a useful ready-reference tool for those reading classical drama in translation.

271. Herzog, Reinhart, and Peter Lebrecht Schmidt, eds. **Handbuch der lateinischen Literatur der Antike**. München: C. H. Beck, 1989- . 8v. (Handbuch der Altertumswissenschaft, Abt.8). ISBN 3-406-31863-0(v.5).

272. Herzog, Reinhart, and Peter Lebrecht Schmidt, eds. **Nouvelle histoire de la littérature latine**. Paris: Brepols, 1993- . 8v. ISBN 2-503-50069-2(v.5).

Herzog and Schmidt are preparing a new major history of Latin literature that will replace that of Schanz-Hosius (entry 280) in the Handbuch der Altertumswissenschaft series. It is being published in both German and French editions. Eight volumes are projected; to date only the fifth, *Restauration und Erneuerung: Die lateinischen Literatur von 284 bis 374 N. Chr.*, has appeared. This volume is the most detailed treatment of its period available. It covers all known authors and works, both major and minor. They are arranged by genre within an overall chronological framework. Sections on major authors are often extensively subdivided. This handbook provides biographical information about the authors, pertinent historical background, summaries and discussions of the literary works, and substantial bibliographies. When completed, this will be the standard history of Latin literature.

✓ 273. Howatson, M. C. **The Oxford Companion to Classical Literature**. 2d ed. New York: Oxford University Press, 1989. 615pp. ISBN 0-19-866121-5. LC 88-27330.

274. Howatson, M. C., and Ian Chilvers. **The Concise Oxford Companion to Classical Literature**. New York: Oxford University Press, 1993. 575pp. ISBN 0-19-211687-8; 0-19-282708-1pa. LC 92-018585.

Paul Harvey's original *Companion*, which appeared in 1937, enjoyed a long life as a standard reference in the field. It has now been replaced by Howatson's revision, which takes into account both recent scholarship and changes in our approaches to the study of classical literature. The work takes the form of a dictionary. Entries, which vary in length from a single line to several columns, cover persons (both authors and historical figures), literary and mythological characters, individual literary works (background material and summaries), and a wide range of topics. While the focus always remains on literature, the *Companion* contains much general information on the ancient world. Its articles are clearly written and provide ample information to assist students and readers in gaining a basic understanding of works of classical literature. A chronological table of historical and literary events and a number of maps appear at the end of the work. Howatson has provided cross-references but not an index. Bibliographical references are also lacking. The abridged version contains about one-third less material than the full edition. This was achieved largely by reducing in length or dropping the long general entries of a historical nature.

Howatson is the best of the general literary handbooks. Feder (entry 268) is adequate but consists mainly of author biographies and plot summaries. She provides much less on the general cultural background than does Howatson. Lang and Dudley (entry 276) also tend to offer author biographies and summaries of literary works, along with a modicum of historical background. Many of their articles include bibliographical notes and suggestions for further reading. Avery (entry 258), which treats only Greek literature, is a slender effort and the least satisfactory of the lot.

275. Kenney, E. J., and W. V. Clausen, eds. **Latin Literature**. New York: Cambridge University Press, 1982. 973pp. (**Cambridge History of Classical Literature,** v.2). ISBN 0-521-21043-7. LC 79-121.

A product of collaboration, this volume counts among its contributors a number of distinguished British and American classical scholars. The work begins with a substantial introduction on "Readers and Critics," which provides an overview of the business end of ancient literature: writing as a profession, publication, the physical production of books, and the reading public. It then proceeds in broadly chronological order from the beginnings of Latin literature through the fourth century A.D. Chapters cover individual authors or genres. The primary focus of the history is on the literary works themselves. The main text is entirely critical, with biographical and bibliographical material relegated to an appendix of authors and works. The bibliographies found there provide a good selection of editions, commentaries, translations, and basic studies. There is also a brief appendix on Latin metrics. This is a solid, reasonably current treatment of Latin literature and is now widely regarded as the standard work in English. Some, especially students, may prefer Conte's recent work (entry 261), which combines a healthy amount of biographical and historical background with a critical appreciation of the literature. The older, more traditional works of Duff (entry 264-265) and Rose (entry 279), now rather dated but still useful, offer biographies of the authors and summaries of their works.

276. Lang, D. M., and D. R. Dudley, ed. **The Penguin Companion to Classical, Oriental, & African Literature**. New York: McGraw-Hill, 1969. 359pp. ISBN 0-07-049281-6. LC 78-158064.

Despite its wide-ranging title, more than half of this book is devoted to classical literature. There is a separate section for each literature (classical, Byzantine, Oriental, and African). The classical section covers Greek and Latin literature from the beginnings to the fifth century A.D.; the Byzantine section extends coverage of Greek literature through the fall of Constantinople (A.D. 1453). Dudley, a Latin scholar, edited the classical and Byzantine portions. A number of British scholars contributed entries on the classics, while the Byzantine section is largely the work of Robert Browning, a notable authority on later Greek. These articles, which are arranged alphabetically, cover authors and genres. Author entries provide basic biographical information and brief descriptions of their works. Entries for genres give their characteristics and provide a summary history of their development. Brief bibliographies accompany most entries. Although there is no index, numerous cross-references are provided. This is a good guide for those concerned primarily with literature, although it does not provide as much historical and cultural background material as Howatson (entries 273-274).

277. Lesky, Albin. **A History of Greek Literature**. Translated by James Willis and Cornelis de Heer. New York: Crowell, 1966. 921pp. LC 65-25033.

This English version is based on the 2d edition of Lesky's *Geschichte der griechischen Literatur* (Bern: Francke Verlag, 1963). Lesky intended "to give a broad outline for the student, intital guidance to the researcher, and to the interested public a speedy but not superficial approach to the literature of Greece." He accomplished this sufficiently well that for many years his work was the standard history of Greek literature. Although now supplanted in this role by the Greek volume of the more recent *Cambridge History of Classical Literature* (entry 266), Lesky is still a valuable guide to Greek literature. He approaches his subject chronologically, assigning a chapter to each major period. Within these major periods, authors and genres are discussed. To keep the size of his book manageable, Lesky omits a number of minor authors, gives somewhat short shrift to the writers of the Roman period, and does not discuss Christian Greek writings at all. He is strongest in his coverage of the early period and the fifth and fourth centuries B.C. Lesky writes traditional literary history, with a healthy dose of biography and historical background, but does not neglect literary criticism. He provides such facts as we have and discusses significant problems. Lesky's notes and bibliographies are a good guide to further study; although not as current as those in the *Cambridge History*, they are sometimes more extensive. A detailed table of contents and full indexing make the work easy to consult.

278. Rose, H. J. **A Handbook of Greek Literature: From Homer to the Age of Lucian**. 4th ed. London: Methuen, 1951. 458pp.

Often reprinted, this work is a traditional literary history, with heavy emphasis on biography and history. Many summaries and descriptions of literary works are provided, but there is little in the way of criticism or interpretation. Rose proceeds in roughly chronological fashion, with his chapters organized around major authors or genres. Discussion of minor authors and works is set in smaller type, and technical matters (e.g., details of chronology) are generally relegated to the footnotes. There is a bibliography (now dated) and an index. Rose is generally dry but informative. Lesky (entry 277), who takes a similar approach (although giving more attention to literary criticism), is fuller and more current. The Greek volume of the *Cambridge History of Classical Literature* (entry 266), which is also more recent, has a more literary and less historical orientation.

279. Rose, H. J. **A Handbook of Latin Literature: From the Earliest Times to the Death of St. Augustine**. 3d ed. Reprinted with a supplementary bibliography by E. Courtney. London: Methuen, 1967. 582pp. LC 67-76490.

This frequently reprinted handbook was long the chief rival to Duff (entries 264-265) as the standard English-language history of Latin literature. Rose is more compact and offers less detail, but, unlike Duff, he extends his coverage through the fourth century A.D. He uses a chronological framework in which each major period receives one or more chapters. The only exception to this is his treatment of technical writers and scholars, whom he places in a separate chapter. Rose follows the traditional approach: His work includes historical background, biographies, and summaries of the various works. It is a readable, if sometimes plodding book. There is a good index. Those who want a more critical approach to the literature should use the Latin volume of the *Cambridge History of Classical Literature* (entry 275), which is also more current. This and Conte's recent work (entry 261) largely supersede Rose.

280. Schanz, Martin. **Geschichte der römischen Literatur bis zum Gesetzgebungswerk des Kaisers Justinian**. 2.-4. Aufl. München: C. H. Beck, 1914-1935. 4v. (Handbuch der Altertumswissenschaft, Abt.8). ISBN 3-406-01390-2(v.1); 3-406-01392-9(v.2); 3-406-01394-5(v.3); 3-406-01396-1(v.4). LC 28-4494.

This massive work is the standard scholarly history of Latin literature. It is often referred to as Schanz-Hosius because the later editions were revised by Carl Hosius. Only the first two volumes appeared in a 4th edition; the third volume is in its 3d edition, and the fourth is in its 2d edition. These four volumes cover the Roman republic, the empire from Augustus to Hadrian, Hadrian to Constantine the Great, and the fourth to sixth centuries A.D. respectively.

Within each volume, material is organized by period and genre. Schanz-Hosius covers virtually every known author and work from the beginnings of Latin literature through the sixth century. Sections for individual authors include biographical information, summaries and discussions of the individual works, and extensive bibliographies. For major authors, Schanz-Hosius also provides general critical discussion and essays on particular aspects of their works. Each volume has its own detailed index; a more sketchy index to the whole work appears at the end of the final volume. Herzog and Schmidt (entries 271-272) are preparing a wholly new history of Latin literature to replace Schanz-Hosius; at this time only the fifth volume, which covers the late third and most of the fourth centuries A.D., has appeared. Pending the completion of this new work, Schanz-Hosius remains the most complete and detailed treatment of Latin literature available. Those who read only English will be best served by Conte (entry 261) or the Latin volume of the *Cambridge History of Classical Literature* (entry 275), although neither is remotely comparable in either size or scope.

281. Schmid, Wilhelm, and Otto Stählin. **Geschichte der griechischen Literatur**. München: C. H. Beck, 1929-1948. 2v. in 7. (Handbuch der Altertumswissenschaft, Abt.7). ISBN 3-406-01376-7(v.1, pt.1); 3-406-01378-3(v.1, pt.2); 3-406-01380-5(v.1, pt.3); 3-406-01382-1(v.1, pt.4); 3-406-01384-8(v.1, pt.5); 3-406-01386-4(v.2, pt.1); 3-406-01388-0(v.2, pt.2). LC 35-14442.

The Greek equivalent of Schanz-Hosius (entry 280), Schmid-Stählin is the most complete and detailed history of Greek literature available. The first volume, in five parts, covers Greek literature from the beginnings to ca. 400 B.C. A sixth part covering the fourth century B.C. was to have been written by Hans Herter; this has never appeared and leaves a major gap in the work. The second volume, which is in two parts, covers 320 B.C. to A.D. 530. Schmid-Stählin is organized by period, with subarrangment by genre. It covers both major and minor authors and works. Sections on individual authors provide biographical information, summaries and discussions of their works, and extensive bibliographies. For major authors Schmid-Stählin also includes extended essays on various aspects of their work. Indexes are provided at the end of each part (except the fourth) of the first volume. The index for the second volume appears at the end of the final part. While no English-language work is comparable in size and scope to Schmid-Stählin, Lesky (entry 277) and the appropriate volume of the *Cambridge History of Classical Literature* (entry 266) will serve the needs of most English readers quite well.

Mythology

282. **Athena: Classical Mythology on CD-ROM**. Boston: G. K. Hall, 1994. 1 disc, accompanied by user's guide. ISBN 0-7838-2119-0 (single-user); 0-7838-2120-4 (network).

Designed for students at all levels, *Athena* is a hypertext-based mythological dictionary. It offers brief articles on the various mythological characters and stories. These articles are linked to both summaries and fulltext translations of the major classical literary sources for the myths. Many entries are accompanied by illustrations, which are mostly drawn from ancient sources. These line drawings, which are uninspiring, are one of the weaker features of the database. A number of genealogical tables are also provided. The most attractive feature of *Athena* is the hypertext links that enable one to move readily to the summaries or the texts of the primary sources and to articles on related myths. The straightforward search procedures permit both keyword access and browsing in the alphabetical list of headings. *Athena* is superior in both content and ease of use to most of the printed dictionaries of mythology, although researchers will still find Grimal (entry 290) better due to his extensive scholarly apparatus.

The same disc contains DOS, Windows, and Macintosh versions. The DOS version currently requires an IBM PC AT or higher with at least 2 MB of RAM; Windows requires Windows 3.x and 2 (preferably 4) MB of RAM. The Macintosh version is designed to run on System 7.1 and requires 8 MB of RAM.

283. Avery, Catherine B., ed. **The New Century Handbook of Greek Mythology and Legend**. New York: Appleton-Century-Crofts, 1972. 565pp. LC 75-183796.

This work is excerpted from the larger *New Century Classical Handbook* (entry 212). It takes the form of a dictionary. Most entries represent the characters of Greek mythology, although there are a few articles on places, events, and objects. The entries vary in length; most run to a paragraph or two, while a few extend to several pages. The articles provide clear identifications and summaries of important stories. A guide to pronunciation is also supplied. There are no bibliographical references. The *Handbook* compares favorably to other basic dictionaries of mythology, such as Schmidt (entry 302), Stapleton (entry 303), and Zimmerman (entry 305), although it lacks some of the detail and the bibliographies found in the larger works of Tripp (entry 304) and Grimal (entry 290).

284. Barthell, Edward E., Jr. **Gods and Goddesses of Ancient Greece**. Coral Gables, FL: University of Miami Press, 1971. 416pp. ISBN 0-87024-165-6. LC 72-129664.

For those who prefer a narrative approach to the myths, Barthell offers a good alternative to the mythological dictionaries described elsewhere in this section. He follows a "chronological" arrangement that proceeds from the older gods through the Olympians and their descendants to the stories of the Trojan War and Odysseus. Barthell's readable text covers the stories in detail; his footnotes provide a good deal of background information and discuss minor variants of the myths. He also includes a large number of detailed genealogical tables. His bibliography lists the primary sources (mainly in *Loeb Classical Library* editions) and a few general handbooks on Greek mythology. A thorough general index completes the work.

✓ 285. Bell, Robert E. **Dictionary of Classical Mythology: Symbols, Attributes, & Associations**. Santa Barbara, CA: ABC-CLIO, 1982. 390pp. ISBN 0-87436-305-5; 0-87436-023-4p. LC 81-19141.

Most dictionaries of mythology use the names of persons and places as access points. Bell's work uses a topical approach. There are entries for objects, animals, attributes of the various mythological characters, and topics. Under each the reader will find the mythical figures associated with the heading. Many of the figures are accompanied by brief notes that clarify the association, although Bell does not usually provide full identifications of characters or summaries of myths. There are also separate lists of surnames, epithets, and patronymics of the characters of classical myth and of participants in various heroic expeditions (e.g., the voyage of the *Argo*). The final section, "Guide to Persona," functions as a name index. Bell provides an excellent companion work to any of the standard mythological dictionaries, such as Grimal (entry 290). Preston (entry 244), whose work is specifically intended for identifying representations of classical myth in art, is similar in form and content.

286. Bell, Robert E. **Women of Classical Mythology: A Biographical Dictionary**. Santa Barbara, CA: ABC-CLIO, 1991; repr., New York: Oxford University Press, 1993. 462pp. ISBN 0-87436-581-3. LC 91-26649.

Another of Bell's works on mythology (see also entries 285 and 404), this volume focuses on women in Greek and Roman mythology. Bell covers approximately 2,600 women mentioned in the classical myths. A few, such as Helen and Medea, are prominent, but the majority are minor figures. The entries present what is known about each and supply references to relevant ancient sources. Although the entries vary in length from a few lines to several pages, most are brief, which in many cases is due to the obscurity of the character. Some of these characters will not be found at all in more general mythological dictionaries. Bell is particularly good for differentiating among characters of the same name and for identifying obscure epithets of the goddesses. He provides numerous cross-references. Bell also provides a list of "the men in their lives," which functions as an index based on the often better-known names of the male characters of classical myth.

287. **The Chiron Dictionary of Greek and Roman Mythology**. Translated by Elizabeth Burr. Wilmette, IL: Chiron, 1994. 312pp. ISBN 0-933029-82-9. LC 93-43989.

Originally published in German as *Herder Lexikon: Griechische und römische Mythologie* (Freiburg im Breisgau, Germany: Herder, 1981), this dictionary provides good coverage of the basic characters, places, and events of classical mythology. Entries, which number more than 1,600, are concise and informative. An unusual feature is the material presented in the margins beside many entries, consisting of small illustrations, genealogical tables, or lists (e.g., the 12 labors of Herakles, the names of the nine muses, the events at the Olympic Games). The dictionary includes cross-references but no bibliography or index. It is an attractive and convenient ready-reference tool for students and readers. Those who require fuller treatment should refer to Grimal (entry 290).

288. Gantz, Timothy. **Early Greek Myth: A Guide to the Literary and Artistic Sources**. Baltimore, MD: Johns Hopkins University Press, 1993. 909pp. ISBN 0-8018-4410-X. LC 92-26010.

For anyone with a serious interest in early Greek literature, art, or mythology, this handbook will be an invaluable resource. Unlike most handbooks that offer composite versions of the myths, Gantz has attempted to determine and present the forms of the myths current in early Greek civilization down to the end of the archaic period. His arrangement is the traditional one, with each cycle treated separately in what might be called the "chronological order" of the myths. In his discussion of each myth, Gantz provides a full discussion of the literary sources. His treatment of the artistic evidence is more selective; those in need of exhaustive coverage are referred to the *Lexicon Iconographicum Mythologiae Classicae* (entry 293). Gantz also supplies an extensive array of genealogical tables and a catalog of artistic representations. The catalog will be opaque to those without a solid grounding in Greek art. Notes (no longer a common feature in handbooks), a bibliography, and a reasonably full subject index complete the book.

289. Grant, Michael, and John Hazel. **Who's Who in Classical Mythology**. London: Weidenfeld and Nicholson, 1973; repr., New York: Oxford University Press, 1993. 447pp. ISBN 0-297-766007. LC 73-177715.

One of the many productions by Michael Grant, this is a good basic dictionary of classical mythology. It includes entries for the characters (but not the places and events) of the myths. The entries range in length from a single sentence to several pages and serve to identify the characters and summarize their stories. For the most part there are no bibliographies, although Grant and Hazel occasionally supply general references to the ancient sources. The work lacks an index but does include many cross-references. In general this is a serviceable ready-reference tool, but not the equal of Tripp (entry 304) or Grimal (entry 290), even in his abridged edition (entry 291).

✓290. Grimal, Pierre. **The Dictionary of Classical Mythology**. Translated by A. R. Maxwell-Hyslop. Oxford, England: Blackwell, 1986. 603pp. ISBN 0-631-13209-0. LC 85-7387.

291. Grimal, Pierre. **The Penguin Dictionary of Classical Mythology**. Edited by Stephen Kershaw from the translation of A. R. Maxwell-Hyslop. New York: Penguin Books, 1991. 466pp. ISBN 0-14-051235-7. LC 92-101281.

Since it first appeared in 1951, Grimal's well-known *Dictionnaire de la mythologie grecque et romaine* has gone through numerous editions and has been translated into several languages. Grimal's entries are chiefly for individual characters of the myths; topics and places are covered indirectly. The compact articles identify each mythic figure and summarize what is known about them. Grimal provides full references to the ancient literary sources for each myth, although these must be sought from a separate section following the text. Amenities include maps of Greece and Italy, a selection of illustrations, and some 40 genealogical tables that elucidate the often complicated family relationships of classical mythology. A comprehensive index rounds out the volume. Grimal provides more detailed accounts of the myths and fuller scholarly apparatus than any of the competing volumes. This excellent work is the best of the many general dictionaries of Greek and Roman mythology in English.

The abridged version, which also appeared under the title *A Concise Dictionary of Classical Mythology*, lacks the many notes and bibliographical references of the full edition. The editor has also deleted material from some articles and greatly reduced the number of genealogical tables.

292. Hunger, Herbert. **Lexikon der griechischen und römischen Mythologie: Mit Hinweisen auf das Fortwirken antiker Stoffe und Motive
in der bildenden Kunst, Literatur, und Musik der Abendlandes bis
zur Gegenwart**. Wien: Hollinek, 1988. 8., erweiterte Aufl. 557pp.
ISBN 3-85119-230-3. LC 89-116531.

Hunger's dictionary covers the full range of classical mythology. His short
articles give basic information and a synopsis of modern studies for each myth
or character. Hunger then lists works of art, literature, and music featuring the
myth. Articles conclude with an extensive bibliographical note. Those who are
seeking only identifications or summaries of myths will be better off with Grimal
(entries 290-291) or one of his competitors. Serious students of myth who have
some German will find Hunger useful, particularly for his rich bibliographies.
His lists of depictions of myth in art are also handy, although Reid's *Classical
Mythology in the Arts* (entry 294) is much more comprehensive.

293. **Lexicon Iconographicum Mythologiae Classicae**. Zürich: Artemis,
1981- . ISBN 3760887511. LC 82-225552.

Commonly referred to as LIMC, this work "is designed to give an account
of the present state of knowledge about the iconography of Greek, Etruscan, and
Roman mythology from after the Mycenaean period down to the beginning of
the early Christian." Six of the projected seven volumes (each in two parts, one
of text, the other of plates) have appeared. It is the most comprehensive source
of information about the depiction of classical myths in ancient art. Because
LIMC is a product of international collaboration, articles are written in English,
French, German, or Italian according to the author's preference. Articles are
arranged alphabetically by the name of the mythical character or event; preference is given to the Greek form if there is one. Each article is in four parts. The
introduction gives a brief identification of the mythical character or subject and
cites the chief literary sources. The second section is a bibliography. Third is a
catalog of depictions of the myth in ancient art, which is exhaustive for early
materials or in other cases where little is available; otherwise it is selective. All
iconographical types and their variations are noted. Within each iconographical
division, subarrangement is by cultural area (Greek, Etruscan, Roman), then by
medium, and then chronological. The fourth section is the iconographical commentary, which offers a brief scholarly study of the development of the iconographical
types, chronological relations, and differences between the various types. Articles
vary greatly in size, ranging from less than a full column to the length of a short
monograph. The longer articles are often subdivided by theme; most supply a table
of contents as a guide to the user. The illustrations, which consist of good-quality
black-and-white plates, equal the text in bulk. This is by far the best source for
locating and studying myths as they appear in ancient art. It is aimed chiefly at
scholars and advanced students. The more casual seeker of images will probably
prefer Rochelle (entry 249).

√ 294. Reid, Jane Davidson. **The Oxford Guide to Classical Mythology in
the Arts, 1300-1990's**. New York: Oxford University Press, 1993. 2v.
ISBN 0-19-504998-5. LC 92-35374.

Of interest to literary scholars and art historians as well as classicists,
Reid's work is an indispensable guide to mythological themes and influences in
late medieval, Renaissance, and modern fine arts, music, dance, and literature.
It contains more than 200 entries for mythological figures and themes. Each entry
gives a brief account of its subject, provides references to the ancient literary

sources, and notes any related entries. Works of art depicting the myth are then listed chronologically, with different formats interfiled. Listings include the name of the artist, title of the work, date, location or (for literary works) publication information, and a short bibliography. This very full work lists more than 30,000 works of art. Reid also provides an exhaustive index of artists. Those seeking depictions of myth in art predating 1300 will find useful references in Rochelle (entry 249).

✓295. Room, Adrian. **Room's Classical Dictionary: The Origins of the Names of Characters in Classical Mythology**. London: Routledge & Kegan Paul, 1983. 343pp. ISBN 0-7100-9262-8. LC 82-16121.

Of interest to etymologists and students of myth, this dictionary lists more than 1,000 proper names from classical mythology. Each entry discusses the origin and meaning of the name. There are separate entries for Greek and Roman versions of the same character (e.g., Jupiter and Zeus), because the etymologies and meanings sometimes vary. Appendices cover such topics as common elements in Greek names and their meanings (mainly prefixes and suffixes), "by-names" of the major gods and goddesses, and the corresponding names of characters (Greek and Roman equivalents). The content is interesting, if sometimes speculative.

296. Roscher, W. H., ed. **Ausführliches Lexikon der griechischen und römischen Mythologie**. Leipzig: B. G. Teubner, 1884-1937; repr., Hildesheim, Germany: Georg Olms, 1992-1993. 6v. in 9. LC 01-9584.

297. Bruchmann, C. H. F. **Epitheta Deorum Quae apud Poetas Graecos Leguntur**. Leipzig: B. G. Teubner, 1893. 225pp. LC 1-15337.

298. Carter, J. B. **Epitheta Deorum Quae apud Poetas Latinos Leguntur**. Leipzig: B. G. Teubner, 1902. 154pp.

299. Berger, E. H. **Mythische Kosmographie der Griechen**. Leipzig: B. G. Teubner, 1904. 40pp. LC 5-15340.

300. Gruppe, O. **Geschichte der klassischen Mythologie und Religionsgeschichte während des Mittelalters im Abendland und während der Neuzeit**. Leipzig: B. G. Teubner, 1921. 248pp. LC 21-12060.

Despite the passage of more than a century since the first volume appeared, Roscher's *Lexikon* remains a fundamental reference work for the study of classical mythology. Its many signed articles treat persons, places, peoples, and topics from mythology. It encompasses even the most obscure and minor figures of Greek and Roman myth. The articles, which vary considerably in length, recount what was known about each subject and include full references to the ancient sources and extensive citations of the modern scholarly literature up to the time of writing. No other dictionary of classical mythology is even remotely comparable in size or scope. Although interpretations have changed greatly and our knowledge of a number of myths has increased, most of the information in Roscher remains useful.

Four supplementary volumes to the *Lexikon* have appeared as well. These are all monographs that treat the Greek and Latin epithets of the gods and goddesses, Greek cosmography, and the history of the study of classical myth and religion. These supplements are normally included in reprint editions.

301. Rose, H. J. **A Handbook of Greek Mythology, Including Its Extension to Rome**. 6th ed. London: Methuen, 1958; repr., London: Routledge, 1991. 363pp. LC 58-1932.

For those who prefer a more connected approach to myth, Rose is a good alternative to the mythological dictionaries. He covers Greek myth well, Roman myth merely adequately. The book is organized by the various cycles in their "chronological" order: origins of the world, the children of Kronos, the queens of heaven, the younger gods, lesser and foreign deities, cycles of saga, Troy, legends of the Greek lands, *Märchen* in Greece and Italy, and Italian mythology. Rose does a good job of assembling the basic stories and citing the primary sources. His style can be rather dry, and his interpretations are generally out-of-date and should be ignored. There are extensive notes and a bibliography. The work also has a good index.

302. Schmidt, Joël. **Larousse Greek and Roman Mythology**. Edited by Seth Benardete. New York: McGraw-Hill, 1980. 310pp. ISBN 0-07-055342-4. LC 80-15046.

Another of the many dictionaries of mythology, *Larousse* provides fairly typical coverage of the characters, events, and places of the classical myths. Its entries tend to be longer than those of Stapleton (entry 303) and Zimmermann (entry 305), but less full than those of Grimal (entry 290). The entries are readable and generally reliable; they do not include any bibliographical references. The work is well illustrated, chiefly with reproductions of ancient paintings and sculptures. Numerous genealogical tables are also provided. A brief listing of the major ancient literary sources for the myths and a detailed index conclude the volume.

303. Stapleton, Michael. **A Dictionary of Greek and Roman Mythology**. London: Hamlyn, 1978; repr., New York: Wings Books, 1993. 224pp. ISBN 0-600-36291-4. LC 78-316936.

The various printings of this work sometimes include the epithets "concise" or "illustrated" in the title, but all have basically the same content. Stapleton offers brief, readable entries that identify the major characters, places, and events of classical mythology. Aside from occasional broad references to ancient sources, Stapleton provides no bibliographical citations within individual articles. There is a short general bibliography. Some illustrations accompany the text. There is a fairly extensive index of minor characters and place-names. This dictionary provides the basic information and is adequate for ready-reference; Grimal (entry 290) is a more substantial work.

304. Tripp, Edward. **Crowell's Handbook of Classical Mythology**. New York: Crowell, 1970. 629pp. LC 74-127614. Reprinted as **The Meridian Handbook of Classical Mythology**, New York: New American Library, 1974.

Presented in a dictionary format, Tripp's handbook is aimed at the general reader who needs help with mythological allusions in literature. He emphasizes the best-known version of each myth, although he frequently includes significant variants as well. Entries, which range from a few words to several pages, cover mostly characters and places. Topics and events are generally treated as aspects of these entries. Many entries include references to their major ancient sources. Tripp also supplies maps and a few genealogical tables. The "Pronouncing Index" is not an index as such, but provides guidance in pronounciation. There are numerous cross-references. Tripp provides a full account of the myths and is second only to Grimal (entry 290) for English readers. Grimal's superiority rests mainly upon his much more extensive scholarly apparatus.

305. Zimmerman, J. E. **Dictionary of Classical Mythology**. New York: Harper & Row, 1964; repr., New York: Bantam Books, 1985. 300pp. LC 63-20319.

This widely available dictionary of mythology contains approximately 2,100 entries covering people, places, events, and objects. The entries, which are generally brief, include a pronunciation guide, a concise identification of the subject, and occasional reference to the ancient sources. Zimmermann provides cross-references from variant forms, but no index. His dictionary is an adequate and reliable ready-reference tool for students and readers; those who want more detailed information should use Grimal's larger work (entry 290) instead.

Philosophy

306. Armstrong, A. H., ed. **The Cambridge History of Later Greek and Early Medieval Philosophy**. New York: Cambridge University Press, 1967. 710pp. LC 66-12305.

This work was planned as a continuation of Guthrie's *History of Greek Philosophy* (entry 307), although it has developed along different lines. Chronologically it covers the period from the fourth century B.C. to the beginning of the twelfth century A.D. Treatment of the earlier period (e.g., of Plato) aims at explaining the background of Neoplatonism rather than giving a complete history of the period, for which one should consult Guthrie. The work is divided into eight parts, each by a different scholar, that cover Greek philosophy from Plato to Plotinus, Philo and the beginnings of Christian thought, Plotinus, the later Neoplatonists, Marius Victorinus and Augustine, the Platonist tradition from the Cappadocians to Maximus and Eriugena, Western Christian thought from Boethius to Anselm, and early Islamic philosophy. A substantial bibliography and several indexes (ancient and medieval works discussed, general, and Greek terms) round out the volume. The work provides a good general survey of later Greek philosophy and its influence, as well as early Christian and medieval thought.

307. Guthrie, W. K. C. **A History of Greek Philosophy**. New York: Cambridge University Press, 1962-1981. 6v. ISBN 0-521-05159-2(v.1); 0-521-29420-7pa. (v.1); 0-521-05160-6(v.2); 0-521-29421-5pa.(v.2); 0-521-07566-1(v.3); 0-521-09666-9pa.(v.3, pt.1); 0-521-09667-7pa.(v.3, pt.2); 0-521-20002-4(v.4); 0-521-31101-2pa.(v.4); 0-521-20003-2(v.5); 0-521-31102-0pa.(v.5); 0-521-23573-1(v.6); 0-521-38760-4pa.(v.6). LC 62-52735.

Long established as the standard work in the field, Guthrie surveys Greek philosophy from its beginnings through Aristotle. The first two volumes cover the Pre-Socratics, the third deals with the fifth-century sophists and Socrates, the fourth and fifth volumes with Plato, and the final volume with Aristotle. Guthrie originally intended to extend the history through the Hellenistic period, but was only able to reach Aristotle, who is treated on a more limited scale. While not neglecting the necessary biographical and historical background material, Guthrie focuses on the philosophical works and provides extensive discussion of them. The treatment is learned but remains accessible to the lay reader. Each volume includes an extensive bibliographical apparatus and full indexes.

308. Peters, F. E. **Greek Philosophical Terms: A Historical Lexicon**. New York: New York University Press, 1967. 234pp. LC 67-25043.

Aimed at the "intermediate student" of Greek philosophy, this is an alphabetical listing of terms used by the Greek philosophers. Peters defines each term and discusses its usage in the various philosophical writers; the discussions include numerous specific references. He supplies numerous cross-references and an English-Greek index that provides access from English versions of the terms. This useful work allows students of philosophy who lack a good command of ancient Greek to get some idea of the actual meanings of Greek philosophical terms and to see some of the problems and uncertainties associated with the standard definitions.

Quotations

309. Bartels, Klaus, and Ludwig Huber. **Veni, Vidi, Vici: Geflügelte Worte aus dem Griechischen und Lateinischen**. 8. Aufl. Zurich: Artemis, 1990. 216pp. ISBN 3-760-81007-1.

For those comfortable in German, this attractive volume provides an excellent selection of quotations and notable phrases from the Greek and Latin classics. Greek and Latin quotations are gathered into separate lists, each alphabetized by keyword. The phrase is given in the original, followed by a German translation and a citation for the ancient source. Occasionally an extended note provides some history of the quotation, such as its adoption by subsequent writers. The excellent selection of material is a tribute to the taste and scholarship of the editors. The latest edition, unlike some of the earlier ones, includes an index.

310. Guterman, Norbert. **The Anchor Book of Latin Quotations with English Translations**. New York: Doubleday, 1990. 433pp. ISBN 0-385-41391-2. LC 90-237.

This compilation includes more than 1,500 quotations from Latin literature. Guterman arranges the quotations chronologically by author (the least useful choice for such a dictionary). The Latin original and the English translation appear on facing pages. While most of the better-known phrases appear in these pages, there are also many surprises. Occasionally Guterman lapses into being an anthologist rather than a compiler of quotations. The majority of the translations are by Guterman, although some are by well-known literary figures. There are indexes of ancient authors, subjects (in English), and Latin keywords. Aside from browsers, most will need to turn to these first.

311. Harbottle, Thomas Benfield. **Dictionary of Quotations (Classical)**. 3d ed. New York: Macmillan, 1906. 684pp. Reprinted as **Anthology of Classical Quotations**, San Antonio, TX: Scylax Press, 1984.

This work is divided into two parts, one for Latin quotations, the other for Greek. Within each, the quotations are arranged alphabetically by the first word. Harbottle supplies the original Latin or Greek, its source, and an English translation. In addition to famous phrases, he includes many less well known quotations. Harbottle provides an author index and subject indexes in Latin, Greek, and English. His dictionary remains useful both for finding and identifying classical quotations. The more recent work of Guterman (entry 310) includes only Latin quotations. Bartels (entry 309), a collection containing both Greek and Latin quotations, is a good alternative but requires at least some knowledge of German. Tosi (entry 314) also offers an excellent dictionary of quotations, but is in Italian.

312. Otto, A. **Die Sprichwörter und sprichwörterlichen Redensarten der Römer**. Leipzig: B. G. Teubner, 1890; repr., Hildesheim, Germany: Georg Olms, 1971. 436pp. LC 31-20573.

313. Häussler, Reinhard, ed. **Nachträge zu A. Otto, Sprichwörter und sprichwörterlichen Redensarten der Römer**. Hildesheim, Germany: Georg Olms, 1968.

Otto's work is the classic compilation of Latin proverbs and *bons mots* that he culled from the whole corpus of Latin literature. The proverbs are arranged alphabetically by keyword. Under each term the selected sayings are quoted in full in the original Latin. Otto also cites the source and sometimes provides a German translation. Occasionally there is some discussion of the proverb. Numerous cross-references are provided.

Häussler gathers a number of reviews and articles by various hands that supplement Otto. He also supplies an index that correlates the additions with the appropriate entry in Otto.

314. Tosi, Renzo. **Dizionario delle sentenze latine e greche: 10.000 citazioni dall'antichità al rinascimento nell'originale e in traduzione con commento storico letterario e filologico**. 8. ed. Milano: Rizzoli, 1993. 885pp. ISBN 88-17-14516-9.

For those who can read Italian, this is perhaps the best general dictionary of classical quotations and sayings. It lists some 1,841 notable quotations and proverbial expressions from ancient and medieval sources. Each is given in the original Latin and Greek, followed by an Italian translation. The commentary to each expression notes its first known use and discusses its meaning. Many entries include citations of the quotation's subsequent appearances in Western literature as well. The quotations are well chosen; the commentary provides many interesting historical sidelights on Western literature and culture. Tosi sensibly employs a thematic arrangement, which is clearly laid out by his table of contents. Latin and Greek indexes also provide alphabetical access for those who need it. Readers who prefer an English-language work might consult Guterman (entry 310) or Harbottle (entry 311).

Ancillary Disciplines

314a. Bischoff, Bernhard. **Latin Palaeography: Antiquity and the Middle Ages**. Translated by Dáibhí O Cróinín and David Ganz. Cambridge, England: Cambridge University Press, 1990. 291pp. ISBN 0-521-36473-6; 0-521-36726-3pa. LC 88-34649.

Translated from the second edition of *Paläographie des romischen Altertums und des abendländischen Mittelalters* (Berlin: Erich Schmidt, 1986), this handbook is the product of one of the foremost Latin palaeographers of the twentieth century. Bischoff covers all aspects of his subject: writing materials and tools, codicology, writing and copying, the history of Latin scripts from the earliest surviving examples through the Renaissance, and the role of manuscripts in cultural history. The text is both readable and authoritative. Numerous illustrations and an extensive bibliography round out the work.

315. Cappelli, Adriano. **Lexicon Abbreviaturarum = Dizionario di abbreviature latine ed italiane usate nelle carte e codici specialmente del medio-evo riprodotte con oltre 14000 segni incisi, con l'aggiunta di uno studio sulla brachigrafia medioevale, un prontuario di sigle epigrafiche, l'antica numerazione romana ed arabica ed i segni indicanti monete, pesi, misure, etc.** 6a ed., corr. Milano: Ulrico Hoepli, 1973. 531pp. ISBN 88-203-1100-3.

316. Pelzer, Auguste. **Abréviations latines médiévales: supplément au Dizionario di abbreviature latine ed italiane de Adriano Cappelli.** 2éme éd. Louvain: Publications Universitaires, 1966; repr., Bruxelles: Editions Nauwelaerts, 1982. 86pp. LC 68-114011.

Cappelli is the standard dictionary of Latin abbreviations found in manuscripts. His work is sometimes useful for deciphering abbreviations in early printed books as well. The work begins with an introductory discussion of medieval shorthand and abbreviations. The dictionary of abbreviations follows. Entries consist of reproductions of the abbreviations in the original scripts, a printed transcription, and the resolution. Cappelli appends several additional lists to the dictionary, including conventional signs, Roman numerals, Arabic numerals, and epigraphic abbreviations. The first three include reproductions of the abbreviations in the original scripts. The epigraphic abbreviations are printed. A substantial bibliography closes the work. Although Cappelli has appeared in a number of editions, there is little difference between them, and most will serve equally well. Pelzer's supplement notes a number of additional abbreviations.

317. Carson, R. A. G. **Coins of the Roman Empire**. London: Routledge, 1990. 367pp. ISBN 0-415-01591-X. LC 89-6207.

Carson, a former keeper of coins and medals at British Museum, provides an excellent account of Roman imperial coinage that is suitable for students and general readers as well as scholars. He covers gold, silver, and the principal bronze coins from Augustus to Anastasius (A.D. 498). The first part of the book is a historical survey, which proceeds emperor-by-emperor. The second part deals with such topics as metals, coin production, mints, and forgeries. Carson focuses on the broader issues; those who want details on particular coins will probably need to consult Sear (entries 326 and 327). Carson's work includes an extensive section of plates, a substantial bibliography, and a detailed index.

318. Gallo, Italo. **Greek and Latin Papyrology**. Translated by Maria Rosaria Falivene and Jennifer R. March. London: Institute of Classical Studies, University of London, 1986. 153pp. (Classical Handbook, 1). ISBN 0-900587-50-4. LC 90-159964.

Intended primarily for graduate students in classics, Gallo's handbook provides a concise overview of the major aspects of papyrology. A series of short chapters cover such topics as writing materials in antiquity, papyrology as an academic discipline, the Herculaneum papyri, literary papyri, documentary papryi, the dating and handwriting of papyri, and editorial conventions. Gallo also provides a reasonably good basic bibliography. His work will provide a basic introduction to the field, although most will find Turner's classic work (entry 331) more readable and informative.

319. Gordon, Arthur E. **Illustrated Introduction to Latin Epigraphy**. Berkeley, CA: University of California Press, 1983. 264pp. ISBN 0-520-03898-3. LC 79-63546.

Gordon's work is really a chrestomathy aimed at students with a strong background in Latin and ancient history who need to acquire a working knowledge of Latin epigraphy. His substantial introduction covers such topics as the definition of epigraphy, the provenance of Latin inscriptions, sources and collections, technical matters (e.g., abbreviations, Roman names, copying inscriptions), the subject matter of inscriptions, and problems (chiefly palaeography and dating). It also includes an extensive bibliographical section that describes the major *corpora* of Latin inscriptions and provides a basic working bibliography. The core of the book is a selection of 100 Latin inscriptions, presented in chronological order. Gordon provides introduction, text, and translation for each. The plate section that follows supplies illustrations for all of the selections. The appendices provide lists of archaic and unusual forms of abbreviations and of words along with their classical equivalents, a basic overview of the Roman calendar and dating systems, and an explanation of conventions used in printing epigraphical texts. There are two indexes, one covering subjects and ancient authors, the other modern authors. Gordon's manual offers a good working introduction to the field for advanced students and scholars. Keppie's informative but less demanding introduction (entry 321) will appeal to those who find Gordon too technical.

320. Jenkins, G. K. **Ancient Greek Coins**. 2d ed. London: Seaby, 1990. 182pp. ISBN 1-85264-014-6. LC 91-148548.

Aimed at a general audience, this richly illustrated work offers a general account of Greek coins from the archaic period to the time of the Roman conquest. Jenkins employs period divisions for his overall arrangement: archaic, fifth century B.C., fourth century B.C., and Hellenistic. Within each of these he organizes his material geographically. His narrative covers technical and artistic developments and supplies much historical background as well. A glossary, a strong bibliography, and a general index complete the work. While this is a good introduction to the subject, those interested in identifying and studying individual coins will want to consult Sear's catalog (entry 325).

320a. Jones, John Melville. **A Dictionary of Ancient Greek Coins**. London: Seaby, 1986. 248pp. ISBN 0-900652-81-0.

Jones, a respected authority on ancient numismatics, compiled this work with the needs of coin collectors and students of ancient history in mind, although scholars also will find it a handy reference work. He treats Greek coins issued under the Roman Empire, as well as the earlier issues. The dictionary covers people, places, and subjects found on coins, technical terms, metals and mining, and metrology and weight standards. In addition, there are a number of entries on coin collecting, which treat the history and terminology of the hobby and provide brief biographies. A brief list of the most important general works on Greek and Roman coins appears at the front of the dictionary. A companion volume covers Roman coins (entry 320b).

320b. Jones, John Melville. **A Dictionary of Ancient Roman Coins**. London: Seaby, 1990. 329pp. ISBN 1-85264-026-X, LC 91-155684.

In this companion work to his *Dictionary of Ancient Greek Coins* (entry 320a), Jones treats Roman coinage from the earliest Republican issues to the beginning of the reign of Anastasius I (A.D. 491). As in the earlier work, entries cover coin types, technical terms, weights and measures, and mining and metals. Jones also devotes some space to the history of collecting Roman coins. While aimed at a broad general audience, his concise and informative entries will also be of use to scholars. Jones does not provide a bibliography; rather he refers the reader to the bibliographical note in his earlier *Dictionary*. A third volume on Byzantine coinage is projected.

321.   Keppie, Lawrence. **Understanding Roman Inscriptions**. Baltimore, MD: Johns Hopkins University Press, 1991. 158pp. ISBN 0-8018-4322-7; 0-8018-4352-9pa. LC 91-19853.

Aimed at the nonspecialist, Keppie's work offers an unusually readable introduction to a technical field. Several short chapters cover the basics: the ancient stonecutter, reading inscriptions (alphabet, abbreviations, Roman names, numerals, etc.), dating inscriptions, the survival of inscriptions, and their recording and publication (an overview of *corpora* of inscriptions, basic reference works, and bibliographical sources). Then Keppie uses a topical approach to survey selected inscriptions and demonstrate their uses as historical sources. Many illustrations accompany the text. Appendices provide a chronological table of Roman emperors, a list of common abbreviations, an overview of the structure of the *Corpus Inscriptionum Latinarum*, and explanations of epigraphical conventions. A good working bibliography and a general index complete the volume. Although Keppie translates all Latin, some knowledge of the language is needed to get full value from his discussion. Those who need a more detailed and scholarly introduction should consult Gordon (entry 319).

322.   Oikonomides, Al. N., comp. **Abbreviations in Greek Inscriptions, Papyri, Manuscripts, and Early Printed Books**. Chicago: Ares, 1974. 204pp. LC 75-302478.

In this volume Oikonomides reprints several valuable works on Greek abbreviations, including M. Avi-Yonah's *Abbreviations in Greek Inscriptions* (Jerusalem: Government of Palestine, 1940), excerpts from Sir Frederic Kenyon's *Palaeography of Greek Papyri* (London: Clarendon Press, 1899), T. W. Allen's *Notes on Abbreviations in Greek Manuscripts* (Oxford, England: Clarendon Press, 1889), and excerpts on abbreviations in early printed Greek books from the *Manual of Foreign Languages for the Use of Printers and Translators* (3d ed., Washington, DC: GPO, 1936). Together these provide a good basic guide to Greek abbreviations for anyone working with inscriptions, manuscripts, or early printed materials.

323.   Reynolds, L. D., ed. **Texts and Transmissions: A Survey of the Latin Classics**. Oxford, England: Clarendon Press, 1983. 509pp. ISBN 0-19-814456-3. LC 84-148890.

In this technical work, Reynolds and his collaborators present concise accounts of the transmissions of the texts of Latin authors from antiquity to the modern era. Reynolds covers all authors and texts, from the beginnings of Latin literature down to Apuleius, who had their own independent transmission. A selection of later authors is also included. The 134 entries are arranged alphabetically and vary in character: Some represent original research, while others summarize and update existing scholarship. In some cases the entries are slender because little is known about the transmission of the author in question. In general, each entry discusses the history and relationships of the more important manuscripts of the author, notes (and frequently summarizes) key studies, and gives some evaluation of major printed editions. A full index of names concludes the volume. This handbook is especially useful for students and scholars who are not primarily interested in palaeography or textual criticism but need information on the transmission of a particular text. Those in need of a more general discussion of the transmission of the ancient classics should consult Reynolds's earlier work, *Scribes and Scholars* (entry 324).

324. Reynolds, L. D., and Nigel Wilson. **Scribes and Scholars: A Guide to the Transmission of Greek and Latin Literature**. 3d ed. Oxford, England: Clarendon Press, 1991. 321pp. ISBN 0-19-872145-5; 0-19-872146-3pa. LC 90-41300.

Designed for beginning graduate students, this work is the only accessible introduction in English to the transmission of the classics from antiquity to the modern era. Reynolds and Wilson describe the nature of the ancient manuscript book and its copying, editing, and preservation from antiquity through the Renaissance. They also discuss the editing of printed editions of the classics during the Renaissance and later periods and introduce the reader to the rudiments of textual criticism. They cover many of the high points in the history of classical scholarship. Their notes provide extensive references to the scholarly literature. Reynolds and Wilson offer an exceptionally lively and readable account of a subject too often considered dry and technical.

325. Sear, David R. **Greek Coins and Their Values**. London: Seaby, 1978-1979. 2v. ISBN 0-900652-46-2(v.1); 0-900652-50-0(v.2). LC 79-309601.

Aimed at hobbyists, this work is also useful for those with a more serious interest in Greek coins or history. Sear covers Greek coinage from its beginnings down to the time of the Roman conquest. The first volume covers the Greek coins of Europe (the northern shore of the Mediterranean from Spain to Greece), while the second deals with the coinage of Greek cities in Asia and North Africa. Both volumes have essentially the same front matter: a brief history of Greek coins, a discussion of coin types, the principal deities found on Greek coins, weight standards and denominations, the dating of Greek coins, a bibliography, and a glossary. Sear arranges the actual catalogs geographically. Under each city he makes entries for every distinct coin known to have been issued. Entries include a detailed description, dates, references to standard works on Greek coins, and an approximate value. The values, which are ephemeral, can be ignored. There are many illustrations. Each volume has a detailed index that includes geographical names, rulers, and deities. Sear is useful for identifying coins and finding information about them. Those who seek a more connected history of Greek coins rather than a catalog should use Jenkins (entry 320) instead.

326. Sear, David R. **Greek Imperial Coins and Their Values: The Local Coinages of the Roman Empire**. London: Seaby, 1982. 636pp. ISBN 0-900652-59-4. LC 82-145157.

In this work Sear lists and describes coins issued by the Greek cities of the Eastern Roman Empire. His introductory material includes discussion of the types of coins and the inscriptions of Greek imperial coins, their denominations and marks of value, and their dating. There is also a short bibliography. Sear divides the catalog into three parts: the actual Greek imperial coinage (chronologically by emperor from Augustus to Diocletian); the quasi-autonomous coinages of Greek cities (arranged geographically); and "contemporary coinage," the coins issued by independent kingdoms and client states of the empire. The 6,034 numbered entries include detailed descriptions of the coins, their dates of issue, references to the standard works on ancient Greek numismatics, and values. Many illustrations accompany the text. A list of Greek mints, several maps, and a selective index conclude the work. Sear is a useful reference both for coin collectors and scholars.

327. Sear, David R. **Roman Coins and Their Values**. 4th ed., rev. London: Seaby, 1988. 388pp. ISBN 0-900652-985. LC 89-135362.

A standard work on Roman coins, Sear's catalog covers both the republican and imperial eras. The extensive introduction includes discussion of the denominations of Roman coins, reverse types, mints and mint marks, and the dating of coins. The catalog is organized chronologically. It contains 4,412 entries ranging from the earliest known Roman coinage to Anastasius I (A.D. 491-518). Entries include a full description, date, bibliographical references, and estimated value. Sear provides many illustrations and a bibliography. His index is selective but adequate. For treatment of Greek coinage under the empire, one should consult his companion volume (entry 326). Those who want a history of Roman coinage rather than a catalog of coins will prefer Sutherland (entry 328) or Carson (entry 317).

328. Sutherland, C. H. V. **Roman Coins**. New York: Putnam, 1974. 311pp. (World of Numismatics). ISBN 0-399-11239-1. LC 73-81400.

Sutherland, an eminent British numismatist, provides a general history of Roman coins from the earliest known issues of the republic through the reign of Romulus Augustulus (A.D. 476). The broad historical narrative gives attention both to technical and artistic developments in Roman coinage. Many illustrations accompany the text. The work is suitable for students and general readers as well as numismatists and historians. It includes a brief bibliography, a glossary, and a general index. Although Sutherland offers the best overall account of Roman coins, Carson (entry 317) supplies a more recent and more detailed history of imperial coinage. Those who want information on specific coins might also consult Sear's work (entry 327).

329. Thompson, Edward Maunde. **A Handbook of Greek and Latin Palaeography**. 3d ed. London: K. Paul, Trench, Trübner, 1906; repr., Chicago: Ares, 1980. (International Scientific Series). 361pp. LC 11-513.

330. Thompson, Edward Maunde. **An Introduction to Greek and Latin Palaeography**. Oxford, England: Clarendon Press, 1912; repr., New York: Burt Franklin, 1973. 600pp. LC 13-9740.

These two works by Thompson, who was for many years Director and Principal Librarian of the British Museum, have long been the standard manuals on the subject for English-speaking students. Though now dated, they remain useful. For Greek palaeography, Thompson is still the only general manual available in English. The *Handbook* first covers a number of general topics: the Greek and Latin alphabets, writing materials, the forms of books in antiquity, shorthand and cryptography, abbreviations, and numerals. Then a series of chapters surveys Greek and Latin scripts of antiquity and the middle ages. Thompson provides many examples of the various scripts. There are a bibliography and index.

The *Introduction* is actually an expanded version of the *Handbook*. It generally follows the same plan as the earlier work, but includes much more material. In particular, the *Introduction* has more and better illustrations of the ancient scripts than does the *Handbook*. Its bibliography is also fuller. While Bischoff's authoritative treatment of Latin palaeography (entry 314a) to some extent supersedes Thompson, there is no more current manual available in English for Greek palaeography.

331. Turner, E. G. **Greek Papyri: An Introduction**. Rev. ed. Oxford, England: Clarendon Press, 1980. 225pp. ISBN 0-19-814841-0. LC 80-40987.

Aimed at students of the classics and the interested lay reader, Turner's classic work provides an eminently readable overview of papyrology. He covers successively the nature of books and writing in antiquity, the history of papyrology as a discipline, the editing of papyri, and the importance of papyri both for social and cultural history and for the study of Greek literature. Several maps, an extensive bibliographical apparatus, and an index of names complete the book. In spite of Gallo's more recent handbook (entry 318), Turner remains the basic work for English readers. Those who are interested primarily in documentary papyri and can read Italian might also consult with profit O. Montevecchi, *La Papirologia*, rev. ed. (Milan: Vita e Pensiero, 1988).

332. West, Martin L. **Textual Criticism and Editorial Technique Applicable to Greek and Latin Texts**. Stuttgart, Germany: B. G. Teubner, 1973. 155pp. ISBN 3-519-07402-8; 3-519-07401-Xpa. LC 73-164029.

Those interested in how modern editions of the classics are constructed will find West's handbook enlightening. In it he provides effective guidance to would-be editors and to readers of critical editions who wish to make use of the apparatus. The first part of the work, which is devoted to textual transmission, gives considerable attention to the common types of errors found in ancient and medieval manuscripts. West also discusses how relationships between manuscripts are established. The second part deals with the mechanics of editing a text: preparation for the task and the presentation of the edition (construction of the preface and critical apparatus). A final section provides sample editions of several passages with discussion of the problems involved. Reading West will give one a keen awareness of the basis and limitations of modern editions.

✓ 333. Woodhead, A. Geoffrey. **The Study of Greek Inscriptions**. 2d ed. New York: Cambridge University Press, 1981; repr., Norman: University of Oklahoma Press, 1992. 150pp. ISBN 0-521-23188-4; 0-521-29860-1pa. LC 80-41198.

Aimed at students of the classics and professional scholars who need an overview of Greek epigraphy, Woodhead is the standard introduction to the field for readers of English. He surveys all aspects of this highly technical subject in a clear and readable fashion. His chapters cover such topics as editorial conventions in printed editions of inscriptions, the Greek alphabet, the classification and dating of inscriptions, restorations, squeezes and photographs, inscriptions and the history of Greek art, epigraphical publications, and miscellaneous information (numbers, chronology, etc.). The chapter on epigraphical publications is especially useful; it provides an excellent guide to sources of bibliography and the major *corpora* of published Greek inscriptions.

History of Scholarship and the Classical Tradition

✓ 334. Highet, Gilbert. **The Classical Tradition: Greek and Roman Influences on Western Literature**. New York: Oxford University Press, 1949. 763pp. LC 49-11655.

A well-known and frequently reprinted book, *The Classical Tradition* provides a guide to the influence of the classics on subsequent Western literature from the early Middle Ages through the early twentieth century. Within a broad chronological framework, Highet devotes chapters to various periods, topics, genres, and, occasionally, to important authors. His eminently readable narrative shows wide learning. While Highet covers most topics in summary fashion, his notes and bibliography furnish excellent leads for further study. This book is a good first choice for anyone seeking general information on the literary and cultural influence of the classics. The full index makes for interesting browsing in itself; some of the less probable entries include: "corpses on stage," "skunkery," and "X, signing with."

✓335. Pfeiffer, Rudolf. **History of Classical Scholarship from the Beginnings to the End of the Hellenistic Age**. Oxford, England: Clarendon Press, 1968. 310pp. ISBN 0-19-814342-7. LC 68-112031.

✓336. Pfeiffer, Rudolf. **History of Classical Scholarship from 1300 to 1850**. Oxford, England: Clarendon Press, 1976. 213pp. ISBN 0-19-814364-8. LC 77-363045.

Pfeiffer, a distinguished Hellenist, is the first writer since Sandys (entry 337) to attempt a history of classical scholarship on such a scale. His first volume offers a magisterial treatment of the origins of classical scholarship among the ancient Greeks. Its early chapters discuss the beginnings of literary criticism in classical Greece. The bulk of the work, however, is devoted to the scholars of the Hellenistic age, especially those of third- and second-century B.C. Alexandria. Although Greek science is not neglected, the central focus remains literary scholarship, especially the editing and interpreting of texts. Pfeiffer's work is indispensable for anyone interested in the history of Greek scholarship or the early transmission of Greek literature and largely supersedes Sandys's treatment of this period. It is likely to be slow going for the nonspecialist, because it is often technical and includes much untranslated Greek.

Pfeiffer skips over late antiquity and the Middle Ages to begin his second volume with the Renaissance. This part of his history, although no less scholarly, is much more accessible to the lay reader. In it Pfeiffer surveys the high points of classical scholarship from the time of Petrarch through 1850. He is highly selective and tends to focus on major figures, such as Lorenzo Valla, Richard Bentley, and F. A. Wolf. Here Pfeiffer serves to supplement and correct, rather than replace, Sandys. Both volumes include detailed general indexes.

✓337. Sandys, John Edwin. **A History of Classical Scholarship**. Cambridge, England: University Press, 1908-1921; repr., New York: Hafner, 1967. 3d ed. (v.1 only). 3v.

Sandys remains the standard comprehensive history of classical scholarship. His magisterial work covers the whole field from the sixth century B.C. to the end of the nineteenth century. Sandys covers virtually every aspect: scribes, editors, textual and literary critics, grammarians, historians, archaeologists, and antiquarians. *History* is of value not only to classicists but also to anyone interested in European intellectual history and the history of manuscripts, books, and printing. The first volume, which covers antiquity and the Middle Ages, was twice revised by the author. The other volumes remain as they originally appeared in 1908. Each includes a detailed table of contents and an extensive index. Sandys's treatment of scholarship through the Alexandrian era has been largely superseded by Pfeiffer (entry 335). The rest of the work, although showing its age, is still without rival. The second volume of Pfeiffer (entry 336) and the brief history by Wilamowitz-Moellendorff (entry 338) supplement it and correct some details, but in no way challenge its preeminence.

338. Wilamowitz-Moellendorff, U. von. **History of Classical Scholarship**. Translated by Alan Harris. Edited by Hugh Lloyd-Jones. Baltimore, MD: Johns Hopkins University Press, 1982. 189pp. ISBN 0-8018-2801-5. LC 81-48182.

Wilamowitz-Moellendorff, the preeminent Hellenist of the nineteenth and early twentieth centuries, published his *Geschichte der Philologie* in 1921. In it he covers the high points of the history of classical scholarship from antiquity to the early years of the twentieth century. Wilamowitz-Moellendorff covers less and offers less detail than Sandys's massive three-volume work (entry 337). However, he takes a more critical approach to the subject and does so with unique authority. The English edition includes a substantial introduction and explanatory and bibliographical notes by Lloyd-Jones, himself a distinguished Greek scholar and former Regius Professor at Oxford. An index of names is also provided.

Miscellaneous Works

338a. Adkins, Lesley, and Roy A. Adkins. **Handbook to Life in Ancient Rome**. New York: Facts on File, 1994. 404pp. ISBN 0-8160-2755-2. LC 93-11213.

Similar in scope to Sandys's *Companion to Latin Studies* (entry 349), but on a less heroic scale, this new work provides a handy companion for contemporary students of ancient Rome. The authors attempt to cover all aspects of Roman civilization from the founding of the city through the fifth century A.D. in a series of nine thematic chapters: republic and empire; military affairs; geography of the Roman world; towns and countryside; travel and trade; written evidence; religion; economy and industry; and everyday life. In each chapter the reader will find numerous concise entries that provide information on people, places, institutions, and the material culture of the ancient Romans. The *Handbook* is especially strong on practical aspects of everyday life. Many lists are provided; these cover, for example, emperors, literary authors, gods and goddesses, and names of Roman legions and fleets. Numerous maps and illustrations accompany the clearly written text. The many bibliographical notes are both up to date and well suited to the needs of students and general readers. The *Handbook*'s wide scope and careful organization make it an exceptionally useful ready-reference source; it would be a good first choice for most queries on ancient Roman civilization. A very detailed index rounds out the volume.

339. Berger, Adolf. **Encyclopedic Dictionary of Roman Law**. Philadelphia: American Philosophical Society, 1953. pp.333-809. (*Transactions of the American Philosophical Society*, n.s., v.43, pt.2). LC 53-7641.

Of interest to legal historians as well as classicists, this work is a guide to the technical terminology of Roman law. Berger defines and discusses each term. Many articles include references to the scholarly literature. Berger provides numerous cross-references for related entries. An English-Latin glossary facilitates access for those interested in a particular legal concept but who lack the Latin term.

340. Crane, Gregory, ed. **Perseus**. Version 1.0. New Haven, CT: Yale University Press, 1992. 1 CD-ROM disc, 1 videodisc, and 1 manual. ISBN 0-300-05087-9 (CD-ROM); 0-300-05086-0 (videodisc); 0-300-05088-7 (manual).

An award-winning multimedia database, *Perseus* is both an outstanding electronic reference source for ancient Greek civilization and a library of electronic versions of classical Greek texts. The database is divided into five sections. The historical overview provides an outline history of Greece that primarily covers the sixth to fourth centuries B.C. and gives pride of place to Athens. The art and archaeology section contains descriptions of various archaeological sites and of individual works of art. It includes many site plans and illustrations. The indexes to this section offer access by site and by artistic medium (architecture, sculpture, pottery, and coins). An atlas provides maps of Greece and the eastern Mediterranean; the software allows one to display different types of information and to zoom in on particular places. The tools and reference works section includes an encyclopedia of Greek civilization, which consists of brief descriptive articles; access is provided by alphabetical and subject indexes. A Greek-English lexicon also resides in this section. The final section contains classical Greek texts, presently including the works of Aeschylus, Apollodorus, Herodotus, Homer, Pausanias, Pindar, Plutarch, Sophocles, and Thucydides. Facing Greek and English versions of each text are displayed; hypertext links enable readers to consult the Greek-English lexicon while reading. A biographical sketch is also supplied for each author. Future versions containing additional material are planned. At the present time, *Perseus* can only be run on Macintosh computers. Further information on *Perseus* is available through the Perseus Project gopher site (entry 613).

341. Cristofani, Mauro, ed. **Dizionario della civiltà etrusca**. Firenze, Italy: Giunti Martello, 1985. 340pp. (Archeologia). LC 85-198607.

The only dictionary of Etruscan civilization available, Cristofani directs his work toward the student and the interested layperson rather than the scholar. Its compact and informative articles cover every aspect of Etruscan culture. There are entries for people, places, objects, and topics. Cristofani has also included entries on major museum collections of Etruscan artifacts and on modern pioneers of Etruscan studies, such as George Dennis. A number of authors, mostly Italian, have contributed to the dictionary; all articles are signed. Many well-chosen illustrations accompany the text. A timeline at the back of the volume offers a comparative overview of Etruscan and other Mediterranean cultures from the fifteenth century B.C. to 200 B.C. The lack of bibliographies and an index is the chief defect of this work. Otherwise, it provides an attractive reference work on this mysterious culture.

342. Fraser, P. M., and E. Matthews, eds. **A Lexicon of Greek Personal Names**. Oxford, England: Clarendon Press, 1987- . ISBN 0-19-864222-9(v.1); 0-19-814990-5(v.2). LC 87-12344.

Intended as a replacement for the nineteenth-century compilation of Wilhelm Pape (entry 347), this work is being produced by an international team of scholars under the sponsorship of the British Academy. When completed it will include all attested Greek personal names, with the exception of most names from mythology and Greek epic poetry. Most, though not all, foreign names in Greek are also excluded. The overall arrangement of the lexicon is geographical; each volume is devoted to a particular region of the Greek world. Two volumes have appeared thus far, the first covering the Aegean islands, Cyprus, and Cyrenaica, and the second covering Attica. Within each volume entries are arranged alphabetically. The same names will often be found in more than one volume. Entries cite the ancient attestations and give approximate dates for each occurrence. Because this work is highly technical and presents the names in Greek characters, it is chiefly of use to graduate students and professional scholars.

✓343. Halporn, James W., Martin Ostwald, and Thomas G. Rosenmeyer. **The Meters of Greek and Latin Poetry**. Rev. ed. Norman, OK: University of Oklahoma Press, 1980; repr., Indianapolis: Hackett, 1994. 137pp. ISBN 0-8061-1558-0. LC 79-6718.

Since it first appeared in 1963, this has been the standard handbook on metrics for English-speaking students of Greek and Latin poetry. The book is divided into two independent sections, one on Greek, the other on Latin meters. Material is repeated as necessary, so that those interested in only one language need refer only to that half. Each unit begins with introductory chapters that discuss the basic terms and concepts of the meters of quantitative verse. Each then proceeds through the basic meters of epic, elegiac, dramatic, and lyric poetry. The presentation is reasonably clear, with many examples given. A glossary of technical terms and a table of meters appear at the end of the volume. There are also indexes of Greek and Latin authors cited in the text. This is a good introductory work on a sometimes complex subject.

344. LaRue, Rodrigue, Gilles Vincent, and Bruno St.-Onge. **Clavis Scriptorum Graecorum et Latinorum = Répertoire des auteurs grecs et latins = Repertoire of Greek and Latin Authors = Repertorium der griechischen und lateinischen Autoren**. Trois-Rivières, Québec: Universitè du Québec à Trois-Rivières, 1985. 4v. ISBN 2-89125-015-X. LC 86-672003.

Essentially an authority list or thesaurus, this manual provides a list of "standard" forms of the names of Greek and Latin authors. It was originally devised to assist its authors in compiling computerized bibliographical databases. *Clavis* includes approximately 21,000 names of Greek and Latin writers from antiquity through the Renaissance. In addition, it contains titles of anonymous works and a number of subject headings (mostly based on those found in *L'Année philologique* [entry 26]). Author and title entries include the standardized form of name or title, date, language, indication of genres, and variant forms of name. The subject entries, which are less well thought out, provide the selected term and its variants. The fourth volume is an index; it must be used for access by variant forms of name, because cross-references are not made in the text. While this work may be of some value to other compilers of computer databases, most will find it useful chiefly for identifying the more obscure or problematic authors.

345. Matz, David. **Greek and Roman Sport: A Dictionary of Athletes and Events from the Eighth Century B.C. to the Third Century A.D.** Jefferson, NC: McFarland, 1991. 169pp. ISBN 0-89950-558-9. LC 90-53509.

This work, the only one of its type for Greek and Roman sports, is handy for ready-reference. Matz's introductory material includes an outline history of the subject and a brief survey of ancient sources and modern works. His bibliography has some curious omissions. The dictionary, which is arranged alphabetically, includes entries for athletes, events, various Greek and Latin technical terms relating to athletics, and specific athletic games and festivals. The length of entries varies. Biographical articles range from a line or two to several pages and often cite primary sources. Other entries tend to offer a brief identification of a place, event, or term. Several special essays are appended to the dictionary that expand on some of the individual entries or pull together in one place materials from related entries. Matz also provides a number of lists (drawn from the ancient sources) of athletes and horses. A glossary of places identifies ancient places by type (city, island, etc.) and locates them. A subject index concludes the volume.

✓346. Nicholas, Barry. **An Introduction to Roman Law**. Oxford, England: Clarendon Press, 1962. 282pp. ISBN 0-19-876003-5. LC 62-4467.

For more than 30 years Nicholas's frequently reprinted work has been the standard introduction to the subject for students in the English-speaking world. An introductory section covers the history and sources of Roman law. Subsequent sections cover various types of law: of persons, of property, of obligations, and succession. Nicholas's focus is on private law, although he occasionally touches on constitutional and other public aspects of the law. The book is well organized and as clear and readable as a work on this complex subject can be. The selective bibliography, though now dated, will direct the reader to the most important fundamental works on Roman law. There is also a good subject index.

347. Pape, W. **Wörterbuch der griechischen Eigennamen**. 3. Aufl. Neu bearb. von Gustav Eduard Benseler. Braunschweig, Germany: Friedrich Vieweg, 1863-1870; repr., Graz, Austria: Akademische Druck- und Verlagsanstalt, 1959. (Handwörterbuch der griechischen Sprache, Bd.3). 2v.

Often referred to as Pape-Benseler, this work is a dictionary of Greek proper names. It is compiled chiefly from literary sources, unlike the Oxford *Lexicon of Greek Personal Names* (entry 342), which emphasizes documentary sources over literary ones. Pape-Benseler also includes geographical names. Each entry includes the name and citations of occurrences. Although dated, Pape-Benseler remains useful and will not be entirely superseded even when the Oxford *Lexicon* is completed.

348. Rosumek, Peter. **Index des périodiques dépouillés dans la Collection de bibliographie classique et dans la Revue des comptes rendus des ouvrages relatifs á l'antiquité classique (publiées par J. Marouzeau) et index des leurs sigles**. Paris: Les Belles Lettres, 1982. 76pp. ISBN 2-25190305-4.

Published as a supplement to volume 51 of *L'Année philologique* (entry 26), this work lists some 1,857 periodicals that have been cited in *L'Année* and its predecessors Lambrino (entry 14) and Marouzeau (entry 15). Rosumek arranges the titles in an alphabetical list. He provides the full title, place of publication, and abbreviation used by *L'Année*. An index of abbreviations refers back to the numbered entries. While Rosumek's compilation can be useful for identifying periodical abbreviations, it has several drawbacks. He has taken his citations from *L'Année* exactly as they appear, mistakes and all. Places of publication in particular are not always current or accurate. Rosumek's decision to include only those abbreviations used in his source also reduces the value of his index. There are variant forms of abbreviation for many of the periodicals, and those found in *L'Année* are not always the most common. Wellington (entry 351), whose guide to abbreviations also appeared in 1982, covers more than twice as many works and attempts (with considerable success) to note all variant forms of abbreviations.

349. Sandys, John Edwin, ed. **A Companion to Latin Studies**. 3d ed. New York: Cambridge University Press, 1935; repr., New York: Hafner, 1968. 891pp. LC 26-5843.

Designed as a *vade mecum* for students of Latin, this venerable work represents the combined efforts of 27 notable British scholars of the early twentieth century. Its articles cover virtually every aspect of Roman civilization: the geography and ethnology of Italy, fauna and flora, an outline of Roman history, religion and mythology, law, finance, population, social organization, industries and commerce, roads and travel, weights and measures, money, the Roman army and navy, art, literature, philosophy, and natural science. Articles are also provided on various specialized fields of study such as epigraphy, palaeography, textual criticism, language, meter, and the history of scholarship. While most of the material is now badly dated, much is still of value if used with some care. Sandys remains a handy source of general information on such topics as flora and fauna, weights and measures, and money. The work's four indexes cover ancient peoples and persons, geographical names, scholars and modern writers, and Latin words.

350. Temporini, Hildegard, and Wolfgang Haase, eds. **Aufstieg und Niedergang der römischen Welt: Geschichte und Kultur Roms im Spiegel der neueren Forschung**. Berlin: W. de Gruyter, 1972- . LC 72-83058.

The ANRW began life as a festschrift in honor of the 75th birthday of the German ancient historian Joseph Vogt, and has since mushroomed into a publishing venture rivalling Pauly-Wissowa (entry 225) in size, if not scope. Approximately 70 volumes have appeared to date, with many more in preparation. This ongoing project, which surveys virtually all aspects of the Roman world, will include contributions by more than 1,000 scholars from around the world when completed. The ANRW consists of three parts. The first, which covers Rome from its origins to the end of the republic, is complete in four volumes. The part that deals with the principate (the early empire) is still in progress, with more than 60 volumes now in print. The third part, which is concerned with late antiquity, is still in preparation.

Each part of the ANRW includes six sections: political history, law, religion, language and literature, philosophy and the sciences, and the arts. Within each area numerous articles, variously written in English, French, German, or Italian, cover major and minor topics. Articles include mainly surveys and reviews, although many contain the results of original research as well. All of the articles are long and scholarly; some are nearly book length. Many include their own tables of contents. Quality varies from item to item, but is generally good.

While the ANRW is an extremely valuable resource for all areas of Roman studies, it has several significant drawbacks. Its sheer size makes it difficult to use; a guide volume with tables of contents for the whole work and some form of index are badly needed. This problem is exacerbated by the lack of a coherent overall plan, which results in some volumes being more like a collection of loosely related articles than part of a well-designed handbook. Another major problem is the time lag from writing to publication. Because of the slow pace of production, some articles languish in press for more than a decade and are already dated when they appear in print; this problem is often not made clear to users.

351. Wellington, Jean Susorney. **Dictionary of Bibliographic Abbreviations Found in the Scholarship of Classical Studies and Related Disciplines**. Westport, CT: Greenwood Press, 1983. 393pp. ISBN 0-313-23523-6. LC 82-21068.

Classical studies boasts more than its share of abbreviations. In addition to idiosyncrasy and inconsistency for their own sake, one must deal with the varying stylistic conventions of scholars and editors working in many different languages. As a result, a single journal is sometimes represented by a half-dozen different abbreviations, while at times the same abbreviation may refer to three or four different journals. Wellington's book provides the means to identify the vast majority of these abbreviations. She includes all the abbreviations that she could find for 4,427 items. These include primarily serial titles, *corpora*, and standard works. Coverage of congresses, festschriften, and papyrological publications is limited. Abbreviations for ancient authors are not included; for these see the preliminaries to Liddell-Scott-Jones (entry 455) and the *Oxford Latin Dictionary* (entry 452). For festschriften one should consult Rounds (entry 40), and for papyri the *Checklist of Editions of Greek and Latin Papyri, Ostraca, and Tablets* (entry 104).

Wellington divides her dictionary into two sections. The first lists abbreviations in alphabetical sequence, with supplementary lists for Greek and Cyrillic (these two are confusingly mislabeled). The second section gives full bibliographical descriptions of the items. Wellington provides much more extensive coverage than Rosumek (entry 348) and is by far the better guide.

352. Whibley, Leonard. **A Companion to Greek Studies**. 4th ed. New York: Cambridge University Press, 1931; repr., New York: Hafner, 1968. 790pp. LC 33-3397.

Similar in design to Sandys's *Companion to Latin Studies* (entry 349), this work contains articles by some 40 prominent British scholars of the early twentieth century. Virtually every aspect of Greek civilization is covered: geography; ethnology; fauna; flora; history; literature; philosophy; science; art; mythology and religion; law; finance; population; commerce and industry; weights and measures; money; war; ships; the calendar; family; birth, marriage, and death; education; books and writing; the position of women; dress; daily life; houses and furniture; and medicine. There are also articles on such topics as Greek dialects, epigraphy, palaeography, textual criticism, meter, and the history of scholarship. In addition to a detailed table of contents, the book includes four indexes that cover ancient peoples and persons, geographical names, scholars and modern writers, and Greek words.

In its day, this manual provided the basic background material and technical knowledge needed by students of Greek literature. Although much of its contents are now very dated, Whibley is still a good source for some types of information. For example, it is a handy reference for such things as weights and measures, calendars, and flora and fauna of the ancient world. But it should always be used with care.

CHAPTER  9

BIOGRAPHICAL SOURCES

A number of different types of works will be found in this chapter. The first part includes dictionaries and other primarily textual works that provide biographical data. The dictionaries tend to deal with the famous figures of antiquity: political leaders, generals, artists, writers, and the like. These titles will accommodate the needs of most people seeking biographical information on the ancients. Prosopographies, on the other hand, cover minor officials, soldiers, and ordinary folk, as well as the famous. They are often based on the more esoteric primary sources, such as inscriptions and papyri. For the most part these works will interest specialists. Several dictionaries and handbooks treating the lives of classical scholars are also listed in this part.

The second part is devoted to collections of portraits. These will be of use to anyone who wishes to find a picture of a particular person from classical antiquity. Some of these works also include basic biographical information.

Biographical Dictionaries and Prosopographies

353. Alföldy, Géza. **Fasti Hispanienses: Senatorische Reichsbeamte und Of-fiziere in den spanischen Provinzen des Römischen Reiches von Augustus bis Diokletian**. Wiesbaden, Germany: Franz Steiner, 1969. 335pp.

The first part of this work (pp. 1-190) consists of prosopographical lists of imperial officials (governors, *iuridici*, legates, tribunes, etc.) in the Roman provinces of Hispania Citerior, Lusitania, and Baetica. The lists are arranged by office and subarranged chronologically. Entries in the prosopography range from about a half page to several pages and give the full name of the individual, date of his office in Spain, and date of consulship, if held. Then literary and epigraphic sources are quoted. The body of the entry discusses the person's family connections and political and military activities, with emphasis on activities in Spain. Extensive bibliographical references are included. An index of personal names provides alphabetical access. There are also indexes of geographical names, ancient sources, and offices and titles. Alföldy is a good supplement to the *Prosopographia Imperii Romani* (entries 388-389) for Romans who served in Spain.

✓ 354. Avery, Catherine B., ed. **The New Century Handbook of Leaders of the Classical World**. New York: Appleton-Century-Crofts, 1972. 393pp. ISBN 0-390-66948-2. LC 71-189007.

Drawn from the larger *New Century Classical Handbook* (entry 212), this work offers short biographies of generals, politicians, kings, queens, and emperors of the Greek and Roman world. Rulers of neighboring states, such as the Persian empire, are included also. Articles range in length from a paragraph to several pages depending on the person's relative importance. Most provide an adequate account of the subject's life and activities. Lack of bibliographies is a major weakness. All entries include a guide to pronunciation. While there is no index, Avery has supplied plentiful cross-references. Those who want a general biographical dictionary that includes cultural as well as military and political figures will find Bowder's two works (entries 357-358) better suited to their needs. Many of the individuals found in Avery are also discussed in more general handbooks and encyclopedias, such as the *Oxford Classical Dictionary* (entry 218).

355. Berve, Helmut. **Das Alexanderreich auf prosopographischer Grundlage**. München: C. H. Beck, 1926; repr., Salem, NH: Ayer, 1988. 2v.

The second volume of Berve's work is a prosopography of more than 800 individuals associated with Alexander the Great. These persons are listed alphabetically (in the Greek alphabet). Entries, which are numbered sequentially, range from a paragraph to several pages. Each provides a brief biography with full citation of primary sources and a bibliography of modern studies. A number of people whom Berve believes to have been incorrectly associated with Alexander have been treated in a separate section at the end of the volume. Although dated, Berve is a useful resource for the period of Alexander the Great.

356. Birley, Anthony R. **The Fasti of Roman Britain**. Oxford, England: Clarendon Press, 1981. 476pp. ISBN 0-19-814821-6. LC 80-41709.

Birley, one of the foremost authorities on Roman Britain, covers the higher Roman officials (e.g., governors, military commanders, procurators) in Britain from its subjugation in 43 A.D. to the expulsion of the Roman governors in 409. After a brief general introduction (which provides a good overview of the senatorial career under the empire), Birley presents biographies of individual officials arranged by office and subarranged chronologically. The biographies are compact and readable. Each entry includes information about its subject's career, family, and personality. There are full references to, and often extensive quotations from, the primary sources, and many references to modern studies. Access is facilitated by several indexes. The index of persons highlights in capitals those who are given biographical entries in the text. There are also geographical and general indexes and an index of sources quoted *in extenso*. Birley is an excellent source for information about any Roman with a British connection.

✓ 357. Bowder, Diana, ed. **Who Was Who in the Greek World, 776 B.C.-30 B.C.** Ithaca, NY: Cornell University Press, 1982. 227pp. ISBN 0-8014-1538-1. LC 82-71594.

Bowder offers biographical sketches of the major historical and cultural figures of the Greek world from the traditional date of the first Olympiad to completion of the Roman conquest of the Greek world. Legendary characters of the early period are largely omitted, although the introduction discusses a few of the more important ones. Some Greek notables of the Roman period (30 B.C.-A.D. 476) appear in Bowder's companion volume for the Roman world (entry 358). Entries are brief and factual; nearly all include one or more bibliographical references for further study. The work is also well illustrated with many contemporary portraits drawn from coins and works of art. Cross-references lead the reader from variant forms of a name to the proper entry. There is also an index of persons mentioned who do not receive an entry of their own. A glossary of technical terms, several maps, selected genealogical tables, and a short general bibliography are provided to aid the user.

358. Bowder, Diana, ed. **Who Was Who in the Roman World: 753 B.C.-A.D. 476**. Ithaca, NY: Cornell University Press, 1980. 256pp. ISBN 0-8014-1358-3. LC 80-67821.

This companion volume to *Who Was Who in the Greek World* (entry 357) provides similar coverage for the ancient Romans. It includes nearly all major historical and cultural figures of the Roman world, which has been broadly defined to include the entire empire, and non-Romans who had a significant impact on Roman history. Overlap with the companion work has been limited, so that both must be used for full coverage. Entries are brief (one or two paragraphs on average) and present basic dates and facts. As in the companion volume, nearly every entry has some bibliographical references to works by or about the subject; these are well chosen. Whenever possible, ancient portraits drawn from coins or sculpture illustrate the entries. A chronological table, genealogical tables of the imperial dynasties, numerous maps, and a glossary of frequently used technical terms aid the reader. There is also an index of people mentioned without receiving full entries of their own. Bowder's two volumes and Radice (entry 390) will cover most routine biographical queries.

359. Bradford, Alfred S. **A Prosopography of Lacedaemonians from the Death of Alexander the Great, 323 B.C., to the Sack of Sparta by Alaric, A.D. 396**. München: C. H. Beck, 1977. 499pp. (Vestigia, Bd.27). ISBN 3-406-04797-1. LC 78-310194.

A continuation of Poralla's *Prosopography of Lacedaimonians* (entry 387), Bradford's work extends coverage to the destruction of Sparta in A.D. 396. Bradford includes citizens of Sparta and members of the families and households of citizens. He also lists foreigners with honorary Spartan citizenship. Like Poralla, Bradford uses an alphabetical arrangement (names are in the Greek alphabet). Individuals of the same name are distinguished by number; various subarrangements are used according to what is known about each person. Cross-references are provided from unused forms, although they do not always make clear the chosen form of entry. Bradford makes no attempt to compose complete biographies for major figures; instead, he offers a summary acccount and refers the reader to published biographies for further information. The standard format of entries is name—sources—biography. The sources consist chiefly of contemporary inscriptions, although literary sources make an occasional appearance. Modern studies are cited in a few entries. The biographical portion tends to concentrate on family connections and offices held. Most entries are very brief, because most of the subjects are known from a single inscription.

Appendices offer lists that bring together related entries (e.g., eponymous officials) and stemmata of the royal houses. Poralla and Bradford are specialized sources best used for obscure Spartans; Bowder (entry 357), the *Oxford Classical Dictionary* (entry 218), or Pauly-Wissowa (entry 225) are better choices for well-known Spartans.

360. Briggs, Ward W., Jr., ed. **Biographical Dictionary of North American Classicists**. Westport, CT: Greenwood Press, 1994. 800pp. ISBN 0-313-24560-6. LC 94-4785.

Briggs and his 170 contributors (all classicists) provide biographical sketches of some 600 deceased classicists from the United States and Canada. Chronologically these individuals range from the seventeenth century to the present; the most recent subject died in 1993. The chief criterion for inclusion, apart from geography and death, was that the individual has made "some kind of significant contribution to the profession." This broad guideline has resulted in a work that includes all the household names along with a sizeable number of the now obscure. The work exhibits a tendency to keep skeletons in the closet; some biographies are less than candid. Often, entries for classicists from the recent past are written by former colleagues and students, which allows for personal knowledge but does not promote objectivity. Aside from this, the *Dictionary* is generally a useful and accurate work. Entries offer an outline of the scholar's career, a short biographical note, and a bibliography. There are also two introductory essays in which William Calder and Alexander McKay review the history of classical scholarship in the United States and Canada. Three indexes round out the volume; these provide access by date of birth, primary institutional affiliation, and the institution that granted each scholar his or her highest degree.

361. Briggs, Ward W., Jr., and William M. Calder III, eds. **Classical Scholarship: A Biographical Encyclopedia**. New York: Garland, 1990. 534pp. ISBN 0-8240-8448-9. LC 89-23294.

Not intended as a comprehensive biographical dictionary, this work aims at selective coverage of influential classicists. It presents accounts of the lives and work of some 50 scholars from C. G. Heyne (1729-1812) to Arnaldo Momigliano (1908-1987). Coverage is uneven, and the work is biased towards German scholars. French scholars in particular receive short shrift. All articles purportedly were written by scholars who are experts in their subject's field, although this is not always obvious. Each entry includes a bibliography of works by and about its subject. There is some variation in length and content of the articles and also in the completeness of the bibliographies. Arrangement is alphabetical, although a chronological listing of entries is provided to facilitate a historical approach. There is also a subject index. While this work brings together much information that is difficult to find elsewhere, it is hoped that a more comprehensive and balanced work will supersede it.

362. Broughton, T. Robert S. **The Magistrates of the Roman Republic**. Chico, CA: Scholars Press, 1984-1986. 3v. (Philological Monographs; no. 15). ISBN 0-89130-706-0(v.1); 0-89130-812-1(v.2); 0-89130-811-3(v.3). LC 84-23590.

The first two volumes are reprinted from the original edition (New York: American Philological Association, 1951-1952), while the third is a supplement including additions and corrections. A standard reference work for Roman historians since it first appeared, MRR provides information on all known Roman magistrates and officials from 509 B.C. to 31 B.C. Its arrangement is chronological, with offices listed in roughly descending order of importance. Each entry lists the incumbent for the year, summarizes his activities in office, and provides references to the relevant ancient evidence. There are occasional references to modern studies. The index of careers in the second volume provides alphabetical access to the work; each individual is listed alphabetically along with offices held and dates. While not primarily a biographical work, MRR is extremely useful for finding information about Romans of the republican period. It is somewhat cumbersome to consult, but, apart from Pauly-Wissowa (entry 225), it is the only readily available source on many of its subjects.

363. Bryant, Donald C., ed. **Ancient Greek and Roman Rhetoricians: A Biographical Dictionary**. Columbia, MO: Artcraft Press, 1968. 104pp. LC 70-1929.

Compiled for the Speech Association of America, this book was originally intended to be part of a comprehensive biographical dictionary of speech educators. Its contributors include both classicists and communications scholars. It covers theorists, critics, authors of treatises or textbooks, and teachers of speech, but not those who were merely performers or composers. Thus it includes Isocrates and Cicero but omits Demosthenes. Many of those listed are relatively obscure. Entries range from two or three sentences to a maximum of 600 words. Each identifies and dates its subject and highlights his rhetorical activities. Arrangement is alphabetical. There is a general bibliography at the beginning of the work; individual entries lack bibliographical references. The work is useful for ready-reference and is handy for speech and communications specialists with historical interests.

364. Buchwald, Wolfgang, Armin Hohlweg, and Otto Prinz. **Tusculum-Lexikon: griechischer und lateinischer Autoren des Altertums und des Mittelalters**. 3., neu bearb. und erw. Aufl. München: Artemis, 1982. 862pp. ISBN 3-7608-1641-X.

365. Buchwald, Wolfgang, Armin Hohlweg, and Otto Prinz. **Dictionnaire des auteurs grecs et latines de l'antiquité et du moyen âge**. Traduit et mis à jour par Jean Denis Berger et Jacques Billen. Turnhout, Belgium: Brepols, 1991. 887pp. ISBN 2-503-50016-1.

Tusculum-Lexikon covers Greek and Latin writers from antiquity through the Renaissance. One or two paragraphs offer essential biographical facts and discuss the scope of each author's work. These include references to editions of the author in the original language and sometimes to translations. Occasionally one or two secondary works are cited as well. The French translation essentially reproduces the content of the German original, with the addition of a few (chiefly French-language) items in the bibliographies. While there are equally good or better English-language sources for standard classical authors (e.g., Grant [entry 374] and Luce [entry 383]), *Tusculum-Lexikon* is useful for later Greek and Latin authors. It also includes articles on many of the more prominent classical scholars of the Middle Ages and Renaissance.

366. Cosenza, Mario Emilio. **Biographical and Bibliographical Dictionary of the Italian Humanists and of the World of Classical Scholarship in Italy, 1300-1800**. 2d ed. Boston: G. K. Hall, 1962-1967. 6v. LC 62-13227.

For those with a serious interest in the history of classical scholarship in Italy or in manuscripts and early printed editions of the classics, Cosenza's remarkable compilation is an invaluable source of information. Cosenza spent most of his scholarly life gathering the materials found in these volumes. He covers the Italian humanists and their patrons, other humanists who studied in Italy, copyists, owners and collectors of classical manuscripts, and users of classical texts (a broad classification that includes, among others, astrologers). Entries include both Latin and vernacular forms of names, a list of any known variants, dates of birth and death, cities in which the subject resided, a brief biographical sketch, a bibliography of the subject's works, and a review of his interests in the classics. When appropriate, entries also include a list of the individual's teachers and students. While there are inevitable lapses and omissions, this is a generally thorough and reliable work. Much of the biographical and bibliographical data supplied by Cosenza cannot be readily obtained from other reference sources.

Cosenza kept his material on index cards; these are photographically reproduced in the first four volumes of the dictionary. These handwritten entries are often cramped and difficult to read. In the fifth volume Cosenza provides summaries of the material in the earlier volumes. This synopsis is easier to use because it is reproduced from typescript, but omits many of the entries and much of the information from main listings. This volume also includes a selected bibliography of works on Italian humanism and the history of classical scholarship. The sixth volume is a supplement that includes additional entries in a second alphabetical sequence. While there is no index, Cosenza supplies numerous cross-references from variant forms of names.

367. Davies, J. K. **Athenian Propertied Families: 600-300 B.C.** Oxford, England: Clarendon Press, 1971. 653pp. ISBN 0-19814-273-0. LC 76-857878.

Although a highly specialized book concerning the relation of wealth and politics in classical Athens, Davies can be a valuable source of biographical information. The heart of the work is a prosopography of wealthy Athenians of the archaic and classical periods. It is arranged alphabetically (with the names in Greek alphabet); entries that correspond to names listed in Kirchner's *Prosopographia Attica* (entry 380) have Kirchner's number in the left margin. Davies tends to treat families in a single entry (that for earliest member listed), with cross-references from individual members. He has also provided indexes of names by *deme* (a political unit), primary sources that are cited, and subjects discussed. Entries focus on the financial affairs and political activities of their subjects. They provide numerous references to source materials and modern studies. There are also many genealogical tables. While primarily of interest to those doing in-depth research on the political and economic history of Athens, Davies provides a partial supplement to Kirchner's very dated work.

368. Della Corte, Francesco, ed. **Dizionario degli scrittori greci e latini**. Milano: Mazorati Editore, 1987. 3v. ISBN 88-280-0053-8.

Della Corte's dictionary covers Greek and Latin authors from the beginnings of Greek literature through the sixth century A.D. Major authors receive separate entries, while minor figures are covered in articles devoted to various genres, philosophical schools, and periods. The articles on individual authors include a biography, a discussion of the works, and a substantial bibliography. Those covering a genre or period also provide biographical and critical material on relevant authors, with a general bibliography at the end of the section. The articles, which tend to be fairly long, are by a variety of hands; all are signed. The content is generally good, but the bibliographies are the most valuable part of the work. Because the *Dizionario* treats so many authors under collective rubrics, it is best approached through the index of names. This also assures finding all the relevant material, because some authors are discussed in more than one place (e.g., Cicero is covered both in his own chapter and in the chapter on epistolography). Although there is no work on a comparable scale in English, those not fluent in Italian will be well served by Luce (entry 383) and Grant (entry 374).

369. Demougin, Ségolène. **Prosopographie des chevaliers romains julio-claudiens (43 av. J.-C.-70 ap. J.-C.).** Rome: Ecole française de Rome, 1992. 715pp. (Collection de l'Ecole française de Rome, 153). ISBN 2-7283-0248-7. LC 93-155994.

Demougin lists all known equestrians of the Julio-Claudian period. His 770 entries are arranged in chronological order and are numbered consecutively. An alphabetical list of names, accompanied by entry numbers, precedes the actual prosopography. Entries provide citations of primary sources and references to modern studies. These are followed by a brief discussion of the person's public career and family connections. Indexes of names and sources conclude the work. Not all of Demougin's subjects can be found in the *Prosopographia Imperii Romani* (entries 388-389) or Pauly-Wissowa (entry 225); his book provides a useful supplement to these works. There is some overlap with Devijver (entry 371).

370. Develin, Robert. **Athenian Officials, 684-321 B.C.** New York: Cambridge University Press, 1989. 556pp. ISBN 0-521-32880-2. LC 88-17765.

Develin's work consists of a year-by-year listing of known Athenian officials, subarranged by office. Some are well known; many are obscure. When available, the entry number from Kirchner's *Prosopographia Attica* is provided (see entry 380). Develin cites primary sources, which are chiefly epigraphical, and occasionally offers discussion of the individual and references to secondary works. The book has a very good index of persons and also an index of tribes and *demes*. It is mainly aimed at political historians, although it is useful for finding information on the more obscure Athenian politicians. Along with Davies (entry 367) it can be used to supplement the dated material in Kirchner.

371. Devijver, H. **Prosopographia Militarum Equestrium Quae Fuerunt ab Augusto ad Gallienum**. Louvain, Belgium: Leuven University Press, 1976- . (Symbolae Facultatis Litterarum et Philosophiae Lovanensis). ISBN 90-6186-046-6(v.1); 90-6186-056-3(v.2); 90-6186-091-1(v.3); 90-6186-234-5(v.4). LC 81-478673.

Devijver's ongoing work is an alphabetical listing of equestrian officers in the Roman army from the time of Augustus (27 B.C.) to Gallienus (died A.D. 268). The first three volumes comprise the basic work; the fourth, which appeared in 1987, is the first supplement. There are approximately 2,000 entries in the basic list. Each includes references to original source material (usually inscriptions and papyri) and to the modern secondary literature. The individual's *cursus* (sequence of military and civil offices held) and place of origin follow.

Entries range from a few lines to a couple of pages. The supplement provides a number of new entries and adds new material to many existing entries. Both the basic work and the supplement have full indexing. In addition to several name indexes and a subject index, there are several geographical indexes and indexes of emperors, gods and goddesses, authors cited, and inscriptions and papyri cited. Although a specialized work, Devijver is an excellent source for biographical information on Roman army officers and equestrians in the early empire, many of whom are relatively obscure and do not appear in most other biographical sources. The work is a very useful supplement to the *Prosopographia Imperii Romani* (entries 388-389).

372. Eckstein, Friedrich August. **Nomenclator Philologorum**. Leipzig: B. G. Teubner, 1871; repr., Hildesheim, Germany: Georg Olms, 1966. 656pp. LC 01-17868.

Eckstein has compiled a biographical dictionary of European classicists from the Renaissance through the nineteenth century. It includes many obscure and minor scholars as well as famous ones. Entries are brief and typically include dates, place of birth, education, and positions held. Some give citations of published biographical notices and obituaries. A short list of notable early printers and publishers of the classics is appended under the title *Nomenclator Typographorum*. A contemporary work by Pökel (entry 386) covers much the same ground as Eckstein. Pökel tends to give more information but lists fewer scholars. Because each work includes individuals and information not found in the other, one is well advised to consult both.

373. Goulet, Richard, ed. **Dictionnaire des philosophes antiques**. Paris: CNRS, 1989- . ISBN 2-271-05193-2(v.1). LC 91-140105.

The *Dictionnaire*, when complete, will provide an exhaustive listing of all known philosophers of classical antiquity. So far only the first volume, which contains some 453 entries covering Abam(m)on to Axiothea, has appeared. Entries begin with the individual's dates and references to Pauly-Wissowa (entry 225) or the *Prosopography of the Later Roman Empire* (entry 378) when these include articles on the person in question. Apart from this, the content and arrangement of each entry can vary greatly. Normally entries include a summary of all known biographical data, a complete list of relevant ancient testimonia and other biographical sources, and a selective bibliography of modern editions and studies. Articles also vary in length; the majority run only a paragraph or two, while some important figures receive many pages (e.g., 10 pages for St. Augustine, 177 pages for Aristotle). However, there are many other sources for major philosophers. Most will find that the real value of this dictionary lies in its extensive coverage of minor and obscure figures. The first volume includes an index of proper names and indexes of Greek and Latin keywords from the titles of philosophical works; presumably such indexes will appear in future volumes as well.

374. Grant, Michael. **Greek and Latin Authors: 800 B.C.-A.D. 1000**. Bronx, NY: H. W. Wilson, 1980. 490pp. (Wilson Authors Series). ISBN 0-8242-0640-1. LC 79-27446.

This book includes 376 entries ranging from the beginnings of Greek literature to A.D. 1000. Among them one can find every important classical author and a selection of the better-known Greek and Latin writers of the early Middle Ages. Each entry provides a biographical sketch followed by a description and critical evaluation of the author's works. Entries also include a bibliography of the best editions and translations, along with a few major secondary works. Arrangement is alphabetical. Appendices provide a list of works of doubtful attribution with references to the appropriate entry and a chronological listing of authors by century. There is also a guide to the pronunciation of the authors' names. An excellent ready-reference tool, this work covers far more authors than Luce's *Ancient Writers* (entry 383). For major authors, however, Luce offers more detailed treatments.

375. Grant, Michael. **The Roman Emperors: A Biographical Guide to the Rulers of Imperial Rome, 31 B.C.-A.D. 476**. New York: Scribner's, 1985. 367pp. ISBN 0-684-18388-9. LC 85-8391.

Grant offers brief lives of 92 Roman emperors, from Augustus to Romulus Augustulus, arranged in chronological order. Usurpers are covered only in passing and do not receive separate listings. The articles are readable and accurate; most are illustrated with contemporary portraits from ancient coins and busts. The work includes genealogical tables of each dynasty, several maps, and a glossary of Latin terms. No alphabetical access is provided to the emperors, although there is a detailed table of contents. There is an index of Greek and Latin authors cited in the text, and another of maps. *Roman Emperors* is well suited to the needs of students and general readers.

376. Hafner, German. **Prominente der Antike: 337 Portraits in Wort und Bild**. Düsseldorf, Germany: Econ Verlag, 1981. 359pp. ISBN 3-430-13742-X. LC 81-152739.

Unlike many of the other biographical dictionaries described here, this one includes both literary and political/historical figures. It also includes both Greeks and Romans. Hafner offers brief biographies of writers, artists, kings and queens, politicians, and generals ranging from Homer to Constantine the Great. Arrangement is alphabetical. One or more portraits drawn from ancient works of art accompany each entry. These are usually "artistic" portraits rather than real likenesses of the subject. Hafner is a useful reference for those fluent in German. However, most of his subjects can be readily found in standard English-language reference sources. His chief value is as a source of portraits.

377. Hofstetter, Josef. **Die Griechen in Persien: Prosopographie der Griechen im Persischen Reich vor Alexander**. Berlin: Dietrich Reimer, 1978. 216pp. (Archaeologische Mitteilungen aus Iran, Ergänzungsband 5). LC 79-340220.

Hofstetter offers brief biographies of Greeks who were in some way associated with Persia. He covers Ionian Greeks who lived under Persian rule and those from the Greek mainland who had a significant connection with Persia. Both well-known and obscure figures are included. The arrangement is alphabetical. A bibliographical note, often extensive, concludes each entry. Several lists at the end of the book gather together types of individuals (e.g., ambassadors). There is also a chronological listing of those included. While specialized, Hofstetter is a good supplementary source for Greek biography.

378. Jones, A. H. M., J. R. Martindale, and J. Morris. **The Prosopography of the Later Roman Empire**. New York: Cambridge University Press, 1971-1992. 3v. in 4. ISBN 0-521-07233-6(v.1); 0-521-201594(v.2); 0-521-20160-8(v.3). LC 77-118859.

A prosopography of the later empire was originally planned and undertaken by Theodor Mommsen as a continuation of the *Prosopographia Imperii Romani* (entries 388-389). This project was a casualty of the two World Wars. A. H. M. Jones launched his effort, now commonly referred to as the PLRE, in 1950. Although Jones and, after his death, Martindale have been primarily responsible for the content, an editorial board of distinguished scholars has contributed much to the work. The PLRE includes a wide range of Roman aristocrats, public officials, military officers, scholars, and literary figures. There are also entries for wives and children. Many non-Romans (Franks, Lombards, Visigoths, Persians, etc.) who are significant to the study of the empire are included as well.

Volume 1 covers A.D. 260-395, volume 2, 395-527, and volume 3 (in two parts), 527-641. Individuals whose careers overlap these boundaries are included in both relevant volumes, although the second entry is in summary form and both must be consulted for a full account. The arrangement of entries within each of these volumes is alphabetical, with cross-references provided from variant forms of names. Entries vary widely in length, ranging from a few lines to several pages; a number of the entries in volume 3 are considerably longer. Entries provide whatever information is known about the person's origin, religion, career, and family. There are full references to primary sources. Few modern studies are cited in the first volume; references to these increase substantially in subsequent volumes. Each volume includes *fasti* (chronological lists of office-holders) and numerous genealogical tables of important families. This is by far the best source of biographical information for the later empire. A further volume of addenda and corrigenda is still in preparation.

379. Kienast, Dietmar. **Römische Kaisertabelle: Grundzüge einer römischen Kaiserchronologie**. Darmstadt, Germany: Wissenschaftliche Buchgesellschaft, 1990. 376pp. ISBN 3-534-07532-3. LC 90-217569.

This chronology covers Roman emperors from Augustus to Theodosius I. Each entry gives date of birth, parents, full form of name, offices, and a chronological list of key events in the life of the emperor. Subentries are provided for other prominent members of the imperial household and for unsuccessful usurpers. Bibliographies list works on the life, family, and chronology of each emperor. Kienast also provides a listing of births, deaths, and major events by date in a single calendar. A very good source for historians and numismatists, this work can be used even by those with modest German.

380. Kirchner, Johannes. **Prosopographia Attica**. Editio altera lucis ope impressa inscriptionum Graecarum conspectum numerorum addidit Siegfried Lauffer. Berolini, Germania: Typis et impensis Walter de Gruyter, 1966; repr., Chicago: Ares, 1981. 2v.

381. Sundwall, J. **Nachträge zur Prosopographia Attica**. Helsingfors, Finland: Akademiska Bokhandeln, 1910. 177pp. (Ofversigt af Finska Vetenskaps-Societetens Förhandlingar, LII, 1909-1910. Afd. B N:o 1). Reprinted as **Supplement to J. Kirchner's Prosopographia Attica**, Chicago: Ares Press, 1981.

Kirchner's work, first published in 1901, is an alphabetical listing of all known Athenian citizens. Although it is billed as a 2d edition, the contents were not updated and remain essentially the same as the original 1901 edition. Entries often include some biographical data, and all offer references to primary sources (often inscriptions) and dates whenever available. Most are only a few lines in length, although for better-known Athenians, entries sometimes extend to a page or more. There are also genealogical tables for some families. There are two additional lists at the end of the main work. One, the *conspectus demotarum*, is essentially an index by *demes* (a political unit) to the list of the citizens. The second list, the *archontum tabulae*, lists known archons from 683/82 to 30/29 B.C. There is also an index to citations of Greek inscriptions. While information about famous Athenians, such Cleisthenes or Pericles, can be found in many sources, Kirchner provides a valuable resource for biographical material on the more obscure ones.

In compiling his supplement to Kirchner, Sundwall noted the need (still unmet 80 years later) for a new edition of the work. Sundwall updates some of Kirchner's entries and adds many new names. He mingles both updated and new entries in a single alphabetical sequence; no attempt is made to follow Kirchner's numbering system, although references to Kirchner's numbers appear at the end of updates to existing entries. Many of Sundwall's entries cite then-unpublished inscriptions in various museum collections; because no inventory numbers are provided for these inscriptions, they can be difficult to identify and track down. Although somewhat different in focus, the more recent works of Davies (entry 367) and Develin (entry 370) can be used to supplement the *Prosopographia Attica*.

382. Kroh, Paul. **Lexikon der antiken Autoren**. Stuttgart, Germany: Alfred Kröner Verlag, 1972. 675pp. (Kröners Taschenausgabe, Bd.366). ISBN 3-520-366-010.

The *Lexikon der antiken Autoren* contains articles on approximately 2,400 Greek and Roman authors from the beginnings to the sixth century A.D. It includes poets, historians, orators, philosophers, and scholarly and technical writers. The articles range from a paragraph to several pages and tend to be brief and factual. The majority of entries include short bibliographies of editions, translations, and secondary literature. The *Lexikon* is chiefly useful for its coverage of minor and obscure authors who are often omitted from such biographical works.

383. Luce, T. James, ed. **Ancient Writers: Greece and Rome**. New York: Scribner's, 1982. 2v. ISBN 0-684-16595-3. LC 82-50612.

This work consists of 47 articles that cover the major classical authors. Each has been written by a leading specialist. While the approach and emphasis vary, all offer biographical information, a description of the author's works, and an orientation to the major aspects of criticism and research. Bibliographies list major editions, translations, commentaries, and the more important scholarly literature (primarily recent studies and standard works). Articles are arranged chronologically. There is an index of names and titles. This is a very good introduction to the major figures of classical literature and a convenient point of departure for more detailed study of the authors.

384. Nicolet, Claude. **L'Ordre équestre a l'époque républicaine (312-43 av. J.-C.)**. Paris: E. de Boccard, 1966-1974. 2v. (Bibliothèque des Ecoles françaises d'Athènes et de Rome, fasc.207). LC 67-75746.

The second volume of Nicolet's work comprises a prosopography of Roman knights. It lists some 404 equestrians of the republican period. Entries are brief, although some extend to several pages. Each entry begins with the person's life dates, place of origin, and rank or offices. A short biography follows; emphasis is on the individual's public career and family connections. There are extensive references to primary and secondary sources. The republican period is not nearly as well served by biographical sources as the empire. Nicolet, Broughton (entry 362), and Pauly-Wissowa (entry 225) are the major resources for Romans of that era.

385. Peremans, W., and E. van't Dack. **Prosopographia Ptolemaica**. Lovanii, Belgium: Bibliotheca Universitatis Lovanii, 1950-1981. (Studia Hellenistica) 9v. LC 53-33025.

This highly specialized work attempts to gather information on all known persons who lived in Ptolemaic Egypt (323-30 B.C.). It includes more than 17,000 individuals, many of whom are painfully obscure. Volumes 1-5 comprise the basic list, while volume 6 is a name index to the earlier volumes. Volumes 8-9 are addenda and corrigenda. Entries are arranged by occupation; the first volume, for example, covers individuals who were part of the civil or financial administration of Egypt. Each major category is subdivided into specific occupations. Arrangement within each list is alphabetical by name. Entries vary in length; most are quite brief. They provide in summary fashion what is known of each person: occupation, family connections, date, and home or place of activity. Primary sources (chiefly papyri) and selected secondary works are cited.

386. Pökel, W. **Philologisches Schriftsteller-Lexikon.** Leipzig: Alfred Krüger, 1882; repr., Darmstadt, Germany: Wissenschaftliche Buchgesellschaft, 1966. 328pp. LC 07-20050.

Along with Eckstein's *Nomenclator Philologorum* (entry 372), this work is one of the basic biographical sources on European classical scholars of the modern era. Pökel's chronological limits run from the mid-fifteenth century to about 1880. His alphabetical listings give for each scholar dates, places of birth and residence, titles and institutions (for those with academic affiliations), and brief citations of major publications. Occasionally Pökel also furnishes references to published obituaries or biographies of his subjects. Pökel's entries generally offer more information than do those of Eckstein. Because there is less than complete overlap between the two works, most users will need to consult both. Users of Pökel should be sure to also check the extensive additions and corrections found at the end of the volume.

387. Poralla, Paul. **A Prosopography of Lacedaimonians from the Earliest Times to the Death of Alexander the Great (X-323 B.C.) = Prosopographie der Lakedaimonier bis auf die Zeit Alexanders des Grossen.** 2d ed. Chicago: Ares Press, 1985. 202pp. ISBN 0-89005-521-1.

Originally presented as Poralla's doctoral dissertation (Breslau, 1913), this work includes Spartan royalty, Spartiates (full citizens), and *perioeci* (free inhabitants of the Spartan domain without citizenship); helots (similar in status to serfs) and resident foreigners are omitted. It records all known individual Lacedaimonians from the archaic and classical periods. Individuals are listed in alphabetical order (names are printed in the Greek alphabet). Those with the same name are arranged chronologically. Each is assigned a number (1-817). Corrupt or false names are printed in smaller characters and not assigned a number. Entries include such biographical data as is known about each and references to primary sources. There are also genealogical tables for some of the more important Spartan families and lists of nauarchs (naval commanders) and ephors (magistrates).

An introduction, addenda, and corrigenda have been provided by Alfred S. Bradford. The addenda and corrigenda (the first appendix) provide additional citations of primary sources and recent studies, as well as correcting errors in the original work. The second appendix adds 45 new entries. Bradford's additions are in English and Greek; Poralla's text is reprinted in the original German and Greek. The work is continued by Bradford's *Prosopography of Lacedaemonians from the Death of Alexander the Great* (entry 359).

388. **Prosopographia Imperii Romani Saec. I. II. III.** Edita consilio et auctoritate Academiae Scientarum Regiae Borussicae. Berolini, Germania: Apud Georgium Reimerum, 1897-1898; repr., Berlin: Walter de Gruyter, 1978. 3v. LC 30-30140.

389. **Prosopographia Imperii Romani Saec. I. II. III.** Consilio et auctoritate Academiae Litterarum Borussicae iteratis curis ediderunt ... Editio Altera. Berolini et Lipsiae, Germania: Apud Walter De Gruyter, 1933- . LC 40-106.

One of the many monumental products of nineteenth-century German scholarship, this work was proposed and planned by Theodor Mommsen and sponsored by the Prussian Academy. The first edition was edited by Elimar Klebs, Paul von Rohden, and Hermann Dessau. The PIR, as it is commonly abbreviated, covers the Roman Empire from Augustus (31 B.C.) to the accession of Diocletian (A.D. 284). The PIR has long been one of the standard sources for biographical information about Romans of the imperial period. It includes Romans of senatorial and equestrian rank and their families, and many other notable Romans. Romans of plebeian rank who are known only from Christian writers are excluded. Greeks and barbarians who were involved in Roman affairs are included selectively. Entries for emperors only include their activities outside of their reigns.

Entries are arranged alphabetically. Each gives an account of the individual's career, lists public offices held, and provides whatever information is known about his family. Primary sources are cited in full. Many entries are brief, sometimes as little as two or three lines, while others are considerably longer. A fourth volume, which was intended to include consular *fasti*, was planned but never published.

Edmund Groag and Arthur Stein, both now deceased, were the original editors of the 2d edition of PIR. They have since been succeeded by Leiva Petersen. The criteria and format of entries generally follow those of the first edition. The second edition includes many new entries and augments old ones with new material and greatly expanded citations of primary sources. Cross-references have also been added to the new edition. There are occasional references to modern studies, but no attempt is made to provide a systematic bibliography. Some genealogical tables are also provided. This is an excellent biographical source for the period and a great improvement over the first edition. The most recent volume to appear (1987) reached the letter O; the first edition must still be consulted for the remainder of the alphabet. Those interested in the late empire (from A.D. 260 to 641) should consult A. H. M. Jones, *The Prosopography of the Later Roman Empire* (entry 378), which continues the work of the PIR.

390. Radice, Betty. **Who's Who in the Ancient World**. New York: Stein and Day, 1971. 225pp. ISBN 0-8128-1338-3. LC 73-127027.

Radice provides a single alphabetical list of Greek and Roman mythological, historical, and cultural figures ranging from the Bronze Age to late antiquity. Entries are brief and informative, with frequent cross-references to related articles. There is also a complete index. The book is aimed at general readers pursuing classical references in modern art and literature. It has a much wider scope but is less comprehensive than Bowder's two *Who's Who* volumes (entries 357-358). Bowder is superior for those seeking strictly historical information, while Radice is better for those with more cultural interests. Together they provide good basic biographical coverage of notable Greeks and Romans.

391. Raepsaet-Charlier, Marie Thérèse. **Prosopographie des femmes de l'ordre sénatorial (Ier-IIe siècles)**. Lovanii: Aedibus Peeters, 1987. 2v. (Fonds René Draguet, t.4). ISBN 90-6831-086-0(v.1); 90-6831-087-9(v.2).

Raepsaet-Charlier's work is intended to remedy, in part, the difficulty in finding information about prominent women of the early empire. In sources such as the *Prosopographia Imperii Romani* (entries 388-389) and Pauly-Wissowa (entry 225), women typically receive only a passing mention in articles concerning their husbands or fathers. The lack of indexes to these works makes it difficult to find them. Raepsaet-Charlier lists all known women of families of senatorial rank, including wives, daughters, sisters, and mothers of senators. Each notice includes the woman's complete name, bibliographical references, primary sources, biographical information and discussion, and family connections. Entries are arranged alphabetically; indexes of men, women, and elements of women's names (which serve as cross-references for the more complicated names) facilitate access to the list. An extensive collection of genealogical tables can be found in the second volume.

This well-organized work is a mine of information on women in the early empire. While few of the names included are likely to be of general interest, it is a valuable reference tool for those doing historical research on women.

392. Smith, William, ed. **A Dictionary of Greek and Roman Biography and Mythology**. London: John Murray, 1890; repr., New York: AMS, 1967. 3v. LC 11-24983.

Nearly every large library holds one or another edition of this venerable work, which first appeared in 1844. Along with Smith's *Dictionary of Greek and Roman Antiquities* (entry 230) and *Dictionary of Greek and Roman Geography* (entry 416) it is part of his *Encyclopedia of Classical Antiquity*. Smith covers real people and characters from myth and legend. His work remains the largest and most comprehensive single dictionary of classical biography in English. It includes the names of nearly all noteworthy individuals from the earliest period through late antiquity. Smith also covers the Byzantine empire, although in less detail. The entries, which range in length from a few lines to several columns, are written in a clear and readable style. They usually provide references to the pertinent ancient sources, as well as to the secondary literature of the time.

While much of the information in Smith remains useful, enough is now outdated or inaccurate that the work should be used with care. When possible, more recent works, such as those of Radice (entry 390) or Bowder (entries 357-358) should be preferred.

393. Veh, Otto. **Lexikon der Römischen Kaiser: von Augustus bis Iustinianus I., 27 v. Chr. bis 565 n. Chr.** Zurich: Artemis, 1990. 3., überarbeitete, ergänzte und mit Bildern versehene Auflage. 158pp. ISBN 3-7608-1035-7.

The articles in this biographical dictionary of Roman emperors are generally based on the corresponding entries in the Artemis *Lexikon der Alten Welt* (entry 224). Each gives the subject's commonly used name, full name, dates of reign or attempted usurpation, and a short biography. Most are a paragraph or two, although some of the more important emperors receive several pages each. References to Pauly-Wissowa (entry 225), *Kleine Pauly* (entry 233), and the *Prosopography of the Later Roman Empire* (entry 378) are provided, when appropriate, at the end of each article. Some noteworthy features of the book include its alphabetical arrangement (works on the emperors tend to be arranged chronologically) and its good coverage of minor emperors, usurpers, and later emperors. While many English-speaking readers will prefer Grant (entry 375), who also offers longer articles on most of the better-known emperors, this is a good alternative. Those working on the later empire especially will find it a handy reference tool.

Portraits

394. Bernoulli, J. J. **Griechische Ikonographie: mit Ausschluss Alexanders und der Diodochen**. München: F. Bruckmann, 1901; repr., Hildesheim: G. Olms, 1969. 2v. LC 03-6659.

Griechische Ikonographie was long the standard work on Greek portraiture; it is now superseded by Richter's *Portraits of the Greeks* (entry 398). Bernoulli provides a series of articles in chronological sequence that cover notable Greeks of the classical and Hellenistic periods. He includes literary figures, philosophers, statespeople, and generals. Most articles are on individuals, although a few are on collective subjects (e.g., the Seven Sages). Each article gives a biographical synopsis and discusses the person's depiction in art. There are some small illustrations in the body of the text and a number of plates at the end of each volume. There are a detailed table of contents and a name and subject index. There is also a geographical index of the sources (i.e., museums) of portraits. Although Bernoulli can still be useful, Richter is both more recent and offers fuller coverage.

395. Bernoulli, J. J. **Römische Ikonographie**. Stuttgart, Germany: W. Spemann, 1882-1894; repr., Hildesheim: G. Olms, 1969. 2v. in 4. LC 06-22528.

Bernoulli's monumental work on Roman portraiture consists of two volumes. The first covers prominent Romans (except for emperors and members of their households) from Romulus to the second century A.D. It includes some legendary figures (e.g., the early kings of Rome), many political and military figures, and the most famous literary authors and philosophers. The second volume, which is in three parts, covers the emperors. Arrangement is chronological. Each article begins with a biographical summary, followed by a discussion of portraits of the individual. While most articles are brief, some (e.g., Julius Caesar) extend to many pages. Most of the portraits are to be found at the end of each volume. There is a detailed table of contents, but no alphabetical access to the work as a whole. There are individual subject indexes in two parts of the second volume, but none for the third part or for the first volume.

Römische Ikonographie is now badly out-of-date. Unfortunately, there is no single source to replace it. Toynbee (entry 402) is generally better for historical portraits down to the time of Augustus. For imperial portraiture, there are more options: Calza (entry 396), Felleti Maj (entry 397), and Schindler (entry 401).

396. Calza, Raissa. **Iconografia romana imperiale: Da Carausio a Giuliano (287-363 d.C.)**. Roma: "L'Erma" di Bretschneider, 1972. (Quaderni e guide di archeologia, III) 1v. (various paging). LC 72-359178.

Calza continues the work of Felletti Maj (entry 397). Unfortunately, she also follows the organizational pattern of the earlier work. She begins by gathering all the literary evidence for the physical appearance of the emperors from Diocletian to Julian. This is arranged by emperor in a chronological sequence. The passages are quoted in both the original Latin or Greek and in Italian translation. The second part is the actual *iconografia*, which offers discussions of the portraits of emperors from Carausius to Julian. The content of this section mainly deals with art history. The illustrations are in a separate section at the end. These portraits are drawn from coins, statuary, reliefs, paintings and mosaics. As in Felleti Maj, the plates are not captioned and are identified only by number; the key (*indice delle illustrazioni*) or the corresponding sections of text must be used as a guide. There are chronological and alphabetical name indexes and an index of museums that hold the portraits used as illustrations. While not intended as a reference tool and difficult to use, Calza provides a valuable source of information on the physical appearance of Roman emperors for the period covered. Her work is useful as a supplement to the corresponding section of Bernoulli (entry 395).

397. Felleti Maj, Bianca Maria. **Iconografia romana imperiale da Severo Alessandro a M. Aurelio Carino (222-285 d.C.)**. Roma: "L'Erma" di Bretschneider, 1958. 309pp. (Quaderni e Guide di Archeologia, II). LC 62-45541.

Felleti Maj's study covers the iconography of Roman emperors and their families for A.D. 222 to 285. The organization of the work is cumbersome. It begins with a general bibliography. Next is a compilation of the ancient literary evidence for the physical appearance of the various emperors. Felleti Maj provides both the Greek or Latin texts of these and an Italian translation on the facing page. The third section consists of a series of entries on individual emperors, which are arranged chronologically. Each begins with a brief biographical note. A discussion of the portraits of the individual follows. The illustrations are in a separate section at the end of the book. The plates are identified only by number; there are no captions. Also, the figure numbers are not entirely sequential. This necessitates constant reference both to the article on a given emperor and to the key (*indice delle illustrazioni*) when seeking a portrait. The indexes, which are located between the text and plates, include chronological and alphabetical name indexes and an index of museums that hold the actual portraits.

This work is more current and contains more portraits than the corresponding section of Bernoulli's *Römische Ikonographie* (entry 395). It can be useful in finding information on and portraits of the more obscure emperors. The extensive collection of source material and the plates are its most valuable features. The book is difficult to use, as noted above. Readers must look in several different places to find information about a single individual. Felleti Maj's study is continued as far as Julian (A.D. 363) by Calza (entry 396).

398. Richter, Gisela M. A. **The Portraits of the Greeks**. London: Phaidon Press, 1965. 3v. LC 66-4110.

399. Richter, Gisela M. A. **The Portraits of the Greeks. Supplement**. London: Phaidon Press, 1972. 24pp.

✓ 400. Richter, Gisela M. A. **The Portraits of the Greeks**. Abridged and revised by R. R. R. Smith. Ithaca, NY: Cornell University Press, 1984. 254pp. ISBN 0-8014-1683-3. LC 83-73222.

Richter wrote this book to replace Bernoulli's *Griechische Ikonographie* (entry 394). It includes "(1) all reliably identified portraits of Greek poets, philosophers, orators, statesmen, generals, and artists; (2) the portraits for which plausible identifications have been proposed; and (3) the portraits merely cited in ancient literature and inscriptions." Unlike Bernoulli, Richter also includes Hellenistic rulers. She follows Bernoulli's chronological arrangement in a modified form, in which she groups her subjects by century and then subdivides them by profession (e.g., poets). Thus, the first volume (after a substantial introduction to the history and study of Greek portraiture) has chapters on the early period and the fifth century B.C.; the second volume covers the fourth, third, and second centuries; and the third treats Hellenistic rulers and Greeks of the Roman period.

This arrangement is inconvenient for someone merely seeking likenesses of an individual, but the detailed table of contents and the index of names provide ready access.

Individual entries begin with a short biography, followed by what is known about the person's physical appearance. Then there is a full discussion and listing of both the ancient literary evidence for portraits and the extant portraits of the subject. The portraits are gathered at the end of each volume. These are perhaps the most valuable part of the work: more than 2,000 portraits of notable Greeks. The *Supplement* published in 1972 adds newly discovered or identified portraits. Richter covers far more individuals than Bernoulli and provides many more portraits for each. Richter is unlikely to be superseded as the standard work in the field for many years.

The abridgement of Richter's three-volume work was begun by the author; after her death Smith completed it. It includes all notable Greeks from the eighth to the first centuries B.C. of whom a portrait has been identified with some certainty. The book covers the same range of material (with the exception of Greeks of the Roman period, whom Smith has largely omitted), but with much less detail. Each entry still includes a brief account of the person's life, portraits recorded in literary sources, evidence for surviving portraits, and the best versions of those portraits. However, much of the detailed scholarly apparatus has been omitted, and the reader often is referred back to the unabridged work. Smith has also changed the arrangement of the material. Most of the entries are now presented in a single alphabetical sequence. An exception is made for the Hellenistic rulers, who are still covered in a separate section that is arranged geographically and subarranged chronologically. Also, the illustrations have been integrated into the text, which is much more convenient for the user. Smith's abridgement should meet most of the reference needs of students and casual readers.

401. Schindler, Wolfgang. **Römische Kaiser: Herrscherbild und Imperium**. Leipzig: Koehler & Amelang, 1985. 219pp.

This study of imperial portraiture covers major emperors from Augustus to Constantine the Great. A preliminary chapter discusses portraits of Roman leaders prior to the principate (27 B.C.). Minor emperors and co-emperors are often omitted (e.g., Lucius Verus, Pertinax, Julius Didianus). While the author's chief concern is the portraiture, each entry provides a short biographical sketch of its subject. The many good-quality photographs of contemporary artworks depicting emperors and members of their families are the most valuable feature of Schindler's book. The arrangement is chronological. There is no index, although a fairly detailed table of contents helps in this regard. Grant (entry 375) is a much better source for imperial biography and provides some portraits as well. Schindler is useful mainly for additional imperial portraits.

402. Toynbee, J. M. C. **Roman Historical Portraits**. Ithaca, NY: Cornell University Press, 1978. 208pp. (Aspects of Greek and Roman Life). ISBN 0-8014-1011-8. LC 75-38428.

Toynbee aims to provide accurate likenesses of prominent figures in Roman history. She uses only portraits made during the subject's life or based on a contemporary portrait. The first part of the work offers portraits of 52 notable Romans ranging from M. Claudius Marcellus (consul in 222 B.C.) to C. Asinius Gallus (consul in 8 B.C.). Toynbee includes only those who played an important role in public life during the republican and early Augustan periods; she omits figures of primarily cultural importance. This part is arranged chronologically.

The second part consists of portraits of about 205 foreign rulers who had dealings with Rome between the third century B.C. and the fifth century A.D. These rulers are arranged geographically and then subarranged chronologically. Spouses and children are sometimes included under a ruler's entry as well. There are some odd placements. For example, Hamilcar and Hannibal are placed under Spain (there is no heading for Carthage). It is best to consult the general index for the person sought. Entries are mainly concerned with the portraits as such, but do include some biographical and historical data. Toynbee is chiefly of value for the illustrations; this is perhaps the only collection that consciously strives to avoid idealized portraits and present real likenesses.

CHAPTER 10

GEOGRAPHICAL SOURCES

All manner of resources pertaining to classical geography will be found in this chapter. The first part includes essentially textual works such as dictionaries, manuals, and the like. The second part covers maps and atlases. Readers should consult the headnote to the second part for a brief discussion of cartographic resources for the ancient world and pertinent bibliography on the topic.

Dictionaries, Handbooks, and Gazetteers

403. Avery, Catherine B., ed. **The New Century Handbook of Classical Geography**. New York: Appleton-Century-Crofts, 1972. 362pp. ISBN 390-66930-X. LC 78-189006.

This work is based on *The New Century Classical Handbook* (New York: Appleton-Century-Crofts, 1962); the material has been updated and a number of new entries included. Its intended audience consists of travelers and students. Arrangement is alphabetical; there is no index, although occasional cross-references are provided. Entries cover "cities, mountains, rivers, and islands of the Mediterranean region." Articles tend to be brief, with a few notable exceptions (e.g., the Acropolis receives six pages). Each gives the pronunciation of the place name, ancient variants, and the modern name (if different). Then it locates the place and describes it concisely. A summary of any legends or historical events associated with the site concludes the entry. There are no bibliographical references. Maps of Italy and Greece are bound in the center of the volume; these are not very detailed and do not include most of the entries. Avery will serve for ready-reference purposes, although Grant (entry 407) is preferable: his work is more up-to-date, is a bit more comprehensive, and has better maps.

404. Bell, Robert E. **Place-Names in Classical Mythology: Greece**. Santa Barbara, CA: ABC-CLIO, 1989. 350pp. ISBN 0-87436-507-4.

Bell's intention is to help place the myths and legends of Greece into their geographical contexts. He limits his coverage to the boundaries of modern Greece. This excludes many important sites in Ionia and Asia Minor, which Bell proposes to treat in a future volume. There are entries for approximately 1,000 place-names, arranged alphabetically by the ancient name, with the modern name (when different) given in parentheses. Cross-references are made from variant names. Each entry identifies and locates the place, be it town, district, river, mountain, or other geographical feature. A brief discussion of its mythological associations follows. Bell cites relevant ancient literary sources in the course of each article. The length of entries ranges from a few lines to several pages, depending upon the importance of the site and the amount of information available. In lieu of indexes, Bell provides lists of modern place-names and of personal names mentioned in the various entries. This readable and accurate book is the only work of its kind.

405. Cary, M. **The Geographic Background of Greek & Roman History**. Oxford, England: Clarendon Press, 1949; repr., Westport, CT: Greenwood Press, 1981. 331pp. LC 49-3013.

Cary provides a geographical survey of the entire Greco-Roman world. He begins with a general overview of the Mediterranean region, followed by separate chapters on each of the major regions of the ancient world. Greece and Italy receive two chapters apiece (a general and a regional one); other areas, such as North Africa or Western Europe, receive only one. Cary covers many topics such as climate, topography, natural resources, plant life, agriculture, and the cultural and social aspects of the geographical environment. It is a useful handbook on the subject, though now dated. One of its major drawbacks is that its coverage is heavily biased in favor of Greece and Italy; other parts of the ancient world receive less detailed, sometimes cursory attention. The number of maps is reasonable, although some lack adequate detail. The bibliography of both ancient and modern works is good but outdated. The index of place-names and geographical features includes both ancient and modern names.

406. Graesse, J. G. T., Friedrich Benedict, and Helmut Plechl. **Orbis Latinus: Lexikon lateinischer geographischer Namen**. Braunschweig, Germany: Klinkhardt & Biermann, 1971. Handausgabe. Lateinisch-Deutsch, Deutsch-Lateinisch. Vierte reviderte und erweiterte Auflage. 579 pp. LC 76-886535.

This is the latest incarnation of a work that has been a standby for more than a century. *Orbis Latinus* is the best guide to Latin place-names employed in antiquity, the Middle Ages, and the Renaissance. It consists of two lists: Latin place-names followed by modern equivalents, and modern place-names followed by Latin equivalents. Many cross-references are provided. The modern names, although in German, are generally recognizable to the English reader. There are many different editions and printings of *Orbis Latinus*; most are serviceable.

407. Grant, Michael. **A Guide to the Ancient World: A Dictionary of Classical Place Names**. Bronx, NY: H. W. Wilson, 1986. 728pp. ISBN 0-8242-0742-4. LC 86-15785.

Grant provides an alphabetical listing of approximately 900 places in the ancient world. He includes primarily towns, cities, provinces, and the like, although rivers, mountains, and lakes are included when appropriate. Grant's chronological limits reach from the first millenium B.C. to the later fifth century A.D. Ancient variant forms of name and modern equivalents are noted by cross-references. Entries begin with geographical facts and offer historical and archaeological information. Material on art and mythology are included when relevant. Entries range in length from a few sentences to several pages. The series of maps, gathered at the front of the book, includes all places listed in the dictionary. A general bibliography of both ancient and modern sources concludes the work. This readable book is a good all-purpose reference work for students, travelers, and general readers.

408. Lauffer, Siegfried, ed. **Griechenland: Lexikon der historischen Stätten von den Anfängen bis zur Gegenwart**. München: C. H. Beck, 1987. 775pp. ISBN 3-406-33302-8. LC 89-211323.

The scope of this work is limited to places of human habitation or activity, mainly cities and towns. Natural geographical features, such as rivers, are omitted. A substantial introduction gives an overview of ancient, Byzantine, and modern Greek history. The lexicon is arranged alphabetically. Headings include the place-name in transliterated form, followed by the Greek form and a map reference. The body of each entry begins with the geographical location (usually fairly exact; for smaller sites, the direction and distance from a larger place is often given). Historical and cultural material on the site follows, including information on prehistoric, ancient, Byzantine, and modern periods. Each entry concludes with extensive bibliographical references. Entries range from a paragraph to several pages. A list of headings, which precedes the lexicon proper, gives an overview of the contents. An index and a set of detailed sectional maps of Greece are provided as well. The *Lexikon* is particularly valuable for locating information about small and obscure places.

409. **Lexicon of the Greek and Roman Cities and Place Names in Antiquity: ca. 1500 B.C.-ca. A.D. 500**. Amsterdam: Adolf M. Hakkert, 1992- . ISBN 90-256-0985-6(fasc.1); 90-256-1033-1(fasc.2).

This new lexicon is being issued in fascicles. It covers chiefly cities and towns, although other types of places are included as well (e.g., military posts, road stations). Articles are usually brief, ranging from a couple of lines up to (rarely) several columns. Each entry locates and describes the place, then provides a historical summary if appropriate. All articles include a bibliography of ancient and modern sources; some of these are extensive. Many entries are accompanied by small maps, which are useful but sometimes hard to read. All articles are signed by the contributor. This is a good source of information, particularly for small and obscure places. It will be a valuable reference work when completed.

410. Lugli, Giuseppe, ed. **Fontes ad Topographiam Veteris Urbis Romae Pertinentes**. Rome: Università di Roma, Istituto di Topografia Antica, 1952- . LC 56-36611.

Lugli gathers the ancient literary sources, inscriptions, and other documentary sources pertaining to the topography and monuments of ancient Rome. The arrangement of material is complex. Lugli begins with references to the city as a whole, then proceeds to large general features of the city (e.g., the various city walls, the Tiber, bridges). He goes through the city by *regiones* (the ancient districts of the city), covering topographical features in each by type (e.g., streets, fountains). Each volume has its own *index topographicus* and a few illustrations and plans. Lugli provides an exhaustive compilation of source material for most of the city (not all volumes have been published).

411. Nash, Ernest. **Pictorial Dictionary of Ancient Rome**. Rev. ed. London: Thames and Hudson, 1968; repr., New York: Hacker, 1981. 2v. LC 72-355732.

The original publication of this work was sponsored by the German Archaeological Institute. Nash provides excellent black-and-white photographs of the archaeological remains and topographical features. He generally follows Platner and Ashby (entry 412) in the "arrangement and denomination" of entries. His bibliographical references are designed to complement and update those of Platner and Ashby. Nash's entries, which are arranged alphabetically, offer a brief description of each site or monument and a bibliography (often extensive), followed by illustrations. Most of the illustrations are modern photographs, although a few reproduce old engravings that provide views or details no longer available. An excellent general index provides access by a number of approaches, including the names of modern streets and squares in which monuments are located. This outstanding contribution to the study of Roman topography is best used in conjunction with Platner and Ashby or with Richardson's recent work (entry 413).

412. Platner, Samuel Ball. **A Topographical Dictionary of Ancient Rome**. Completed and revised by Thomas Ashby. London: Oxford University Press, 1929; repr., Rome: "L'Erma" di Bretschneider, 1965. 608pp. LC 30-10804.

This classic work covers the buildings, places, and natural features of ancient Rome. It includes those that have survived and those known only from ancient literary and documentary sources. Entries, which are arranged alphabetically, range from a line or two to several pages. Platner and Ashby cite the ancient sources extensively. Selective bibliographies of secondary literature appear at the end of some entries. The small number of illustrations is a major drawback in a work of this type. There is a single map, small and crowded. The only index is a chronological one to dated monuments. Platner and Ashby are now largely superseded by Richardson (entry 413). For extensive illustrations of the sites covered by both of these see Nash (entry 411).

413. Richardson, L., Jr. **A New Topographical Dictionary of Ancient Rome**. Baltimore, MD: Johns Hopkins University Press, 1992. 458pp. ISBN 0-8018-4300-6. LC 91-45406.

This recent work covers all significant sites, monuments, and buildings from the earliest settlements at Rome to the sixth century A.D., with the exception of most Christian churches and tombs. The entries are arranged alphabetically, with cross-references where appropriate. The clearly written articles identify and describe the sites and monuments, and concisely provide what is known of their histories. Many include references to ancient sources and to the modern secondary literature. The introduction includes a wide-ranging survey of source materials and the history of the study of Roman topography. Richardson provides a substantial bibliography, although he refers readers to Platner and Ashby (entry 412) for earlier works and to Lugli (entry 410) for a full conspectus of the ancient sources. The work includes a fair number of maps and plans, but for illustrations of most sites it is necessary to refer to Nash (entry 411). Richardson, who has devoted a lifetime of study to his subject, has a close personal knowledge of the remains of ancient Rome. This is now the best single source and the starting point for further studies on the Roman monuments and topography.

414. Rivet, A. L. F., and Colin Smith. **The Place-Names of Roman Britain**. Princeton, NJ: Princeton University Press, 1979. 526pp. ISBN 0-691-03953-4. LC 79-21616.

This unusual work lists alphabetically all known place-names of Roman Britain. Each entry gives sources for the name, its derivation, and an identification (type of place and location). An index of modern names in England, Scotland, and Wales is provided. There is also a massive introduction that discusses the source material employed by the editors. The work serves as an exhaustive gazetteer for Roman Britain.

415. Schoder, Raymond V. **Ancient Greece from the Air**. London: Thames and Hudson, 1974. 256pp. ISBN 0-500-05016-3; 0-500-27045-7pa. LC 74-196316.

Schoder's well-known work, which was also published under the title *Wings over Hellas*, is of both geographical and archaeological interest. He provides spectacular aerial views (all in color) of the principal Greek archaeological sites. The work is arranged alphabetically by the modern Greek name of the sites. Each section offers a brief description of the site, which includes historical, geographical, and archaeological information. This is followed by one or more photos and often plans of the site and its buildings. A brief chronology, bibliographies for each site, and an index conclude the work. This is an excellent source of pictures of Greek archaeological sites. There is one curious omission: the book lacks a map locating all the sites.

416. Smith, William, ed. **Dictionary of Greek and Roman Geography**. London: Walton and Maberly; John Murray, 1854-1857. 2v. LC 01-21133.

Part of Smith's *Encyclopedia of Antiquity* (see also entries 230 and 392), these two massive volumes cover Greek, Roman, and Biblical geography. Names of cities, towns, rivers, and mountains are included. Each entry locates and briefly describes its subject, gives relevant historical and mythological data about it, discusses its name, and lists any known variant names. Smith does a good job of citing ancient sources, although most of the secondary literature cited is now outdated. There are many small illustrations.

This work is now antiquated and contains much obsolete and erroneous information. It remains, however, one of the most comprehensive works on ancient geography and one of the most widely available. It may be used with caution.

416a. Steinby, Eva Margareta, ed. **Lexicon Topographicum Urbis Romae**. Roma: Edizioni Quasar, 1993- . ISBN 88-7097-019-1 (v.1). LC 94-117766.

This work-in-progress is intended to replace the venerable dictionaries of Platner and Ashby (entry 412) and Nash (entry 411). It covers the places and moments of the city of Rome from its beginnings through the seventh century A.D. The contributors incude many well-known archaeologists; all have first-hand knowledge of the sites and monuments they discuss. Most of the articles are written in Italian, although some are in English or French. Entries attempt to present the current state of research in a concise manner. Each includes the ancient and medieval names of the site or monument, its history (drawn fron literary sources), archaeological data, and brief bibliographies. Many cross-references are provided. Plates and figures appear at the end of each volume; these consist of photographs of the actual remains, plans, sketches, and reconstructions. When completed, this promises to be the most comprehensive reference work available on the topography of Rome. While the *Lexicon* is indispensable for scholars, students and casual inquirers will find Richardson's recent work (entry 413) more suited to their needs.

✓ 417. Stillwell, Richard, ed. **The Princeton Encyclopedia of Classical Sites**. Princeton, NJ: Princeton University Press, 1976. 1019pp. LC 75-30210.

This aim of this work is "to provide a one-volume source of information on sites that show remains from the classical period." The encyclopedia covers the entire classical Mediterranean world. Its chronological limits run from the mid-eighth century B.C. to the sixth century A.D.; early Christian sites of the fourth and fifth centuries A.D. are generally omitted. There are entries by nearly 400 authors on about 3,000 sites. Entries normally represent sites with actual remains and are arranged alphabetically under the ancient name. Each entry includes description and location (with a map reference), followed by a brief history with references to the ancient sources. Each also has a bibliography. There are no site maps or illustrations. A series of general maps is supplied at the end of the book for locating the sites. This work is extremely useful for the study of geography, history, and archaeology.

418. Travlos, John. **Bildlexikon zur Topographie des antiken Attika**. Tübingen, Germany: Ernst Wasmuth, 1988. ISBN 3803010365. LC 89-160506.

A companion to Travlos's earlier work on Athens (entry 419), this title also was sponsored by the German Archaeological Institute. It covers the whole of ancient Attica. The format and features resemble the earlier volume. Travlos covers the districts of Attica in alphabetical sequence. In each section a brief introduction provides a historical and archaeological overview of the district, followed by a bibliography and plates. The illustrations are the heart of the work; Travlos provides numerous maps, plans, and photos of the archaeological remains. Unfortunately, it has not yet been translated into English.

419. Travlos, John. **Pictorial Dictionary of Ancient Athens**. New York: Praeger, 1971; repr., New York: Hacker, 1980. 590pp. LC 70-89608.

This dictionary was sponsored by the German Archaeological Institute and was published simultaneously in German and English. It is the Athenian equivalent of Nash's work on Rome (entry 411). Travlos arranged his material alphabetically by name of site or monument (e.g., Agora, Parthenon). Each entry includes location, description, history, and a detailed bibliography followed by many plans, sketches, and black-and-white photographs. The illustrations are of high quality. There is a full general index and an index of inscriptions. The author had a close personal knowledge of the monuments. His work is a valuable resource for students of ancient topography, archaeology, and history. His *Bildlexikon zur Topographie des antiken Attika* (entry 418) extends coverage to all of Attica.

Atlases

None of the existing classical atlases is entirely satisfactory. Those listed here are the most readily available and useful ones. A major new atlas of the classical world, edited by Richard J. A. Talbert, is now in preparation under the aegis of the American Philological Association (with a projected publication date of 1999). The APA is also sponsoring a forthcoming survey, *Map Resources for the Greek and Roman Worlds*, edited by W. V. Harris. The complex history of modern attempts to map the ancient world is ably covered by Talbert in his article "Mapping the Classical World: Major Atlases and Map Series, 1872-1990," *Journal of Roman Archaeology* 5 (1992): 5-38. Interested readers might also consult the comparative study by Clive Foss, "Classical Atlases," *Classical World* 80 (1987): 337-65.

420. Bengtson, Hermann, and Vladimir Milojcic, eds. **Grosser historischer Weltatlas. Teil 1. Vorgeschichte und Altertum**. 5. überarbeitete und erweiterte Auflage. München: Bayerischer Schulbuch Verlag, 1972. 1v. (various paging). LC 71-650154.

This excellent atlas offers a wide range of color maps for the study of the ancient world. It begins with a series of maps of prehistoric Europe. Next are several maps of the world as conceived by ancient geographers, followed by a series of maps covering the Ancient Near East and the world of the Old Testament. The classical world then receives full coverage. There are separate maps for nearly every major period of Greco-Roman civilization that often include insets of city and battle plans. The maps are designed and arranged to show historical development. For example, maps of the same region or province at different times are often grouped together to show changes. The maps offer much topographical and historical information. GHW extends to ca. A.D. 600 and includes maps of India and China. The extremely detailed index will assist in locating a large number of places. This is the best all-around choice for those willing to deal with German; actually, it does not really require that much German, because the place-names are the same as or very similar to those used in English.

421. Cornell, Tim, and John Matthews. **Atlas of the Roman World**. New York: Facts on File, 1982. 240pp. ISBN 0-87196-652-2. LC 81-19591.

"The purpose of this Atlas is to give a comprehensive general view of the Roman world in its physical and cultural setting." It follows the recent trend in thematic atlases and offers more text and illustration while relegating maps to more of a supporting role. Cornell and Matthews cover the topography and climate of Italy well, but do little for the rest of the empire. They focus on historical and cultural developments. The maps are attractively designed and make effective use of color. As a whole they show the development and expansion of the Roman world throughout the Mediterranean. There are good basic maps of the city of Rome during the republican and imperial eras. Maps are also provided for other major cities and archaeological sites. Coverage of the provinces is better than average. The text and illustrations are excellent. A gazetteer and an index conclude the book.

This is a good atlas for students of Roman history. It is weak for those interested primarily in topographical information, because relief is provided only in one map (of Italy), and the total of places shown on the maps is too few for effectively locating any but the best-known sites. This work is a companion to Levi's *Atlas of the Greek World* (entry 430).

422. Finley, M. I. **Atlas of Classical Archaeology**. New York: McGraw-Hill, 1977. 256pp. ISBN 0-07-021025-X. LC 76-16761.

Finley covers Greek and Roman civilization from roughly 1000 B.C. to A.D. 500. He surveys major sites throughout the Greco-Roman world, moving west to east, from Britain to the Euphrates. Finley supplies a brief textual description of each site, accompanied by illustrations and maps, and provides some bibliographical references. There are many regional maps (based on provinces of the Roman empire) and numerous city maps and plans of archaeological sites. A general index concludes the work. This is a useful supplement to the broader historical atlases, and particularly useful when information about a specific site is needed.

423.   Grant, Michael. **Atlas of Classical History**. 5th ed. New York: Oxford University Press, 1994. 116pp. ISBN 0-19-521074-3; 0-19-521078-6pa. LC 93-48331.

Previously published under the titles *Ancient History Atlas* and *Atlas of Ancient History*, this work covers the Ancient Near East, the classical world, and Biblical history. Its chronological span reaches from 1700 B.C. to A.D. 565. Maps are arranged in chronological sequence and tend to be simple and lacking in detail; all are black-and-white (mostly white). The focus of the maps is historical rather than geographical. There are, for example, maps of the various kingdoms and empires at particular times, of the expansion of Rome, and of trade and agricultural products. The atlas is useful for the study of political and economic history, although even then it must be used with care. There are a number of inaccuracies in the information provided. Grant's atlas is exceptionally poor for locating places or forming any idea of the actual topography. The short index of place-names highlights the work's lack of detail.

✓ 424.   Grundy, G. B., ed. **Murray's Small Classical Atlas**. London: John Murray, 1917. 2d ed. 1v. (various paging). LC 21-949.

This compact atlas is easy to use but somewhat deficient in the range of information provided. It provides maps of the Ancient Near Eastern empires, two general maps of the Roman empire, maps of the provinces, city plans (several each of Rome and Athens), and plans of the principal battles in Greek and Roman history. A number of these maps, which are actually insets in larger ones, are small. Grundy is not much use for historical study, because there are too few maps (14), and he does not give a good picture of different periods. There is an index. Grundy will serve for locating places, although Kiepert (entry 428), the *Grosser historischer Weltatlas* (entry 420), and Hammond (entry 425) all offer a larger number of toponyms.

✓ 425.   Hammond, Nicholas G. L., ed. **Atlas of the Greek and Roman World in Antiquity**. Park Ridge, NJ: Noyes Press, 1981. 56pp. ISBN 0-8155-5060-X. LC 81-675203.

This atlas, which includes a number of distinguished historians and archaeologists among its contributors, covers the Greco-Roman world from the neolithic period to the sixth century A.D. Its large format provides for maps of generous size and detail. Both topographical and historical information are provided. The atlas does have a number of drawbacks. The heart of the work, a series of topographical maps of the entire region at the same scale (1:1,500,00), has been rendered difficult to use by the Procrustean manner in which they have been chopped up to fit the pages. The symbols and labeling on some of the historical maps are confusing and hard to follow. The maps are all in black-and-white. However, the atlas is generally serviceable and is one of the best all-round choices available at the present.

426.   Jones, Barri, and David Mattingly. **An Atlas of Roman Britain**. Oxford, England: Blackwell, 1990. 341pp. ISBN 0-631-13791-2. LC 90-675155.

Britain is the best known archaeologically of all the provinces of the Roman Empire. Jones and Mattingly have taken advantage of this fact to provide an extremely detailed atlas. Separate chapters cover such topics as the topography and climate, Britain as viewed by the ancient geographers, Britain before the conquest (A.D. 43), the conquest and garrisoning of Britain, the economy, and religion. The many maps present all sorts of general and specialized information. In addition, numerous site plans, aerial photographs of sites, and reproductions of antique maps and plans enrich the work. A large bibliography and detailed general index complete the work. This atlas is an indispensable aid for the study of Roman Britain.

427. Kiepert, Heinrich. **Atlas Antiquus: Zwolf Karten zur Alten**. Berlin: Dietrich Reimer, 1902. 12. berichtige Aufl. LC 3-14223.

Although outdated in some ways, this old standard is still useful. The atlas covers the Ancient Near East as well as the classical world. It has a limited number of maps, but these are very detailed and show more than 9,000 place-names, which are fully indexed. Kiepert also does a fairly good job of showing relief. Thus, his maps remain a good source of topographical information. However, they are not very good for historical study, because they do not show changes over time in the political boundaries of antiquity. *Atlas Antiquus* appeared in numerous editions and printings and is widely available.

428. Kiepert, Heinrich, and Ch. Huelsen. **Formae Urbis Romae Antiquae. Accedit Nomenclator Topographicus**. Berolini, Germania: Apud D. Reimer, 1912. Editio altera auctior et emendata. 162pp. LC 14-14626.

Kiepert and Huelsen has long been a fundamental work. It was intended for those who found Lanciani (entry 429) too detailed. Although now badly out-of-date, its maps are still useful. The four maps, which are clear and readable and stored in a pocket, cover Rome in the time of the republic, the early empire, and the late empire. The fourth map is a more detailed plan of the heart of the city as it was in the imperial era. Due to the acidic paper on which they were printed, the maps now are in delicate condition and must be handled with care.

429. Lanciani, Rodolfo. **Formae Urbis Romae**. Mediolani, Italia: Apud Ulricum Hoepli, 1893-1901; repr., Roma: Edizioni Quasar, 1989. 12 p., 46 double maps.

Lanciani provides a series of extremely valuable detailed maps of Rome that show the entire city at a scale of 1:1,000. (The reprint edition has maps at a scale of 1:2,000.) The known remains of the ancient city are superimposed on the modern city streets and buildings. The maps are quite readable, although sections cover such small areas that it is easy to lose a sense of perspective. One index covers the monuments and places of the ancient city, another the buildings and places of the modern city.

✓ 430. Levi, Peter. **Atlas of the Greek World**. New York: Facts on File, 1980. 239pp. ISBN 0-87196-448-1. LC 81-122477.

Like its companion volume, *Atlas of the Roman World* (entry 421), this work is more a cultural than a geographical atlas. While there are a significant number of maps, the accompanying text and illustrations comprise a history of ancient Greek civilization. The illustrations are good, but the text is quirky and not always reliable. The maps, especially the historical ones, are usually acceptable, but there are occasional inaccuracies. There is also insufficient topographical detail. Those interested in basic geographical information would do better to consult Kiepert (entry 427), *Grosser historischer Weltatlas* (entry 420), or Hammond (entry 425).

431. Muir, Ramsay. **Muir's Atlas of Ancient and Classical History**. 6th ed. Edited by R. F. Treharne and Harold Fullard. London: George Philip, 1963. ISBN 0-540-05433-X.

This is a useful basic atlas for students. It begins by presenting various ancient conceptions of the world (i.e., those of Herodotus, Erastosthenes, Strabo, and Ptolemy). Then there is a chronological sequence of maps of the Ancient Near East and the classical world. The attractive color maps provide adequate detail. Many of the larger maps have useful insets (e.g., the general map of

Greece includes insets of the Acropolis, Athens, the Propontis, and Crete). While the number of maps is modest (47 on 20 plates), they provide a good overall picture of the ancient world and manage to cover key places and periods.

432. Myers, J. Wilson, Eleanor Emlyn Myers, and Gerald Cadogan, eds. **The Aerial Atlas of Ancient Crete**. Berkeley, CA: University of California Press, 1992. 318pp. ISBN 0-520-07382-7. LC 91-20649.

This atlas covers one of the most important centers of early Greek civilization. The substantial introduction includes essays on the geomorphology and history of Crete. The atlas surveys some 44 archaeological sites in Crete, arranged alphabetically. Each article includes a general discussion of the site and its history, the history of the excavation and location of finds, and a bibliography. Plans of the sites and spectacular color aerial photographs follow. The text of each entry has been prepared by the current director of research at each site. A full index concludes the work. The atlas is a valuable geographical and archaeological resource.

433. Oliphant, Margaret. **The Atlas of the Ancient World: Charting the Great Civilizations of the Past**. New York: Simon and Schuster, 1992. 220pp. ISBN 0-671-75103-4. LC 91-38075.

Oliphant covers the entire ancient world: the Near East, prehistoric Europe, Greece, Rome, India, China, and the Americas. She follows the recent trend of combining relatively few maps with a general cultural and historical text and many illustrations. Greece and the Aegean receive six small maps and several plans of individual sites and buildings. A general map of Greece presents topographical information but is not very detailed. Other maps are historical in character, covering topics or periods. The maps of the Roman world are similar in number and type. The work is colorful and offers a readable, if sketchy and basic, text. Its focus is cultural rather than geographical. This work might be suitable for high school students or the less-demanding general reader, but is not recommended as an atlas.

✓ 434. Shepherd, William R. **Shepherd's Historical Atlas**. 9th ed., revised and updated. New York: Barnes & Noble, 1964. 1v. (various paging). ISBN 0-06-013846-7. LC Map 64-26.

Shepherd, a general historical atlas, has long been a standard reference work. It has a reasonably strong section of maps covering the Ancient Near East and the classical world. Shepherd is more than adequate for historical study. It includes a variety of maps covering the major periods of ancient history. For example, the development of the Roman empire is covered by a series of maps, and the provinces are shown at several different times in the history of the empire. There are a number of plans of major cities (e.g., Athens, Rome, Alexandria, Jerusalem). Sufficient topographical information is given; many maps show relief and a fairly large number of places are shown. Unfortunately, many of the maps are too small and crowded for easy consultation. There is a substantial general index to aid in locating places. This is a serviceable atlas, although *Grosser historischer Weltatlas* (entry 420) is better as a general historical atlas. Hammond (entry 425) and Talbert (entry 437) offer far more specific help to students of Greek and Roman history.

435. Stier, Hans-Erich, and Ernst Kirsten, eds. **Westermanns Atlas zur Weltgeschichte. Teil I: Vorzeit und Altertum**. Berlin: Georg Westermann, 1963. 44pp. LC 66-220.

This atlas includes the Ancient Near East and prehistoric Europe as well as the classical world. The many attractive color maps offer a wealth of detail. There are numerous maps of cities and parts of cities and of individual provinces of the Roman empire at various periods. The sequence of maps is roughly chronological. Overview maps are inserted at appropriate points. *Westermann's Atlas* will serve well those engaged in historical studies. However, this otherwise admirable work lacks an index.

436. **Tabula Imperii Romani**. 1930- .

The *Tabula Imperii Romani* is an international project under the sponsorship of the Union Académique Internationale. Its aim is to produce, in sections, a complete map of the Roman empire at a scale of 1:1,000,000. There are a number of problems in finding and using such parts as are available. Because it is an international project, the mapping and publication of each part of the empire is the responsibility of its modern successsor state. The result has been chaotic. Not all of the sections (usually called sheets) have been completed or published; many have appeared only in provisional form. Each has a different publisher and place of publication. Those that have appeared definitively consist of a gazetteer and bibliography in book form, with the map in a folded pocket. In general the maps are attractively printed and convey a great deal of information. For a complete list of sheets available in some form, provisional or definitive, see R. J. A. Talbert, "Mapping the Classical World 1872-1990," *Journal of Roman Archaeology* 5 (1992): 35-37. No library is known to have a complete set, and it is difficult to locate or obtain copies of many sheets.

437. Talbert, Richard J. A., ed. **Atlas of Classical History**. New York: Macmillan, 1985; repr., London: Routledge, 1988. 217pp. ISBN 0-02-933110-2. LC 85-675113.

This atlas, which focuses almost entirely on the Greco-Roman world, is aimed at college students. There is a good range of maps that cover key places and periods. Unfortunately, they are all in black-and-white. An extensive amount of text accompanies the maps, providing a historical summary for the period or events covered by each map. The maps are presented in chronological sequence. A strong point of the atlas is the use of many smaller maps and insets to present towns, archaeological sites, and battle plans, although these are sometimes too small and crowded. The larger maps include enough detail to be really useful, but are rarely crowded. The bibliography at the end, which is arranged by period to correspond with sections of maps and text, rounds up the usual suspects to provide a good basic reading list. A gazetteer concludes the work. Talbert's atlas is weak in the topographical department; few of the maps show relief, and the atlas shows only half as many places as Hammond (entry 425) and the *Grosser historischer Weltatlas* (entry 420). It is, however, useful and up-to-date for historical purposes.

438. Van der Heyden, A. A. M., and H. H. Scullard, eds. **Atlas of the Classical World**. London: Nelson, 1959. 221pp. LC 61-1130.

This work was the first classical atlas to include extensive text and illustrations. The text is pedestrian and often irrelevant to the needs of those consulting an atlas. The atlas is weak in topography: its maps include relatively few place-names and almost never show relief. On the other hand, there is a wide range of maps for historical study. They cover the major periods and events of Greco-Roman history adequately. There are also some unusual topical maps, such as "Greek Buildings and Monuments in the Mediterrranean Area" and a map of the birthplaces of important Greek authors and scholars. This atlas is an adequate work for students of history and is widely available. However, the *Grosser historischer Weltatlas* (entry 420), Hammond (entry 425), and Talbert (entry 437) are all more recent and offer equal or better coverage.

439. Warrington, J. **Everyman's Atlas of Ancient and Classical Geography**. Rev. ed. New York: E.P. Dutton, 1952. 256pp. LC 53-270.

This atlas includes 43 color and 20 line maps. The maps are small in size and weak in showing relief. A set of maps at the beginning shows various ancient conceptions of the world. Then follows a series of maps of the Ancient Near Eastern empires, Greece, Rome, and the Roman empire. There are some detailed maps of cities (Rome and Athens). The atlas also includes maps to assist students (the voyage of the *Argo,* the voyages of Aeneas, and plans of famous battles). A gazetteer covers major sites only, but does so in considerable detail. It locates the places and gives extended topographical descriptions of them. There is also a good index of place-names. While it has its faults as a geographical tool, *Everyman's Atlas* provides a serviceable companion to students and general readers.

CHAPTER

GREEK AND LATIN LANGUAGE

This chapter lists a selection of basic works on the Greek and Latin languages. These titles include general works on the history of the languages and standard dictionaries and reference grammars. A few dictionaries that list and gloss Latin phrases commonly used in English are also noted. Smaller dictionaries and grammars designed for the use of students are, for the most part, excluded. Many valuable specialized lexica and grammatical works have also been omitted because of their narrow focus.

General Works

440.   Hammond, Mason. **Latin: A Historical and Linguistic Handbook**. Cambridge, MA: Harvard University Press, 1976. 292pp. ISBN 0-674-51290-1. LC 75-33359.

Hammond intends "to present a historical and linguistic introduction to Latin." His work is aimed at teachers of Latin, particularly at the secondary level, and students. The book assumes relatively little knowledge beyond a basic grasp of Latin. The first four chapters supply some background material in linguistics and show the relation of Latin to the Indo-European language family and to the other languages of ancient Italy. Subsequent chapters focus on specific aspects of the Latin language: alphabet, pronunciation, morphology, formation of compounds, syntax, and versification. The concluding chapters cover postclassical Latin and its relation to the romance languages, and Latin and English. There are an adequate bibliography and a general index. Hammond is sometimes superficial and does not do as much as his introduction claims; Palmer (entry 442) is a much better book overall. Still, Hammond covers a few topics that Palmer does not (e.g., the alphabet, versification, the relation of Latin and English). The work is an adequate source of general information on the Latin language.

157

441. Palmer, L. R. **The Greek Language**. Atlantic Highlands, NJ: Humanities Press, 1980. 355pp. (Great Languages). ISBN 0-391-01203-7. LC 79-26758.

This forms a companion work to Palmer's earlier volume on the Latin language (entry 442). "Like its predecessor, the book is divided into two parts: the first concentrates on tracing the development and ramifications of the language as a vehicle and instrument of a great culture.... The second part is a condensed Comparative-Historical Grammar." Part 1 covers the prehistory of the Greek language, Linear B, dialects, the development of the literary language, and postclassical Greek. Part 2 offers chapters on writing and pronunciation, phonology, and morphology; syntax was omitted for reasons of space. A brief bibliography points the way for those who wish to pursue a topic further. There are indexes to subjects, Greek words, and Linear B words. Palmer summarizes a vast amount of research on the Greek language in a manageable and readable volume, and is now the standard work on the subject in English.

442. Palmer, L. R. **The Latin Language**. London: Faber and Faber, 1954; repr., Norman, OK: University of Oklahoma Press, 1988. 372pp. (Great Languages). LC 54-3075.

Considered a standard work since its publication in 1954, *The Latin Language* is the best general work on Latin available in English. Palmer's intention is "to summarize for classical students, for fellow scholars working in other fields, and for the interested laity the results reached by research into the history of Latin from the Bronze Age down to the breakup of the Roman Empire." The book consists of two parts. The first is an outline history of the language; its chapters cover Latin in relation to other Indo-European languages and to other Italic languages, Latin dialects and early texts, spoken Latin, the development of the literary language, Vulgar Latin, and Christian Latin. Palmer's discussions of spoken Latin and of the literary language are highly regarded. The second part is a brief comparative-historical grammar, with chapters on phonology, morphology, and syntax. Palmer then provides a good, if short, bibliography, with some useful annotations. There are also indexes of subjects and Latin words.

Dictionaries and Thesauri

443. Bauer, Walter. **A Greek-English Lexicon of the New Testament and Other Early Christian Literature**. 2d ed. Revised and augmented by F. Wilbur Gingrich and Frederick W. Danker from Walter Bauer's 5th edition, 1958. Chicago: University of Chicago Press, 1979. 900pp. ISBN 0-226-03932-3. LC 78-14293.

This is a translation and adaptation of Bauer's *Griechisch-Deutsches Wörterbuch zu den Schriften des Neuen Testaments und der übrigen urchristlichen Literatur* by William Arndt and Gingrich. Bauer-Arndt-Gingrich is the standard lexicon for New Testament Greek. In addition to the New Testament and early Christian writers, it frequently cites the Septuagint, Hellenistic Jewish authors such as Philo and Josephus, a wide range of papyri, and some Byzantine authors. Articles provide definitions and discussions of forms; many also cite pertinent secondary works. A useful tool for all who deal with Hellenistic and later Greek, this lexicon forms a valuable supplement to Liddell-Scott-Jones (entry 455) and other Greek-English dictionaries.

444. Boisacq, Emile. **Dictionnaire étymologique de la langue grecque: étudiée dans ses rapports avec les autres langues indo-européenes.** 4e éd., augmentée d'un index par Helmut Rix. Heidelberg, Germany: Carl Winter Universitätsverlag, 1950. 1,256pp. LC 51-2358.

A respected, if now dated, work on Greek etymology, Boisacq is primarily concerned with the relation of Greek to other Indo-European languages. The history of words within the Greek language receives less attention; for this one should consult Chantraine (entry 446). Boisacq's entries provide extensive bibliographical references. There are frequent cross-references from words and forms that are treated as part of a larger article. Boisacq also provides indexes to non-Greek words by language; these are arranged by language family. Although Boisacq remains useful, Frisk (entry 451) is more up-to-date and should be preferred.

445. Branyon, Richard A. **Latin Phrases & Quotations.** New York: Hippocrene Books, 1994. 242pp. ISBN 0-7818-0260-1.

Intended as an aid to readers of English literature, this compendium lists more than 4,200 Latin phrases along with their English equivalents. These phrases include both quotations from literary works and common Latin expressions that are sometimes used in English. Quotations are generally identified by author, although Branyon does not provide full references. Branyon arranges the phrases alphabetically. Appendices list the Latin mottos of selected states and the Latin phrases most frequently found in English.

Branyon's translations leave a good deal to be desired. They generally provide the gist of the original but often fail to communicate its tone and force. Ehrlich's similar work (entry 447) offers far superior translations. No index of any sort is provided.

446. Chantraine, Pierre. **Dictionnaire étymologique de la langue grecque: histoire des mots.** Paris: Editions Klincksieck, 1968-1980. 2v. ISBN 2-252-02210-8. LC 68-136031.

Chantraine's work is modelled on Ernout-Meillet's Latin etymological dictionary (entry 448); its relation to Frisk's etymological dictionary (entry 451) is similar to that of Ernout-Meillet's to Walde-Hofmann (entry 466). Chantraine is more concerned with the histories of the words than with their origins and linguistic affiliations. He provides much information on the forms and meanings of words at various periods in the history of Greek. His etymologies draw heavily on Frisk, although he occasionally offers an alternative etymology. Also, because Chantraine's dictionary is younger, he is able to take into account extensive recent work on the early history of Greek as revealed by the Linear B tablets. Indexes to Mycenaean Greek words and non-Greek words conclude the work.

447. Ehrlich, Eugene. **Amo, Amas, Amat and More: How to Use Latin to Your Own Advantage and to the Astonishment of Others.** New York: Harper & Row, 1985. 328pp. ISBN 0-06-181249-8. LC 84-48594.

This extremely useful book is a dictionary of Latin expressions and tags used in English. In addition to those expressions that used to be common among the literate, it includes scholarly abbreviations, mottos, proverbs, and technical terms from various fields such as law. Each entry includes the Latin word or phrase, a guide to pronunciation, and an idiomatic translation. The translations reflect the spirits rather than the letters of the originals. A descriptive passage concludes many of the entries, giving the literal meaning (if not covered by the translation) and explaining when and how English speakers might use the expression. An index gives English phrases and refers to the Latin equivalent. Ehrlich is a great help both in translating Latin phrases found in reading English and for discovering how to "say something in Latin."

448. Ernout, A., and A. Meillet. **Dictionnaire étymologique de la langue latine: histoire des mots**. Quatrième édition, deuxième tirage augmentée de corrections nouvelles. Paris: Librairie C. Klincksieck, 1967. 827pp. LC 68-68022.

This work is generally considered to be the standard Latin etymological dictionary. Ernout, one of the foremost French Latinists of this century, is responsible for providing the history of each word from early Latin through late antiquity. Meillet discusses the Indo-European roots of each word. Many of the entries include references to modern studies. Less problematic word histories are often treated in less detail and equipped with a smaller bibliographical apparatus; for further information on these, one can consult Walde-Hofmann (entry 466). Many cross-references are provided from forms that are treated under another entry. There are also word indexes for non-Latin words; these are divided by language.

449. Estienne, Henri. **Thesaurus Graecae Linguae**. Post editionem Anglicam novis additamentis auctum, ordineque alphabetico digestum tertium ediderunt Carolus Benedictus Hase, Gulielmus Dindorfius, et Ludovicus Dindorfius. Parisiis: Excudebat Ambrosius Firmin Didot, 1831-1865. 8v. in 9. LC 06-39594.

Long the basic compendium for the study of classical and Byzantine Greek lexicography, the *Thesaurus Graecae Linguae* is based on obsolete texts and methods. The work of a Renaissance Hellenist, it was revised and expanded in the nineteenth-century by a trio of distinguished German classical scholars. It is much larger than Liddell-Scott-Jones (entry 455) and is only partly superseded by it. For exhaustive citations of all known uses of a particular word or form, the computerized *Thesaurus Linguae Graecae* (entry 464) is a far better tool. However, the TLG database does not offer definitions or other lexicographical information at present. Specialists will still find Estienne's venerable work of use on occasion.

450. Forcellini, Egidio. **Totius Latinitatis Lexicon**. In hac editione post tertiam auctam et emendatum a Josepho Furlanetto ... amplissime auctum atque emendatum cura et studio Doct. Vincentii De-Vit. Prati, Italia: Typis Aldinianis, 1858-1875. 6v. LC 09-25614-5.

Forcellini's large Latin dictionary was his life's work. He completed it in 1753; it was published posthumously in 1771. A number of scholars have since reworked it. Vincenzo De Vit's edition is both the most commonly cited and the most readily available. Long the fullest and most complete Latin dictionary, Forcellini is gradually being superseded by the *Thesaurus Linguae Latinae* (TLL) (entry 465). Even the *Oxford Latin Dictionary* (entry 452), which in terms of currency and lexicographical method is far superior, offers fewer examples and citations. For those parts of the alphabet not yet covered by the TLL, Forcellini remains a valuable resource.

451. Frisk, Hjalmar. **Griechisches Etymologisches Wörterbuch**. Heidelberg, Germany: Carl Winter Universitätsverlag, 1973-1979. Zweite, unveränderte Auflage. 3v. (Indogermanische Bibliothek). ISBN 3-533-00652-2(v.1-2); 3-533-02203-X(v.3).

Frisk is the standard etymological dictionary for the Greek language. His compact entries provide a wealth of information on the forms and meanings of Greek words, although his chief concern is to present their linguistic connections and etymologies. Frisk also supplies numerous references to the scholarly literature. Corrigenda and addenda are found in the third volume, which also includes a number of indexes to non-Greek words. The indexes are arranged by language. Frisk is complemented by Chantraine's somewhat later work (entry 446), which concentrates primarily on word histories.

✓ 452.   Glare, P. G. W., ed. **Oxford Latin Dictionary**. Oxford, England: Clarendon Press, 1982. 2,126pp. ISBN 0-19-864224-5. LC 82-8162.

This is the first entirely new comprehensive dictionary of classical Latin to appear in this century. Based on a fresh reading of the Latin sources, it is completely independent from its predecessor, Lewis and Short (entry 454), and from the *Thesaurus Linguae Latinae* (entry 465). Editorial work began in 1933. The dictionary was issued in fascicles as the work progressed; the final fascicle and the single-volume edition were published in 1982. The dictionary treats "classical Latin from its beginnings to the end of the second century A.D." The lower limit is somewhat fuzzy; coverage occasionally extends to the third century, while patristic authors of the late second century are generally omitted. Christian Latin is out of scope; for both this and late antique pagan authors, one must consult Souter's glossary (entry 463). Within its chronological limits the dictionary treats all known words thoroughly; a sizeable number of proper names (place-names, Roman family names, and mythological characters) are covered as well. In general the OLD follows the same lexicographical principles and imitates the formal layout of the *Oxford English Dictionary*. One of the OLD's strengths is the large number of examples cited in the entries. Brief etymological notes are supplied also. This is now the standard Latin-English dictionary. It is considerably larger and much more up-to-date than Lewis and Short. However, those working in late Latin or requiring detailed etymological information or exhaustive citations of examples of a particular usage still will have to consult other works.

453.   Lampe, G. W. H., ed. **A Patristic Greek Lexicon**. Oxford, England: Clarendon Press, 1961. 1,568pp. ISBN 0-19-864213-X. LC 77-372171.

A Patristic Greek Lexicon serves as a companion volume to the 9th edition of Liddell-Scott-Jones (entry 455), which excluded all post-Biblical Christian writers. It covers Christian authors from Clement of Rome (first century A.D.) to Theodore of Studium (d. A.D. 826). The focus of the lexicon is on theological and ecclesiastical vocabulary. Words found in Liddell-Scott-Jones are not generally repeated unless they are of particular interest to the reader of the Fathers of the Church. Nor are common meanings of words covered by those authors repeated; so that a Greek word may be listed with a single uncommon meaning, although its usual meanings also appear in patristic literature. Because the scope of the dictionary is restricted to patristic usage, it also does not cover the usage of the Septuagint or New Testament. Lampe covers many Greek words not found in other dictionaries, and is of use to the general student of later Greek as well as to patristic scholars.

✓ 454.   Lewis, Charlton T., and Charles Short. **A Latin Dictionary**. Oxford, England: Clarendon Press, 1879. 2,019pp. ISBN 0-19-864201-6.

This work, popularly called Lewis and Short, has a long history. It is based on E. A. Andrews's 1850 translation of Wilhelm Freund's *Wörterbuch der lateinischen Sprache* (Leipzig: Hahn, 1834-1840). Freund's own work was, in turn, based largely on Forcellini (entry 450). Lewis and Short extensively reworked the earlier dictionary. Their dictionary, which has been reprinted frequently, remained the standard Latin-English dictionary until the completion of the *Oxford Latin Dictionary* (entry 452) in 1982. Lewis and Short cover the entire classical period, from the beginnings of Latin literature to the fourth century A.D. The dictionary is based on antiquated principles and obsolete editions; it also contains many errors. In general, the *Oxford Latin Dictionary* should be preferred to Lewis and Short. However, Lewis and Short is widely available and remains a serviceable dictionary if used with some care.

✓ 455. Liddell, Henry George, and Robert Scott. **A Greek-English Lexicon**. 9th ed. Revised by Henry Stuart Jones with Roderick McKenzie and others. Oxford, England: Clarendon Press, 1968. 2042, 153pp. ISBN 0-19-864214-8. LC 71-2271.

✓ 456. Liddell, Henry George, and Robert Scott. **A Lexicon Abridged from Liddell and Scott's Greek-English Lexicon**. Oxford, England: Clarendon Press, 1871. 804pp.

✓457. Liddell, Henry George, and Robert Scott. **An Intermediate Greek-English Lexicon**. Oxford, England: Clarendon Press, 1889. 910pp.

A Greek-English Lexicon, which is commonly referred to as LSJ, is the standard Greek-English lexicon. The most recent edition is the 9th (1940), which is now accompanied by a supplement edited by E. A. Barber and others. The supplement has been included in all printings of LSJ since 1968; it is also available in a separate edition from Clarendon Press (1968). The lexicon covers the Greek language from Homer to approximately A.D. 600. It addresses itself primarily to meanings of words; discussion of etymology is largely omitted. The authors have supplied many citations and examples in the entries. Their coverage of the classical authors is quite strong. While LSJ does include many words and citations from epigraphical and papyrological texts, those with interests in these areas will need the assistance of more specialized works. Mycenaean Greek (i.e., Linear B texts) is not covered at all and also requires consultation of specialized publications.

LSJ is also available in two abridged versions intended for students. These are both based on earlier editions of the larger work. While these smaller works are suitable for everyday use, those requiring the fullest and most accurate information should consult the 9th edition.

458. Packard Humanities Institute. **PHI CD-ROM #5.3**. Los Altos, CA: Packard Humanities Institute, 1991. 1 disc.

459. Packard Humanities Institute. **PHI CD-ROM #6**. Los Altos, CA: Packard Humanities Institute, 1991. 1 disc.

These two CD-ROM products allow one to do word searches of a large body of Latin and Greek texts. *PHI CD-ROM #5.3* includes the full text of more than 350 Latin authors; virtually all Latin literature through the end of the second century A.D. is covered, along with a few later texts. This disc also contains a number of versions of the Bible, including the Hebrew text, the Septuagint, the Greek New Testament, the Latin Vulgate, the Coptic New Testament, and the Authorized and Revised Standard versions. *PHI CD-ROM #6* is a database of Greek and Latin inscriptions and papyri. A selection of Coptic texts is also provided on this disc.

These CD-ROMS can be used with either DOS or Macintosh computers. Search software is not supplied by the Institute and must be obtained through various third-party vendors. Usually the same software can be used for both PHI discs and *Thesaurus Linguae Graecae* discs (entry 464).

460.   Smith, William, and Theophilus D. Hall. **A Copious and Critical English-Latin Dictionary**. New York: American Book Company, 1871. 964, 709-754pp.

461.   Smith, William. **Smaller English-Latin Dictionary**. London: John Murray, 1870. 719pp.

This frequently reprinted work is the most complete English-Latin dictionary available. Its original audience (which, to a large extent, no longer exists) consisted of students of Latin prose composition. Entries generally cite authorities and often provide examples of usage. A dictionary of proper names, which gives the correct Latin forms of these names, is appended. There is also an abridged version, which will serve the needs of most students.

462.   Sophocles, E. A. **Greek Lexicon of the Roman and Byzantine Periods (from B.C. 146 to A.D. 1100)**. Memorial edition. Cambridge, MA: Harvard University Press, 1914; repr., Hildesheim, Germany: Georg Olms, 1992. 1,188pp.

Sophocles first published his lexicon in 1870. Subsequent editions include a few corrections but no additions or revisions of any substance. It remains the only Greek-English lexicon for the Byzantine period; as such, it is a useful supplement to Liddell-Scott-Jones (entry 455) and Lampe (entry 453). It is also sometimes helpful for Greek authors who flourished under the Roman empire, although these are, for the most part, covered by LSJ. A new Byzantine Greek lexicon remains a desideratum.

463.   Souter, Alexander. **A Glossary of Later Latin to 600 A.D.** Oxford, England: Clarendon Press, 1949. 459pp. LC 50-7994.

Souter, one of the editors of the *Oxford Latin Dictionary* (OLD) (entry 452), compiled this glossary to cover the gap between the OLD's coverage and the beginning of the medieval period. "The glossary is intended to include all known 'common' words that, according to the witness of surviving writings and documents, do not occur in the period before A.D. 180 and yet may be certainly or reasonably assigned to a date earlier than A.D. 600." Souter gives only the basic form of the word and its definition, and does not discuss forms or quote examples. Citations of specific works are given only for those words for which Souter found no more than three or four occurrences. This is a handy tool for those working in Late Latin and the Church Fathers.

464.   **Thesaurus Linguae Graecae**. Irvine, CA: Thesaurus Linguae Graecae Project, University of California, Irvine.

The *Thesaurus Linguae Graecae* (TLG) is a computerized database of ancient Greek literature. It now contains virtually all extant Greek literary texts from Homer (eighth century B.C.) to A.D. 600, and the texts of many Byzantine historiographical, lexicographical, and scholiastic writers as well. Documentary texts (e.g., most inscriptions and papyri) are not included in the database; these are included in other databases produced by the Packard Humanities Institute (see entries 458-459). At the present time, TLG functions strictly as a gigantic concordance to Greek literature. Through it one can find all occurrences of a particular word, form of a word, or phrase. However, definitions and other lexicographical information are not provided. TLG is available for lease in both magnetic tape and compact disc formats. Updated discs are issued approximately every two years. TLG does not supply search software; several third-party vendors offer software to run TLG on DOS and Macintosh computers. The *Thesaurus Linguae Graecae Canon of Greek Authors and Works* (entry 56) lists all authors and works included in the database; it also specifies which editions were used. The most current source of information about TLG is the TLG gopher server (entry 615) at the University of California at Irvine.

465. **Thesaurus Linguae Latinae**. Editus auctoritate et consilio Academiarum Quinque Germanicarum Berolinensis, Gottingensis, Lipsiensis, Monacensis, Vindobonensis. Lipsiae, Germaniae: B. G. Teubner, 1900- . LC 77-11275.

This project began in 1893, at the instigation of Theodor Mommsen. The first fascicle of TLL appeared in 1900; subsequent fascicles have appeared at irregular intervals. The volumes for A through O are now complete, and parts of P have appeared as well. Several supplementary volumes covering proper names have also been published. Work continues on the remaining fascicles at the TLL offices in Munich. The *Thesaurus* is intended to cover Latin in full from the beginnings to the Antonine age, with selective coverage extending up to the seventh century A.D. Individual scholars prepare the entry for each word; all articles are signed. Entries discuss forms, gender, and, when appropriate, vowel quantities. They then give the full history of the word. The treatment is exhaustive; each entry includes a massive number of examples and citations. The TLL is the best and fullest source available for the study of Latin lexicography. For the parts of the alphabet not yet covered by the *Thesaurus* one must rely on the *Oxford Latin Dictionary* (entry 452) supplemented by Forcellini (entry 450). The Packard Humanities Institute CD-ROMs (entries 458-459) are also useful for locating occurrences of particular Latin words.

466. Walde, A. **Lateinisches Etymologisches Wörterbuch**. 4. Auflage von J. B. Hofmann. Heidelberg, Germany: Carl Winter Universitätsverlag, 1965. 3v. (Indogermanische Bibliothek). LC 68-83380.

This edition is essentially a reproduction of the 3d edition (1938-1956). It is the German counterpart of Ernout-Meillet (entry 448); because both works went through a number of editions, they cite each other frequently. Walde-Hofmann generally offers a much more detailed treatment, with longer entries and more citations of texts and secondary literature. Occasionally, Ernout-Meillet offers fuller treatment of a particular word. Walde-Hofmann tends to offer more hardcore Indo-European etymology and pays less attention to the history of words within the Latin language. While a denser, less readable work, Walde-Hofmann is a valuable and informative dictionary. Those who are concerned with the Latin language proper rather than Indo-European linguistics will prefer Ernout-Meillet in most instances. The third volume of Walde-Hofmann consists of extensive indexes of non-Latin words grouped by language family and language.

467. Woodhouse, S. C. **English-Greek Dictionary: A Vocabulary of the Attic Language**. 2d ed. London: Routledge & Kegan Paul, 1932. 1029pp. LC 39-8394.

Woodhouse compiled his dictionary as an aid to writers of Greek prose compositions in schools and universities. Although this use is now rare, the work is still useful for those seeking the Greek equivalent for an English expression. The supplement that accompanies the 2d edition is a list of proper names, many of them famous Romans of antiquity, which provides the correct

Greek equivalent. Woodhouse has been reprinted a number of times and is both more readily available and more up-to-date than Yonge's slightly larger dictionary (entry 468).

468. Yonge, C. D. **An English-Greek Lexicon: With Many New Articles, an Appendix of Proper Names, and Pillon's Greek Synonyms**. Edited by Henry Drisler. New York: American Book, 1870. 1v. (various paging).

Yonge's lexicon, which first appeared in 1849, was aimed at the student writer of Greek prose and verse. It is based strictly on classical authors, chiefly those of the fifth and fourth centuries B.C. His goal was to provide "a complete English vocabulary, so far, at least, as there are words in the Greek language by which the English words can be literally or adequately rendered, and where this cannot be done, to supply, wherever practicable, the deficiency by phrases." Yonge's *Lexicon*, with its small type and densely packed columns, is actually a bit larger than Woodhouse's *Dictionary* (entry 467). It is, however, based on older scholarship and is less readily available. Yonge exists in a number of nineteenth-century editions and reprints; there are relatively few differences among them.

Grammars

469. Allen, Joseph H., and J. B. Greenough. **Allen and Greenough's New Latin Grammar for Schools and Colleges: Founded on Comparative Grammar**. Edited by J. B. Greenough, G. L. Kittredge, A. A. Howard, and Benj. L. D'Ooge. Boston: Ginn, 1903; repr., New Rochelle, NY: Caratzas Brothers, 1988. 490pp. LC 03-23416.

The original edition of this old standby appeared in 1872. It reached its final form in the 1903 revision and has since been reprinted regularly. Allen and Greenough remains a reliable descriptive grammar of Latin, possibly the best available in English. It covers the morphology, syntax, and prosody of Latin more than adequately, although it lacks the massive thoroughness of the Kühner-Stegmann (entry 475). Its manner of presentation is clearer and less quirky than that of Hale and Buck (entry 472). A detailed table of contents and ample word and subject indexes make the book easy to consult.

470. Blass, F., and A. Debrunner. **A Greek Grammar of the New Testament and Other Early Christian Literature**. Chicago: University of Chicago Press, 1961. 325pp. ISBN 0-226-27110-2. LC 61-8077.

This is a translation and revision of the 9th-10th German edition, incorporating supplementary notes from A. Debrunner, by Robert Funk. Blass-Debrunner-Funk, as it is frequently called, is the standard grammar of New Testament Greek and serves as a companion volume to Bauer-Arndt-Gingrich, *A Greek-English Lexicon of the New Testament* (entry 443). Blass's *Grammatik des neutestamentlichen Griechisch* first appeared in 1896 and has been frequently revised (from 1913 to 1954 by Albert Debrunner, currently by Friedrich Rehkopf). The English edition also includes new material by Funk. Blass-Debrunner-Funk does not treat the New Testament in isolation; it also covers a wide range of Hellenistic Greek writings, including the Septuagint, early Christian authors, papyri, and some Byzantine authors. The work deals with all standard aspects of grammar: phonology, accidence and word formation, and syntax. The grammar includes many illustrative examples from Greek texts and frequently cites pertinent scholarly literature. It is a valuable tool for the study of Hellenistic Greek. There are indexes of subjects, Greek words and forms, and passages cited. The 16th German edition of the grammar revised by Rehkopf (Göttingen, Germany: Vandenhoeck & Ruprecht, 1984) contains much new material; those who read German should consult it in preference to the English edition.

✓ 471. Buck, Carl Darling. **Comparative Grammar of Greek and Latin**. Chicago, IL: University of Chicago Press, 1933. 405pp. LC 33-11254.

Although there is no compelling linguistic reason for the comparative study of Greek and Latin, the subject has become a traditional one because of the cultural affinities of the Greeks and Romans. Buck has long been the standard comparative grammar for Greek and Latin. The introduction covers the Indo-European languages and various features of linguistic history in general and provides outline histories of Greek and Latin languages. The major sections of the grammar cover phonology, inflection, and word formation. Syntax was deliberately omitted. There is still much useful information in Buck, although the book is now badly dated. Andrew Sihler's recent *New Comparative Grammar of Greek and Latin* (entry 479) should replace Buck as the standard work on this topic.

472. Hale, William Gardner, and Carl Darling Buck. **A Latin Grammar**. Boston: Ginn, 1903; repr., University: University of Alabama Press, 1966. 388pp. LC 03-17596.

Hale and Buck is a reliable and readily available descriptive grammar of Latin. It is considerably less detailed than Kühner-Gerth's large work (entry 473), but will generally serve the needs of English-speaking students. Hale and Buck occasionally arrange or present their material in an unusual manner, so that many prefer their chief English-language competitor, *Allen and Greenough's New Latin Grammar* (entry 469). Allen and Greenough also has superior indexing.

473. Kühner, Raphael, Friedrich Blass, and Bernhard Gerth. **Ausführliche Grammatik der griechischen Sprache**. 3. Aufl. Hannover, Germany: Hahnsche Buchhandlung, 1890-1904. 4v. LC 01-2623.

474. Calder, William M., III. **Index Locorum zu Kühner-Gerth**. Darmstadt, Germany: Wissenschaftliche Buchgesellschaft, 1965. 164pp. LC 67-74716.

Kühner's nineteenth-century work remains the fundamental descriptive grammar of Greek. The first part (in two volumes) covers phonology and morphology. It was revised by Friedrich Blass and is usually referred to as Kühner-Blass. This part, while still useful, is somewhat dated; Schwyzer (entry 478) is generally superior for such information. The second part (also in two volumes) deals with syntax. It is routinely called Kühner-Gerth because it was revised by Bernhard Gerth. This sound and detailed treatment of Greek syntax is still frequently cited. Both parts of the grammar have full indexes to subjects and Greek words. While they do not have indexes to Greek and Latin passages cited, an *index locorum* to Kühner-Gerth has been published by W. M. Calder. There have been several reprintings of Kühner's Greek grammar, some of which advertise themselves as 4th editions. These are, however, merely reprints. There is no work of comparable scope in English; those who read only English will have to make do with Smyth's much smaller *Greek Grammar* (entry 480).

475. Kühner, Raphael, Friedrich Holzweissig, and Carl Stegmann. **Ausführliche Grammatik der lateinischen Sprache**. 2. Aufl. (T. 1) and 5. Aufl. (T. 2). Hannover, Germany: Hahnsche Buchhandlung, 1976-1982. 2v. in 3. ISBN 3-7752-5189-8(T.1); 3-7752-5284-3(T.2, Bd.1); 3-7752-5284-3 (T.2, Bd.2).

476. Schwartz, Gary S., and Richard L. Wertis. **Index Locorum zu Kühner-Stegmann "Satzlehre."** Darmstadt, Germany: Wissenchaftliche Buchgesellschaft, 1980. 254pp. ISBN 3-5340-4341-3. LC 86-672472.

Like his companion work on Greek grammar (entry 473), Kühner's massive nineteenth-century Latin grammar remains a standard work. The first volume, which covers phonology and morphology, was revised by Holzweissig in 1912. Holzweissig's revision was never satisfactory and has largely fallen into disuse. The second volume, as revised by Carl Stegmann, is a different matter. Kühner-Stegmann covers Latin syntax in great detail and offers a vast array of examples drawn from the ancient authors. It has been revised several times since Stegmann's original reworking in 1914. Kühner-Stegmann is the best descriptive Latin grammar available. A separately published index to Latin and Greek authors cited in Kühner-Stegmann now makes up one of the few deficiencies of this important work. For comparative and historical grammar one should consult Leumann-Hofmann-Szantyr (entry 477). There is no satisfactory English equivalent; the school grammars of Allen and Greenough (entry 469) and of Hale and Buck (entry 472) are serviceable but offer far less.

477. Leumann, Manu, J. B. Hofmann, and Anton Szantyr. **Lateinische Grammmatik**. München: C. H. Beck, 1972-1979. 3v. (Handbuch der Altertumswissenschaft; Abt. 2,2). ISBN 3-406-01426-7(v.1); 3-406-01347-3(v.2); 3-406-06072-2(v.3). LC 72-374136.

This is the best available comprehensive Latin grammar. While Kühner-Stegmann (entry 475) is a better descriptive grammar, Leumann-Hofmann-Szantyr is the standard reference work for all other aspects of Latin grammar, especially comparative and historical grammar. The first volume covers phonology and morphology; it is much superior to the corresponding volume of Kühner. The second volume, which is the work of Szantyr, offers a valuable treatment of syntax and stylistics. Appended to this is a brief history of Latin and a general introduction to the grammar as a whole. Indexes of subjects and words appear at the end of each volume. Fritz Radt and Abel Westerbrink compiled the *index locorum* and the index of non-Latin words that comprise the third volume.

478. Schwyzer, Eduard. **Griechische Grammatik: Auf der Grundlage von Karl Brugmanns Griechischer Grammatik**. München: C. H. Beck, 1966-1971. 4v. (Handbuch der Altertumswissenschaft; Abt. 2,1). ISBN 3-406-01339-2(v.1); 3-406-01341-4(v.2); 3-406-01343-0(v.3); 3-406-03397-0(v.4).

Along with Kühner-Gerth (entry 473) this is one of the two standard reference grammars for ancient Greek. The first volume, now in its 4th edition, covers phonology, word formation, and morphology. It is far better than the corresponding volume of Kühner. This is also the only part that Schwyzer himself completed before his death in 1943. Albert Debrunner is responsible for the second volume, which deals with syntax and stylistics. It offers extensive illustrative examples from Greek literature and a generous array of citations from the secondary literature. However, Kühner-Gerth is often more helpful for purely descriptive grammar. The remaining two volumes consist of indexes. The third contains the word indexes, which were compiled by Demetrius J. Georgacas. The final volume is an *index locorum* by Fritz and Stephen Radt. Both index volumes include corrections and additions to the grammar.

479. Sihler, Andrew L. **New Comparative Grammar of Greek and Latin**.
New York: Oxford University Press, 1995. 686pp. ISBN 0-19-508345-8.
LC 93-38929.

Originally begun as a revision of Buck's *Comparative Grammar of Greek
and Latin* (entry 471), Sihler's grammar ended as an entirely new work. It is
nearly twice as long as Buck and includes the results of much new work in the
field. Sihler's introduction provides a brief overview of the Indo-European
family of languages and of the history of the Greek and Latin languages. Various
parts of the book cover phonology, declension, pronouns, numerals, and conju-
gation. To make room for new material, Sihler omitted several topics covered
by Buck, such as the fundamentals of historical linguistics and word formation.
Like Buck, Sihler also does not cover syntax. This valuable new book should
largely supersede Buck as the standard work in the field.

✓480. Smyth, Herbert Weir. **Greek Grammar**. Revised by Gordon M. Messing.
Cambridge, MA: Harvard University Press, 1956. 784pp. ISBN 0-674-36250-0.
LC 57-2203.

481. Schumann, Walter A. **Index of Passages Cited in Herbert Weir Smyth,
Greek Grammar**. Cambridge, MA: Greek, Roman, and Byzantine Studies,
1961. 28pp. (Greek, Roman, and Byzantine Studies. Scholarly Aids, v.1).

Originally published as *A Greek Grammar for Colleges*, this work has
been for more than 70 years the standard reference grammar of ancient Greek
for English-speaking students. In the 1956 edition Messing has revised the
historical and comparative sections to reflect more recent linguistic scholarship.
Otherwise, the work remains much as when it first appeared. It is, for the most
part, a descriptive grammar. Smyth provides a clear guide to the complexities of
Greek morphology and syntax. This venerable work serves well the needs of
students; scholars will need to supplement it with the larger German grammars
of Kühner (entry 473) and Schwyzer (entry 478). Smyth includes English and
Greek indexes. There is a separately published *index locorum*, which was
compiled under the direction of Walter A. Schumann.

CHAPTER  12

PRIMARY SOURCES IN TRANSLATION

While translations of the works of both major and minor classical authors are readily available in the Loeb Classical Library series, the Penguin Classics, and other editions, English versions of documentary sources can be difficult to find. Tracking down primary sources on a given topic can also present formidable challenges. Fortunately, in recent years many anthologies of source material in English translation have appeared. Most cover a particular place and period, such as Greece in the fourth century B.C., or a particular subject, such as women in antiquity. The works described below include both general and specialized collections of primary sources. Most of these works are intended to be used in conjunction with other books (e.g., textbooks) or in the framework of a course, although they can be used independently. Those unfamiliar with the nature of the ancient sources and the problems involved in using them might also wish to consult Michael Crawford's *Sources for Ancient History* (New York: Cambridge University Press, 1983), which discusses some types of primary sources used by classicists and ancient historians.

482. Austin, M. M. **The Hellenistic World from Alexander to the Roman Conquest: A Selection of Ancient Sources in Translation**. New York: Cambridge University Press, 1981. 488pp. ISBN 0-521-22829-8; 0-521-29666-8pa. LC 81-6136.

The most comprehensive of the three general sourcebooks for the Hellenistic period (see also entries 483 and 486), Austin offers some 279 selections from literary, epigraphical, and papyrological sources. Austin is much better than his rivals in presenting the literary sources, both major and minor, and nearly their equal in documentary texts. His arrangement combines chronological and geographical approaches. He begins chronologically with two chapters covering Alexander and his successors. Then Austin shifts to a geographical division with chapters on Macedon and the Greek mainland, the Greek cities (social and economic conditions), the Seleucids and Asia, the Attalids of Pergamum, and the Ptolemies and Egypt. The individual selections range from a few lines to several pages in length. Some have brief introductions; all include short bibliographies and explanatory notes. With a few exceptions, all translations are by Austin; they are clear and generally reliable. Austin also provides a number of maps, chronological tables, a general bibliography, an index of ancient sources, and a general index. Austin offers a better balanced selection than Bagnall and Derow (entry 483), and a substantially larger one than Burstein (entry 486). However, these other works include some material not found in Austin, and sometimes provide better explanatory matter.

483. Bagnall, Roger S., and Peter Derow. **Greek Historical Documents: The Hellenistic Period**. Chico, CA: Scholars Press for the Society of Biblical Literature, 1981. 270pp. (Sources for Biblical Study, no.16). ISBN 0-89130-496-7. LC 81-5604.

This volume provides translations of documentary sources for the history of the Greek world from 336 B.C. to 30 B.C. It includes only epigraphical and papyrological texts; literary materials are excluded. Bagnall and Derow designed the book to serve as a companion volume to C. B. Welles's *Alexander and the Hellenistic World* (Toronto: A. M. Hakkert, 1970) and have generally followed his organization. The first and longest section deals with political history for the whole period; the documents in it are arranged chronologically. Subsequent chapters cover various broad topics in social, economic, and cultural history. While their scope extends to the entire Hellenistic world, Bagnall and Derow devote more than half of their space to Ptolemaic Egypt. This bias accurately reflects the distribution of the surviving documents, but also means that the volume is most useful to those interested in Ptolemaic history. Bagnall and Derow have equipped each selection with an informative introduction that supplies background material. They also provide some explanatory notes and a glossary of Greek terms. A concordance of sources and a general index conclude the volume. Burstein (entry 486), whose work treats the same period, offers better coverage of the other Hellenistic kingdoms. Austin (entry 482) also covers the same ground; his work offers both a combination of literary and documentary sources and a more balanced treatment of the various Hellenistic kingdoms.

484. Barker, Andrew, ed. **Greek Musical Writings**. New York: Cambridge University Press, 1984-1989. 2v. (Cambridge Readings in the Literature of Music). ISBN 0-521-23593-6(v.1); 0-521-30220-X(v.2). LC 83-20924.

Ancient music is widely considered to be a complex and difficult subject. Barker's work provides translations of relevant ancient works. His first volume, *The Musician and His Art*, is reasonably accessible to the nonspecialist. It includes 196 selections concerning music from Greek writers ranging from Homer to Athenaeus. Barker presents the selections in chronological sequence, with introductions and extensive notes. The volume concludes with a bibliography and a general index.

The second volume, *Harmonic and Acoustic Theory*, is highly technical and much more challenging than the first. In it, Barker translates and comments on some 12 texts, chiefly by philosophers. For the most part, these are complete works rather than excerpts or selections. Barker again employs a chronological arrangement. He also provides a bibliography, an index of words and topics, and an index of proper names.

485. Braund, David C. **Augustus to Nero: A Sourcebook on Roman History, 31 BC-AD 68**. Totowa, NJ: Barnes & Noble, 1985. 334pp. ISBN 0-3892-0536-2. LC 84-20368.

Intended as a supplementary text for students, this work covers one of the best-known and most frequently studied periods of Roman history. Braund gathers 849 texts from inscriptions, papyri, coin legends, and the lesser-known literary sources; he deliberately excludes the major literary sources (i.e., Tacitus, Suetonius, and Cassius Dio). He organizes the texts into eight topical chapters that cover social and economic matters as well as political and military affairs. In addition to the translations, entries include references to published versions of the Greek or Latin original and to related primary sources, date and place (for documentary texts), and occasional notes that provide background or explanatory information. Because Braund assumes that his collection will be used in conjunction with a good narrative history (several are suggested in his bibliographical note), the notes tend to be sketchy. He does provide a substantial introduction that offers an excellent discussion of the different types of primary sources and how to use them properly. Indexes of personal names and sources conclude the volume.

486. Burstein, Stanley M., ed. and trans. **The Hellenistic Age from the Battle of Ipsos to the Death of Kleopatra VII**. New York: Cambridge University Press, 1985. 173pp. (Translated Documents of Greece and Rome, v.3). ISBN 0-521-23691-6; 0-521-28158-Xpa. LC 84-29251.

Burstein has gathered and translated a selection of primary sources for the history of the Hellenistic period from 300 B.C.to 30 B.C. His intended audience includes both students and scholars. He covers social and cultural as well as political history. Although Burstein includes some passages from literary authors, the bulk of the volume consists of documentary texts drawn from inscriptions and papyri. Because the Hellenistic states spread over such a wide area and were so diverse in character, Burstein has departed from the chronological arrangement customarily used in this series in favor of a geographical arrangement. Each chapter is devoted to the history of a specific region. Within the chapters, a brief description, date, and short bibliography precede each selection. The explanatory notes that follow the texts supply the necessary background information to enable students to understand the text. Burstein also provides a glossary of Greek terms, several lists of Hellenistic kings, and a short discussion of chronology. There are indexes for personal and geographical names, subjects, and sources. While Burstein covers essentially the same period as Bagnall and Derow (entry 483), there is remarkably little overlap in the texts selected for each. Burstein offers better coverage of the Hellenistic kingdoms other than Egypt, while Bagnall and Derow cover Ptolemaic Egypt in much greater detail. Austin's similar work (entry 482) offers perhaps the best balanced treatment of the period as a whole and also includes a good selection of literary sources as well as documentary texts.

487. Campbell, Brian. **The Roman Army, 31 BC-AD 337: A Sourcebook**. London: Routledge, 1994. 272pp. ISBN 0-415-07172-0; 0-415-07173-9pa. LC 93-9032.

Designed for students of ancient and military history, this work gathers and translates a wide array of materials about the Roman army from the rise of Augustus to the death of Constantine the Great. While Campbell makes use of literary sources when appropriate, he draws most heavily on inscriptions and papyri. He groups the texts under nine rubrics: the soldiers; the officers; the emperor as commander-in-chief; the army in the field; the army in peacetime; the army, the local community, and the law; the army in politics; veterans; and the army in the later empire. Campbell further subdivides most of these into several topical sections. He provides an introduction for each section and occasional commentary on individual selections. His selections are well chosen to illustrate the various aspects of Roman military history, including the social, political, and economic impact of the army on the empire. The translations are clear and generally readable, although the content is sometimes dry. A number of maps, charts, and illustrations supplement the text. A good working bibliography and indexes of translated passages and of names and subjects conclude the volume.

488. Chisholm, Kitty, and John Ferguson, eds. **Rome, the Augustan Age: A Source Book**. New York: Oxford University Press with the Open University Press, 1981. 708pp. ISBN 0-19-872108-0; 0-19-872109-9pa. LC 82-126744.

Originally compiled as a textbook for an Open University course on Rome in the Augustan age, this work's temporal limits actually go well beyond the title's implications. While the book focuses on the era of Augustus, it also provides much material concerning the last years of the Roman republic and the early empire in general. It is the most complete collection of source material in English on the Augustan period. The editors have arranged their material by subject under such rubrics as politics, administration, art and architecture, and the provinces. In addition to generous selections from well-known literary sources, the editors have included a number of passages from minor authors and many important inscriptions and papyri. Brief introductions to each chapter and selection supply the necessary background material. The translations, which are by a variety of hands, are generally accurate and readable. There is an index of sources, which is helpful for users who need a translation of a particular document. One of the few drawbacks to this work is the lack of a good subject index.

489. Cohen, Morris R., and I. E. Drabkin. **A Source Book in Greek Science**. New York: McGraw-Hill, 1948; repr., Cambridge, MA: Harvard University Press, 1966. 579pp. (Source Books in the History of the Sciences). LC 48-009579.

Compiled by two distinguished philosophy professors who had a strong interest in ancient science, this volume gathers some of the most significant passages from the surviving scientific writings of the ancient Greeks. It also includes Latin writings that reflect Greek thought and methods. The authors represented range from the sixth century B.C. through the second century A.D. The material is organized into nine broad subject categories: mathematics, astronomy, mathematical geography, physics, chemistry and chemical technology, geology and meteorology, biology, medicine, and physiological psychology. Each of these is subdivided into a number of topical sections. Extensive notes accompany each selection. The authors have generally employed existing translations. Although now dated in terms of its scholarship, this collection should still serve its intended audience of students and general readers reasonably well.

490. Crawford, Michael H., and David Whitehead. **Archaic and Classical Greece: A Selection of Ancient Sources in Translation**. New York: Cambridge University Press, 1983. 634pp. ISBN 0-521-22775-5; 0-521-29638-2pa. LC 82-4355.

Crawford and Whitehead have compiled a comprehensive sourcebook for Greek history from the eighth through fourth centuries B.C. They draw their selections from both major (e.g., Herodotus, Thucydides) and minor literary authors and from the surviving inscriptions. Their overall arrangement is chronological; the four major divisions of the book cover the archaic period, the fifth century, the Peloponnesian War, and the fourth century. Within each division, Crawford and Whitehead group sources under several broad topics. The general introduction provides a useful discussion of the nature of the surviving sources, while introductions to the various sections supply historical overviews and bibliographies. The selections are furnished with explanatory notes as necessary. There are also many maps and illustrations. Supplementary materials include a glossary of Greek terms, chronological tables, and a full set of indexes. Crawford and Whitehead is the best one-volume collection of primary sources for Greek history. Fornara (entry 494), Lewis (entry 503), and Wickersham and Verbrugghe (entry 523) all cover shorter periods and are more restricted in scope. However, all include valuable materials that are not in Crawford and Whitehead. For Greek history after the fourth century see Austin (entry 482), Bagnall and Derow (entry 483), and Burstein (entry 486).

491. Croke, Brian, and Jill Harries. **Religious Conflict in Fourth Century Rome: A Documentary Study**. Sydney, Australia: Sydney University Press, 1982. 139pp. (Sources in Ancient History). ISBN 0-424-00091-1. LC 82-100681.

Croke and Harries assemble and translate some 94 documents that are key sources for the conflict between Christians and pagans during the fourth century A.D. These documents primarily include selections from literary and legal texts, along with a few inscriptions. Many were not previously readily available in English versions. They are well chosen to illuminate the religious conflicts of the era. Most focus on two events: the Altar of Victory debate and the short reign of the pagan usurper Eugenius. Croke and Harries employ a thematic arrangement. Their introductory comments place each document in context and supply necessary background. Relevant scholarly studies are discussed in the notes, while the general bibliography lists translations and important general studies. A glossary, an index of documents, and a general index complete the work.

492. Dudley, Donald R. **Urbs Roma: A Source Book of Classical Texts on the City and Its Monuments**. London: Phaidon, 1967. 339pp. LC 67-100815.

In this book, Dudley collects literary testimonia on notable places and structures of the city of Rome from its founding to the death of Constantine (A.D. 337). The excerpts come from numerous classical authors, both famous and obscure, and from ancient inscriptions. Dudley translated all the selections himself. In a number of cases where the original is exceptionally important or not readily accessible, he provides the Latin text as well. Dudley divides his collection into three sections: the site of Rome, buildings and monuments, and praises of Rome. The section on buildings and monuments is extensively subdivided and includes passages on virtually every monument of consequence. Dudley's introductions and notes provide useful background material and bibliography. He has also included a large number of black-and-white plates to illustrate the sites and monuments discussed in the testimonia. There are indexes of ancient authors, inscriptions, names, and places.

493. Ferguson, John. **Greek and Roman Religion: A Source Book**. Park Ridge, NJ: Noyes Press, 1980. 208pp. ISBN 0-8155-5055-3. LC 79-23009.

Designed for students and general readers, this work contains more than 150 translated passages concerning religion in the classical world. Ferguson organizes these into eight chapters by subject: the Olympians, the religion of the countryside, ritual and observance, political religion, philosophical religion, fears and needs, beliefs about death, and the mystery religions. He presents the translations within a loose narrative framework that provides both context and continuity for the reader. Brief explanatory notes and comments, set in smaller type, sometimes follow the selections. Ferguson draws most of his material from literary sources, particularly poets and philosophers. He also includes some documentary texts from inscriptions and papyri. The passages are well chosen to illustrate the various aspects of Greek and Roman religion. The translations, which are Ferguson's own, are generally accurate, although occasionally stilted. An index of passages cited and a general index round out the volume.

494. Fornara, Charles W., ed. and trans. **Archaic Times to the End of the Peloponnesian War**. New York: Cambridge University Press, 1983. 2d ed. 241pp. (Translated Documents of Greece and Rome, v.1). ISBN 0-521-25019-6; 0-521-29946-2pa. LC 79-054018.

Fornara's compilation was originally published by Johns Hopkins University Press in 1977; this edition includes some additions and corrections. It is aimed at college and graduate-level students of ancient history. Fornara intends to supplement standard and readily available sources for the period covered (roughly 776 B.C to 403 B.C.). Hence, he does not include selections from the major literary sources (e.g., Herodotus, Thucydides), but rather draws his material from less well known authors and from inscriptions. Fornara includes such texts as city foundation stories, laws, official and private letters, accounts, and dedications. Although fifth-century Athenian documents predominate (reflecting the nature of the surviving evidence), Fornara has made an effort to provide a selection of the more important non-Athenian documents. Presentation follows the pattern of the series. The selections are arranged in chronological sequence. Each is supplied with a descriptive title, date, and selected bibliography. Notes furnish background information to assist in understanding passages. The appendices include a useful glossary of Greek terms and information about Athenian political organization. Full indexes provide access by name and subject. Crawford and Whitehead (entry 490) cover the same period plus the fourth century. Unlike Fornara, they also include excerpts from the major literary sources. However, their coverage of documentary sources is considerably weaker than Fornara.

495. Gardner, Jane F., and Thomas Wiedemann. **The Roman Household: A Sourcebook**. London: Routledge, 1991. 210pp. ISBN 0-415-04421-9; 0-415-04422-7pa. LC 90-8691.

Compiled by two well-known scholars of Roman social history, this book focuses on "the activities and the often conflicting aspirations of individuals within the household (Latin *domus*)." Because the Roman household was often a large one that included extended family, slaves, servants, and various other dependents, it is different from its modern counterpart in size and scope. Gardner and Wiedemann cover all the social, economic, and legal aspects of the Roman household. Their 217 selections, which are arranged topically, are drawn from both literary and documentary sources. These selections span a wide range of dates (from the second century B.C. to the sixth century A.D.) and represent all parts of the Roman world except Egypt. The brief introductions that accompany most entries provide useful background information and set the passages in context. A good bibliography and a general index round out the volume.

496. Harding, Phillip, ed. **From the End of the Peloponnesian War to the Battle of Ipsus**. New York: Cambridge University Press, 1985. 210pp. (Translated Documents of Greece and Rome, v.2). ISBN 0-521-23435-2; 0-521-29949-7pa. LC 83-15444.

In this volume Harding gathers more than 140 selections from the lesser-known literary and documentary sources for fourth century B.C. Greek history. The majority are drawn from inscriptions. In keeping with the nature of the surviving evidence, Athens receives proportionally more coverage than other parts of the Greek world. Harding arranges his numbered selections (some of which include two or more related texts) in chronological sequence. Each has a descriptive title and date; some have additional introductory material as well. Harding also equips each with a short bibliography and explanatory notes. All translations are Harding's own. They are reliable and generally readable, although the requirements of the series that translations of inscriptions be line-by-line have resulted in some strained versions. The end matter includes a glossary of technical terms and offices, short appendices covering chronological matters and money, and a full array of indexes (names, subjects, and translated passages). Harding largely supersedes the earlier collection of Wickersham and Verbrugghe (entry 523). Those who need broader chronological coverage that includes the fourth century should consult Crawford and Whitehead (entry 490).

497. Ireland, S. **Roman Britain: A Sourcebook**. New York: St. Martin's Press, 1986. 266pp. ISBN 0-312-68964-0. LC 86-1764.

Prepared by a scholar with impeccable credentials, this work offers an extensive selection of primary sources for the study of Roman Britain. Ireland draws on the full range of literary, epigraphical, and numismatic sources. Because of the bulk of material available, he has been extremely selective. His translations are readable and accurate; the brief comments that accompany them serve to set them in context. Ireland marshalls his material into three sections: geography and people of Britain; political and military history; and religion, commerce, and society. The second part, political and military affairs, is by far the longest. It is arranged chronologically, while the other two parts are arranged thematically. Ireland also provides a bibliography, separate indexes for literary sources and inscriptions, and a general index. Although an extremely useful tool for students of Roman Britain, this work may present some difficulties for the uninitiated because Ireland's commentary is fairly abbreviated.

498. Jones, A. H. M., ed. **A History of Rome Through the Fifth Century**. New York: Walker, 1968-1970. 2v. (Documentary History of Western Civilization). LC 68-13332.

The title of this volume misleadingly suggests a narrative history of Rome, although it is really a collection of primary sources in translation. The first volume, which contains 150 selections, covers the Roman republic. The bulk of the volume consists of four chapters that cover Roman military and political history from the origins of the city to 44 B.C. The remaining chapters cover major topics in greater detail: the constitution, politics, Italy, and the provinces. Most of the selections are from fairly well known literary and legal texts; there are relatively few documents and no surprises. Jones's introductions do an adequate job of setting the scene for each text. The volume includes a short general bibliography and a subject index. This is a serviceable work but lacks the breadth and balance of the corresponding volume of Lewis and Reinhold (entry 506).

The second volume, which covers the empire, is a far superior work. This is not surprising, because Jones was one of the foremost twentieth-century historians of the Roman empire. His approach in this volume is strictly topical; the chapters cover all aspects of Roman imperial history rather than merely political and military matters. While not neglecting the literary sources, Jones makes much greater use of documentary texts, such as inscriptions and papyri, in this part of this work. He presents 184 texts with brief but informative introductions. Again the volume includes its own bibliography and index. While Lewis and Reinhold are the better overall collection of sources for Roman history, those interested primarily in the empire will find Jones well worth consulting.

499. Jones, John R. Melville. **Testimonia Numaria: Greek and Latin Texts Concerning Ancient Greek Coinage**. London: Spink, 1993. 544pp. ISBN 0-907605-40-0(v.1).

Aimed primarily at scholars, this work gathers the majority of extant documents relevant to the study of ancient Greek coinage. Jones draws them from a wide range of sources, including literary texts, inscriptions, and papyri. The first volume contains the texts, with the Latin or Greek originals and English translations on facing pages, arranged by topic. Chapters cover, for example, particular Greek cities, mints, forgeries, hoards and treasures, money changers, and weights and denominations. An *index locorum* is provided at the end of the volume. The second volume, which has not yet been published, will contain commentary and essays.

500. Kraemer, Ross S. **Maenads, Martyrs, Matrons, Monastics: A Sourcebook on Women's Religions in the Greco-Roman World**. Philadelphia: Fortress Press, 1988. 429pp. ISBN 0-8006-0855-0; 0-8006-2071-2pa. LC 87-45899.

Kraemer pulls together a generous selection of texts concerning women's religious activities in classical antiquity. Her 135 passages are drawn from a variety of literary and documentary sources and include, for example, excerpts from Euripides, letters of St. Jerome, and funerary inscriptions. Religions represented include the traditional cults of the Olympians, various pagan mystery religions, Judaism, and Christianity. Kraemer arranges her material in broad subject categories: observances, rituals, and festivals; documents from, by, and to women; religious offices; new religious affiliation and conversion; holy, pious, and exemplary women; and the feminine divine. A source reference and date are given at the beginning of each entry; no background notes or commentary are provided. A short appendix supplies biographical and historical notes on the authors and texts that appear in the volume. Indexes of sources, personal names, and divine names conclude the work.

501. Lefkowitz, Mary R., and Maureen B. Fant. **Women's Life in Greece & Rome: A Source Book in Translation**. 2d ed. Baltimore, MD: Johns Hopkins University Press, 1992. 387pp. ISBN 0-8018-4474-6; 0-8018-4475-4pa. LC 92-6845.

This well-received compendium gathers a wide array of ancient writings and documents concerning women, including excerpts from literary, philosophical, legal, and medical works; private letters and legal documents; and funerary inscriptions. Many are drawn from relatively obscure sources, and a number of the texts were not previously available in English translation. Lefkowitz and Fant arrange the texts in broad subject categories: women's voices, men's opinions, philosophers on the role of women, legal status, public life, private life, occupations, medicine, and religion. Subarrangement within each category is chronological. Each selection begins with a brief descriptive title and a reference to the Greek or Latin original. Many also have introductory notes that supply useful background material. The authors have provided a concordance of sources, an index of women and goddesses, and a general index. Those interested primarily in women and religion should also refer to Kraemer's more specialized work (entry 500).

502. Levick, Barbara. **The Government of the Roman Empire: A Sourcebook**. London: Croom Helm, 1985. 260pp. ISBN 0-7099-1622-1; 0-7099-1668-Xpa.

In this book Levick presents 228 selections concerning the governing of the Roman empire from 27 B.C. to A.D. 285. She draws the selections from both literary and documentary sources. Less readily accessible sources, such as legal texts, inscriptions, papyri, and coin legends, are especially well represented. Levick organizes the selections into a series of topical chapters. She supplies a brief introduction for each chapter and background notes for many of the individual passages. Levick also provides much supplementary material: maps, a chronological list of emperors, and a table of weights, measures, and currencies. The bibliography, which is arranged to correspond to the various chapters, offers reliable guidance for further study. Two indexes close the work. The first, an index of passages cited, includes bio-bibliographical notes about the various authors and works. The second is a geographical index.

503. Lewis, Naphtali. **The Fifth Century B.C.** Toronto: A. M. Hakkert, 1971. 124pp. (Greek Historical Documents). ISBN 0-88866-503-2; 0-88866-504-0pa. LC 75-148096.

This slim volume deals primarily with Athens during the fifth century B.C. In fact, it is divided into two parts: Athens (which consumes more than half Lewis' space) and "Elsewhere." Within each of these sections Lewis arranges his material chronologically by the event described. Most of the selections are documents (chiefly inscriptions), although excerpts from a few minor literary authors are included. Lewis omits standard authors, such as Herodotus and Thucydides, because they are readily available. Most of the passages selected focus on politics, war, and diplomacy; there is not much in the way of social history. The brief introductions to each selection supply background material needed to understand the document, and sometimes refer to important studies. Lewis also provides a glossary of Greek terms, a short bibliography, a general index, and a concordance of texts translated. This work offers a good general collection of materials for the study of fifth-century Greek political history. Those with broader interests would do well to consult one of the more general sourcebooks on Greek history, such as Fornara (entry 494) or Crawford and Whitehead (entry 490).

504. Lewis, Naphtali. **The Ides of March**. Sanibel, FL: Samuel Stevens, 1984. 164pp. ISBN 0-89522-026-1; 0-89522-027-Xpa. LC 84-24118.

Despite its ominous title, this work covers the entire career of Julius Caesar, not just his assassination. Lewis collects and translates the most important primary sources for Caesar's life. They cover the years 60 B.C. (the First Triumvirate) to 42 B.C. (the Battle of Philippi). The excerpts are all from literary authors: Caesar himself, Cicero, Suetonius, Velleius Paterculus, Appian, Dio Cassius, Plutarch, and Nicolaus of Damascus. Because most of these are readily available in translated editions, Lewis's chief service is in gathering all the relevant passages in one place. He also provides an introduction, a glossary, and a short bibliography. There is no index.

505. Lewis, Naphtali. **The Roman Principate, 27 B.C.-285 A.D.** Toronto: A. M. Hakkert, 1974. 149pp. (Greek Historical Documents). ISBN 0-88866-574-4; 0-88866-548-2pa. LC 73-94074.

In this volume Lewis collects primary source material for the Greek-speaking portion of the Roman empire from the Augustan era to the accession of Diocletian. Although he includes excerpts from a few minor authors, Lewis chiefly focuses on documentary sources (i.e., inscriptions and papyri). He marshalls the excerpts into four groups: government, economy, society, and religion. Each of these is further subdivided by topic. Lewis is particularly good for material on economic and social history, because he includes many documents on such topics as the imperial cult, taxes, prices and inflation, trade, professions, entertainment, and slaves. His selection of documents is interesting and includes many not found in other sourcebooks. The translations are readable. Some have introductions, while others do not. In general, the editorial material is minimal. Indexes provide access by Roman emperors, proper names (very selectively), and subject. There is no concordance of sources.

506. Lewis, Naphtali, and Meyer Reinhold, eds. **Roman Civilization: Selected Readings**. 3d ed. New York: Columbia University Press, 1990. 2v. ISBN 0-231-07054-3; 0-231-07055-1pa. LC 90-33405.

This venerable work first appeared as part of the famous Columbia Records of Civilization series in 1951. It is a massive gathering of primary sources for the study of Roman history and culture from the founding of the city through the fourth century A.D. Lewis and Reinhold include excerpts from both major and minor classical authors (the bulk of the collection), legal writings, inscriptions, papyri, and coin legends. They generally use a chronological approach in arranging the selections, although occasionally, as in the chapter on Roman women, they adopt a topical approach instead. The first volume covers the republic and the Augustan era, while the second is devoted to the empire. The introduction provides an excellent description of the different types of sources and of many of the authors and works excerpted in *Roman Civilization*. While Lewis and Reinhold tend to draw heavily on well-known authors, they also offer strong coverage of minor and technical works. Their selection of documentary sources is adequate, but not as extensive as that found in the various collections by Sherk (entries 519-520). They supply a glossary, bibliographies, and a brief subject index in each volume. Unfortunately, there is no index of sources. This omission creates difficulties for those seeking a particular passage or document.

Roman Civilization is the best single collection of sources for Roman history. It offers more up-to-date scholarship and a stronger, better balanced selection of materials than Jones (entry 498), the only work of comparable scale. However, Jones's volume on the empire is still worth consulting because of his exceptional knowledge of the period. Some of the more narrowly focused works, such as those of Sherk, offer better coverage of documentary materials and better indexing, but none equal Lewis and Reinhold in scope and comprehensiveness.

507. Luck, Georg. **Arcana Mundi: Magic and the Occult in the Greek and Roman Worlds**. Baltimore, MD: Johns Hopkins University Press, 1985. 395pp. ISBN 0-8018-2523-7; 0-8018-2548-2pa. LC 84-28852.

The study of magic and the occult in classical antiquity has become fashionable in recent years. Luck's volume, one of the early products of this trend, gathers 122 selections under six rubrics: magic, miracles, daemonology, divination, astrology, and alchemy. His sources include both well-known authors, such as Homer and Vergil, and those who are seldom read, such as Iamblichus and Artemidorus. He also incorporates a number of inscriptions and papyri in his collection. Luck provides a substantial introduction to each chapter. Individual selections also have introductory notes that give historical background and discuss content. A general bibliography, an index of ancient sources, and a general index conclude the volume. This is a very useful selection of primary source materials for students and for general readers with an interest in the area. Many of the texts are otherwise inaccessible.

508. Meijer, Fik, and Onno van Nijf. **Trade, Transport, and Society in the Ancient World: A Sourcebook**. London: Routledge, 1992. 201pp. ISBN 0-415-00344-X; 0-415-00345-8pa. LC 91-46010.

Intended for both college students and general readers with a serious interest in ancient history, this work deals primarily with ancient trade. Meijer and van Nijf draw their material from literary and documentary sources. Their 238 selections are organized into thematic sections. These sections, with their numerous subdivisions, cover the ideology and practice of trade, commodities traded, and means of transport. Brief introductions to each section and passage provide background information. The compilers have used existing English translations whenever possible and have provided new translations for the remaining selections. The introductory matter includes discussion of Greek and Roman measures, weights, and coins (with modern equivalents). A general bibliography, an index of passages cited (which also dates and identifies the authors of literary texts), and a selective general index conclude the volume. This is a very useful work for anyone seeking primary source material on ancient economic activity.

508a. Meyer, Marvin W., ed. **The Ancient Mysteries: A Sourcebook**. San Francisco: Harper & Row, 1987. 267pp. ISBN 0-06-065577-1; 0-06-065576-3pa. LC 86-45022.

Compiled by an established scholar in the field, this volume gathers a generous selection of texts concerning the Greco-Roman mystery religions. Meyer draws his materials from a variety of literary and documentary sources; some of these were not previously accessible to students or general readers. The selections are presented in topical chapters that cover respectively: the Eleusinian mysteries, the Andanian mysteries, Dionysus, the Magna Mater, Isis and Osiris, Mithras, and "mysteries within Judaism and Christianity." Many of the texts are of substantial length. Although no notes are provided, Meyer prefaces each text with a brief introduction. The translations, which are by a variety of hands, are quite readable. Meyer has also equipped the book with a good general introduction and a glossary. There is no index.

509. Miller, Stephen G. **Arete: Greek Sports from Ancient Sources**. 2d ed. Berkeley, CA: University of California Press, 1991. 226pp. ISBN 0-520-07508-0; 0-520-07509-9pa. LC 90-28646.

Designed as a supplementary textbook for college courses on Greek athletics, *Arete* is a collection of translations from literary texts, papyri, and inscriptions, arranged thematically. The passages are well chosen and illustrate all major aspects of ancient Greek athletics. Miller has made his own translations, which are not only accurate but readable and idiomatic as well. He has also equipped each selection with introductory notes to set the context and provide historical information. A short general bibliography and a combination index and glossary conclude the volume. Miller is more up-to-date and accurate than his rivals Robinson (entry 516) and Sweet (entry 522). Those who strongly prefer a chronological arrangement might wish to use Robinson. Sweet's work has two major virtues: he covers a much wider range of sports and recreation than the other books, and his work is heavily illustrated.

510. Monroe, Paul. **Source Book of the History of Education for the Greek and Roman Period**. New York: Macmillan, 1901. 515pp. LC 01-25603.

This old volume is still the only general collection of primary sources on education in the classical world. It is available in a number of unaltered reprint editions (the last appearing in 1932). Separate sections cover Greek and Roman education. Within these sections, Monroe combines chronological and topical approaches to organizing his material. Each chapter begins with a substantial introductory note that sets the stage and supplies background information. Monroe then presents translated selections from one or more classical authors. He draws chiefly on philosohical and rhetorical authors, although he also includes selections from the poets. His excerpts are much longer on average than those found in most sourcebooks. A general index is provided. While Monroe's translations have not always aged well and his scholarship is now dated, the book is still usable. Some more recent volumes, such as Shelton (entry 518), include primary materials on education in the ancient world, but they are much less extensive than Monroe.

511. Platthy, Jenö. **Sources on the Earliest Greek Libraries: With the Testimonia**. Amsterdam: Adolf M. Hakkert, 1968. 203pp. LC 67-16334.

Unlike most of the works found in this chapter, Platthy's volume is aimed at scholars rather than students. In it he gathers passages from literary, epigraphical, and papyrological sources to illustrate the early history of book collecting and libraries in classical Greece. Platthy restricts himself to Greece and Asia Minor; he does not cover the Alexandrian library or libraries of the Roman era. After a lengthy introduction, Platthy presents the primary sources in a geographical arrangement. Each of the 182 passages is presented both in the original Greek or Latin and in English. A selective bibliography and an index of sources close the volume.

512. Pollitt, J. J. **The Art of Ancient Greece: Sources and Documents**. 2d ed. New York: Cambridge University Press, 1990. 298pp. ISBN 0-521-25368-3; 0-521-27366-8pa. LC 90-1494.

Originally published as *The Art of Greece, 1400-31 B.C.* (Englewood Cliffs, NJ: Prentice-Hall, 1965), this volume presents a comprehensive collection of the ancient literary evidence for the study of Greek art. After a brief introductory chapter that treats the earliest period as a whole, Pollitt arranges his translated passages by media: sculpture, painting, architecture, and decorative arts. Each section is subarranged chronologically. A final chapter covers art history, aesthetics, and comparative criticism. Pollitt draws his material from a wide range of sources, including both famous and obscure authors. His running commentary sets the passages in context and provides background information and references for further study. Additional explanatory material and bibliography appears in the footnotes. Pollitt also provides an extensive, well-organized bibliography (arranged by subject) and indexes covering artists, places, and general subjects.

513. Pollitt, J. J. **The Art of Rome, c. 753 B.C.-337 A.D.: Sources and** ✓
    Documents. Englewood Cliffs, NJ: Prentice-Hall, 1966; repr., Cam-
    bridge: Cambridge University Press, 1983. 252pp. (Sources and Docu-
    ments in the History of Art Series). LC 66-18490.

In this companion volume to *The Art of Ancient Greece* (entry 512), Pollitt
gathers and translates the literary testimonia for Roman art. His selections come
from a wide range of authors, many of them seldom read except by specialists.
These passages show the Romans' views on art and describe both extant and lost
works of art. Pollitt employs a chronological arrangement. When the material
under a given period warrants it, he subdivides it by artist, work, or medium. His
introductions and notes supply much historical and biographical information.
Special indexes provide access by artist and geographical location. Pollitt also
provides a good general index. This work covers Roman art as a whole. Those
interested specifically in the monuments of city of Rome should also consult
Dudley (entry 492).

514. Reinhold, Meyer. **Diaspora: The Jews Among the Greeks and Ro-**
    mans. Sarasota, FL: Samuel Stevens, 1983. 182pp. ISBN 0-89522-020-2;
    0-89522-021-0pa. LC 81-9361.

Reinhold has collected a wide array of source materials concerning the
Jews in the Greco-Roman world. He presents a good balance of literary and
documentary texts. His literary sources include the Bible, Philo, Josephus,
Tacitus, Suetonius, and others. He draws documentary material from inscriptions, papyri, and coin legends. The overall framework is chronological; the
major divisions include Jews in the Greek world, Jewish statehood, Jews in the
Roman world, and Christians and Jews. A number of topical subdivisions appear
under each of these rubrics. His annotation is light; brief introductions to the
each section set the context, while individual selections rarely receive more than
a sentence or two of comment or background information. Most selections are
unannotated. There are many maps and illustrations. A glossary, a bibliography,
and a selective general index conclude the volume. Kraemer (entry 500), although her focus is different, also has relevant primary source materials on Jews
in the ancient world.

515. Rhodes, P. J. **The Greek City State: A Source Book**. Norman, OK:
    University of Oklahoma Press, 1986. 266pp. ISBN 0-8061-2010-X;
    0-8061-2013-4pa. LC 86-3375.

The purpose of Rhodes's book is to gather primary sources that illustrate
the workings of the Greek city-state. His intended audience includes college-
level students of ancient history and of political science. Rhodes presents a good
mix of well-known and obscure materials drawn from literary texts, inscriptions,
and papyri. His overall arrangement is chronological. Sparta and Athens, each
of which receives its own chapter, get considerably more attention than the other
cities. Rhodes prepared his own translations for this collection. His introductory
notes to the sections and to individual passages supply much useful background
information. Rhodes provides an index of passages cited and a selective index
of names and subjects. The indexes double as glossaries; a number of their entries
include explanatory notes.

516. Robinson, Rachel Sargent. **Sources for the History of Greek Athletics**
    in English Translation: With Introductions, Notes, Bibliography, and
    Indices. Cincinnati, OH: Rachel Sargent Robinson, 1955; repr., Chicago:
    Ares Publishers, 1984. 289pp. LC 56-27699.

Robinson gathers a large number of texts, chiefly from literary sources, concerning Greek sports. She arranged the sources chronologically; chapters consist of passages concerning a single period. Although this format gives an overview of the development of Greek athletics as a whole, it creates obvious difficulties for anyone seeking material on a single athletic event or activity. Long the only work of its type, Robinson has now been largely superseded by the more recent works of Sweet (entry 522) and Miller (entry 509). Both of these offer more up-to-date scholarship in their editorial and bibliographical matter. Miller in particular is stronger in coverage of documentary material, much of which has come to light only in recent years.

517. Rodewald, Cosmo. **Democracy: Ideas and Realities**. London: J. M. Dent, 1974. 138pp. (Ancient World). ISBN 0-460-10302-4; 0-460-11302-Xpa. LC 76-364816.

Suitable for students of ancient history and of political science, this volume brings together approximately 60 translated passages concerning democracy in the classical world. Not surprisingly, most concern Athens. Rodewald takes his selections mainly from literary works; excerpts from the Greek philosophers, orators, and historians predominate. He arranges the selections under several broad topics: Athens in the fifth and fourth centuries, the origins of Greek democracy, democracy and society, attitudes to democracy in Greece, democracy and empire (the period of Alexander), and democracy in the Roman empire. Brief introductions set each selection in context; Rodewald also provides occasional explanatory notes that supply background information and define technical terms. A general index concludes the volume. Readers primarily interested in early Athenian politics should consult Stanton (entry 521), whose work offers more primary materials and much better notes.

✓ 518. Shelton, Jo-Ann. **As the Romans Did: A Source Book in Roman Social History**. New York: Oxford University Press, 1988. 492pp. ISBN 0-19-504176-3; 0-19-504177-1pa. LC 87-1582.

Those interested in everyday life in the ancient world will find this anthology quite useful. Shelton covers a wide range of topics, such as families, marriage, housing, domestic and personal concerns, education, work, slaves, government and politics, the army, women, leisure, and religion. She gathers her selections from many sources: letters, legal documents, graffiti, agricultural handbooks, medical texts, contracts, and funerary inscriptions. Her well-chosen texts are presented in accurate and readable translations. Arrangement is by subject; numerous cross-references and an index facilitate access. Shelton generally provides brief introductory comments under each heading and explanatory notes throughout the work. Several genealogical tables and diagrams accompany the text. Appendices supply background information about the ancient authors and documentary sources used in the book, a brief discussion of Roman money, and a chronological table that covers 753 B.C to A.D. 565. Shelton provides the best overall collection of source materials on Roman social history; those interested in specific topics may find other collections listed in this chapter helpful as well.

519. Sherk, Robert K., ed. and trans. **The Roman Empire: Augustus to Hadrian**. New York: Cambridge University Press, 1988. 302pp. (Translated Documents of Greece and Rome, v.6). ISBN 0-521-33025-4; 0-521-33887-5pa. LC 87-24204.

This volume, like others in its series, is intended for university students in ancient history. In it, Sherk gathers some 200 readings drawn from lesser-known classical authors, inscriptions, and papyri. He deliberately omits the works of major literary authors (e.g., Tacitus), because these are readily available elsewhere. Sherk divides his material into two parts. The first, which deals with the imperial government, is arranged into sections by emperor. The second covers various aspects of Roman society during the period. Sherk provides short bibliographies and notes for many of the texts. The indexes cover personal, divine, and geographic names, subjects, and translated passages. There is some overlap with Chisholm and Ferguson (entry 488), although Sherk extends coverage considerably later. Sherk also concentrates much more on less-accessible source materials than do either Chisholm and Ferguson or Lewis and Reinhold (entry 506).

520. Sherk, Robert K., ed. and trans. **Rome and the Greek East to the Death of Augustus**. New York: Cambridge University Press, 1984. 181pp. (Translated Documents of Greece and Rome, v.4). ISBN 0-521-24995-3; 0-521-27123-1pa. LC 83-1833.

Aimed at college and graduate-level students of ancient history, this volume offers a selection of translated source materials on Roman relations with the Greek-speaking East from the end of the third century B.C. to the death of Augustus in A.D. 14. The selections cover political, diplomatic, and military matters. Sherk omits commonly available authors, such as Livy and Polybius, in order to concentrate on less-accessible sources such as inscriptions, papyri, coin legends, and excerpts from minor authors. He arranges the material chronologically. For each selection Sherk provides a brief description, a date, a short bibliography, and helpful explanatory notes. The translations are sometimes stilted because they are designed to reflect the originals as closely as possible. Supplementary materials include a glossary of Greek and Latin technical terms and appendices covering Roman names, consuls (200 B.C. to A.D. 14), and Greek and Roman chronology. Indexes provide access by name, subject, and source. Sherk includes a number of documents that are not available in English elsewhere.

521. Stanton, G. R. **Athenian Politics, c. 800-500 BC: A Sourcebook**. London: Routledge, 1990. 226pp. ISBN 0-415-04060-4; 0-415-04061-2pa. LC 89-71345.

In this volume Stanton collects in translation nearly all of the relevant primary sources for early Athenian politics. These include a large number of epigraphical texts as well as selections from literary authors. Stanton organizes the material by period, with topical subdivisions. His introductory comments to the various sections provide the context for the selections. The extensive notes that accompany each selection go far beyond providing explanatory material and will interest scholars as well as students. This exemplary volume also includes maps, genealogical tables, and a good working bibliography. Stanton has provided indexes of sources translated and of names and subjects.

522. Sweet, Waldo E. **Sport and Recreation in Ancient Greece: A Sourcebook with Translations**. New York: Oxford University Press, 1987. ISBN 0-19-504126-7; 0-19-504127-5pa. LC 86-18209.

Sweet's compilation, like those of Robinson (entry 516) and Miller (entry 509), is aimed at college students. Sweet, however, covers a much wider range of activities than do his competitors. He goes beyond the traditional focus on competitive athletics to include chapters on such topics as walking and mountaineering, swimming and boating, hunting, dance, and the like. His 33 topical chapters cover virtually every aspect of Greek sport and recreation. Introductions and notes provide historical background and possible interpretations. An index of testimonia and a combined general index and glossary conclude this heavily illustrated work. While Miller is better for coverage of the traditional Greek athletic events and competitions, Sweet is really the only source of translated primary materials for the study of most other sports and recreational activities.

523. Wickersham, John, and Gerald Verbrugghe. **The Fourth Century B.C.** Toronto: Hakkert, 1973. 129pp. (Greek Historical Documents). ISBN 0-88866-527-X; 0-88866-528-8pa. LC 73-83517.

A companion volume to Naphtali Lewis's *The Fifth Century B.C.* (entry 503), this work presents primary sources for Greek history from the end of the Peloponnesian War (403 B.C.) to the rise of Alexander the Great (336 B.C.). Although Wickersham and Verbrugghe include a few excerpts from the literary sources, the bulk of the 76 texts are epigraphical. Their emphasis is on political, military, and diplomatic history. They have equipped each text with a short commentary that provides background material. Supplementary materials include a glossary of Greek terms and a number of tables providing information on chronological and monetary matters. A concordance of sources and indexes of personal and geographic names close the work. Harding (entry 496) covers roughly the same period; he offers more material, and his notes and bibliography are more current. Those in need of material covering a wider temporal span might consult Crawford and Whitehead (entry 490), who provide sources for the whole of the archaic and classical period. They also tend to emphasize literary authors more, while, for this period, both Harding and Wickersham and Verbrugghe are stronger for documentary sources.

524. Wiedemann, Thomas. **Greek and Roman Slavery**. London: Croom Helm, 1981; repr., London: Routledge, 1988. 284pp. ISBN 0-7099-0388-X; 0-7099-0389-8pa.

The primary sources concerning slavery in the ancient world are exceptionally diverse and scattered. Wiedemann's collection makes a generous selection of these sources accessible to students and general readers. He presents some 243 documents under the following topics: the slave as property, debt-bondage and serfdom, manumission, moral inferiors, status symbol or economic investment, sources of slaves, slaves owned by the state, treatment of slaves, resistance, rebellion, and Stoics and Christians. Because of space limitations, Wiedemann focuses on Athens in the fifth and fourth centuries B.C. and Rome in the first centuries B.C. and A.D. He draws his texts primarily from literary sources, although he does include some inscriptions and papyri. Roman legal writings are well represented in his compilation. Brief introductory notes supply context and background for each selection. Wiedemann also provides a bibliography, an excellent index of passages cited (which includes notes on the authors and texts), and a general index.

CHAPTER  13

CORE PERIODICALS

Several criteria have governed the selection of titles for this chapter. The chief aim has been to provide broad general coverage of the leading journals from all areas of classical studies. Journals with a narrowly specialized focus (e.g., papyrology, epigraphy) have been excluded. Most of the selected journals are well established; a number of them have been published for more than a century. In the case of these older titles, the back runs are important resources for research. The journals chosen are, for the most part, widely indexed. Virtually all journals listed here are abstracted in *L'Année philologique* (entry 26); many are indexed in other standard humanities and social science indexes as well. The English-language titles are widely held by American academic libraries; the foreign-language ones are commonly found in American research libraries that collect in classical studies. Information about title changes and publication history, if significant, are to be found in the annotations.

525. **American Journal of Ancient History**. Cambridge, MA: Harvard University, 1976- . Semiannual. ISSN 0362-8914. LC 76-641269.
      Launched in 1976 to fill the perceived need for an American journal devoted solely to ancient history, this journal is edited and published by E. Badian with support from the Department of History at Harvard. It publishes articles on Greek and Roman history and occasional items on the Ancient Near East. Despite an amateurish physical appearance, the quality of the content is good; many distinguished historians are found among the contributors. The publication schedule tends to be erratic.

526. **American Journal of Archaeology**. Boston: Archaeological Institute of America, 1885- . Quarterly. ISSN 0002-9114.

American Journal of Archaeology covers the "art and archaeology of ancient Europe and the Mediterranean world, including the Near East and Egypt, from prehistoric to late antique times." It publishes field reports, articles, newsletters, necrologies, and a substantial number of scholarly book reviews. The proceedings of the Archaeological Institute of America's (entry 643) annual conference appear in the April issue each year. This is the single most important English-language journal for classical archaeology and is very widely indexed.

527. **American Journal of Philology**. Baltimore, MD: Johns Hopkins University Press, 1880- . Quarterly. ISSN 0002-9475. LC 05-31891.

Founded by Basil Lanneau Gildersleeve, AJP is one of the oldest and best classical journals published in America. Early issues covered philology in the widest sense of the term, including articles on Germanic, Romance, and Oriental philology as well as classical. In time the *Journal*'s focus narrowed to classical studies only. It now publishes articles and scholarly book reviews on Greek and Roman literature and history. The Johns Hopkins University Press is now making available via the Internet tables of contents for recent and forthcoming issues of AJP. These can be reached at the following address: gopher://jhunix.hcf.jhu.edu:10003/11/JHU_Press/.zjournals/.class

528. **Ancient Philosophy**. Pittsburgh: Mathesis Publications, 1980- . Semiannual. ISSN 0740-2007. LC 83-3286

Most of the articles in this journal deal with mainstream classical Greek philosophers. Material on ancient science and religion can also be found in its pages. There are contributions by both philosophers and philologists. A typical issue has eight to ten articles and notes and 20 or more reviews. It is a good general journal on classical philosophy.

529. **Annual of the British School at Athens**. London: British School at Athens, 1895- . Annual. ISSN 0068-2454. LC 19-19615.

The *Annual* primarily publishes articles in Greek art and archaeology. Topographical and historical studies and, very rarely, literary ones appear as well. The journal also includes excavation reports on British digs in Greece. A few of the articles deal with medieval Greece. Most of the articles are by members of the School (entry 624). Abstracts in English and Greek follow the table of contents. A cumulative index covers the first 32 volumes.

530. **Antike Welt: Zeitschrift für Archäologie und Kulturgeschichte**. Mainz am Rhein, Germany: Philipp von Zabern, 1970- . Quarterly. ISSN 0003-570X. LC 76-641505.

Most articles in this general archaeology periodical deal with the ancient Mediterranean; many are on classical topics. Other areas (e.g., Mesoamerican archaeology) are covered as well. The approach is a blend of popular and scholarly writing. Many color illustrations supplement the text. *Antike Welt* also provides a calendar of museum exhibits (in Europe) relating to ancient art and archaeology and brief notices of recent books. In many ways it can be considered a German version of *Archaeology* (entry 532), but the content of *Antike Welt* is often more challenging.

531. **Apeiron: A Journal of Ancient Philosophy and Science**. Edmonton, AB: Academic Printing and Publishing, 1966- . Quarterly. ISSN 0003-6390. LC 88-30374.

Apeiron publishes "papers of historical and philosophical interest in the area of ancient history and philosophy." A typical number includes three or four articles, although sometimes the content may consist of only one or two long articles. In recent years there have been frequent theme issues that have guest editors and are often equipped with indexes. *Apeiron* is one of the few journals that regularly features articles on ancient science.

532. **Archaeology**. New York: Archaeological Institute of America, 1948- . Bimonthly. ISSN 0003-8113. LC 50-37022.

Archaeology is a general archaeological journal with a strong classical component. It is geared toward students and general readers. In addition to classical and Near Eastern archaeology, articles cover Asia and the Americas. Articles are generally well written and accompanied by many illustrations. Each issue lists current museum exhibits (mostly American) of archaeological and historical interest. There are also book reviews. *Archaeology* frequently includes information on travel to archaeological sites as well.

533. **Arethusa**. Baltimore, MD: Johns Hopkins University Press, 1968- . Semiannual. ISSN 0004-0975. LC 79-10240.

Arethusa focuses on classical literature. A typical issue contains a half-dozen articles. There are no book reviews. *Arethusa* tends to be less traditional than most of the journals included in this chapter. Many articles feature more recent approaches and critical theories. Some issues are theme-oriented. Nonspecialists will find *Arethusa* one of the more interesting and approachable journals. Johns Hopkins University Press is now making available via the Internet tables of contents for recent and forthcoming issues of Arethusa. These can be reached at the following address: gopher://jhunix.-hcf.jhu.edu:10003/11/JHU_Press/.zjournals/.class

534. **Arion: A Journal of Humanities and the Classics**. Boston: Boston University, 1962- . Triannual. ISSN 0004-1351.

This is a nontraditional and occasionally controversial journal. *Arion* is one of the few genuinely interdisciplinary journals in classical studies. Articles tend to be literary. Many are comparative studies. The latest (at least for classical studies) methodological approaches and critical theories are likely to be found here. Indeed, *Arion* has a reputation as something of an "antiphilological" journal. In addition to articles, most issues include translations of classical literature, original poetry, and book reviews.

535. **Athenaeum: studi di letteratura e storia dell'antichità**. Pavia, Italy: Università di Pavia, 1913- . Semiannual. ISSN 0004-6574. LC 83-645627.

Athenaeum is the best general Italian journal of classical studies. It publishes articles on both literary and historical topics. It also includes reviews, often substantial ones. The journal publishes studies in English, French, and German as well as Italian; book reviews tend to be in Italian. The substantial issues usually contain around 20 articles and notes and as many more reviews. Indexes of authors and book reviews appear in the final issue each year.

536. **Bulletin de correspondance hellenique**. Paris: De Boccard for the Ecole Française d'Athenes, 1877- . Annual (in 2v.). ISSN 0007-4217. LC 09-13099.

This venerable French journal is devoted to Greek archaeology and history. It publishes articles and excavation reports, most by French scholars connected with the Ecole (entry 632) . It appears in two substantial volumes that routinely total 800-1,000 pages. The *Bulletin* is a valuable resource for the hellenist.

537. **Bulletin of the Institute of Classical Studies**. London: University of London, Institute of Classical Studies, 1954- . Annual. ISSN 0076-0730.

Many of the articles published in this annual are the work of scholars connected to the Institute (entry 636) in one way or another. Articles tend to deal with Greek literature, history, and art; there are occasional contributions on Latin literature and Roman history. Notices on special programs and seminars at the Institute also appear in the *Bulletin*. Each issue includes a review of "Research in Classical Studies for University Degrees in Great Britain and Ireland." This review is divided into two sections: work in progress and work completed. Each is arranged alphabetically by university and lists candidates for advanced degrees and their thesis topics.

538. **Classical and Modern Literature**. Terre Haute, IN: CML, 1980- . Quarterly. ISSN 0197-2227. LC 81-640263.

This journal is devoted to studies of the influence of the classics on modern literature (English, European, and American). It includes articles and occasional book reviews. From 1984 to 1992, one issue per year consisted of an "Annual Bibliography of the Classical Tradition," which listed publications on the *Nachleben* of the classics. This was prepared by the Institute for the Classical Tradition (entry 635); future installments of this bibliography are to appear in the Institute's own *International Journal for the Classical Tradition*.

539. **Classical Antiquity**. Berkeley, CA: University of California Press, 1982- . Semiannual. ISSN 0278-6656. LC 83-640320.

This journal began life in 1968 as *California Studies in Classical Antiquity*. The original journal primarily published the work of University of California faculty and students. The change of title in 1982 reflected a broadening of the contributor pool. *Classical Antiquity* includes a wide range of articles in history, literature, philosophy, art, and archaeology. The content is generally of good quality. The University of California Press intends to make *Classical Antiquity* available in electronic as well as print form in the near future.

540. **Classical Bulletin**. Wauconda, IL: Bolchazy-Carducci, 1925- . Semiannual. ISSN 0009-8337. LC 78-648960.

This journal originally appeared monthly during the academic year (November-April). It was published over the years by several different university classics departments (most notably at St. Louis University) before being acquired by a commercial publisher in 1987. Never one of the more prestigious journals, *Classical Bulletin* traditionally offered short articles and reviews covering the entire field of classical studies. In 1992, a new subtitle was added: "Abstracts, Bibliographies, and History of World-Wide Classical Scholarship." The contents have changed to reflect this as well. Recent issues have consisted primarily of articles on the history of classical scholarship, review articles, bibliographies, and book reviews. Extensive coverage has been devoted to Eastern European classical scholarship, which is, perhaps, the journal's most important contribution.

541. **Classical Journal**. Charlottesville, VA: Classical Association of the Middle West and South, 1905- . Bimonthly. ISSN 0009-8353. LC 08-6753.

A typical issue includes several articles on various topics in classical literature and ancient history, one or two notes of pedagogical interest, and a half-dozen substantial book reviews. While similar in content and format to *Classical World* (entry 545), *Classical Journal* is generally ranked a bit higher.

Two cumulative indexes have been issued. The first, compiled by Franklin H. Potter, covers volumes 1-25 (1905-1930); the second, compiled by Dorrance S. White, covers volumes 26-50 (1930-1955).

542. **Classical Outlook**. Oxford, OH: American Classical League, 1923- . Quarterly. ISSN 0009-8361. LC 40-2196.

As the official organ of the American Classical League (entry 640), this journal is aimed at teachers of classics at all levels. It includes short articles concerning pedagogy and reviews of new books in classical studies. Regular columns deal with teaching resources and with computing and the teaching of the classics. Another recurrent feature is "Classica Americana," which offers biographical sketches of noted American classicists.

543. **Classical Philology**. Chicago: University of Chicago Press, 1906- . Quarterly. ISSN 0009-837X. LC 07-22643.

Edited by the classics department of the University of Chicago since its inception, this is one of the most distinguished classical journals produced in North America. A typical issue includes a half-dozen articles, a review article, and a half-dozen book reviews. In keeping with the title, articles are primarily on Greek and Latin languages and literature, although there are significant numbers of articles and reviews that deal with ancient history and philosophy.

544. **Classical Quarterly**. Oxford, England: Oxford University Press for the Classical Association, 1907- . Semiannual. ISSN 0009-8388. LC 08-19521.

Classical Quarterly's scope includes Greek and Roman literature, history, and philosophy. Each issue contains about 20 articles and nearly as many notes. The journal is characterized by austere, traditional scholarship, often heavily philological in orientation. Its standards are uniformly high. Author and subject indexes appear in the final issue of each year. There are no reviews; its sister publication *Classical Review* (entry 45) is devoted entirely to book reviews.

545. **Classical World**. Pittsburgh: Department of Classics, Duquesne University for the Classical Association of the Atlantic States, 1907- . Bimonthly. ISSN 0009-8418. LC 10-2751.

This journal was originally called *Classical Weekly*; the name changed with the frequency. Most issues offer two or three scholarly articles, one or more notes on pedagogy, and a large number of brief book reviews. The journal features studies in Greek and Roman literature and history. *Classical World* is especially valuable for the many topical review essays and bibliographical surveys it publishes. In the past these have often been reprinted in collections of *Classical World* bibliographies. Its many news items and announcements concerning matters of scholarly, professional, and pedagogical matters are also quite useful. One quirk of the journal has been its refusal to deal with Greek type; all Greek is printed in transliterated form.

546. **Electronic Antiquity**. Hobart, Australia: University of Tasmania, 1993- . Monthly. ISSN 1320-3606.

This was the first classical journal to be published solely in electronic form. It includes short articles and reviews, position advertisements, conference notices, and a column on electronic resources for the study of classics. It is especially useful for its news features because it is generally the most current journal in the field. Subscriptions are free; for information, contact the editors via the Internet at: antiquity-editor@classics.utas.edu.au. Subscriptions consist of electronic notification when a new edition becomes available; the notice includes a table of contents and instructions for access. *Electronic Antiquity* is also available on the Internet through a number of gophers.

547. **Glotta: Zeitschrift für griechische und lateinische Sprache**. Göttingen, Germany: Vandenhoeck und Ruprecht, 1909- . Semiannual. ISSN 0017-1298. LC 15-21054.

Glotta is the only journal devoted entirely to Greek and Latin languages and linguistics. Articles, written chiefly in German and English, deal with etymology, lexicography, phonology, dialects, Indo-European philology, and related topics. The final issue each year includes a keyword index of words discussed; this is subarranged by language.

548. **Greece and Rome**. Oxford, England: Oxford University Press for the Classical Association, 1931- . Semiannual. ISSN 0017-3835. LC 34-30109.

Greece and Rome is aimed at a broad general audience of students, teachers, and scholars within the field of classics. It publishes "scholarly but not technical articles" on all aspects of classical civilization. Each issue contains a half-dozen articles. A particularly valuable feature is the series of review essays that appear in each issue. These survey recent work in the following areas: Greek literature, Roman literature, Greek history, Roman history, archaeology and art, philosophy, and general works. *Greece and Rome* is exceptionally useful for undergraduates because of its readable articles on topics of general interest in classical studies.

549. **Greek, Roman and Byzantine Studies**. Durham, NC: Department of Classical Studies, Duke University, 1958- . Quarterly. ISSN 0072-7482. LC 64-29901.

This journal includes studies of Greek civilization from the beginnings to the fall of the Byzantine empire. "Roman" in the title refers to the Greek world under Roman rule; articles on primarily Roman topics and Latin literature are excluded. Early issues tended to focus more on Byzantine subjects, while recent ones have been weighted more toward mainstream classical Greek topics. A typical volume consists of five to eight articles. The final issue of each year includes author, subject, and Greek word indexes.

550. **Gymnasium: Zeitschrift für Kultur der Antike und humanistische Bildung**. Heidelberg, Germany: Carl Winter Univeritätsverlag, 1890- . Bimonthly. ISSN 0017-5943. LC 86-12570.

Originally called *Das Humanistische Gymnasium*, this began as a general humanities journal aimed at teachers in the humanistic *Gymnasia* (preparatory schools) in Germany. It has always had a considerable classical content, which came eventually to predominate. It now offers articles on Greek and Roman history and literature, classical archaeology, the history of classical scholarship, and humanism. *Gymnasium* also carries book reviews. A subject index appears in the final issue each year.

551. **Harvard Studies in Classical Philology**. Cambridge, MA: Harvard University Press, 1890- . Annual. ISSN 0073-0688. LC 44-32100.

Harvard Studies in Classical Philology, since its inception, has consisted primarily of contributions by faculty and graduates of the Harvard classics department, although works by others also appear in it. Articles tend to be strictly philological, with an occasional foray into ancient history or archaeology. *Harvard Studies* also includes summaries of Harvard dissertations in classics, an especially useful feature because these are not available through *Dissertation Abstracts*.

552. **Helios: A Journal Devoted to Critical and Methodological Studies of Classical Culture, Literature and Society**. Lubbock, TX: Texas Tech University Press, 1976- . Semiannual. ISSN 0160-0923. LC 82-643482.

Previously the journal of the Classical Association of the Southwestern United States, *Helios* has been published by the Department of Classical and Romance Languages at Texas Tech and the Texas Tech University Press since 1981. In its original incarnation, it was an undistinguished general journal of classics and comparative literature. With its relatively recent subtitle, *Helios* has found a niche publishing "articles that explore innovative approaches to the study of classical culture, literature, and society." Recent critical methodologies such as anthropological, deconstructive, feminist, reader response, social history, and text theory are featured in its pages, many times under the rubric of a thematic issue.

553. **Hermes: Zeitschrift für klassische Philologie**. Wiesbaden: Franz Steiner Verlag, 1866- . Quarterly. ISSN 0018-0777. LC 10-32853.

A typical issue of this venerable journal includes around eight articles and several notes (*Miszellen*). While most articles are in German, a substantial number of English contributions appear as well. Articles tend to be philological, although history and philosophy are by no means excluded. The quality of contributions is generally above average. Indexes of names and subjects, of Greek and Latin words discussed, and of passages discussed appear in the final issue each year.

554. **Hesperia**. Princeton, NJ: Institute for Advanced Study for the American School of Classical Studies at Athens, 1932- . Quarterly. ISSN 0018-098X. LC 32-17696.

The primary focus of this journal is Greek art and archaeology. It generally includes three to four articles and excavation reports per issue. Articles are often substantially longer than those found in other journals. Epigraphical and literary studies also appear in *Hesperia* occasionally. *Hesperia* is a fundamental journal for the study of classical Greek archaeology.

555. **Historia: Zeitschrift für Alte Geschichte**. Wiesbaden, Germany: Franz Steiner Verlag, 1952- . Quarterly. ISSN 0018-2311. LC 53-31306.

Historia is one of the best journals devoted to ancient history. Its main focus is Greek and Roman history. A typical issue contains a half-dozen articles and two or three notes. Articles are usually in German or English, with a sprinkling of French and Italian contributions. Early issues included book reviews, but these are no longer carried.

556. **Illinois Classical Studies**. Atlanta, GA: Scholars Press, 1976- . Seminannual. ISSN 0363-1923. LC 76-645935.

Despite its title, this is, perhaps, the most international classical journal published in America. It includes articles in all of the standard languages of classical scholarship and counts many prominent European scholars among its contributors. While articles cover the full range of classical studies, most tend to be in literature, philology, and philosophy. Traditional classical scholarship is emphasized.

557. **Journal of Hellenic Studies**. London: Society for the Promotion of Hellenic Studies, 1880- . Annual. ISSN 0075-4269. LC 09-20515.

This journal covers all aspects of ancient Greece: archaeology, art, history, literature, and philosophy. It often publishes longer-than-average articles. The quality tends to be high. The *Journal* also includes a large number of critical book reviews, which together provide a good survey of recent work in the field.

558. **Journal of Roman Archaeology**. Ann Arbor, MI: University of Michigan, Department of Classical Studies, 1988- . Annual. ISSN 1047-7594. LC 89-656368.

This relatively new journal is "concerned with Italy and all parts of the Roman world from about 700 B.C. to about 700 A.D." It interprets archaeology broadly and includes much material on Roman history in general. The annual volume is substantial, typically running more than 400 pages. In addition to articles and notes, each volume includes an extensive array of reviews and review articles that provide an excellent survey of recent work in Roman archaeology. While English predominates, contributions in the standard European languages are fairly common. The *Journal* is a valuable resource for both archaeologists and historians.

559. **Journal of Roman Studies**. London: Society for the Promotion of Roman Studies, 1911- . Annual. ISSN 0075-4358. LC 26-2981.

While the *Journal* covers the full range of Roman studies, emphasis tends to be on history and literature. It resembles its sister publication, the *Journal of Hellenic Studies* (entry 557), in format. Many of its articles are of above-average length, and the content is generally of high quality. The many critical book reviews and review essays provide an excellent overview of recent work in Roman studies.

560. **Latomus: revue d'études latines**. Tournai, Belgium: Société d'Etudes Latines de Bruxelles, 1937- . Quarterly. ISSN 0023-8856. LC 41-16538.

Latomus publishes articles on Latin language and literature and on Roman history. A typical issue contains a dozen articles and a substantial number of book reviews. Articles are in English and a variety of European languages; reviews are normally in French. The quality of the contents is good but rarely outstanding. The final issue of each year contains an author index and an index of books reviewed.

561. **Mnemosyne: Bibliotheca Classica Batava**. Leiden, Netherlands: E. J. Brill, 1852- . Semiannual. ISSN 0026-7074.

This old and distinguished Dutch journal includes work on Greek and Latin literature and philosophy. The journal has a strong philological bent and includes many textual notes. In addition to articles and notes, each volume includes a substantial number of reviews. While early volumes were in Dutch and Latin, currently English and German predominate. Indexes of authors and books reviewed appear in the final number of each volume.

562. **Oxford Journal of Archaeology**. Oxford, England: Blackwell, 1982- . Triannual. ISSN 0262-5253. LC 0262-5253.

This is a general journal of European and Near Eastern archaeology. Chronologically, it covers antiquity and the Middle Ages. A large part of its content is devoted to Bronze Age Mediterranean and classical archaeology. It also includes a number of articles concerning technical and theoretical aspects of archaeology.

563. **Oxford Studies in Ancient Philosophy**. New York: Oxford University Press, 1983- . Annual. ISSN 0265-7651. LC 84-645022.

Oxford Studies offers papers on a wide variety of topics in ancient philosophy, although primary emphasis is on classical Greek philosophy. It includes both articles and substantial (usually article-length) reviews. Its contributors include many well-known scholars, and the quality is generally high. An *index locorum* appears at the end of each volume.

564. **Papers of the British School at Rome**. London: British School at Rome, 1902- . Annual. ISSN 0068-2462. LC 10-13288.

This annual publishes articles on the "archaeology, history, and literature of Italy and other parts of the Mediterranean up to early modern times." Articles tend to be substantial. Most are by the staff of the school (entry 625) and its present and former members. This is a very useful publication for Roman archaeology and history. While it includes articles on medieval and Renaissance Italy, classical topics usually predominate.

565. **Philologus: Zeitschrift für klassische Philologie**. Berlin: Akademie der Wissenschaften der DDR, Zentralinstitut für Alte Geschichte und Archaeologie, 1846- . Semiannual. ISSN 0031-7985. LC 05-26859.

Philologus offers articles in the traditional German style on philology, ancient history, and philosophy. Each issue has approximately 10 articles and five notes. Articles are mainly in German; a few are in English or other languages. The second issue each year includes indexes of subjects, passages discussed, and Greek and Latin words discussed. The back run is particularly valuable, as its contributors comprise a virtual who's who of nineteenth-century German classical scholars.

566. **Phoenix**. Toronto: Classical Association of Canada, 1946- . Quarterly. ISSN 0031-8299. LC 52-15373.

Phoenix is the journal of the Classical Association of Canada. It publishes articles in English and French (mostly in English) on all aspects of classical studies. While the majority of contributions are by Canadians, U.S. scholars frequently publish in it as well. *Phoenix* is a solid journal of classics. An author index appears in the final issue of each year.

567. **Phronesis: A Journal for Ancient Philosophy**. Assen, Netherlands: Van Gorcum, 1955- . Triannual. ISSN 0031-8868. LC 59-35648.

Phronesis deals primarily with mainstream ancient Greek philosophy. A typical issue runs to four or five articles. A piece called "Editor's Notes," which selectively noted recent work in the field, frequently appeared at the end of an issue. Since 1993, this feature seems to have been replaced by actual reviews and review articles. Articles are mostly in English, with a sprinkling of German, French, and Italian pieces.

568. **Revue des études anciennes**. Bordeaux, France: Université de Bordeaux III, 1899- . Semiannual. ISSN 0035-2004. LC 43-43754.

The *Revue* publishes articles and reviews on Greek and Roman history, literature, and archaeology, written chiefly in French. Extensive literature reviews (*chroniques*) appear on a regular basis, covering Roman France and late antiquity. Indexes of authors and of works reviewed usually appear in the second issue each year. Sometimes other indexes are printed as well.

569. **Revue des études grecques**. Paris: Société d'Edition "Les Belles Lettres," for Société des Etudes Grecques, 1888- . Semiannual. ISSN 0035-2039. LC 09-13102.

This journal publishes articles on all aspects of classical Greek culture. It also includes the proceedings of the Société des Etudes Grecques. A substantial number of brief reviews appear as well. Two substantial bibliographical surveys appear regularly in the *Revue*: the *Bulletin archéologique* and the *Bulletin épigraphique*.

570. **Revue des études latines**. Paris: Société d'Edition "Les Belles Lettres," for Société des Etudes Latines, 1928- . Annual. ISSN 0373-5737.

This is roughly the French equivalent of the *Journal of Roman Studies* (entry 559), although not quite as good. It publishes articles and reviews concerning Latin language and literature. All are in French; nearly all are by French scholars. The reviews cover the full range of Roman studies and can be useful, although they are never timely. The *Revue* also includes a list of French doctoral theses in Roman studies each year, which provides author, title, and university.

571. **Rheinisches Museum für Philologie**. Frankfurt, Germany: J. D. Sauerlaender's Verlag, 1827- . Quarterly. ISSN 0035-449X.

August Boeckh and B. G. Niebuhr were among the founding editors of *Rheinisches Museum*; over the years its contributors have included virtually every German philologist of importance. Its contents are primarily philological, with some attention to ancient history and philosophy. It represents a traditional Germanic style of scholarship. A typical issue consists of five to eight articles and two to four notes. The majority of contributors are German, although a significant number of Anglo-American scholars publish in it as well. While remaining nominally quarterly, since 1977 *Rheinisches Museum* has appeared triannually (with nos. 3-4 combined).

572. **Transactions of the American Philological Association**. Atlanta, GA: Scholars Press for the American Philological Association, 1870- . Annual. ISSN 0360-5949. LC 76-646066.

The official journal of the American Philological Association (entry 641), this is the oldest classical journal published in North America. Early volumes had a general philological content and included articles on Indo-European, Germanic, and Romance language topics, among others. Gradually both the association and the journal shifted to a strictly classical orientation. The journal now publishes articles on all aspects of classical studies. Its reputation has varied over time. In the past decade its standing has been greatly improved by a series of vigorous editors. There is an index to the first 100 volumes by J. W. Spaeth: *Index to the Transactions and Proceedings of the American Philological Association, Volumes 1-100, 1870-1969* (Cleveland, OH: Case Western Reserve University for the Association, 1971).

The journal is also making preprints of forthcoming articles available electronically through the Internet. These can be found through various gopher servers; the "official" version is located at: gopher://ccat.sas.upenn.edu:70/11/Journals%2c%20Newsletters%20and%20Publications/TAPA.

573. **Yale Classical Studies**. New York: Cambridge University Press for Department of Classical Studies, Yale University, 1928- . Irregular. ISSN 0084-330X. LC 28-23551.

In its early years this journal contained only articles by Yale faculty and graduates; over time its list of contributors has broadened substantially. YCS sometimes publishes considerably longer articles than the typical classical journal. Its contents consist chiefly of literary and philological studies, but often include works on ancient history and philosophy as well. Recent volumes (since 1966) have tended to be thematic.

CHAPTER 14

DIRECTORIES

This chapter includes a variety of directories that list either university departments of classics or individual classicists. Many are produced by professional associations; most are updated more or less regularly. Others appear as special issues of journals. In order to assure a reasonable degree of currency, only directories that have been published or updated within the last five years are listed below. Users should be aware that even recently published directories quickly become out of date.

574. American Philological Association. **Directory of Members**. Worcester, MA: American Philological Association, 1970- . ISSN 0044-779X. LC 74-644044.

The American Philological Association (entry 641) currently publishes its directory biennially. It lists the names, addresses, and telephone numbers of members of the association. E-mail addresses are provided when available. Information is taken from the APA membership records. The membership of the APA includes most, but by no means all, classicists working in North American colleges and universities. It also includes a few overseas members. Individual members are listed alphabetically; a separate list of institutional members (mostly university libraries) follows. Access is only by name, because no indexes are provided. Gaichas's *Directory of College and University Classicists in the United States and Canada* (entry 580) is more inclusive, provides more information, and has better access. However, the APA directory is usually more current because it is revised at regular intervals. Supplements and corrections to the directory are sometimes included in the Association's newsletter.

575. **APA Guide to Graduate Programs in the Classics in the United States and Canada**. 3d ed. Worcester, MA: American Philological Association, 1994. 180pp.

Intended for those contemplating graduate study, this guide describes programs offering master's and doctoral degrees in classics, ancient history, and classical archaeology. There are two lists, one each for the United States and Canada. Arrangement in both is alphabetical by institution. There are multiple entries for universities that offer more than one graduate program (e.g., separate programs in classics and in archaeology). Each entry includes mailing address, telephone and fax numbers, degrees offered, a brief description of facilities available, and a list of current faculty and their research interests. There is an index of faculty members.

576. **Association Internationale de Papyrologues**. Bruxelles, Belgium: Association Internationale de Papyrologues, 1993. 29pp.

The Association (entry 644) produces lists of its members on an irregular basis; this is the first since 1987. Its membership includes most of the working papyrologists in the world, along with some other classicists and ancient historians who have an interest in the field. Entries, which are arranged alphabetically, usually consist of name, address, telephone and fax numbers, and E-mail address. Frequently they include institution and title as well. The directory also provides a list of institutes and centers for papyrological study.

577. **Classical and Modern Literature. Directory of Scholars**. Terre Haute, IN: CML, 1992- .

This directory of scholars interested in the comparative study of classical and modern literature is published annually as a supplement to the journal *Classical and Modern Literature* (entry 538). Subscribers to the journal are listed free, while others are charged a small fee to be included. Needless to say, this policy makes for an incomplete directory. The list includes a mix of classics, English, modern language, and other faculty in colleges and universities; some teachers in secondary schools; and a few independent scholars. Entries consist of name, title, institution, office address and telephone number, home address and telephone number, and fields of specialization. Occasionally E-mail addresses are added. All information is supplied by the individuals. The arrangement is alphabetical; indexes provide access by specialty and geographical location.

578. Classical Association of South Africa. **CASA Directory of Classical Scholars and Research for Higher Degrees in Sub-Saharan Africa**. Pretoria: Classical Association of South Africa, 1993- .

Prepared for the Association by William Dominik, this relatively new directory is intended to appear every two years. It includes university faculty and graduate students in Sub-Saharan Africa. Future issues are expected to extend coverage to North Africa as well. Arrangement is by universities, which are listed in a single alphabetical sequence. Faculty and other relevant academic staff are listed under each, with further subdivisions by department if appropriate. Entries include name, academic credentials, research interests, telephone and fax numbers, and E-mail addresses. Mailing addresses are provided only at the head of each section. Graduate students are listed after faculty. Entries for students include only name and topic of research. Although a name index is provided, the format is cumbersome for those seeking information about an individual.

The 1993-94 edition has also been made available in electronic form through *Electronic Antiquity* (see entry 546); it appears in volume 1, no. 5 (October 1993). The editor anticipates that future directories will also be made available through *Electronic Antiquity*.

579. **Classicists in British Universities**. Cambridge, England: Classical Association. Irregular.

Formerly called *Classics Departments in British Universities*, this directory is issued irregularly. The last edition appeared in 1992. The former title was more accurate because the directory actually covers classics departments in colleges and universities in the United Kingdom. Entries are arranged alphabetically by institution and include the college address and telephone number, the department name, contact name, and a description of the department. They also provide E-mail addresses for faculty members when available.

580. Gaichas, Lawrence E., ed. **Directory of College and University Classicists in the United States and Canada**. 3d ed. Pittsburgh: Classical Association of the Atlantic States, 1992. [*Classical World* 85:5 (May-June, 1992): 385-658.]

Gaichas's volume, the most comprehensive directory of North American classicists, appeared as a special issue of *Classical World* (entry 545). Its scope is actually wider than the title suggests, because it includes academic administrators, librarians, secondary school teachers, and independent scholars as well as college teachers. Gaichas took great pains to find and list as many classicists as possible. The directory contains more than 1,800 entries in an alphabetical arrangement. Each includes name, title, institution, address, telephone and fax numbers, E-mail address, degrees (with institution and date), home address and telephone number, and up to three fields of specialization. All information was supplied by the individuals. Indexes provide access by specialization and geographical location. Although much more complete and informative than the American Philological Association directory (entry 574), this directory is not updated frequently enough to remain current; the first edition appeared in 1974, the second in 1985.

581. Kinzl, K. H., ed. **Classical Studies in Canadian Universities**. New ed. Peterborough, ON: Department of Classical Studies, Trent University, 1993. 36pp. ISBN 0-9697240-0-4.

Previous editions of this directory were called *Classics in Canadian Universities*. The present version lists Canadian universities that offer courses in classics and university-level teachers of classics (excluding those with emeritus status and part-time appointments). Arrangement is alphabetical by university. Under each Kinzl, supplies mailing address, telephone and fax numbers, and a brief description of programs offered in classical studies. Faculty with classical interests are then listed by department. Faculty subentries include academic degrees, rank, and research interests. Several research centers and museums of interest to Canadian classicists are noted in an appendix. An index of classics faculty is also provided. The listings reflect the 1993-1994 academic year; a new edition is expected in two to three years.

Chapter 15

Internet
Resources

The Internet offers access to a variety of new sources of information in classical studies. Most are quite unlike traditional printed sources. Those noted in this chapter include electronic discussion groups (listservs), electronic journals, gophers and World Wide Web servers, and text archives. At present, most of these sources function primarily as current awareness tools. The discussion groups provide news about recent publications, research in progress, and pedagogical matters. They also offer a convenient means of communicating directly with a large body of scholars, students, and others interested in the listserv's subject area; queries posted to listservs often draw helpful responses. Electronic journals in classics currently tend to concentrate on reviews and news items, although several also publish articles. Gophers and World Wide Web site gather a wide range of materials on particular subjects; they include informational files and direct links to other Internet resources. Ftp (file transfer protocol) sites and text archives provide access to public domain software and to electronic versions of texts. A few Internet resources have been treated in other chapters, when appropriate. The headnote for each section below supplies references to these entries.

Information about access is generally limited to addresses, URLs (Uniform Resource Locators), and paths within gophers and ftp sites. Those who need help with particular processes should consult their Internet service provider. Many books on the Internet are now available; two good choices for basic information are Brendan Kehoe's *Zen and the Art of the Internet: A Beginner's Guide*, 2d ed. (Englewood Cliffs, NJ: Prentice-Hall PTR, 1993) and Ed Krol's

The Whole Internet: User's Guide and Catalog, 2d ed. (Sebastopol, CA: O'Reilly, 1994). Readers of this chapter should also note that the Internet is in constant flux: Addresses change and various resources come and go rapidly. Such changes are sometimes, but not inevitably, noted on the appropriate discussion groups. Ian Worthington's "Electronic Forums and Repositories for the Classics," which appears regularly in *Electronic Antiquity* (entry 546), is an excellent source of current information. A frequently updated list of academic discussion groups is maintained at Kent State University (available by anonymous ftp from ksuvxa.kent.edu). The "Europe in Bits & Bytes" column in the *Western European Specialists Section Newsletter* (Chicago: Association of College and Research Libraries, 1976-) also frequently notes new Internet resources of interest to classicists. More general sources include the *Directory of Electronic Journals, Newsletters and Academic Discussion Groups* (issued periodically by the Association of Research Libraries) and *Internet World's On Internet* (Westport, CT: Mecklermedia, 1994-).

Electronic Discussion Groups

These are also called listservs because many of them run on Listserv software. Some are moderated (i.e., the listserv owner reviews all postings before forwarding them to the listserv), while others allow any subscriber to post directly to the list. Many discussion groups allow only subscribers to post messages. In most cases, it is possible to subscribe by sending the following message to the subscription address: subscribe <LIST NAME><FIRST NAME><LAST NAME>.

582. **AEGEANET**. Subscription address: majordomo@acpub.duke.edu
Based at Duke University, this discussion group focuses on all aspects of Aegean Bronze Age archaeology. Most subscribers are professional archaeologists or ancient historians. To subscribe to this list, just send the message "subscribe aegeanet" to the above address; do not include your name.

583. **AIA-L**. Subscription address: listserv@cc.brynmawr.edu
The Archaeological Institute of America (entry 643) sponsors this discussion group. While the list is open to any topic, it is especially intended for the discussion of technical issues by professional archaeologists. The list is moderated.

583a. **ANAHITA**. Subscription address: listserv@ukcc.uky.edu
This forum discusses women and gender in antiquity. The listowners also maintain a related World Wide Web site called Diotima (entry 609a).

584. **ANCIEN-L**. Subscription address: listserv@ulkyvm.louisville.edu
The history of the ancient Mediterranean world is the focus of this listserv. It covers the Ancient Near East as well as the classical world. Content is generally scholarly, with some popular material included. Traffic on the list is usually moderate.

585. **ARCH-L**. Subscription address: listserv@dgogwdg1.bitnet
This is a general discussion group for archaeology. It is especially concerned with current research and excavations.

586. **CLASSICS**. Subscription address: listproc@u.washington.edu
The CLASSICS listserv concentrates on the study and teaching of Greek and Latin language and literature, with occasional digressions into history and archaeology. Content is geared toward an academic audience. Traffic on the

listserv runs from moderate to heavy. This listserv has a decided tendency to get sidetracked on minor or irrelevant issues. It is, however, an excellent news source and a good place to post queries on classical topics.

587. **Deremi-L**. Subscription address: listserv@ukanaix.cc.ukans.edu

Maintained by the organization De Re Militari (entry 652), this listserv is devoted to the discussion of classical and medieval military history. Postings include discussions and announcements concerning all aspects of the study of ancient and medieval warfare and related matters. Further information about the listserv and its archives can be found on the De Re Militari information server (entry 609).

588. **ELENCHUS**. Subscription address: listserv@acadvm1.uottawa.ca

While primarily of interest to scholars of religion, this discussion group occasionally addresses topics of interest to classicists. Its scope includes the thought and literature of Christianity through the sixth century A.D. The discussion often tends toward technical matters. Volume is usually light.

588a. **HOMER-L**. Subscription address: listproc@lists.missouri.edu

This discusion group is sponsored by the Center for Studies in Oral Tradition at the University of Missouri-Columbia. While its primary focus is on the Homeric epics, epic poetry from other cultures may also be discussed when appropriate.

589. **IOUDAIOS-L**. Subscription address: listserv@lehigh.edu

This listserv is devoted to first-century Judaism, with special emphasis on Philo of Alexandria and Flavius Josephus. The discussion generally assumes knowledge of Greek and sometimes Hebrew as well. This tends to be an active list.

590. **LATIN-L**. Subscription address: listserv@psuvm.psu.edu

Intended for those interested in Latin language and literature, this listserv accepts postings in Latin or English. Many of the active participants are high school Latin teachers. Common topics include pedagogical matters and discussion of how to translate various English expressions into Latin. The volume of postings tends to be light.

591. **LEXI**. Subscription address: listserv@uci.edu

A forum for the discussion of Greek and Latin lexicography, LEXI also includes some material on lexicography in general. Postings tend to be sporadic.

592. **LT-ANTIQ**. Subscription address: listserv@univscvm.csd.scarolina.edu

This discussion group covers all aspects of late antiquity (defined as ca. A.D. 260-640). Postings on religious and philosophical topics are the most common, although general historical and literary topics also receive attention. Volume on the listserv is usually moderate, although it can be heavy.

593. **MEDTXTL**. Subscription address: listserv@vmd.cso.uiuc.edu

Although aimed primarily at medievalists, this list is useful for anyone interested in palaeography and the transmission of classical literature during the Middle Ages. The listserv's normal topics include philology, codicology, and the analysis of medieval texts.

594. **NT-Greek**. Subscription address: nt-greek-request@virginia.edu

Based at the University of Virginia, this listserv is concerned with the scholarly study of the Greek New Testament.

595. **NUMISM-L.** Subscription address: listserv@univscvm.csd.scarolina.edu

Aimed at both collectors and scholars, this listserv offers a discussion forum on ancient and medieval coinage. Chronologically, its scope extends to the fall of Byzantium (A.D. 1454). The listserv is a good source of current information on this specialized field.

596. **PAPY.** Subscription address: listserv@igl.ku.dk

Based at the University of Copenhagen, this listserv focuses on papyrology and the study of Greco-Roman Egypt. Postings tend to be sporadic, and their contents are often technical. This is a good source of information about recent publications and developments in the field.

597. **PERSEUS.** Subscription address: listserv@brownvm.brown.edu

This relatively low-volume list is for anyone interested in *Perseus* (entry 340), a multimedia database on classical Greece. Discussion includes both technical issues and pedagogical applications. There is also a gopher server (entry 613) that provides information on *Perseus*.

597a. **ROMARCH.** Subscription address: majordomo@rome.classics.lsa.umich.edu

Sponsored by the Interdepartmental Program in Classical Art and Archaeology at the University of Michigan, ROMARCH is a discussion group concerned with the art and archaeology of ancient Italy and the provinces of the Roman empire. There is a related World Wide Web site, the ROMARCH Homepage (entry 613a).

598. **SOPHIA.** Subscription address: listserv@liverpool.ac.uk

This listserv provides a general forum for the discussion of ancient philosophy. Its scope extends from Hesiod to Iamblichus and from Spain to Palestine.

599. **TALAROS.** Subscription address: listserv@listserv.acns.nwu.edu

TALAROS is a relatively new listserv. Its focus is Hellenistic Greek history and literature.

600. **THUC-L.** Subscription address: listserv@vm.temple.edu

Part of a recent trend toward more specialized discussion groups on classical topics, this listserv provides a forum for those interested in the Greek historian Thucydides.

Electronic Journals

Several of the most important electronic journals have been discussed elsewhere in this book. These include the *Bryn Mawr Classical Review* (entry 44), *Electronic Antiquity* (entry 546), and *Scholia Reviews* (entry 50). Other classical journals currently published in electronic form are listed below. Some of these are available by subscription, while others can be accessed through ftp or a gopher. All electronic journals noted here are available for free at present.

600a. **Arachnion: A Journal of Ancient Literature and History on the Web.**
URL: http://www.cisi.unito.it/arachne/arachne.html

Originally titled *Arachne*, this journal is based in Italy. Contributions, which are in a variety of languages, deal with all aspects of Greek and Roman literature and history. Current and back issues are available for reading or downloading from the web site.

601. **Canadian Classical Bulletin/Bulletin canadien des études anciennes**. Peterborough, ON: Canadian Classical Association, 1994- . ISSN 1198-9149.

Of particular interest to Canadian classicists, this newsletter is intended to appear on a monthly basis. It contains notices of conferences, scholarships, fellowships, job openings, museum exhibits, and the like. The *Bulletin* is distributed to subscribers over the Internet; subscription requests should be sent to Professor Konrad Kinzl at KKINZL@TRENTU.CA. The journal is also available by means of gopher; its URLs are gopher://tornade.ere.umontreal.ca:7071 and http://137.122.12.15/HumCanada.html.

602. **Classics Ireland**. Dublin: Classical Association of Ireland, 1994- .

This journal appears in both print and electronic form. It includes articles, mostly by Irish classicists, on history, literature, archaeology, and teaching the classics. Electronic access is by gopher; the home location is gopher.ucd.ie. The journal is also available through a number of other gopher and World Wide Web servers.

603. **Didaskalia: Ancient Theatre Today**. Hobart, Australia: University of Tasmania, 1993- .

This unique journal publishes announcements and reviews of contemporary productions of ancient plays. It also includes short articles, book reviews, and notices of conferences relating to classical theater. A "subscription" consists of advance notice (with a table of contents) when a new issue is published; to subscribe send a request to Didaskalia-editor@classics.utas.edu.au. One may access the journal itself through gopher at: info.utas.edu.au. *Didaskalia* is in a folder labeled "Publications." The journal is also available by ftp from: ftp.utas.edu.au following the path departments/classics/didaskalia.

Gophers and World Wide Web Servers

Gopher servers offer menu access to Internet resources. A particular gopher server can be reached directly by pointing your gopher at its Uniform Resource Locator (URL) or by "burrowing" through other gophers. World Wide Web servers are similar to gophers but are based on hypertext; these servers often provide images and sound as well as text. Their URLs are prefixed by http. Some sites offer both gopher and World Wide Web servers; if so, URLs are provided for both. Readers should note that URLs, unlike normal E-mail addresses, can be case-sensitive. Only a few servers that offer unusual or exceptionally rich resources for classical studies are listed here.

604. **ACL Gopher**. URL: http://www.umich.edu/~acleague

This server contains information about the American Classical League (entry 640). In addition to membership information and various ACL documents, the server includes teaching materials for classics courses and information about Internet resources. Those who lack World Wide Web access can gopher to gopher://classics.lsa.umich.edu and select the ACL gopher from the first menu.

605. **ARIADNE**. URL: gopher://ithaki.servicenet.ariadne-t.gr:70/1

Located in Greece, this gopher server offers access to the Hellenic Civilization database, which includes materials on medieval, modern, and classical Greece. Among other things, the database contains information about Greek museums, images of works of art, and portions of classical Greek texts.

606. **Center for Computer Analysis of Texts, University of Pennsylvania**.
URL: gopher://ccat.sas.upenn.edu

This gopher contains extensive material on classical studies, as well as much on the humanities in general. James O'Donnell, a professor in the classics department at the University of Pennsylvania, is largely responsible for the classical portion of the gopher. Most of the resources are found under the menu choice "Electronic Publications and Resources." Among other things, this sub-menu provides access to nearly all available electronic journals in the classics, electronic versions of university press catalogs, and several other bibliographical tools for classicists, including the TOCS-IN service (entry 38). This gopher also offers access to several collections of texts, which include electronic versions of various classical texts either in Latin or in English translation (there are relatively few Greek texts available over the Internet because of technical difficulties with the display and transmission of Greek characters).

607. **Centre for Computing in the Humanities, University of Toronto**. URL: gopher://alpha.epas.utoronto.ca:70/11/cch/disciplines/classics

In addition to providing information about classical studies at the University of Toronto, this server offers access to many other Internet resources. For example, its menu choices include the *Bryn Mawr Classical Review* (entry 44), TOCS-IN (entry 38), *Electronic Antiquity* (entry 546), and files containing preprints or advanced content information from several classical journals. It also supplies links to other servers with classical materials.

607a. **Classics Alcove**. URL: http://nervm.nerdc.ufl.edu/~blaland/class.html

Created and maintained by Blake Landor at the University of Florida, the Classics Alcove is an excellent starting point for exploring Internet resources for classical studies. This well-organized site presents materials by type: guides, journals, texts, databases, discussion groups, images, software, teaching resources, and other resources. Its coverage is extensive and up to date. The guides section is particularly helpful for the inexperienced; it offers direct links to several introductory works, including Landor's own "Burrowing in Classical Antiquity: A Guide to Internet Resources."

608. **Classics and Mediterranean Archaeology**. URL: gopher://rome.classics.las.umich.edu:70+/11/General or http://rome.classics.las.umich.edu/welcome.html

One of the best collections of classical material on the Internet, this is both a gopher and a World Wide Web site. Its many files and links to other sites provide descriptions of electronic discussion groups, information about undergraduate and graduate programs in classical studies, various teaching materials, and electronic versions of a number of academic press catalogs. Other resources available include archaeological field reports, papyrological files from Yale and Heidelberg, and direct links to backfiles of most electronic journals concerning classics (*Bryn Mawr Classical Review* [entry 44], *Electronic Antiquity* [entry 546], etc.). There are also links to several collections of electronic texts, which include classical authors (chiefly in translation). This server does an exceptional job of gathering relevant materials and arranging them conveniently.

609. **De Re Militari Information Server**.
URL: http://kuhttp.cc.ukans.edu/history/deremil/deremain.html

De Re Militari (entry 652), an association for the study of ancient and medieval military history, maintains this World Wide Web server. It contains material about the association (e.g., its newsletter, membership information, a directory of members) and announcements of conferences and recent publications. The server also includes a number of bibliographical resources for the study of ancient and medieval warfare. Finally, the archives of the association's electronic discussion group, Deremi-L (entry 587), are located here.

609a. **Diotima: Materials for the Study of Women and Gender in Antiquity**.
URL: http://www.uky.edu/ArtsSciences/Classics/gender.html

This World Wide Web site is devoted to the study of women and gender in antiquity. Diotima covers the Ancient Near East as well as the classical world. Material is arranged by type. Contents include an impressive array of bibliographies, a few translations of primary sources (more will be added in the future), a wide range of course materials (syllabi, outlines, study guides), and direct links to a number of relevant essays and reviews now available on the web. Diotima is maintained by the listowners of ANAHITA (entry 583a).

610. **Gods on File**. URL: http://www.the-wire.com/culture/mythology/mythtext.html

For anyone interested in mythology, this World Wide Web site offers a wide range of material. It covers myths from around the world, including those of Greece and Rome. Among the many files on the server are a dictionary of gods and goddesses, a dictionary of heroes (still under construction at present), a collection of bibliographies, and a number of short works on mythology. The server also provides links to other servers that have electronic versions of such works as *Bulfinch's Mythology* and Grimm's *Fairy Tales*. This is a particularly useful resource for the study of comparative mythology.

611. **Heidelberg Institut für Papyrologie**. URL: gopher://gopher.urz.uni-heidelberg.de:70/11/institute/papyrologie

This gopher assembles electronic resources for the study of papyrology. Among other things, it contains an index of published documentary papyri from Egypt and descriptions of some collections of papyri (e.g., Yale). The log of the electronic discussion group on papyrology (entry 596) is also maintained at this site.

612. **Less Commonly Taught Languages Gopher**. URL: gopher://lc tl.acad.umn.edu

Sponsored by the Center for Advanced Research on Language Acquisition at the University of Minnesota, this gopher is a directory of institutions where all "less commonly taught languages" (i.e., languages other than English, French, German, and Spanish) are taught. The directory covers two- and four-year colleges and universities in North America. It contains individual lists for each language. Entries usually give the name of a contact person, an address, and a telephone number. No information about actual programs or courses is provided. The Latin listings include more than 450 institutions; those for Greek more than 500. The Greek listings are not well organized; there are separate lists for ancient Greek, classical Greek, Hellenistic Greek, Homeric Greek, Modern

Greek, and New Testament Greek. There is also a list for "Greek," which appears to include all those institutions found in the other lists, plus a good many more.

612a. **Papyrology Homepage**. URL: http://www-personal.umich.edu/~jmucci/papyrology/home.html

Based at the University of Michigan, this World Wide Web site offers a reasonably complete guide to papyrological resources on the Internet. The Papyrology Homepage provides links to the electronic resources of other institutions with major collections of papyri, images of papyri, and a guide to recent scholarly literature in the field. Other resources include a directory of working papyrologists in North America and descriptions of major projects and research in progress. This site is much more extensive than that of the Heidelberg Institut für Papyrologie (entry 611).

613. **Perseus Project**. URL: gopher://perseus.harvard.edu:70/1

This server offers current information about *Perseus* (entry 340), a multimedia database on ancient Greek culture. The various files provide both technical information and material on the use of *Perseus* as a teaching tool. There is also an electronic discussion group on *Perseus* (entry 597).

613a. **ROMARCH Homepage**.
URL: http://www-personal.umich.edu/~pfoss/ROMARCH.html

This World Wide Web site is sponsored by the Interdepartmental Program in Art and Archaeology at the University of Michigan. It covers the art and archaeology of Italy and the Roman provinces from ca. 1000 B.C. to A.D. 700. The page is colorful and easy to navigate. Its major divisions include *Acta Tempestiva* (notices of recent archaeological discoveries, etc.), the archives of the ROMARCH discussion group (entry 597a), and a geographical index (by Roman province) to Internet resources for Roman archaeology. Many more archaeological and historical resources are also noted.

613b. **Rome Project**. URL: http://www.nltl.columbia.edu/groups2/rome/index.html

Designed for students of ancient Rome, this World Wide Web site is maintained by the New Laboratory for Teaching and Learning at the Dalton School. Its colorful icons offer access to Internet resources in the following areas: literature, military history, archaeology, political history, general materials, philosophy, drama, religion, and maps of the Roman empire. While there is not much original here, it provides many useful links to other sites.

614. **TELA**. URL: http://scholar.cc.emory.edu

Maintained by Scholars Press, this World Wide Web site provides information both about the Press and the organizations affiliated with it, including the American Philological Association (entry 641) and the American Society of Papyrologists (entry 642). Types of material found on this gopher include descriptions of professional organizations in classics and religious studies, catalogs of academic presses, and announcements concerning conferences, grants, and employment opportunities.

615. **TLG Gopher**. URL: gopher://tlg.cwis.uci.edu:7011/1

Based at the University of California, Irvine, this gopher provides the most up-to-date information about *Thesaurus Linguae Graecae* products (entry 464). Files include a contents list for the current CD-ROM release, prices and a copy of the standard TLG licensing agreement, technical data, and a list of third-party software suppliers.

615a. **University of New Hampshire Classics Department Homepage**.
URL: http://www.circe.unh.edu/classics/home_page.html
This useful World Wide Web site offers several noteworthy features. It provides information about the Classical Association of New England (entry 651) and the *New England Classical Newsletter & Journal* (including recent tables of contents). The page also includes a section on classics resources on the Internet. This consists of two parts "Starting Points" and "Electronic Resources for Classicists: The Second Generation" by Maria Pantelia. The former is a list of major resources with brief descriptions of each. The latter, a much fuller list, originally appeared as a printed article in the *New England Classical Journal* (22.3 [Feb. 1995]). The electronic version is regularly updated and includes direct links to all of the resources noted. These are arranged by type; rubrics include: project reports, electronic publications, journal indexes, collections of images, electronic text archives, software ftp sites, course materials, professional organizations, and classics departments. This site and the Classics Alcove (entry 607a) are particularly helpful for the less-experienced user.

616. **University of Virginia**. URL: gopher//lib.virginia.edu:70 or http://gwis.virginia.edu:80
This site is particularly noteworthy for containing the "official" copies of the *Bryn Mawr Classical Review* (entry 44) and TOCS-IN (entry 38). Many of the other gopher servers that provide access to these sources do so through links to Virginia. A number of other electronic journals in classics can also be found on this gopher. These are all in the subdirectory "Electronic Journals."

Text Archives

These are sites on the Internet that collect information about electronic version of texts; some also supply texts. The text archives and other sites noted below have significant listings of classical texts. Many of these are in English translation; some are in Latin. Due to the technical difficulties involved in the display and transmission of Greek characters, there are relatively few Greek texts available over the Internet. Many of the gopher servers noted in the preceding section also provide access to electronic texts, either through files residing on the server or through links to other sites.

617. **Catalogue of Projects in Electronic Texts**. URL: gopher://gopher.george-town.edu/1
CPET is a project of the Center for Text & Technology at Georgetown University. It is a directory of projects that create and analyze electronic texts in the humanities. The descriptions of these projects are organized by language and subject. A number of projects involving Greek and Latin texts are listed. These entries often include detailed lists of electronic texts and information about their availability. While CPET does not itself supply electronic texts, it is a good means of locating those that are available. The easiest way to gain access to CPET is via gopher; CPET has its own directory within the Georgetown University gopher. CPET files can also be obtained by anonymous ftp from guvax.george-town.edu; once logged into this server, it is necessary to change directories by typing: cd cpet_projects_in_electronic_text at the ftp prompt.

618. **Oxford Text Archive**. ftp address: black.ox.ac.uk
The Oxford Text Archive holds extensive collections of electronic versions of literary works in many languages. Its collections include a large number

of Greek and Latin works. A complete catalog of currently available texts can be obtained by anonymous ftp from the Internet address given above. It is under the directory /ota. Texts in the public domain may also be obtained directly by anonymous ftp. However, most of the Archive's collection is under some form of copyright restriction, although copies are frequently available at cost for scholarly use. These texts must be ordered from the Archive and are supplied on tape or disk or over the network. Further information can be obtained by means of anonymous ftp or by sending a query to archive@vax.oxford.ac.uk.

619. **Project Libellus**. ftp address: ftp.uwashington.edu

This project makes electronic versions of basic Latin texts available. It currently offers works by such authors as Caesar, Catullus, Cicero, Livy, and Vergil. In addition to other texts, a Latin grammar and a Latin-English dictionary are in preparation. Project Libellus also intends to include Greek texts as soon as technical problems are resolved. All texts are scanned from older editions that are now in the public domain. As a result, these texts are not always reliable for scholarly study. Texts may be obtained by anonymous ftp from the above address. Once in the server, the directory to follow is /pub/user-supported/libellus.

Miscellaneous Resources

620. **Classics Resource List**. URLs: ftp://ftp.std.com or gopher://gopher.epas.utoronto.ca/0ftp%3aftp.epas.utoronto.ca%40/pub/cch/classics /classics_resource_list

Compiled by Michael Sikillian, this list contains information about associations, publishers of classical materials, booksellers, teaching materials, and electronic resources. While a useful compendium, the list has not been adequately maintained and now includes a fair amount of obsolete information. The whole list can be obtained by ftp from its home address above. For username type ftp and use your E-mail address as a password. The list is under the "Pub" directory and is called "cls." The Classics Resource List is also available through various gopher sites; the second URL noted above is for one of these.

PART 3

ORGANIZATIONS

CHAPTER 16

RESEARCH CENTERS

Here are noted a number of special research centers for classical studies in both North America and Europe. Some are residential centers for scholars, while others primarily exist to maintain collections of resources. Centers that function mainly as graduate programs are generally omitted. The list is selective but includes those centers most likely to be of interest to North American students and scholars. While the directory information for research centers is less subject to change than that for associations (chapter 17), current addresses and telephone numbers can be verified in such annual reference works as *The World of Learning*. Readers unfamiliar with international calling should note that all non-U.S. telephone numbers listed below include the applicable country and city codes for calls placed from North America.

621. **American Academy in Rome**. Via Angelo Masina 5, 00153 Rome, Italy. Tel.: (39 6) 58461. Fax: (39 6) 581-0788. U.S. Office: 7 East 60th St., New York, NY 10022. Tel.: (212) 751-7200. Fax: (212) 751-7220.

Founded in 1894, the American Academy in Rome is a residential center for research in the fine arts, classical studies, art history, Italian studies, and archaeology. The Academy offers a number of fellowships for graduate students and established scholars. It also sponsors annual summer programs aimed primarily at high school Latin teachers and college students in classical studies. The Academy maintains an outstanding research library, which now numbers more than 100,000 volumes. Its monographic series, the *Memoirs,* publishes works on Roman literature, history, and archaeology.

622. **American Center of the International Photographic Archive of Papyri**. c/o Prof. Maryline Parca, Dept. of the Classics, 4072 FLB, University of Illinois, 707 S. Mathews, Urbana, IL 61801. Tel.: (217) 333-1008.

This archive, which is the result of a project funded by the National Endowment for the Humanities, is a collection of photographs and negatives of papyri held in American collections. Although some of the largest and most important collections (e.g., those of the University of Michigan and Columbia University) are not part of the archive, it includes papyri from the majority of American collections. A partial listing of its holdings can be found in E. W. Wall, "Interim Report of IPAP," *Bulletin of the American Society of Papyrologists* 18:3-4 (1981): 161-64. The archive is housed in the Rare Book Room of the University of Illinois Library but is administered by the University's classics department. Materials are available for consultation on site; in some cases, photographs can be supplied by mail. For papyri held by collections outside North America, see the International Photographic Archive of Papyri (entry 638).

623. **American School of Classical Studies at Athens**. Odos Souidas 54, 106 76 Athens, Greece. Tel.: (30 1) 723-6313. U.S. address: 993 Lenox Dr., Ste. 101, Lawrenceville, NJ 08648. Tel.: (609) 844-7577. Fax: (609) 844-7524.

Founded in 1881, the School is a research institute devoted to ancient Greek literature, history, and archaeology. It offers various fellowships for scholars and provides programs of study for graduate students during the academic year. The School also conducts summer sessions for advanced undergraduates, graduate students, and high school and college faculty. Two research libraries are maintained: the Blegen Library (55,000 volumes), which focuses on classical studies, and the Gennadius Library (see entry 198), which concentrates on Byzantine and modern Greek studies. Over the years, the School has sponsored or cosponsored important excavations in Greece (most notably the Athenian Agora). In addition, it publishes a highly regarded journal, *Hesperia* (entry 554).

624. **British School at Athens**. Odos Souidias 52, 106 76 Athens, Greece. Tel.: (30 1) 721-0974. Fax: 723-6560. British Office: 31-34 Gordon Square, London, WC1H 0PY, England. Tel.: (44 71) 387-8029. Fax: (44 71) 383-0781.

Established in 1886, the School is a center for the study of Greek literature, history, and archaeology. It maintains a research library of more than 50,000 volumes and an archaeological laboratory. Among other activities, the British School sponsors archaeological excavations. It also publishes the *British School Annual* (entry 529) and *Archaeological Reports*.

625. **British School at Rome**. Piazzale Winston Churchill 5, 00197 Rome, Italy. Tel.: (39 6) 323-0743.

The British School at Rome, which was founded in 1901, is a residential research center for British scholars working in classical studies, medieval and modern archaeology, history, art history, and the fine arts. Thus, while much of its focus is on classical studies, it is really a general institute for the study of Italian and Mediterannean history and culture. The School possesses a library of approximately 72,000 volumes. In addition to sponsoring various research projects and excavations, the School publishes the *Papers of the British School at Rome* (see entry 564), a semiannual newsletter, and occasional monographs.

626. **Canadian Academic Center in Italy**. Piazza Cardelli 4, 00186 Rome, Italy. Tel.: (39 6) 687-3677. Fax: (39 6) 687-3693.

This is one of the smaller and newer centers in Rome. Founded in 1978, it assists Canadian scholars working in Italy. The Center has a modest library of 2,000 volumes.

627. **Canadian Archaeological Institute at Athens**. Gennadiou 2B, 115 21 Athens, Greece. Tel.: (30 1) 722-3201. Fax: (30 1) 722-8318.

This recently established institute is much smaller than its British and American counterparts. It is intended to be the main center for Canadian classical archaeologists working in Greece.

628. **Center for Epigraphical and Palaeographical Studies**. Ohio State University, 190 Pressey Hall, 1070 Carmack Rd., Columbus, OH 43210-1002. Tel.: (614) 292-3280.

The Center was established in 1986 as a comprehensive research facility for the study of Greek and Latin inscriptions. In 1992 its scope was enlarged to embrace palaeography as well. The Center maintains a working library and substantial collections of squeezes (paper impressions) and photographs of inscriptions. It offers both postdoctoral fellowships and short-term fellowships for established scholars. The Center is also involved in a project to make Greek inscriptions available in electronic form (entry 459).

629. **Center for Hellenic Studies**. 3100 Whitehaven St. NW, Washington, DC 20008. Tel.: (202) 234-3738. Fax: (202) 797-3745.

Established in 1961, the Center for Hellenic Studies is administered by the Trustees of Harvard University. It supports research on all aspects of ancient Greek civilization. The Center maintains a substantial research library. It awards eight junior fellowships each year. Fellows normally reside at the Center during the academic year. The Center has also recently instituted a "Summer Scholars" program, which allows up to nine researchers to make use of its facilities during the summer.

630. **Deutsches Archäologisches Institut**. Via Sardegna 79, 00187 Rome, Italy. Tel.: (39 6) 481-7812.

One of oldest foreign research institutes in Rome, the DAI was established in 1829. Its primary focus is on classical archaeology. The DAI is well known for its excellent library of more than 160,000 volumes; both a printed catalog (see entry 202) and, for materials published since 1956, a computerized database (entry 33) are available. The Institute also publishes the journal *Römische Mitteilungen*.

631. **Deutsches Archäologisches Institut, Abteilung Athen**. Odos Fidiou 1, 106 78 Athens, Greece. Tel.: (30 1) 362-0270. Fax: (30 1) 361-4762.

Founded in 1874, this branch of the Deutsches Archäologisches Institut is concerned with preclassical and classical Greek archaeology. It maintains a research library (currently 60,000 volumes) and sponsors excavations in Greece. The Institut also published an annual journal, *Athenische Mitteilungen*, and a monographic series, the *Beihefte*.

632. **Ecole Française d'Athènes**. Odos Didotou 6, 106 80 Athens, Greece. Tel.: (30 1) 361-2518. Fax: (30 1) 363-2101.

Established in 1846, the Ecole Française supports historical and archaeological research on classical Greece. It has long sponsored important excavations, most notably that at Delphi. The school's library currently numbers more than 80,000 volumes. The Ecole Française also carries out a major publishing effort, which includes both an annual journal, the *Bulletin de correspondance hellénique* (entry 563), and several monographic series.

633. **Ecole Française de Rome**. Piazza Farnese 67, 00186 Rome, Italy. Tel.: (39 6) 86011. Fax: (39 6) 874-4834.

The Ecole Française, which was founded in 1873, devotes its activities to Italian archaeology and history, with emphasis on the ancient and medieval periods. The school maintains a research library that now stands at more than 140,000 volumes. It also supports an active publication program, which produces a journal, the *Mélanges de l'Ecole Française de Rome*, and several monographic series.

634. **Institute for Antiquity and Christianity**. Claremont Graduate School. 831 N. Dartmouth Ave., Claremont, CA 91711-6178. Tel.: (909) 621-8066. Fax: (909) 621-8390.

While focusing primarily on early Christianity, the Institute for Antiquity and Christianity also supports research on the Ancient Near East and the classical world. Activities of particular interest to classicists include projects on Greek rhetoric, papyrology, and epigraphy. The Institute maintains a small museum and various teaching collections of papyri and other antiquities. In addition, its facilities include a reference library of approximately 3,000 volumes. The Institute offers graduate courses (through the Claremont Graduate School) and continuing education programs open to the public. Its publications include a quarterly bulletin and a variety of monographs and project reports.

635. **Institute for the Classical Tradition**. Boston University, 745 Commonwealth Ave., Boston, MA 02215. Tel.: (617) 353-7370. Fax: (617) 353-2053.

This Institute, which is closely associated with the International Society for the Classical Tradition (entry 657), supports research on the later influence of the classics. Its facilities at Boston University include a growing library of books and offprints on topics relating to the classical tradition. The Institute compiles an annual bibliography of work in the field, which previously appeared in *Classical and Modern Literature* (entry 538) and is now to be published in the Institute's own journal, the *International Journal of the Classical Tradition*. In addition to its various publishing projects, the Institute sponsors regular meetings.

636. **Institute of Classical Studies**. 31-34 Gordon Square, London, WC1H 0PY, England. Tel.: (71) 387-7696.

Established in 1953, the Institute of Classical Studies is part of the University of London. Although it primarily functions as a graduate program in classical studies, the Institute also participates in a number of activities of broader interest. In collaboration with the Societies for the Promotion of Hellenic and Roman Studies (entries 664-665), the Institute maintains a major research library for classical studies. The Institute carries out an extensive publication program as well; it produces an important journal, the *Bulletin* (entry 537), and a monographic series (the *Bulletin Supplements*).

637. **International Centre for Classical Research**. 47 Alopekis St., 140 Athens, Greece.

Founded in 1959 by the Hellenic Society for Humanistic Studies, the Centre supports scholarly research and popular educational programs on classical Greek culture. Its facilities include a library of 20,000 volumes. The Centre sponsors conferences and several publications, including *Antiquity and Contemporary Problems* and *Studies and Research*.

638. **International Photographic Archive of Papyri**. Fondation Egyptologique Reine Elisabeth, Parc du Cinquantenaire 10, B-1040 Bruxelles,
Belgique. Primary Contact: Prof. Adam Bülow-Jacobsen, Kobenhavns
Universitet, Institut for Graesk og Latin, Njalsgade 90, DK 2300 Koben-
havn S., Denmark. Fax: 45 32 96 11 15. Internet: bulow@coco.ihi.ku.dk

Founded by Ludwig Koenen and continued by Bülow-Jacobsen and Revel
Coles, the International Photographic Archive of Papyri holds negatives and
photographs of papyri from a number of European and Egyptian collections.
These include, among others, the Cairo Museum in Egypt, the Bodleian Library,
and collections in Oslo, Lund, and Athens. Reports detailing the holdings of the
archive are published on an irregular basis; the most recent is Adam Bülow-
Jacobsen, "Report on the 1987 Mission for the International Photographic
Archive of Greek Papyri," *Zeitschrift für Papyrologie und Epigraphik* 70 (1987):
63-64.

Access to the archive is complex. While the primary repository is at the
Fondation Egyptologique Reine Elisabeth in Brussels, a significant part of the
collection resides with Adam Bülow-Jacobsen in Copenhagen. A satellite archive,
which includes either negatives or color slides of the entire collection, is located at
the Institut für Altertumskunde at the University of Cologne. Inquiries about
holdings or access to the archive should be directed to Professor Bülow-Jacobsen.

639. **Warburg Institute**. University of London, Woburn Square, London
WC1H 0AB, England. Tel.: (71) 580-9663. Fax: (71) 436-2852.

Aby Warburg and his associate Fritz Saxl founded the Warburg Institute
in Hamburg in 1921. Saxl moved the Institute to England in 1934; it became part
of the University of London in 1944. The Institute supports interdisciplinary
work on the classical tradition in European thought, art, and history. To this end
it maintains a noted research library (see entries 210-211) and sponsors a number
of research fellowships. The Institute also carries out an extensive publication
program, which includes a monographic series (*Studies*) and the *Journal of the
Warburg and Courtauld Institutes*.

CHAPTER 17

PROFESSIONAL ASSOCIATIONS AND SOCIETIES

Listings in this chapter include national and international organizations whose primary concern is with some aspect of classical studies. National organizations are limited to those based in North America or the United Kingdom. A few of the more important regional associations in the United States are also described below. Many of these organizations, especially the smaller ones, do not have permanent business addresses. Often, the mailing address provided is that of the secretary of the association and is subject to change on a regular basis. It is always wise to verify the address in the current edition of the *Encyclopedia of Associations*, *The World of Learning*, or a similar reference work.

640. **American Classical League**. Miami University, Oxford, OH 45056. Tel.: (513) 529-7741. Fax: (513) 529-7741.

The primary purpose of the American Classical League, which was organized in 1919, is to promote the teaching of Latin and related subjects. Most of its members are high school and college Latin teachers. The ACL operates a placement service for Latin teachers and maintains a resource center that supplies instructional materials for Latin and Greek. It also publishes a journal, *Classical Outlook* (entry 542), and holds annual meetings. There is now an ACL gopher (entry 604) available on the Internet that provides current information about the organization and its activities. The ACL also sponsors a second organization, the Junior Classical League (entry 659), for high school students.

641. **American Philological Association**. Dept. of Classics, College of the Holy Cross, Worcester, MA 01610-2395. Tel.: (508) 793-2203. Fax: (508) 793-3428.

Founded in 1869, the APA is one of the oldest professional associations in North America and the principal one for classics. In its early period the Association had a wider scope and included scholars working in a variety of languages and literatures. By 1919, however, the APA had come to focus exclusively on classical languages and literatures. Its membership now consists mainly of college and university professors of classics and related fields, although a number of secondary school teachers and independent scholars also belong to the association. The APA has an active publishing program that produces a biennial directory (see entry 574), a bimonthly newsletter, and an annual journal, *Transactions of the American Philological Association* (entry 572). It also publishes two monograph series (Philological Monographs and American Classical Studies) and a textbook series. In conjunction with the Archaeological Institute of America (entry 643), the APA holds an annual conference, which always takes place December 27-30. A number of other American classical organizations also hold annual meetings at this conference. Current information about the APA is available electronically through the TELA World Wide Web site (entry 614).

642. **American Society of Papyrologists**. Dept. of Classics, St. Joseph's University, 5600 City Ave., Philadelphia, PA 19131-1395.

This society, which was organized in 1961, promotes study of ancient Greek and Latin papyri. Its membership is composed primarily of scholars working in the field. The ASP publishes a journal, the *Bulletin of the American Society of Papyrologists*, and a monograph series, American Studies in Papyrology. The society meets annually in conjunction with the American Philological Association's conference (entry 641). Current information about the ASP is available through the TELA World Wide Web site (entry 614).

643. **Archaeological Institute of America**. 675 Commonwealth Ave., Boston, MA 02215. Tel.: (617) 353-9361. Fax: (617) 353-6550.

While the Institute is concerned with archaeology in general, it also functions as the primary organization for Americans interested in classical archaeology. Unlike many of the other societies listed in this chapter, the AIA blends both scholarly and popular activities. For professional archaeologists the Institute publishes the *American Journal of Archaeology* (entry 526), *Archaeological Fieldwork Opportunities*, and a monograph series. It also maintains close associations with a number of research centers in the Mediterranean region and Middle East. In conjunction with the American Philological Association (entry 641), the Institute holds an annual conference in December. For the interested nonspecialist the Institute publishes a popular magazine, *Archaeology* (entry 532) and, through its local branches, sponsors numerous public lectures on archaeological topics.

644. **Association International de Papyrologues**. c/o Fondation Egyptologique Reine Elisabeth, Parc du Cinquantenaire 10, B-1040 Brussels, Belgium. Tel.: (2) 741-7364.

An international society devoted to the study of papyri, this organization was formed in 1946. Its members include primarily working papyrologists and ancient historians. The AIP promotes international cooperation in papyrological research and sponsors a triennial international congress. It also publishes a directory of members at irregular intervals.

645. **Association Internationale d'Epigraphie Grecque et Latine**. C.I.D., Bibliotheque de la Sorbonne. 47 rue des Ecoles, F-75230 Paris, Cedex 05, France.

This international organization for researchers in Greek and Latin epigraphy was founded in 1972. Its membership consists chiefly of scholars working in the field. The Association produces three annual publications: *L'Année epigraphique*, *Epigraphica*, and *Supplementum Epigraphicum*. It also sponsors a quinquennial congress.

646. **Association of Ancient Historians**. c/o Prof. Diana Delia, Dept. of Classics, Brown University, Box 1856, Providence, RI 02912. Tel.: (401) 863-2993.

This group, which is affiliated with the American Historical Association, promotes the study and teaching of ancient history. The majority of its members are university professors and graduate students. The Association publishes a newsletter and holds an annual conference.

647. **Classical Association**. c/o Dr. Malcolm Schofield, St. John's College, Cambridge, CB2 1TP England. Tel.: (223) 338-6444.

The Classical Association, which dates to 1903, is the largest British organization devoted to classical studies. Its membership consists of classicists working in schools and universities. The Association sponsors an annual conference. It publishes an annual *Proceedings* and, through Oxford University Press, three important periodicals: *Classical Review* (entry 45), *Classical Quarterly* (entry 544), and *Greece and Rome* (entry 548).

648. **Classical Association of Canada**. c/o J. I. McDougall, Dept. of Classics, University of Winnipeg, Winnipeg, MB R3B 2 E9 Canada.

The Classical Association of Canada is the major professsional organization for classical studies in Canada. It publishes two journals, *Phoenix* (entry 566) and *Classical Views* (also called *Echoes du monde classique*). The Association also sponsors a directory of Canadian classicists (entry 581) and recently inaugurated an electronic newsletter (entry 601). The Association now also has its own World Wide Web site at http://137.122.12.15/Docs/Societies/ClassAc/ClassicsAddresses.html.

649. **Classical Association of the Atlantic States**. 4331 F St., SE, Washington, DC 20019. Tel.: (202) 806-6747.

Founded in 1906, this group consists largely of high school and college teachers of classics. Like the other regional classical associations, its interests include both scholarly and pedagogical matters. The Association publishes *Classical World* (entry 545). It also holds semiannual meetings.

650. **Classical Association of New England**. c/o Prof. Matthew I. Wrencke, Dept. of Classics, Dartmouth College, Hanover, NH 03755.

This organization for high school and college teachers of classics was founded in 1906. It publishes a quarterly newsletter, the *New England Classical Newsletter & Journal*, and holds an annual conference. Information about CANE and its activities is available through a World Wide Web site based at the University of New Hampshire (entry 615a).

651. **Classical Association of the Middle West and South**. c/o Prof. John Hall, Dept. of Classics, Brigham Young Universtiy, 118 KMB, Provo, UT 84602. Tel.: (801) 378-2074.

CAMWS is the largest and most active of the regional classical associations in the United States. Its territory covers most of the central and southern part of the nation. Members include a mix of high school and college faculty. The Association focuses on both scholarly and pedagogical activities in classics. It publishes *Classical Journal* (entry 541) as well as a newsletter. CAMWS holds an annual conference. In the years when the main meeting is held in a northern venue, the southern section also generally holds a smaller second conference. An electronic membership directory for CAMWS is now available on the World Wide Web at: http://www.umich.edu/~acleague/cmwsdirectory.html.

652. **De Re Militari**. c/o Monte Turner, 2913 University Drive, Lawrence, KS 66049.

Organized in 1991 at the 26th International Congress on Medieval Studies in Kalamazoo, Michigan, this professional organization promotes the study of classical and medieval military affairs. The Association has sponsored sessions at subsequent Congresses, and has recently inaugurated an electronic newsletter (entry 609). It also maintains an electronic discussion list (entry 587) and plans to make other electronic resources available through the Internet.

653. **Egypt Exploration Society**. 3 Doughty Mews, London WC1N 2PG England. Tel.: (071) 242-1880.

Founded in 1880 as the Egypt Exploration Fund, this is a society for those with scholarly interests in ancient Egypt. It has long supported excavations in Egypt (including those of W. M. Flinders Petrie and of B. P. Grenfell and A. S. Hunt.) and maintains an active publishing program. The Society has been particularly active in promoting the study of Greco-Roman Egypt. Its publications include the *Journal of Egyptian Archaeology* and the Graeco-Roman Memoirs (an important series of papyrological publications).

654. **Federation Internationale des Associations d'Etudes Classiques**. Chemin Aux-Folies 6, CH-1293 Bellevue, Switzerland. Tel.: 22 7742656.

The Federation was founded in 1948 under the auspices of UNESCO to promote the study of classical antiquity. It is a society of societies: its membership includes some 69 societies in 38 countries and 13 international groups. The chief role of the Federation is to serve as a coordinating body for international efforts in classical studies. The Federation sponsors a quinquennial congress.

655. **International Association for the Study of Ancient Baths**. c/o Dr. Jane Biers, Museum of Art and Archaeology, 1 Pickard Hall, University of Missouri, Columbia, MO, 65211. Tel.: (324) 882-3591.

Formed in 1992, this organization is devoted to the study of Greco-Roman baths and bathing customs. Its interests also extend to the bathing practices of medieval, Byzantine, and early Islamic cultures. In addition to organizing conferences, the Association publishes a biannual newsletter called *Balnearia* and an annual bibliography.

656. **International Plutarch Society (North American Branch)**. c/o Prof. A. J. Podlecki, Dept. of Classical, Near Eastern and Religious Studies, University of British Columbia, VN, V6S 1B8, Canada.

This society is devoted to the study of the life, writings, and influence of Plutarch. It publishes a newsletter and frequently sponsors sessions at the annual meetings of the American Philological Association (entry 641).

657. **International Society for the Classical Tradition**. Boston University, 745 Commonwealth Ave., Boston, MA 02215. Tel.: (617) 353-7369. Fax: (617) 353-2053.

Established in 1991 and based at the Institute for the Classical Tradition at Boston University (entry 635), this organization promotes the study of the influence of the classics on other cultures in all time periods. The Society publishes both a newsletter and a journal, the *International Journal of the Classical Tradition*. The final issue of the journal for each year now includes the "Analytical Bibliography of the Classical Tradition," which formerly appeared yearly in *Classical and Modern Literature* (entry 538). The Society also sponsors periodic meetings and conferences.

658. **International Society for the Study of Greek and Roman Music**. c/o Dr. Andrew Barker, Dept. of Classics, University of Otago, P.O. Box 56, Dunedin, New Zealand.

This is a new society (formed in 1994) devoted to fostering research and teaching in the area of ancient Greek and Roman music. Its interests include not only technical aspects of ancient music but also its cultural importance and its influence on subsequent music. The Society intends to publish a newsletter that will include notices about current research projects, new publications, and pertinent conferences.

659. **Junior Classical League**. Miami University, Oxford, OH 45056. Tel.: (513) 529-7741. Fax: (513) 529-7741.

Founded in 1936 by the American Classical League (entry 640), the Junior Classical League is an organization for high school Latin students. Its purpose is to promote classical studies at the secondary level. The League publishes a quarterly magazine, the *Torch*, and holds an annual meeting.

660. **National Committee for Latin and Greek**. c/o Virginia Barrett, Chair, 6669 Vinahaven, Cypress, CA 90630. Tel.: (714) 894-0938.

The Committee, whose membership consists of national and regional classical associations in the United States, was formed in 1978 to initiate and coordinate efforts to promote the study of Latin and Greek. The activities of the Committee include various public relations initiatives, gathering statistics on enrollment in classical language courses and teacher supply and demand, and monitoring federal legislation affecting language study. The Committee publishes a newsletter, *Prospects*, which features brief articles on the current state of and future outlook for classical studies.

661. **Petronian Society**. c/o Prof. Gareth Schmeling, Dept. of Classics, University of Florida, Gainesville, FL 32611. Tel.: (904) 392-2075. Fax: (904) 846-0297.

The Petronian Society, which was established in 1970, has a broader scope than is implied in its name. Its international membership consists of scholars interested in all aspects of the ancient novel. The Society publishes a newsletter that includes scholarly notes, book reviews, an annotated bibliography of recent publications on the ancient novel, and reports on relevant conferences. The Society sometimes sponsors sessions at the annual meeting of the American Philological Association (entry 641).

662. **Society for Ancient Greek Philosophy**. c/o Prof. Anthony Preus, Dept. of Philosophy, Binghampton University, Binghampton, NY 13902-6000. Tel.: (607) 777-2886. Fax: (607) 777-4000.

This society is for philosophers and classicists with interests in ancient philosophy. Its membership consists mainly of college and university professors. The Society publishes a newsletter and holds meetings in conjunction with the conferences of the American Philological Association (entry 641) and the American Philosophical Association. It also publishes occasional collections of essays on Greek philosophy.

663. **Society for Ancient Medicine**. Dept. of Classical Studies, 720 Williams Hall, University of Pennsylvania, Philadelphia, PA 19104. Tel.: (215) 898-6465. Fax: (215) 898-0933.

This group is interested in the study of all aspects of ancient medicine. It generally meets annually in conjunction with the American Philological Association's conference (entry 641). The Society also issues a substantial annual publication, the *Society for Ancient Medicine Review*. Formerly called the *Newsletter*, it provides detailed information about conferences and recent publications.

664. **Society for the Promotion of Hellenic Studies**. 31-34 Gordon Square, London WC1H 0PP England. Tel.: (071) 387-7495.

Founded in 1879 to advance the study of Greek language, literature, history, and art, the Society has long shared quarters with its sister organization, the Society for the Promotion of Roman Studies (entry 665). The two societies maintain a research library in association with the Institute of Classical Studies of the University of London (entry 636). The Society for the Promotion of Hellenic Studies sponsors various lectures and publishes two periodicals: the *Journal of Hellenic Studies* (entry 557) and *Archaeological Reports*.

665. **Society for the Promotion of Roman Studies**. 31-34 Gordon Square, London WC1H 0PP England. Tel.: (071) 387-8157.

This slightly younger counterpart to the Society for the Promotion of Hellenic Studies (entry 664) was founded in 1910. The two organizations share quarters and, in association with the Institute of Classical Studies of the University of London (entry 636), maintain a major research library for classical studies. The Society's aim is to advance the study of Roman history, archaeology, literature, and art. To this end it sponsors public lectures and publishes two journals: the *Journal of Roman Studies* (entry 559) and *Britannia*.

666. **Vergilian Society of America**. c/o John Dutra, Executive Secretary, P.O. Box 817, Oxford, OH 45056. Tel.: (513) 529-1482. Fax: (513) 529-1516.

Organized in 1937, the Vergilian Society promotes the study of Latin literature and Roman history, with special emphasis on the life and writings of Vergil. Its members include primarily teachers and students of Latin from both high schools and colleges. The Society maintains a study center in Italy and sponsors an annual summer school there. It publishes a newsletter and two journals, *The Augustan Age* and *Vergilius*. The Society also regularly meets at the annual conference of the American Philological Association (entry 641).

667. **Women's Classical Caucus**. c/o Prof. Barbara McManus, 5 Chester Dr., Rye, NY 10580.

This group, whose membership includes those working in all areas of classical studies, has two aims. The first is to support the professional status of women in classical studies. The second is to promote the study of women in antiquity. The Caucus publishes a newsletter and meets during the American Philological Association's annual conference (entry 641).

AUTHOR/TITLE INDEX

Reference is to entry number. References followed by "n" are to annotations. References preceded by "p" are to page numbers. Initial articles are inverted for English-language publications; foreign-language works are filed by initial articles (e.g., Das Humanistische Gymnasium is found under "D").

SUBJECT INDEX

Reference is to entry number. References followed by "n" are to annotations.
References preceded by "p" are to pages.

Browning, Robert, 276n
Byzantine authors, 443n, 470n
Byzantine empire, 94
  indexes, 40
Byzantine Greek literature, 11n
Byzantine studies, 8n
  review journals, 42

Caesar. *See* Julius Caesar
Cairo Museum, 638n
Calendars, Greek and Roman, 250, 256
Callimachus, 144
Cambridge Ritualists, 52n
Canada
  directories, classics, 581
  professional organization, 648
Cappadocians, 306n
Carausius
  portraits, 396
Catilinarian conspiracy, 74
Catiline, 74n
Catullus, 79n
  bibliographies, 145-47
Children and youth
  in antiquity, 91
Christianity and Christians
  early, 94
  electronic discussion group, 588
  encyclopedias, 220
  grammars, 470
  lexicons, 443
  mysteries within, 508a
  research centers, 634
  women, 500
Cicero, 74n, 78, 81, 363n, 504n
Classical studies, 8n
  dictionaries, 223, 232
  electronic discussion groups, 601
  electronic journal, 546
  encyclopedias, 213, 214, 216,
    225-28, 233
  essays, 41
  gophers and World Wide Web
    sites, 606, 607a
  graduate directories, 575
  handbooks, 212
  indexes, 26, 31, 35, 36, 38
  Internet resources, p201
  Italian introductions to, 11n

journals, 534, 535, 537, 540, 541,
    542, 550, 556, 567, 573
  library catalogs, 197-211
  professional associations, 641,
    647-51, 657, 667
  research bibliographies, 37
  research centers, p213, 635, 636,
    637, 639
  research guides, 18, 21
  review journals, 42, 44, 45, 46, 50
Classicists
  Canadian electronic journal, 601
  directories, 574, 579, 580, 581
  European, 372, 386
  international, 361
  Irish electronic journal, 602
  Italian, 366
  North American, 360
Cleisthenes, 381
Coins and coinage. *See also*
    Numismatics
  ancient, 70, 131
  ancient Greek, 320, 320a, 325, 499
  Greek imperial, 326
  Roman, 317, 320b, 327, 328, 485
  Roman Republican, 25
Columbia Records of Civilization
    series, 506n
Columbia University, p73, 622n
Comedy, Roman, 269n
Concordances, Greek literature, 464
Constantine the Great, 255n, 280n,
    487n
Constantinople, fall of, 5n, 276n
Cowley, Abraham, 93n
Crete, ancient
  aerial maps, 432
Criticism, textual
  Greek texts, 332
  Latin, 332
Cyprus, 342n
Cyrenaica, 342n

Democracy, primary sources, 517
Dessau, Hermann, 389n
Diaspora, primary resources, 514.
    See also Judaism
Dictionaries, specialized
  bibliographic abbreviations, 348, 351
  classical literature, 273, 274

Fiction, ancient. *See also* Literature
    Roman, 79
File transfer protocol sites, p201
Flavius Josephus, 76n, 443n, 589n
    bibliographies, 158-61
France, Latin studies in, 7n
FTP. *See* File transfer protocol sites

Galba, 179
Gallienus, 371n
Genealogy, Athens, 381
Gennadius, Johannes, 200n
Geography, classical, 1n, 11n. *See*
    also Atlases; Maps
    atlases, p150, 420-39
    dictionaries, 407, 411, 413, 416, 418
    encyclopedias, 417
    handbooks, 403
    lexicons, 406, 408, 416a, 418
    resources, p145
    surveys, 405
Gods and goddesses, ancient
    Greece, 284. *See also* Religion
Gopher servers, p205, 604-16
Government, Roman empire, 502
Graduate programs, directories, 575
Great Britain, classical periodicals
    survey, 208. *See also* Eng-
    land; Roman Britain
Greco-Romans, archaeology, 27
Greece
    aerial views of ancient, 415
    children and youth, 91
    dictionaries, 218
    electronic discussion group, 597
    geographic surveys, 405
    handbooks, 217, 222
    indexes, 40
    journals, 548, 557
    lexicons, 408, 409
    primary sources, 503
    women in, 501
    World Wide Web site, 613
Greek authors, topical bibliographies,
    56
Greek civilization
    electronic reference sources, 340
    reference sources, 352
Greek history
    electronic discussion group, 600

    essays, 41
    geographic background, 405
    journals, 536, 555, 568
    primary sources, 496, 515, 523
    research centers, 623, 624
    topical bibliographies, 76
Greek language
    CD-ROM products, 458, 459, 464
    dictionaries, 443, 446, 451, 453,
        467
    electronic discussion group, 586
    gopher sites, 612, 615
    grammars, 470, 471, 473, 474,
        478-81
    journal, 547
    lexicons, 455, 456, 457, 462, 468
    reference works, 441
    thesauri, 449, 464
Greek literature, 3, 4n
    beginnings of, 5n
    bibliographical guides to, 5, 10n,
        16, 17, 19, 82, 92, 108, 119,
        125a
    electronic discussion group, 599
    encyclopedias, 216
    essays, 41
    guides, 324
    handbooks, 258, 278
    histories, 263, 266, 276, 277, 281
    journals, 544, 561
    library catalogs, 203
    research centers, 623, 624
    research guides, 3, 4, 5, 13
    Roman empire, 262
    text archives, 618
    thesauri, 464
    topical biographies, 52
Greek studies, 7n
    electronic discussion group, 597
        in French colleges and
        universities, 2
    journals, 569
    professional society, 664
    research centers, 629, 637
Greek tragedy, dictionaries, 260
Greeks, art, 25
Groag, Edmund, 389n
Guides, specialized
    classical mythology in art, 284
    Greek and Roman chronology, 256
    Greek civilization, 352